ENGLAND
AND
THE ENGLISH

.

Classics of British Historical Literature

JOHN CLIVE, EDITOR

Edward Lytton Bulwer

—

England
and
the English

EDITED AND WITH AN INTRODUCTION BY

STANDISH MEACHAM

The University of Chicago Press
CHICAGO AND LONDON

ISBN: 0-226-08014-5 (clothbound); 0-226-08015-3 (paperbound)
Library of Congress Catalog Card Number: 71-114959
The University of Chicago Press, Chicago 60637
The University of Chicago Press, Ltd., London
© 1970 by The University of Chicago
Published 1970
Printed in the United States of America

Contents

Series Editor's Preface

This series of reprints has one major purpose: to put into the hands of students and other interested readers outstanding—and sometimes neglected—works dealing with British history which have either gone out of print or are obtainable only at a forbiddingly high price.

The phrase Classics of British Historical Literature requires some explanation, in view of the fact that the two companion series published by the University of Chicago Press are entitled Classic European Historians and Classic American Historians. Why, then, introduce the word *literature* into the title of this series?

One reason is obvious. History, if it is to live beyond its own generation, must be memorably written. The greatest British historians—Clarendon, Gibbon, Hume, Carlyle, Macaulay—survive today, not merely because they contributed to the cumulative historical knowledge about their subjects, but because they were masters of style and literary artists as well. And even historians of the second rank, if they deserve to survive, are able to do so only because they can still be read with pleasure. To emphasize this truth at the present time, when much eminently solid and worthy academic history suffers from being almost totally unreadable, seems worth doing.

The other reason for including the word *literature* in the title of the series has to do with its scope. To read history is to learn about the past. But if, in trying to learn about the British past, one were to restrict oneself to the reading of formal works of history, one would miss a great deal. Often a historical novel, a sociological inquiry, or an account of events and institutions couched in semifictional form teaches us just as much about the past as does the "history" that calls itself by that name. And, frequently, these "informal" historical works turn out to be less well known than their merit deserves. By calling this series Classics of British Historical Literature it will be possible to include such books without doing violence to the usual nomenclature.

Bulwer's *England and the English* is precisely such a book. It is, as Professor Meacham points out in his introduction, a mixture of history and sociology, all attractively presented by the author with the art of a practiced novelist. Considering the date of its publication it is indeed a remarkable production—nothing less than an account, both descriptive and analytical, of English society, culture, and modes of thought in the early eighteen thirties. As such, it is as much a source for historians of the period as it is a pioneering kind of sociohistorical inquiry in its own right.

England and the English is by no means a "value-free" work. Bulwer, like many of his contemporaries, saw that English society was in need of change. He inveighed against the all-pervasive and debilitating effect of the aristocratic principle, and he used his book to propagandize for Benthamism. What is worthy of note and admiration is how, writing before Tocqueville and many years before the systematic analysis of national character had been developed as a field of inquiry, Bulwer nonetheless succeeded as a complete "amateur" in depicting English class attitudes and divisions, currents of literary taste, and the state of morals and manners at various levels of society in an intelligent and perceptive way. It was a brilliant accomplishment on his part and is still very much worth reading today, not least because of the grace of its style and the liveliness of its examples and illustrations.

JOHN CLIVE

Editor's Introduction

Bulwer's *England and the English* may well be as much sociology as history. It inhabits a borderland between disciplines, along with though not on a level with Montesquieu's *De l'esprit des lois* and Tocqueville's *De la democratie en Amerique*. These books, and those of writers as seemingly disparate as Locke, Rousseau, and Adam Smith represent a tradition born of the Enlightenment. They describe society framed by something other than religious determinants and treat human beings as the products of that society.

Impossible, perhaps, to fix with a particular label, these men analyzed and explained society in terms of what they saw around them. Experience, rather than transcendental mystery, provided the clues they sought. Law, custom, economy, literature—these became the materials for this new sort of investigation. "There is nothing mystical," Melvin Richter writes of Montesquieu, "no notion of a Volksgeist, for example, nothing transcending reason and experience in Montesquieu's concept of the general spirit of society."[1] And the same could be said of all those who undertook studies of this sort. *England and the English* has a place within this tradition. Bulwer is trying to explain the private sources of public attitudes. He wants his readers to understand a frame of mind—what it is and what has produced it. To do so, he draws his evidence from a variety of sources, from the "reason and experience" of the age in which he finds himself.

1. Melvin Richter, "Montesquieu," *International Encyclopedia of Social Sciences* (New York, 1968), 10:473.

This by no means makes him either historian or sociologist. Although he writes at length about class, he writes intuitively, and in terms of social orders. Nor does he deal with the concepts of equality, power, and centralization with the analytical assurance of a Tocqueville. *England and the English* bears a resemblance to Hazlitt's *Spirit of the Age,* treating in part as that book does with what can be called the sociology of literature. It more closely parallels Emerson's *English Traits,* whose conclusions often reflect those of Bulwer's earlier work. Both these books deal with the past, and with society. But both are impressionistic in a way that sociology is not. And both have as their focus the contemporary to a degree that marks them as something at one remove from history.

Bulwer's book declares itself the work of a novelist, a journalist, and a politician. It is "up-to-date," reflecting its author's interests and inclinations. He knows his England and his Englishmen and is anxious to impart that knowledge. Sir Harry Hargrave, William Muscle, Samuel Square, Mr. Worm—these men are real to us. But they are a novelist's, not a sociologist's, ideal types. His descriptions of the poor benefit from his recognition of the value of Parliamentary evidence and his willingness to use it. As a politician he is ready to propose solutions to the problems which, as a reporter, he has described.

All this makes the book—whether history, sociology, or not quite either—of great value to both historians and sociologists. Those interested in debating the relative strengths of aristocratic and middle-class values and traditions, for example, will profit from its study. Others concerned to follow the threads of recent scholarly controversy concerning Bentham, Benthamism, and their influence will find Bulwer's opinions on this point worth heeding.[2] Those who study social change will appreciate the manner in which Bulwer chronicles transition, as well as the way in which he manages to endow a period of transition with order and meaning.

2. See O. M. MacDonagh, "The Nineteenth Century Revolution in Government: A Reappraisal," *Historical Journal* 1 (1958): 52–67; Henry Parris, "The Nineteenth Century Revolution in Government: A Reappraisal Reappraised," *Historical Journal* 3 (1960): 17–37; Jenifer Hart, "Nineteenth Century Social Reform: A Tory Interpretation of History," *Past and Present* 31 (1965): 39–61.

The kaleidoscopic coming together of opposites so characteristic of England in transition was no less characteristic of Bulwer's
own life. His dedications in *England and the English*—to Talleyrand, the diplomatist, to Chalmers, the theologian, to D'Israeli,
the litterateur, and to the English people—disclose a mind open
to impressions from all directions. In the preface to his novel
Pelham, he describes his hero as he might have described himself.
"A fop, a philosopher, a voluptuary, and a moralist—a trifler in
appearance but rather one to whom trifles are instinctive, than one
to whom trifles are natural—an Aristippus on a limited scale, accustomed to draw sage conclusions from the follies he adopts, and
while professing himself a votary of pleasure, desirous in reality
to become a disciple of wisdom."[3] His mind was an intellectual
patchwork, as much a product of the age as this book which attempts to describe it. The book and the mind are in that sense of a
piece. To understand the book one must therefore know the mind.
And to know the mind one must know more of the man.

As he begins his *Portrait of an Age,* G. M. Young suggests that
a young Englishman in the year 1831, "whichever way his temperament led him" would, if he reflected, discover himself "controlled and animated by an almost universal faith in progress."[4]
Bulwer, born in 1803, was one of those young men impelled forward by the spirit of the age. In his own case, however, he was
driven by more than his confidence in the destiny of the human
race. Bulwer believed that he was himself born to succeed. In an
autobiographical sketch of his early life, written years later, he
recounted a madman's prediction that he would one day be
"something remarkable."[5]

The vision must have helped to sustain Bulwer through a miserable childhood, an unhappy youth, and a generally melancholy
lifetime. Son of General William Earle Bulwer, a testy Norfolk
gentleman, and of Elizabeth Lytton, daughter of an eccentric,
bookish spendthrift, he grew up in a household oppressed by

3. *Pelham* (London, 1848), p. iv.
4. G. M. Young, *Victorian England: Portrait of an Age,* 2d edition (London, 1952), p. 1.
5. The Earl of Lytton, *The Life of Edward Bulwer, First Lord Lytton* (London, 1913), 1:27–28. Hereafter, *Life.*

disaffection. General Bulwer despised his mother-in-law; Mrs. Bulwer in turn grew to loathe her husband, who not only had banished her mother from his house, but had refused to acknowledge her own right to a voice in the rearing of their first-born son, William. Forced to accede to her husband's demands, Mrs. Bulwer next allowed her mother to carry off her second child, Henry, to be raised in London. When Edward was born in 1803, Elizabeth determined that he would belong to her alone. Much of what was to come grew from that determination.

General Bulwer never developed an affection for the son who was so much his mother's child. After the general's death, Edward's grandfather offered to undertake his grandson's education. Elizabeth agreed and shipped Edward to Ramsgate for extended visits, where old Mr. Lytton's library began to cast a spell upon him. When the books were shipped to London in 1810, following Lytton's death, Edward spoke of their arrival as "the cardinal event of my infancy." For twelve months he plundered them joyfully and reverently. At the end of a year, however, Mrs. Bulwer determined to move with Edward out of London to Knebworth, an estate entailed upon her in Hertfordshire. The books were sold, the move accomplished, and, soon after, Edward dispatched to school in Fulham. He hated it and came home in two weeks. His mother sent him out twice more before he found a comparative haven at a fashionable establishment in Rottingdean. There he remained until it was time for Cambridge. Once more he took a dislike to the place chosen for him, and moved from Trinity into Trinity Hall. The Union took up the time he chose to spend away from books. He consorted with "reading men," enjoyed the company of his more buckish brother, Henry, and took his degree in 1825, carrying off with him as well a gold medal for a prize poem on sculpture, pleased to think "that I had at last done something my dear mother was proud of."[6]

Close ties with his mother had not kept him from the company of other women. When not at school, Bulwer had lived in London. His tutor persuaded Mrs. Bulwer to publish a volume of her son's poetry, and the book won him a reputation as a sort of prodigy. He was handsome, and loved dancing. "The middle-aged ladies

6. Ibid., 1:80.

took me home in their carriages, for I was but a boy. The young ones did not disdain me for a partner—for I was almost a man."[7] Ready for love, he conceived a passion for an unnamed maiden —"well born"—whom he met daily in a suburban arcadia near by Rottingdean. Believing "that we were born for each other," Bulwer was crushed when the girl's family forced her to marry another. She died three years later, declaiming on her deathbed her love for Bulwer and her hope that he might seek out her grave to mourn her.

Bulwer treasured the memory of this melancholy initiation. He grasped at experience in the hope that he might savour romance. Once when he was on a walking tour, a young gypsy girl brought him into her camp to live with her. Far grander, Caroline Lamb bestowed her favors upon him for a few months, and he endured that *rite de passage* which Byron's example demanded.

None of this left him any better prepared for the romance that was to blight his life. Rosina Wheeler had been bred, like Bulwer, in a desperately unhappy household. Her father was a drunken Irish landlord, her mother a flighty, pretentious climber. She had lived in Ireland, Guernsey, and France before returning to London in 1825 to the house of her great-uncle. Bulwer met her that year among the blue-stockings. She was witty and very beautiful. Mrs. Bulwer, who had voiced no objections to her son's past flirtations, sensed a serious infatuation. She remonstrated; he persisted. For a time he broke the engagement; reconciliation led Rosina to become his mistress. They married in 1827 and galloped off to a life of social extravagance, for a time in the country, later in London. Mrs. Bulwer continued to express disapproval. For a year and a half she refused to see Bulwer or to send him money, thereby assisting her son to run up his debts without lessening his determination to make a go of his marriage.

That task proved impossible. Both husband and wife were selfish. Rosina, whose slapdash mind could admire but never understand her husband's talents, grew jealous of his work and naturally resented Mrs. Bulwer's opposition and interference. Edward's closeness to his mother made it hard for him to ignore her imprecations; his open, attractive sociability soon led him to tire

7. Ibid., 1:59.

of Rosina's pettish whims. A trip to Europe in 1833, planned with the hope that a change of scene might work to save the marriage, probably set the seal on its eventual disintegration. Bulwer chose the occasion to pursue in Paris an affair he had already begun at home. Rosina countered by encouraging a Neapolitan prince. Bulwer, enraged, dragged her back to London, where together they endured a further twenty-seven months together before signing a final deed of separation in 1836.[8]

Bulwer had embarked upon the trip hoping to save more than his marriage. His health was in tatters because of the work he had undertaken to keep himself and Rosina afloat. Neither could exist without spending money lavishly. They lived at a rate of £ 3000 per year. Bulwer earned almost all of it by writing, putting his talent to work for him with an energy that by 1833 had almost burned him out.

Fortunately there was a ready market for his product. Postwar England had money to spend on the fashionable literature that was Bulwer's forte. Aristocratic-sounding names—Mordaunt, Godolphin, Maltravers;[9] exotic localities, both domestic and foreign; sudden changes of fortune and fate; a chance to recognize the high and mighty behind the mask of fiction: these were the staples of Bulwer's early novels, as they were of all the elaborate and artificial productions of the silver-fork school. Bulwer joined Theodore Hook, Benjamin Disraeli, John Sterling and the now forgotten T. S. Surr, Lady Lydia Scott, William Harrison Ainsworth, and others in delivering to an audience ever ready to devour them, a series of rich fictional sweetmeats confected to suit the taste of an over-indulged *arriviste* market. *Falkland, O'Neill, Pelham, The Disowned, Devereux, Paul Clifford, Eugene Aram, Godolphin* all appeared between 1826 and 1833.

Meanwhile Bulwer conceived an interest in radical politics that

8. The quarreling did not cease, however, until both were in their graves. In 1880, two years before Rosina's death and seven years after Edward's, a book entitled *A Blighted Life* appeared, a memoir by Rosina full of scandalous accusations against her husband. It was, however, published without her knowledge. See Michael Sadleir, *Bulwer: A Panorama: Edward and Rosina* (Boston, 1931), pp. 395–96.

9. Michael Sadleir makes the point that Bulwer's own name, metamorphosed at last to Edward George Earle Lytton Bulwer-Lytton, Lord Lytton, was itself almost a parody of his own inventions. Ibid., p. 195.

led him to contribute to the *Westminster Review* and helped persuade him to assume the editorship of Henry Colburn's *New Monthly Magazine* in 1831. He stood successfully as a candidate for Saint Ives in Huntingdonshire the same year. His accounts of the debates in the House reflect the exhilaration engendered by reform agitation. Althorp's speech on the third reading of the Reform Bill was "something like the entrance of a new world into active politics when a Minister condescended to be a Philospher."[10] When his constituency disappeared after 1832 he accepted nomination and won election as a radical at Lincoln. Political affiliation of this stripe called down upon him the vindictive wrath of such men as John Gibson Lockhart, Scott's son-in-law and editor of the *Quarterly,* and of William Maginn, editor of *Fraser's,* who employed Thackeray to bait him mercilessly during the early 1830s.

Most of his critics tried to dismiss him as an ambitious, social-climbing, money-hungry hack. Carlyle called him "a poor fribble," and enveighed against the dandyism of *Pelham* in *Sartor Resartus*. But Carlyle began to change his mind after John Stuart Mill persuaded him to read *England and the English*. "The astonishing thing," he was forced to admit, "is the contrast of the man and his enterprise."[11] The book was an outgrowth of ideas he had already expressed in the *New Monthly* and of an earlier effort—"History of the British Public"—which he had begun in 1824 but never finished. The chapters, completed before he left for Italy in 1833, were written with a straightforward conviction the novels lacked.[12] Bulwer set out both expectations and apprehensions honestly. The book is critical and questioning; it provides no pat answers. Of the author it suggests the kind of levelheaded sensitivity that the novels, by their very nature, were designed to mask. Of the nation he describes it suggests the confusion and uncertainty that beset it in the post-Napoleonic years. Belief in prog-

10. *Life,* 1:418.
11. Ibid., p. 180.
12. He set out his hatreds forthrightly as well. Sneak, who appears at the end of book 4 under "Supplementary Characters" was a caricature of Charles Molloy Westmacott, editor of *The Age,* an anti-radical blackmailer who had insulted Bulwer's friend the Countess of Blessington, and who subsequently accused Bulwer of plagiarism.

ress may well have been, as Young suggests, an article of faith. The strange, unnerving facts of politics and society, however, demanded of many a reexamination of that belief. They asked themselves if they could any longer acknowledge as true what they had allowed themselves to take so long for granted.

John Stuart Mill had been driven to do just that in the series of articles he published in *The Examiner* in the spring of 1831 on "the spirit of the age." Anxious to rationalize revolutionary change, he borrowed from positivism the notion that the fragmented present could be fitted together into a larger pattern encompassing past and future. Apparent chaos was but the particular "character" of an age which was transposing civilization from a lower to a higher form of social organization. The very expression "the spirit of the age" betokened a willingness to mark off progressive periods for analysis and reflection. Soon England would reach a new plateau, a "natural" period when those fittest to govern would be the governors. Meanwhile she could console herself with the knowledge that present confusions were an expression of a larger design and need not therefore be feared; that change, far from being senseless, had a meaning worth discovering and a purpose worth encouraging. Others found themselves impelled to the same conclusion. Harriet Martineau, looking back upon the period when writing her *History* in 1850, quoted Thomas Arnold approvingly on the necessity for change and pronounced her own benediction upon a positivistic theory of progress.[13] Whigs like Jeffrey of the *Edinburgh Review* were prepared to appreciate the impulses of historical development and in consequence could view the French Revolution as beneficial.[14]

Bulwer's *England* echoes these same sentiments, acknowledging, if not welcoming, change. "The English of the present day are not the English of twenty years ago."[15] More tolerant, they are becoming citizens of the world. Outgrowing their nationalistic past, they recognize good in others. Indeed, he reports happily to Talleyrand, to whom he dedicates book 1, *"We no longer hate*

13. *A History of England during the Thirty Years Peace* (London, 1850), 2:72.

14. See John Clive, *Scotch Reviewers: The Edinburgh Review, 1802–1815* (London, 1957), p. 122.

15. See below, p. 19–20.

the French." Commerce has contributed as much as anything to such change. Bulwer describes a society forced to accommodate itself to a world in which feudal relationships have all but disappeared. Strain, under these circumstances, is inevitable, and much of Bulwer's task is to demonstrate that the tensions of the present, unnerving though they may be, are but natural results of a phenomenon which Englishmen must learn to live with. Literature reflects those tensions: Wordsworth "the apostle . . . of those who cling to the most idealized part of things that are"; Shelley "the spiritualizer of all who forsake the past and the present, and, with lofty hopes and a bold philanthropy, rush forward into the future";[16] Byron, whose poems had so captured the mood of Romantic postwar disillusion, and who with his death allowed men to awake from "the morbid, the passionate, the dreaming" and address themselves "to the active and daily objects" which lay before them.[17] Bulwer's own talents mirrored these contradictions. His literary romanticism, his political radicalism, and the striving to keep the two divergent strains in balance need to be understood against this background of shifting and questioning, of weary disillusion and ardent hopefulness.

Bulwer admits that the idea of transition can fill him with terror. "I have said that we live in an age of visible transition—an age of disquietude and doubt—of the removal of time-worn landmarks, and the breaking up of the hereditary elements in society—old opinions, feelings—ancestral customs and institutions all crumbling away, and both the spiritual and temporal worlds are darkened by the shadow of change. . . . To me such epochs appear but as the dark passages in the appointed progress of mankind—the times of greatest unhappiness to our species—passages into which we have no reason to rejoice at our entrance, save from hope of being sooner landed on the opposite side."[18] Despite the terror, Bulwer believes that he will eventually walk ashore safe and sound. It will be a new country to which the age of transition has transported him, more democratic, more serious of purpose.[19] But hopefully it will "lose less of the good it already enjoys in

16. See below, p. 283.
17. See below, p. 286.
18. See below, p. 319.
19. See below, p. 107.

working itself free from the evil" than has been the case with the nations on the continent.[20]

The engine of this transformation, Bulwer is certain, will prove to be the philosophy of Jeremy Bentham. He calls it "a philosophy of visible transition."[21] Englishmen need only open their eyes to what is happening around them to see it at work. So important is it to their understanding of the age they live in that Bulwer provides them with special appendixes on Bentham (written for him by John Stuart Mill) and on James Mill. Bulwer does not accept Benthamism uncritically. The greatest happiness principle is "an excellent general rule, but it is not an undeniable axiom."[22] He is sensitive enough, however, to recognize the extent to which current changes owe their initial impetus to utilitarian thinking. He acknowledges the subtlety of the process, and perceives that Bentham himself influenced no more than a handful—"a minute fraction of the few people who think—from them the broad principles travelled onward—became known (their source unknown) —because familiar and successful."[23]

Much in *England and the English* stands as an illustration of that very process. Its central assertion—the danger of an aristocratically-biased constitution—reflects ideas expressed in an article by James Mill, "Men and Things in 1823," in the first number of the radical *Westminster Review*. Bulwer adopts the theme and develops it to an extent that, as a later critic wrote, his book might as well have been titled "An Exposition of the Influences of the Aristocracy."[24] He was not alone in remarking upon the surprising vitality of the aristocratic tradition in a period of increasing democratization. Tocqueville found himself suffused in the "parfum d'aristocratie" when he paid his first visit to England in 1833. He could hardly credit its pervasiveness.[25] Surely, he insisted, these were the stale vapors of the eighteenth century. Almost at once, however, he recognized his mistake. It was an understandable one. In the light of the alarms of the previous several

20. See below, p. 319–20.
21. See below, p. 318.
22. See below, p. 321.
23. See below, p. 318.
24. R. H. Horne, *A New Spirit of the Age* (London, 1844), 2:193.
25. See Seymour Dresher, *Tocqueville in England* (Cambridge, Mass., 1964), pp. 38, 60.

years, one might be forgiven for supposing that the aristocratic governing class could no longer postpone the surrender of its powers and prerogatives. Tocqueville and Bulwer both knew better. There is no evidence that either one directly influenced the other. Both looked about them, however, and concluded that as change came it would be tempered by aristocratic traditions in a society where custom rather than law had always determined the shape and substance of its institutions.

Bulwer devotes a major portion of his book to discussions of the strength of the aristocratic tradition. He recognizes the importance of its social as well as its political influence. Its vitality derives in part from its attachment to land. More important, it derives from the very democratic tendencies that one might logically expect would seal its doom. English society is marked by fluctuation and instability. No sharp line demarcates aristocrats from all the others. Hence, "these shot-silk colours of society produce this effect: That people have no exact and fixed position—that by acquaintance alone they may rise to look down on their superiors—that while the rank gained by intellect, or by interest, is open but to few, the rank that may be obtained by fashion seems delusively open to all."[26] Such apparent opportunity induces Englishmen to act up to a part they expect in time to be allowed to play. Free to adopt the opinions and attitudes of the aristocracy, they hope that the masquerade will at least trick their peers into mistaking illusion for reality. "With us the fusion of all classes, each with the other, is so general, that the aristocratic contagion extends from the highest towards the verge of the lowest. The tradesmen in every country town have a fashion of their own, and the wife of the mercer will stigmatize the lady of the grocer as 'ungenteel.' "[27]

26. See below p. 31. Interesting, in this connection, is Tocqueville's comment on the adaptability of the English aristocracy in *The Old Regime and the French Revolution* (trans. Stuart Gilbert [New York, 1955]): "The reason why the English middle class, far from being actively hostile to the aristocracy, inclined to fraternize with it was not so much that the aristocracy kept open house as that its barriers were ill defined; not so much that entrance into it was easy as that you never know when you had got there. The result was that everyone who hovered on its outskirts nursed the agreeable illusion that he belonged to it and joined forces with it in the hope of acquiring prestige or some practical advantage under its aegis," pp. 88–89.

27. See below, p. 33.

Aristocratic influence operates on many levels to retard progress. Industry has made England a great nation. Yet bounties, prohibitions, and monopolies—all products of the aristocratic temper and designed to further the aristocratic interest—these artificialities are "amputating the sinews of action."[28] The army "commands order by suppressing the faculties, not by inciting the ambition."[29] The Church, led by an aristocratically inclined clergy, cannot "harmonize with the people in political opinion," taking instead "a severe and active course in direct opposition to the wishes of the Popular Heart." The doctrine which demands that a clergyman be a gentleman makes the pastor "a member of the aristocratic profession," "passionless in the pulpit, but decorous in his habits," leaving him respected, perhaps, but without influence within his community.[30] Public schools attract pupils by virtue of their general reputation as aristocratic nurseries. The curriculum may be worthless—indeed, in Bulwer's opinion it generally is—but as long as a mother can convince herself that since "my son is very intimate with little Lord John, he will get, when of age, into the best society!"—and perhaps, in consequence ally himself with little Lady Mary—as long as doting parents reason thus, Bulwer declares, they will remain content to "combat their conviction that their sons are better cricketers than scholars."[31] Schools which should teach moral principle teach toadying instead, encouraging a young man to set his sights on social rather than intellectual horizons.

Thus taught to recognize personal advancement as his only goal, the young aristocratically-tempered gentleman is ready to receive whatever patronage a corrupt political system can provide to help him on his way. "What son—what brother—what nephew —what cousin—what remote and unconjectured relative in the Genesis of the Greys has not fastened his limpet to the rock of the national expenditure?" And yet, when reform is demanded, and the king's son compelled to resign the appointment of the Tower, not one Grey limpet is pried loose. "The tongue so mute for the King's son, rolls in thunder about the revered heads of the in-

28. See below, p. 58.
29. See below, p. 68.
30. See below, p. 191.
31. See below, p. 149.

numerable and unimpugnable Greyides."[32] Such is the power of the aristocratic tradition.

Most debilitating is its tendency to broadcast a kind of flaccid respectability throughout England. Later in the century critics, when condemning this same conformity, would blame its existence upon democracy. Tocqueville and Mill spring immediately to mind. Here Bulwer is suggesting that aristocracy, based as it increasingly seems to be upon wealth, can as easily reduce a nation to dull mediocrity. Merchants entertain lavishly to prove themselves the equal of noblemen. Noblemen retaliate in kind, "and ostentation becomes the order of the day. We do not strive, as should be the object of a court, to banish dullness from society. No! We strive to render dullness magnificent."[33] "Respectability" taints everything. The Royal Society, in order to maintain itself respectably, has cluttered its membership rolls with men of rank and property who know nothing of science. Appearance is all. "Mr. Warm" sees his friend fail in business and forswears his acquaintance. He seduces a young lady and later forswears that connection as well. Yet he subscribes to charities, goes to church, and is in bed at twelve o'clock. "Well, well, all that's very proper; but is Mr. Warm a good father, a good friend, and active citizen? Or is he not avaricious, does he not love scandal, *is not his heart cold,* is he not vindictive, is he not unjust, is he not unfeeling? Lord, sir, I believe he *may* be all that; but what then? *Everybody allows Mr. Warm is a most respectable man.*"[34]

The power of this spirit is immense. And, because so few recognize it for what it is, it is insidious. "Its power is not in a tapestried chamber, or in a crimson woolsack, or in ribbons and stars, in coronets and titles; its power, my friends, is in yourselves; its power is in the aristocratic spirit and sympathy which pervade you all."[35]

It is against such power that "thinking and dispassionate men" must direct the liberalism of the age.[36] Bulwer offers explicit remedies to combat the disease which, unless arrested, will keep En-

32. See below, p. 367.
33. See below, p. 85.
34. See below, p. 76.
35. See below, p. 371.
36. See below, p. 365.

gland from its deserved future. The tonic is Benthamism; but Benthamism must be administered by the state if it is to effect a cure. Bulwer concludes that nothing less than a strong central government will achieve for England what its citizens are loath to undertake as individuals. A "directive" government, Bulwer calls it, "strong not for evil but for good."[37] Liberalism need not mean laissez-faire. "The great mistake of modern liberalism is, to suppose that a government is never to interfere, except through the medium of the tax-gatherer. A government should represent a parent; with us, it only represents a dun, with the bailiff at his heels!"[38]

Bulwer brings little comfort to those who rely upon political parties to engineer reform. Like so many thoughtful politicians immediately after 1832, he appears to consider parties a thing of the past.[39] All the parties are in pieces. To put them together again would be a waste of time. Instead, he grounds his hopes on the formation of a national, independent coalition whose objectives must be to further economic retrenchment, reward industry, downgrade the aristocracy, support the king, purify the church, and foster education.[40] The goals sound remarkably akin to those the Conservative Sir Robert Peel set himself. Yet Bulwer's specific proposals are too radical to be labeled Peelite. He wants trusts broken, so that funds can be freed for public education. He wants teaching colleges established, so that men and women may "not only learn to know, but learn to teach."[41] He wants state patronage for scientists, professorships which will diffuse a respect for both theory and technology throughout society. The state's task is not necessarily to create Newtons or Michelangelos. It is to instill throughout the community a more general "respect for intellect."[42]

Schools are but one of several means of accomplishing that end. An enlightened state will encourage a free press to represent and to originate opinion. One of Bulwer's major political crusades was

37. See below, p. 398.
38. See below, p. 120 n.3.
39. See Norman Gash, *Reaction and Reconstruction in English Politics, 1832–1852* (Oxford, 1965), p. 123.
40. See below, p. 395 ff.
41. See below, p. 224.
42. See below, p. 325.

against the newspaper tax, levied on the presumption that the poor were better off unread, while ignoring the inseparable association of illiteracy and crime. The state must also make better use of its clergymen. Like Tocqueville, Bulwer recognized the strength a religion might impart to society. It must be encouraged "to combat and counterbalance the Titan passions, which, for ever touching earth, for ever take from earth new and gigantic life." In one of the most sensitive passages in the book, Bulwer describes the way in which he believes the life-stream of any community must be infused with religious ardor. "To defeat the passions, the passions must feed [religion]! It can be no lukewarm and dormant principle, hedged in, and crippled by that reason which, in our actions, fetters nothing else. It has nothing to do with rationalism; it must be a sentiment, an emotion, for ever present with us—pervading, colouring and exalting all. . . . Religion wanes from a nation as poetry vanishes from religion. The creeds of states, like their constitutions, to renew their youth, must return to their first principles. It is necessary for us at this time to consider deeply on these truths; for many amongst us, most anxious, perhaps to preserve religion, are forever attempting to attenuate its powers."[43]

Bulwer was not a particularly devout man himself. Although controlled and animated by belief in progress, he was not apparently subject to that "imponderable pressure" G. M. Young describes as predominant along with faith in progress: the evangelical discipline. His religious impulses, as his analysis suggests, stemmed from his Romantic temper. Like Coleridge, he senses a need for a clergy that will spread civilization while dispelling ignorance. State schools, directed by a minister of public instruction, must teach religion, but not established religion. England's mistake has been to recognize but two alternatives: Anglican or secular teaching. What is wanted is a "universal" system, "establishing one fixed and certain standard of morals, which, containing all the broader principles, need not forbid the more complicated." Such a system would provide the nation with what it now sorely lacks—a moral science, "a standard which shall keep us from wandering very far into the multiform theories and schisms

43. See below, p. 186.

in which the vagaries of mere speculative moralists have so often misled morality."[44]

Lack of such a standard has allowed England to rely in the past on common sense, which all too often has simply meant a "general indifference to political theories; our quiet and respectable adherence to the things that are."[45] The result is muddle: the prison system and the penal code, which Bulwer exposed in his novel of 1830, *Paul Clifford;* the system of poor relief, which he criticizes severely in this book. His attack on the dole echoes the philosophical radicals. The poor are cosseted, sacrificing their independence for the "sleek indolence and lazy comfort" of the poorhouse.[46] Rate payers suffer at the expense of men and women who refuse to seek employment. "Idleness and vice, then, are the chief parents of crime and distress; viz., the indisposition to work, not the want of work."[47] Upon this "great truth" Bulwer urges the government to erect a reformed administration. His proposals come close to those adopted in 1834: no relief to the able-bodied poor; abolition of outdoor relief; centralization and rationalization. The state has its positive role to play in this as in all schemes for the welfare of its citizens. Factory conditions, about which Bulwer writes compassionately, must be corrected by state-imposed legislation and state-supervised education. "The principle of legislation in this country has long been that merely of punishing. The proper principle is prevention. A good government is a *directive government.* It should be in advance of the people—it should pass laws *for* them, not receive all laws *from* them."[48] He has learned his Bentham well.

Yet Bulwer understands and appreciates humanity in a way most Benthamites did not. "I know not how it is, sir, but it seems to me that wherever a man is very active on some point of humanity, he always finds himself suddenly surrounded by the great body of the English people."[49] Bulwer rejoices in that fact. Utilitarian impatience is softened by Romantic understanding. The book itself is an accurate reflection of its author—factual, anec-

44. See below, p. 218.
45. See below, p. 49–50.
46. See below, p. 129.
47. See below, p. 126.
48. See below, p. 140.
49. See below, p. 193.

dotal, impassioned, analytical—and an amalgam as well of the age in which it was written.

The age had faith in itself. Despite the vast uncertainties, there was optimism. Progress was "the prerogative of our race."[50] Reform the franchise, strengthen the state, educate a new public opinion, and the world will see tremendous change for the better. For Bulwer it was to prove a false dawn. Whig support for free trade set him drifting toward the Tory camp. His 1842 novel, *Zanoni,* dwelt upon the excesses of the French Revolution. Two years before, he had lost his seat over the free-trade question. When he returned to the House in 1852, it was as a Conservative M.P. for Hertfordshire.[51] Derby appointed him secretary for the colonies in 1858 and raised him to the peerage as a baron in 1866. Before he died in 1873, he wrote an essay entitled "The Genius of Conservatism," an expression of the distance he had traveled in forty-three years. Far from castigating the aristocratic temper, he celebrated it. "The ideal aim of Conservatism," he wrote, "in its relation to popular liberty, would be to elevate the masses, in character and feeling, to that standard which Conservatism seeks in aristocracy—in other words, to aristocratise the community, so than the greatest liberty to the greatest number might not be the brief and hazardous effect of a sudden and revolutionary law, but the gradual result of that intellectual power to which liberty is indispensable."[52] Now Conservatism, not Radicalism, is to insure a beneficent transposition from the old world into the new.

In the introductory memoir to his edition of his father's speeches, Bulwer's son declares that his father was really a conservative throughout his life. Enough evidence exists to suggest he may be right. All the more remarkable, then, this lengthy pamphlet, written at a time when even a philosophical conservative, unable to withstand the force of contradictory intellectual pressures, spun round to face the world as a humanitarian radical. For that very reason, *England and the English* bespeaks the spirit of the age.

50. See below, p. 401.
51. He succeeded to his mother's estate, Knebworth, upon her death in 1843. At that time he also assumed her family surname.
52. Edward Robert Bulwer Lytton, ed., *Speeches of Edward Lord Lytton* (London, 1874), 1:ci–cii.

A Note on the Text

The text for this edition of *England and the English* is the first edition, published by Richard Bentley, New Burlington Street, London, in 1833. It was originally published in two volumes, the first containing books 1–3 and an appendix on education, the second books 4–5, and the appendixes on Bentham (by John Stuart Mill) and on Mill.

STANDISH MEACHAM

Further Reading

The best life of Bulwer remains *The Life of Edward Bulwer, First Lord Lytton,* by his grandson the Earl of Lytton, published in 1913. Also of interest is *Speeches of Edward Lord Lytton* (1874) edited by his son, the first Earl. It is especially valuable for its prefatory memoir. *Bulwer: A Panorama: Edward and Rosina,* by Michael Sadleir (1931) is the first volume of an unfinished life that skillfully sets Bulwer against the background of his age. Readers should compare Bulwer's analysis with that of John Stuart Mill's *The Spirit of the Age* (1942), with an introduction by Friedrich A. von Hayek, and with Emerson's *English Traits* (1966), edited by Howard Mumford Jones. For a general modern account of the period, the best survey is Asa Briggs, *The Age of Improvement* [1783–1867] (1959); the most imaginative interpretation is G. M. Young's *Victorian England: Portrait of an Age* (1952).

ENGLAND
AND
THE ENGLISH

Analytical Table of Contents

BOOK THE SECOND
SOCIETY AND MANNERS
INSCRIBED TO ——— ———, ESQ.

CHAPTER I
SOCIETY AND MANNERS

CHAPTER II
CONVERSATION AND LITERARY MEN

BOOK THE THIRD
SURVEY OF THE STATE OF EDUCATION, ARISTOCRATIC AND POPULAR, AND OF THE GENERAL INFLUENCES OF MORALITY AND RELIGION IN ENGLAND

Inscribed to Thomas Chalmers, D.D.

CHAPTER I
THE EDUCATION OF THE HIGHER CLASSES

CHAPTER II
STATE OF EDUCATION AMONG THE MIDDLING CLASSES

CHAPTER III
POPULAR EDUCATION

CHAPTER IV
VIEW OF THE STATE OF RELIGION

CHAPTER V
THE SABBATH

CHAPTER VI
STATE OF MORALITY

CHAPTER VII
WHAT OUGHT TO BE THE AIM OF ENGLISH MORALISTS IN THIS AGE

APPENDIX
A
POPULAR EDUCATION

BOOK THE FOURTH
VIEW OF THE INTELLECTUAL SPIRIT
OF THE TIME
Inscribed to I. D'Israeli, Esq.

CHAPTER I

CHAPTER II
LITERATURE

CHAPTER III

CHAPTER IV
STYLE

CHAPTER VII
PATRONAGE

CHAPTER VIII
THE STATE OF SCIENCE

CHAPTER IX
THE STATE OF THE ARTS

CHAPTER X
SUPPLEMENTARY CHARACTERS

BOOK THE FIFTH
A VIEW OF OUR POLITICAL STATE
Inscribed to the English People

CHAPTER I

CHAPTER VI
THE STATE OF PARTIES

CHAPTER VII

A PICTURE OF THE PRESENT
HOUSE OF COMMONS

CHAPTER VIII

CHAPTER THE LAST

THE AUTHOR'S APOLOGY

APPENDIX

Book the First

View of
the English
Character

INSCRIBED TO HIS EXCELLENCY

THE PRINCE TALLEYRAND

Before you can rectify the disorders of a state, you must examine the character of the people.   VOLTAIRE

I am he
Have measured all the shires of England over,
For to these savages I was addicted
To search their natures and make odd discoveries.
The New Inn. BEN JOHNSON. Act 5, Scene 5.

I

View of the English Character

I am about, in this portion of my work, to treat of the character of my countrymen: for when a diplomatist like your Excellency is amongst them, they may as well be put upon their guard. I shall endeavour to tell my countrymen the causes that have stamped with certain impressions the National Character, in the belief that the knowledge of self is a better precaution against deceit, than even the suspicion of others. I inscribe this portion of my work to your Excellency on the same principle as that on which the Scythian brought to Darius a mouse, a bird, a fish, and a bundle of arrows:—they were the symbols of his nation, and given as instructions to its foe. I make up also my bundle of national symbols, and I offer them to the representative of that great people with whom for eight centuries we have been making great wars, occasioned by small mistakes. Perhaps if the symbols had been rightly construed a little earlier, even a mouse and a fish might have taught us better. A quarrel is, nine times out of ten, merely the fermentation of a misunderstanding.

I have another reason for inscribing these preliminary chapters to Prince Talleyrand: this is not the first time he has been amongst us—great changes have been over the world during the wide interval between his first and his present visit to England. Those changes which have wrought such convulsions in states, have begun by revolutions in the *character* of nations;—every change in a constitution is occasioned by some change in the people. The English of the present day are not the English of twenty years ago. To whom can I dictate my observations on the causes that influence character so fittingly as to the man who can read character at a glance. The consciousness that I set over my testimony so penetrating a judge must make me doubly scrupulous as to its accuracy: and my presumption in appealing to such an arbiter, is an evidence, indeed, of temerity; but it is also a proof of my honesty, and a guarantee for my caution.

I remember to have read in an ancient writer[1] of a certain district in Africa remarkable for a fearful phenomenon. "In that climate," says our authority, "the air seemed filled with gigantic figures of strange and uncouth monsters fighting (or in pursuit of) each other. These apparitions were necessarily a little alarming to foreigners, but the natives looked upon them with the utmost indifference." Is not this story an emblem of national prejudices? The shadowy monsters that appal the stranger seem ordinary enough to us; we have no notion of a different atmosphere, and that which is a marvel to others is but a commonplace to ourselves. Yet if the native is unobservant, your Excellency will allow that the traveller is credulous; and if sometimes the monsters are unremarked by the one, sometimes also they are invented by the other. Your Excellency remembers the story of the French Jesuit, who was astonished to find priesthood in China; the man who practised it in the name of the Virgin thought it a monstrous piece of impudence to practise it in the name of Fo! In the same spirit of travel you read of an Englishwoman complaining of rudeness in America, and a German prince affecting a republican horror at an aristocracy in England.

His Excellency, Prince Talleyrand, knows better than the whole *corps* of diplomatists how small a difference there is really between man and man—the stature and limbs vary little in proportions—it is the costume that makes all the distinction. Travellers do not sufficiently analyze their surprise at the novelties they see, and they often proclaim that to be a difference in the several characters of nations, which is but a difference in their manners. One of the oldest illustrations of national prejudice is to be found in Herodotus. The Greeks in the habit of *burning* their parents were wonderfully indignant at the barbarity of the

1. Diodorus Siculus.

Callatii, who were accustomed to *eat* them. The Persian king summons the Callatii before him in the presence of the Greeks:—
"You eat your fathers and mothers—a most excellent practice—
pray, for what sum will you burn them?" The Callatii were exceedingly disgusted at the question. Burn their parents! They
uttered yells of horror at so inhuman a suggestion! The Callatian
and the Greek experienced filial affection in an equal degree, but
the man who made a dinner of his father, would have considered
it the height of atrocity to have made a bonfire of him.

The passions are universally the same—the expression of
them as universally varying. Your Excellency will allow that the
French and the English are both eminently vain of country—so
far they are alike—yet if there be any difference between the
two nations more strong than another, it is the manner in which
that vanity is shewn. The vanity of the Frenchman consists (as I
have somewhere read) in belonging to so great a country: but
the vanity of the Englishman exults in the thought that so great
a country belongs to himself. The root of all our notions, as of all
our laws, is to be found in the sentiment of property. It is *my*
wife whom you shall not insult; it is *my* house that you shall not
enter; it is *my* country that you shall not traduce; and by a species
of ultra-mundane appropriation, it is *my* God whom you shall
not blaspheme!

We may observe the different form of the national vanity in
the inhabitant of either country by comparing the eulogia which
the Frenchman lavishes on France, with the sarcastic despondency
with which the Englishman touches upon England.

A few months ago I paid a visit to Paris: I fell in with a French
marquis of the Bourbonite politics: he spoke to me of the present
state of Paris with tears in his eyes. I thought it best to sympathize
and agree with him; my complaisance was displeasing:—he
wiped his eyes with the air of a man beginning to take offence.
"Nevertheless, sir," quoth he, "our public buildings are superb!"
I allowed the fact. "We have made great advances in civilization." There was no disputing the proposition. "Our writers are
the greatest in the world." I was silent. "*Enfin*—what a devil of
a climate yours is, in comparison to ours!"

I returned to England, in company with a Frenchman, who
had visited us twenty years since, and who was delighted with the

improvements he witnessed in London; I introduced him to one of our patriots.—"What a superb street is Regent Street," cried the Frenchman.

"Pooh, sir, mere lath and plaster!" replied the patriot.

"I wish to hear your debates," said the Frenchman.

"Not worth the trouble, sir," groaned the patriot.

"I shall do homage to your public men."

"Mere twaddlers, I assure you—nothing great now-a-days."

"Well, I am surprised; but, at least, I shall see your authors and men of science."

"Really, sir," answered the patriot, very gravely, "I don't remember that we *have any*."

The polished Frenchman was at a loss for a moment, but recovering himself—"Ah!" said he, taking a pinch of snuff, "but you're a very great nation—very!"

"*That* is quite true," said the Englishman drawing himself up.

The Englishman then is vain of his country! Wherefore? because of the public buildings? he never enters them.—The laws? he abuses them eternally.—The public men? they are quacks.— The writers? he knows nothing about them. He is vain of his country for an excellent reason—IT PRODUCED HIM.

In his own mind the Englishman is the pivot of all things—the centre of the solar system. Like Virtue herself, he

> Stands as the sun,
> And all that rolls around him
> Drinks light, and life, and glory, from this aspect

It is an old maxim enough among us that we possess the sturdy sense of independence; we value ourselves on it;—yet the sense of independence is often but the want of sympathy with others.

There was a certain merchant sojourning at an inn, whom the boots by mistake called betimes in the morning.

"Sir," quoth the boots, "the day's breaking." The merchant turned round with a grim look—"Let it break," growled he, "it owes *me* nothing!" This anecdote is rather characteristic: it shows the connexion between selfishness and independence. The trait in our character of which I speak, has been often remarked; none, however, have, to my mind, very clearly accounted for it. Your Excellency knows, to be sure, that all the Frenchmen who ever wrote a syllable about us have declared it the result of our haughty consciousness of liberty. But we are better aware now-a-days than formerly what the real effects of liberty are. The feeling I describe is entirely selfish; the feelings produced by the consciousness of liberty rather run into the wildest extremes of universal philanthropy. Union and fraternity are the favourite cant words of popular power; and unsociability may be the accompaniment, but is certainly not the characteristic, of freedom.

A Frenchman, indeed, has long enjoyed the same security of property, and the same consciousness of liberty, which are the boast of the Englishman; but this advantage has rather tended to widen than concentrate the circle of his affections. In becoming a citizen he has not ceased to mingle with his kind; perhaps, he thinks that to be at once free and unsocial would be a union less characteristic of a civilized, than a savage, condition. But your Excellency has observed, that all amongst us, save those of the highest ranks, live very much alone. Our crowded parties are not society; we assemble all our acquaintance for the pleasure of saying nothing to them. *"Les Anglais,"* says one of your countrymen, *"les Anglais ont une infinite de ces petites usages de convention,—pour se dispenser de parler."* Our main element is home; and if you believe our sentimentalists, we consider it a wonderful virtue to be unhappy and disagreeable every where else. Thus (the consequence is notable) we acquire that habit of attaching an undue importance to our own circle, and viewing with indifference all the sphere beyond, which proverbially distinguishes the recluse, or the member of a confined coterie. Your Excellency has perhaps conversed with Mr. Owen;—that benevolent man usually visits every foreigner whom he conceives worthy of conversion to parallelogrammatisation; and, since I remember the time when he considered the Duke of Wellington and the Archbishop of Canterbury among the likeliest of his proselytes, it is not out of the range of possibilities that he should imagine he may make an Owenite of the Ex-Bishop of *Autun*. If, by any accident, Mr. Owen is wrong upon that point, he is certainly right in another; he is right when, in order to render philanthropy universal, he proposes that individuals of every community should live in public together—the unsocial life is scarcely prolific of the social virtues.

But if it be not the consciousness of liberty, what causes are they that produce amongst us that passion for the Unsocial, which we dignify with the milder epithet of the Domestic? I apprehend that the main causes are two: the first may be found in our habits of trade; the second, in the long established influence of a very peculiar form of aristocracy.

With respect to the first, I think we may grant, without much difficulty, that it is evidently the nature of Commerce to detach the mind from the pursuit of amusement; fatigued with promiscuous intercourse during the day, its votaries concentrate their desires of relaxation within their home; at night they want rest rather than amusement: hence we usually find that a certain apathy to amusement, perfectly distinct from mere gravity of disposition, is the characteristic of commercial nations. It is not less observable among the Americans, and the Dutch, than it is among the English; the last indeed have, in their social state, great counterbalances to the commercial spirit. I had the honour of being introduced the other day to a young traveller from Amsterdam. "Have you been to the play since your arrival in London?" was a natural question.

"No, sir, those amusements are very expensive."

"True; but a man so enviably rich as yourself can afford them."

"No, sir," was the austere and philosophic reply, "I can afford the amusement, but *not the habit* of amusement."

A witty countryman of your Excellency's told me that he could win over any Englishman I pleased to select, to accompany him to a masquerade that was to be given at the Opera House. I selected for the experiment a remarkably quiet and decorous father of a family—a merchant. The Frenchman accosted him—"Monsieur never goes to masquerades, I believe."

"Never."

"So I thought. It would be *impossible* to induce you to go."

"Not quite impossible," said the merchant, smiling; "but I am too busy for such entertainments; besides I have a moral scruple."

"Exactly so. I have just bet my friend here three to one that he could not persuade you to go to the masquerade given to-morrow night at the Opera House."

"Three to one!" said the merchant, "those are long odds."

"I will offer *you* the same bet," rejoined the Frenchman gaily, "in guineas, if you please."

"Three to one!—done," cried the Englishman, and he went to the Opera House in order to win his wager; the masquerade in this case had ceased to be an amusement—it had become a commercial speculation![2]

But the same class that are indifferent to amusement, are yet fond of show. A spirit of general unsociability is not incompatible with the love of festivals on great occasions, with splendid entertainments, and a luxurious hospitality. Ostentation and unsociability are often effects of the same cause; for the spirit of commerce, disdaining to indulge amusement, is proud of displaying wealth; and is even more favourable to the Luxuries, than it is to the Arts.

The second cause of our unsociability is more latent than the first: so far from springing out of our liberty, it arises from the restraints on it; and is the result, not of the haughtiness of a democracy, but the peculiar influences of aristocratic power. This part of my inquiry, which is very important, deserves a chapter to itself.

2. So, in the United States, a traveller tells us that he observed in the pit of the theatre two lads of about fifteen years of age, conversing very intently between the acts. Curiosity prompted him to listen to the dialogue. Were they discussing the merits of the play—the genius of the actor—the splendour of the scene? No such thing; they were attempting to calculate the number of spectators, and the consequent profits to the manager.

II

The proverbial penetration of your Excellency has doubtless remarked, that England has long possessed this singular constitution of society—the spirit of democracy in the power of obtaining
honours, and the genius of an aristocracy in the method by which
they are acquired. The highest offices have been open by law to
any man, no matter what his pedigree or his quarterings; but influences, stronger than laws, have determined that it is only
through the aid of one portion or the other of the aristocracy that
those offices can be obtained. Hence we see daily in high advancement men sprung from the people, who yet never use the
power they have acquired in the people's behalf. Nay, it may be
observed, even among the lawyers, who owe at least the *first* steps
of promotion to their own talents or perseverance, though for
the crowning honours they must look to oligarchical favour, that,
as in the case of a Scott or a Sugden, the lowest plebeian by birth,
has only to be of importance to become the bitterest aristocrat in
policy. The road to honours is apparently popular; but each person rising from the herd has endeavoured to restrain the very
principle of popularity by which he has risen. So that, while the
power of attaining eminent station has been open to all ranks, yet
in proportion as that power bore any individual aloft, you might
see it purifying itself of all democratic properties, and beautifully
melting into that aristocratic atmosphere which it was permitted
to attain.—Mr. Hunt, whom your Excellency may perhaps have
heard of, as a *Doctrinaire,* in a school once familiar to yourself,

had a peculiar faculty of uttering hard truths. "You speak," quoth he, one evening in the House of Commons, "of the mob of demagogues whom the Reform Bill will send to parliament; be not afraid, you have one sure method of curing the wildest of them; choose your man, catch him, place him on the Treasury bench, and be assured you will never hear him accused of being a demagogue again."

Lord Lachrymal (it is classical, and dramatic into the bargain, to speak of the living under feigned names) is a man of plebeian extraction. He has risen through the various grades of the law, and has obtained possession of the highest. No man calls him *parvenu*—he has confounded himself with the *haute noblesse;* if you were to menace the peers' right of voting by proxy, he would burst into tears. "Good old man," cry the Lords, "how he loves the institutions of his country!" Am I asked why Lord Lachrymal is so much respected by his peers—am I asked why they boast of his virtues, and think it wrong to remember his origin?—I would answer that question by another, Why is the swallow considered by the vulgar a bird that should be sacred from injury?—Because it builds under their own eaves! There is a certain class of politicians, and Lord Lachrymal is one of them, who build their fortunes in the roofs of the aristocracy, and obtain, by about an equal merit, an equal sanctity with the swallow.

In nearly all states, it is by being the tool of the great that the lowly rise. People point to the new Sejanus, and cry to their children, "See the effect of merit!"—Alas, it is the effect of servility. In despotic states, the plebeian has even a greater chance of rising than in free. In the east, a common water-carrier to-day is grand vizier to-morrow. In the Roman Republic the low born were less frequently exalted, than they were in the Roman Despotism. So with us—it was the Tories who brought forward the man of low or *mediocre* birth; the Whigs, when they came into power, had only their *grands seigneurs* to put into office. The old maxim of the political adventurer was invariably this: To rise from the people, take every opportunity to abuse them! What mattered it, then, to the plebeians that one of their number was exalted to the Cabinet? He had risen by opposing their wishes; his very characteristic was that of contempt for his brethren. A nobleman's valet is always super-eminently bit-

ter against the *canaille:* a plebeian in high station is usually valet
to the whole peerage!

The time has long past when the English people had any
occasion for jealousy against the power of the crown. Even at
the period in which they directed their angry suspicions against
the king, it was not to that branch of the legislature that the
growing power of corruption was justly to be attributed. From
the date of the aristocratic revolution of 1688, the influence of
the aristocracy has spread its unseen monopoly over the affairs
of state. The king, we hear it said, has the privilege to choose
his ministers! Excellent delusion! The aristocracy choose them!
the heads of that aristocratic party which is the most powerful
must come into office, whether the king like it or not. Could
the king choose a cabinet out of men unknown to the aristocracy—persons belonging neither to whig nor tory? Assuredly
not; the aristocratic party in the two Houses would be in arms.
Heavens, what a commotion there would be! Imagine the
haughty indignation of my Lords Grey and Harrowby! What
a "prelection" we should receive from Lord Brougham, "deeply
meditating these things!" Alas! the *king's* ministry would be
out the next day, and the aristocracy's ministry, with all due
apology, replaced. The power of the king is but the ceremonial
to the power of the magnates. He enjoys the prerogative of seeing two parties fight in the lists, and of crowning the victor.
Need I cite examples of this truth? Lord Chatham is the dread
and disgust of George III.—the stronger of the two factions
for the time being force his majesty into receiving that minister.
The Catholic question was the most unpalatable measure that
could be pressed upon George IV.—To the irritability of that
monarch no more is conceded than was granted to the obstinacy
of his royal father, and the Catholic Relief Bill is passed amidst
all the notoriety of his repugnance. In fact, your Excellency,
who knows so well the juggling with which one party in politics
fastens its sins upon another, may readily perceive that the monarch has only been roasting the chestnuts of the aristocracy;[1] and

---

1. The nation had begun to perceive this truth, when Burke thought fit once
more to blind it. "One of the principal topics," saith he, in his *Thoughts on the
Cause of the present Discontents,* "which was then, and has been since much
employed by that political school, is an effectual terror of the growth of an

the aristocracy, cunning creature, has lately affected to look quite shocked at the quantity of chestnuts roasted.

In a certain savage country that I have read of, there is a chief supposed to be descended from the gods; all the other chiefs pay him the greatest respect; they consult him if they should go to war, or proclaim peace; but it is an understood thing, that he is to be made acquainted with their determination beforehand. His consent is merely the ratification of their decree. But the chiefs, always speaking of his power, conceal their own; and while the popular jealousy is directed to the *seeming* authority, they are enabled quietly to cement and extend the foundations of the *real*. Of a similar nature have been the relations between the English king and the English aristocracy; the often odious policy of the last has been craftily fastened on the first; and the sanctity of a king has been too frequently but the conductor of popular lightning from the more responsible aristocracy.

The supposed total of constitutional power has always consisted of three divisions; the king, the aristocracy, and the commons: but the aristocracy (until the passing of the Reform Bill), by boroughs in the one house, as by hereditary seats in the other, monopolized the whole of the three divisions. They ousted the people from the commons by a majority of their own delegates; and they forced the king into their measures by the maxim, that his consent to a bill passed through *both* houses could not with safety be withheld. Thus then, in state affairs, the government of the country has been purely that of an aristocracy. Let us now examine the influence which they have exercised in social relations. It is to this, I apprehend, that we must look for those qualities which have distinguished their influence from that of other aristocracies. Without the odium of separate privileges, without the demarcation of feudal rights, the absence of

---

aristocratic power, prejudicial to the rights of the crown, and the balance of the constitution," &c. He goes on to argue, that the influence of the crown is a danger more imminent than that of the peerage. Although in the same work that brilliant writer declares himself "no friend to the aristocracy," his whole love for liberty was that of an aristocrat. His mind was eminently feudal in its vast and stately mould, and the patrician plausibilities dazzled and attracted him far more than the monarchical. He could have been a rebel easier than a republican.

those very prerogatives has been the cause of the long establishment of their power. Their authority has not been visible:
held under popular names it has deceived the popular eye;—and
deluded by the notion of a Balance of Power, the people did
not see that it was one of the proprietors of the power who held
the scales and regulated the weights.

The social influence of the aristocracy has been exactly of a
character to strengthen their legislative. Instead of keeping
themselves aloof from the other classes, and "hedging their
state" round with the thorny, but unsubstantial barriers of her-
aldic distinctions; instead of demanding half a hundred quarterings with their wives, and galling their inferiors by eternally
dwelling on the inferiority, they may be said to mix more
largely, and with seeming equality, with all classes, than any
other aristocracy in the savage or civilized world. Drawing their
revenues from land, they have also drawn much of their more
legitimate[2] power from the influence it gave them in elections.
To increase this influence they have been in the habit of visiting
the provinces much more often than any aristocracy in a monarchical state are accustomed to do. Their hospitality, their field
sports, the agricultural and county meetings they attend, in order
"to keep up the family interest," mix them with all classes; and,
possessing the usual urbanity of a court, they have not unfre-
quently added to the weight of property, and the glitter of station, the influence of a personal popularity, acquired less, perhaps, by the evidence of virtues, than the exercise of politeness.

In most other countries the middle classes rarely possessing
the riches of the nobility, have offered to the latter no incentive
for seeking their alliance. But wealth is the greatest of all levellers,
and the highest of the English nobles willingly repair the fortunes of hereditary extravagance by intermarriage with the families of the banker, the lawyer, and the merchant: this, be it observed, tends to extend the roots of their influence among the
middle classes, who, in other countries are the natural barrier of
the aristocracy. It is the ambition of the rich trader to obtain the
alliance of nobles; and he loves, as well as respects, those
honours to which himself or his children may aspire. The long-

2. And yet the power that has been most frequently inveighed against, merely
because it was the most evident.

established custom of purchasing titles, either by hard money or the more circuitous influence of boroughs, has tended also to mix aristocratic feelings with the views of the trader; and the apparent openness of honours to all men, makes even the humblest shopkeeper, grown rich, think of sending his son to College, not that he may become a wiser man or a better man, but that he may *perhaps* become my lord bishop or my lord chancellor.

Thus, by not preserving a strict demarcation, as the German nobles, round their order, the English aristocracy extended their moral influence throughout the whole of society, and their state might thus be said, like the city of the Lacedemonians, to be the safer in internal force, from rejecting all vulgar fortifications.

By this intermixture of the highest aristocracy with the more subaltern ranks of society, there are far finer and more numerous grades of dignity in this country than in any other. You see two gentlemen of the same birth, fortune, and estates—they are not of the same rank,—by no means!—one looks down on the other as confessedly his inferior. Would you know why? His *connexions* are much higher! Nor are connexions alone the dispensers of an ideal, but acknowledged consequence. Acquaintanceship confers also its honours: next to being related to the great, is the happiness of knowing the great: and the wife even of a *bourgeois*, who has her house filled with fine people, considers herself, and is tacitly allowed to be, of greater rank than one, who, of far better birth and fortune, is not so diligent a worshipper of birth and fortune in others; in fact, this lady has but her own respectable rank to display—but that lady reflects the exalted rank of every duchess that shines upon her[3] cardrack.

These mystic, shifting, and various shades of graduation; these shot-silk colours of society produce this effect: That people have no exact and fixed position—that by acquaintance alone they may rise to look down on their superiors—that while the rank gained by intellect, or by interest, is open but to few, the rank that may be obtained by fashion seems delusively to be open to all. Hence,

3. It may be observed that the power of fashion has increased in proportion as the aristocracy have blended themselves more with the gentry and merchants. There was a time when the English were as remarkable among foreigners for their independence and indifference to the mode, as they are now noted for their servile obsequiousness to fashion.

in the first place, that eternal vying with each other; that spirit of show; that lust of imitation which characterize our country-men and countrywomen. These qualities so invariably observed by foreigners have never yet been ascribed to their true origin. I think I have succeeded in tracing their cause as national characteristics to the peculiar nature of our aristocratical influences. As wealth procures the alliance and respect of nobles, wealth is affected even where not possessed; and, as fashion, which is the creature of an aristocracy, can only be obtained by resembling the fashionable; hence, each person imitates his fellow, and hopes to purchase the respectful opinion of others by renouncing the independence of opinion for himself.

And hence, also, proceeds the most noticeable trait in our national character, our reserve, and that *orgueil,* so much more expressive of discontent than of dignity, which is the displeasure, the amazement, and the proverb of our continental visiters. Nobody being really fixed in society, except the *very* great (in whom, for the most part, the characteristics vanish), in any advance you make to a seeming equal, you may either lower yourself by an acquaintance utterly devoid of the fictitious advantages which are considered respectable; or, on the other hand, you may subject your pride to the mortification of a rebut from one, who, for reasons impossible for you to discover, considers his station far more unequivocal than your own. *La Bruyère* observes, that the rank of single men being less settled than that of the married, since they *may* exalt themselves by an alliance, they are usually placed by society in one grade higher than their legitimate claim. Another French writer commenting on this passage has observed, that hence one reason why there is usually less real dignity and more factitious assumption in the single men of polished society, than in the married;—they affect an imaginary situation. With us all classes are the same, as the bachelors of *La Bruyère:* all aim at some ideal situation a grade above their own, and act up to the dignity of this visionary Barataria. The ingenious author of *The Opium Eater* has said, that the family of a bishop are, for the most part, remarkable for their pride. It is because the *family* of a bishop hold an equivocal station, and are for ever fearful that they are not thought enough of: a bishop belongs to the aristocracy, but his family to the gentry.

Again, natural sons are proverbial for arrogance and assumption
—it is from the same cause. In fact, let us consult ourselves. Are
we not all modest when we feel ourselves estimated at what we
consider our just value, and all inclined to presume in proportion
as we fear we are slighted?

In all other countries where an aristocracy is or has been
exceedingly powerful, the distinctions they have drawn between
themselves and society have been marked and stern; they have
chiefly lived, married, and visited among their own appointed
circle. In Germany the count of eighty quarterings does not fear a
rivalry with the baron of six; nor does the baron of six quarterings
dread the aspiring equality of the merchant or the trader; each
rank is settled in its own stubborn circumvallation: fashion in
Germany is, therefore, comparatively nugatory in its influence;
there is no object in vying, and no reward in imitation. With us
the fusion of all classes, each with the other, is so general, that
the aristocratic contagion extends from the highest towards the
verge of the lowest. The tradesmen in every countrytown have a
fashion of their own, and the wife of the mercer will stigmatize
the lady of the grocer as "ungenteel." When Mr. Cobbett, so
felicitous in nicknames, and so liberal in opinions, wished to
assail Mr. Sadler, he found no epithet so suitable to his views
or sentiments as the disdainful appellation of *"linendraper!"* The
same pride and the same reserve will be found every where; and
thus slowly and surely, from the petty droppings of the well of
manners, the fossilized incrustations of national character are
formed.

To the importance which wealth receives from the aristocracy
we must add the importance it receives from trade. What men
are taught to respect, gradually acquires the distinction of a
virtue—to be rich becomes a merit; to be poor, an offence. A
foreign writer has thus justly observed, that we may judge of the
moral influence of this country by the simple phrase, that a man
is *worth* so much; or, as he translates the expression, *digne tant.*

In a work upon England, published at Paris in 1816, which has
stolen much from the more important one of M. Ferri de St. Constant; but which, while often wrong in its facts, is, *when* right in
them, usually profound in its deductions, the writer, after observing that in England, *l'argent décide en tout,* philosophically re-

marks—*"De cette manière, quoique les richesses augmentent à certains égards la puissance d'un état, il arrive qu'elles ne servent qu'à le détruire sitôt qu'elles influent sur le choix de ceux qui sont à la tête du gouvernement."*

In other countries poverty is a misfortune,—with us it is a crime.

The familiar meaning of a word often betrays the character of a people: with the ancient Romans virtue signified valour: with the modern, a virtuoso is a collector. The inhabitants of the Tonga Islands, with whom all morals are in a state of extraordinary confusion, have no expression for virtue in a man which is not equally applicable to an axe: they recognize virtue only in what does *them* an evident service. An axe or a man may be the instrument of murder, but each continues to be a good axe or a good man. With us the word *virtue* is seldom heard, out of a moral essay; I am not sure whether it does not excite a suspicion of some unorthodox signification, something heathen and in contradistinction to religion. The favourite word is "respectability"— and the current meaning of "respectability" may certainly exclude virtue, but never a decent sufficiency of wealth: no wonder then that every man strives to be rich—

Et propter vitam vivendi perdere causas.

Through the effects they thus produce on the national character, the aristocracy have insensibly been able to react upon the laws. Poverty being associated in men's minds with something disreputable, they have had little scruple in making laws unfavourable to the poor! they have clung without shame to the severities of a barbarous criminal code—to an unequal system of civil law, which almost proscribes justice but to the wealthy—to impressment for seamen—to taxes upon knowledge—and to imprisonment by mesne process. Such consequences may be traced to such levities. The Laws of a Nation are often the terrible punishment of their foibles.

Hence also arises one of the causes[4] for the noticeable want

4. One of the causes. Another is the growth of religious sectarianism; but I am apt to believe, that if amusements were within the reach of the poor, there would be far less of the gloom of fanaticism. Excitement of one sort or the other must be sought for, as a counterpoise to toil; at present the poor find it only in two sources—the conventicle or the alehouse.

of amusement for the poorer classes. Where are the cheap *guinguettes* and gardens for the labourer, which make the boast of France? Where the consecrated greensward, formerly the theme of our poets,

> Where all the village train from labour free,
> Lead up their sports beneath the hawthorn tree?

We are told that the Arcadians, as their climate was peculiarly chill and gloomy (in modern phrase "English"), sought to counteract its influence by assemblies, music, and a gay and cheerful education. Thus did legislation conquer nature; nor with unhappy effects, for the Arcadians were no less remarkable for their benevolence and piety than for their passion for music and for their gaiety of disposition.[5] It is reserved for us to counteract the gloomiest climate by the dullest customs!

I do not say, however, that direct legislation should provide amusement for the poor—but at least it should never forbid it. The very essence of our laws has been against the social meetings of the humble, which have been called idleness, and against the amusements of the poor which have been stigmatized as disorder.[6] But what direct legislation itself cannot effect, could be effected by the spirit by which legislation is formed. That prejudice of respect for the wealthy, and contempt for the poor, which belongs to us, would probably soon close any institutions for popular amusements if established to-morrow; if they were cheap they would be considered disreputable. In France, the humbler shopkeepers mix in festivity with the peasantry; the aristocratic spirit would forbid this condescension in England (unless an election were going on), and the relaxation being thus ungraced by the presence of those a little their superiors would perhaps be despised by the labourers themselves.[7]

5. Polybius
6. A few half-sighted politicians, like Windham, have indeed advocated popular amusements, but of what nature?—Bull-baiting and boxing; amusements that brutalize. These are they who turn the people into swine, and then boast of their kindness in teaching them to be savage. Admirable philanthropists! the object of recreation is to soften and refine men, not to render them more ferocious.
7. They might be licentious from the same cause. In France the amusements of the peasantry are so decently conducted, because the presence of some of the middle class produces an unconscious, but most salutary restraint.

It were to be wished on many accounts that this were otherwise;
Amusement keeps men cheerful and contented—it engenders a
spirit of urbanity—it reconciles the poor to the pleasures of their
superiors which are of the same sort, though in another sphere;
it removes the sense of hardship—it brings men together in those
genial moments when the heart opens and care is forgotten. Deprived of more gentle relaxations the poor are driven to the alehouse, they talk over their superiors—and who ever talks of
others in order to praise them? they read the only cheap papers
permitted them, not usually the most considerate and mild in
spirit;—their minds in one respect are benefited; for they advance,
even by this intercourse, in their progress to better government;
but they clog this benefit by a rancour to all its obstacles, which
is at once natural and to be lamented.[8] Woe to the legislator who
succeeds by vexatious laws and petty tyrannies, in interdicting enjoyment to those who labour!—above all, in an age when they
have discovered what is due to themselves; he will, indeed, expedite reform—if that to legislators be an agreeable contemplation—but it will be by souring and exacerbating the spirit which
extorts it!

8. All passion blinds even the best-founded opinions. A passionate indignation against the aristocracy would, if once put into action, frustrate the good
objects it sought to effect. The great Marius saw all the vices of the aristocracy
with the wrath of a wronged plebeian. Marius was the Incarnation of Popular
Passion—he scourged the Patricians for their disorders, by committing more
tumultuous and deadly disorders himself.

III

There is a tale (your Excellency may have read it, it is to be found in the writings of a French missionary—a species of literature that must have manifold attractions for one who was once Bishop of Autun)—there is a tale of a certain Chinese emperor, who conceived great displeasure at the grand historian of the Celestial Empire, for having with too accurate and simple a fidelity, narrated in his chronicle all the errors and foibles of the prince. "I admire your effrontery," said the emperor frowning, "You dare then to keep a diary of my offences for the benefit of posterity?"

"Yes!" said the historian boldly, "I put down faithfully all that can convey to a later age a just impression of your character; accordingly, the instant your majesty dismisses me, I shall hasten to insert in my chronicle the threats and the complaints that you have made me for telling the truth."

The emperor was startled, but the Chinese have long been in the habit of enjoying very sensible monarchs—"Go," said he, after a short pause and with a frank smile, "Go, write down all you please; henceforth I will strive at least that Posterity shall have little to blame in me."

Upon the principle on which the historian wrote of the sovereign, I now write of the people. Will they be indignant at my honesty in painting their foibles? No, they will not be less generous nor less wise than the Emperor of China;—if they are, I shall avenge myself like my model, by a supplement, containing their reproaches! I do not, like the herd of faultfinders, declaim vaguely on the faults of the people, I attempt in honesty, if in error, to trace their causes. This is the first time in which, in a detailed and connected shape, the attempt has been made; the best way to find remedies for a disease is to begin by ascertaining its origin.

I think your Excellency must have perceived, since your first visit to England, there has been a great change from what formerly was a strong national characteristic;—*We no longer hate the French*. We have a greater sympathy with, than an aversion to, foreigners in general. We have enlarged the boundaries of patriotism, and are becoming Citizens of the World. Our ancient dislike to foreigners was not a vague and ignorant prejudice alone, nor was it solely the growth of an insular situation in the map of the globe; it was a legacy which was bequeathed to us by our history. The ancient record of our empire is a series of foreign conquests over the natives. The Roman, the Saxon, the Dane, the Norman, successively taught to the indigenous inhabitant a tolerably well-founded antipathy to foreigners. When the soreness of a conquered people wore off, the feeling was kept alive by the jealousy of a commercial one. Foreigners settled amongst us as traders; and the industry of the Flemish monopolized for centuries, to the great disgust of the natives, a considerable portion of our domestic manufactures. National dislikes, once formed, are slow of conversion; and a jealousy of foreigners, conceived with some cause by our forefathers, was easily retained, when the cause had ceased to exist. Our warlike aristocracy found it indeed expedient to keep alive so pugnacious a characteristic: and Nelson thought the best mode of conquering the French was seriously to inculcate, as a virtue, the necessity of detesting them. This settled hatred to our neighbours began, however, to break up from its solid surface at the close of the last century. The beginning of the French revolution—an event which your Excellency has probably forgotten—taught the more liberal of our populace that the French had no inherent desire to be slaves; they began to feel an union with their neighbours, from the common sentiment of liberty. The excesses of the Revolution checked the nascent charity, or at least confined it to the few; and a horror of the crimes of the French superseded a sympathy with their struggles. Still the surface of national antipathy was broken up; a party was formed to praise your countrymen, in opposition to the party that reviled them. By degrees the general principles of the first party came more into vogue than those of the last; and among those principles, a better estimation of the characters of foreign nations. The peace, of course, bringing us into more actual connexion with the continent, has strengthened the kindly sentiment: and, finally, your last Revolution has removed all trace of the fearful impression left upon us by the first. On the whole, therefore, a hatred of foreigners has ceased to distinguish us; and, of the two extremes, we must guard rather against a desire of imitating our neighbours, than a horror of resembling.

To be sure, however, our toleration of foreigners is more catholic than individual. We suspect them a little when some half a dozen of them in braided coats and mustacios pay us a midsummer visit; a respectable lodging-house keeper would rather be excused letting them apartments. They are driven, like the Jews of old, to a settled quarter, abandoned by the rest of the world; they domicile together in a dingy spot, surrounded by alleys and courts; you may see them matutinally emerging from the desolate gloom of Leicester-square, which is a sort of Petty France in itself, and where they have established a colony of hostels. But assuredly the unoffending frigidity, evinced to them in less familiar regions, is the result of no unhandsome prejudice. We do not think them, as we once did, *inherently,* but *unfortunately,* guilty!—in a word, we suspect them of being *poor.* They strike us with the unprepossessing air of the shabby genteel. Mrs. Smith is sorry her first floor is engaged—not because she thinks the foreign gentleman may cut her throat, but because she fears he may forget to pay his rent. She apprehends that he can scarcely give the "respectable reference" that she demands, for the use of her goods and chattels. Foreigners remark this suspicion, and not guessing the cause, do us injustice by supposing it is solely directed against them. No such thing; it is directed against Poverty ubiquitously; it is the abstract quality, not the material man, that excites in the Smithian breast the sentiment of distrust. Our hostess would be equally lukewarm to any Englishman she considered equivocally poor;— in short, it is a commercial, not a national apprehension. A rich foreigner, as your Excellency well knows, with huge arms on his carriage, half a dozen valets, and a fur great-coat, is sure to be obsequiously treated enough. Hence the wealthy visiter from the continent usually avers that we are a most civil people to foreigners; and the needy one declares that we are exactly the reverse. I hope that what I have said on this point will right us with our neighbours; and assure them that the only stories which we now believe to the practical inconvenience of Monsieur, are those which accuse him of living on a hundred Napoleons a-year, pocketing the sugar at his coffee, and giving the waiter something under a penny halfpenny!

A Russian of my acquaintance visited England, with a small portmanteau, about two years ago. Good heavens! how he abused us!—never was so rude, cruel, suspicious, barbaric a people! I saw him a few months since, having just paid us a second visit: he was in raptures with all he saw; never was a people so improved; his table was crowded with cards—how hospitable we were! The master of the hotel had displaced an English family to accommodate him; what a refined consideration for a stranger! Whence rose this difference in the Russian's estimate of us? His uncle was dead, he had come into a great property. In neither case had our good people looked at the *foreigner;* they had looked the first time at the small portmanteau, and the second time at the three carriages and four!

But if the commercial spirit makes us attach undue importance to wealth, it keeps alive also a spirit of honesty as the best means to acquire it. Thus the same causes that produce our defects, conspire to produce many of our merits. The effect of commerce is to make men trustworthy in their ordinary dealings and their social relations. It does this, not by the sense of virtue, but that of self-interest. A trader soon discovers that honesty is the best policy. If you travel through Italy, and your carriage break down, there is perhaps but one smith in the place; he repairs your carriage at ten times the value of the labour; he takes advantage of your condition and his own monopoly of the trade. Whoever has had the misfortune to make the tour of the Netherlands in a crazy *calèche,* can speak from ample experience of the similar extortion practised also in that country, where the standard of morality is much higher than in Italy. This would rarely, if ever, be the case in England. There might be no other smith in the village for you to apply to, but there would be a public spirit, a common conscience in the village, which would insensibly deter the monopolist from acting towards you dishonestly. To this we must, to be sure, add the consideration, that population being more dense, the monopoly is more rare, and the temptation less frequent.

It is the property of an enlightened aristocracy—I mean one that is comparatively enlightened—to foster the sentiments of honour. Honour is their creed; they sacrifice even virtues to a single one of its prejudices. Thus, in our relations with foreign states, we have been less wise than honurable: and we have sustained our national character, by paying with rigid punctuality the national loans.

Rogues among traders, and swindlers among gentlemen, there are in this, as in all countries; but they do not suffice to stamp the character of the People. There is no systematic mockery of principle with us—nor that sort of *maison de jeu* morality, which you find among the philosophical *élégans* of Paris and of Vienna. A fine gentleman in London is a formidable person to young heirs; but of these fine gentlemen there are, thank Heaven, not above a dozen or two. In private character, as in the national, an English patrician is rather the dupe than the deceiver:—at least, he keeps his deceits for his parliamentary career.

The English are also an eminently generous people. I do not mean generous in the vulgar signification of the epithet, though that they would deserve, if but from the ostentatious and artificial spirit I have already described—but the loftier and more moral one. Their sympathies are generous; they feel for the persecuted, and their love is for the fallen.

But it is mainly *the People,* (properly so speaking,) the mass —the majority that generosity characterizes; nor do I trace this virtue to the aristocratic influences: among the aristocracy it is not commonly found. As little, perhaps, is it to be traced to the influences of trade; it is rather connected with our history and our writers—and may be considered a remnant of the chivalric spirit which departed from the nobles ere it decreased among the people. It is the multitude who preserve longest the spirit of antiquity—the aristocracy preserve only the forms.

Let us recall for a moment the trial of Queen Caroline: in my own mind, and in the minds of the majority of the public, she was guilty of the crime imputed to her. Be it so; but the people sympathized, not with the crime, but the persecution. They saw a man pampered in every species of indulgence, and repudiating his wife in the first instance without assignable cause; allowing her full licence for conduct if she consented to remain abroad, and forbore to cross the line of his imperial Sybaritism of existence; but arming against her all the humiliations, and all the terrors of law, the instant she appeared in England, and interfered with the jealous monopoly of royal solemnities. They saw at once that this was the course of conduct natural rather to a man of passion than to one of honour: to a man of honour disgrace to his name would have seemed equally punishable whether perpetrated in Italy or in England. The queen ceased to be the defendant in a court of law, and seemed to the public the victim of a system of oppression. The zeal with which the lower orders supported her, was the zeal of Chivalry; the spirit which Burke invoked in vain from a debased nobility, leaped at once into life among a generous people. Compare the subservient and smothered disgust of the aristocracy with the loud indignation of the people;—which was the more indicative of the nobler emotions, or which preserved in the higher shape our national characteristic of generosity? Who are they that feel the most deeply for the negro slave —the people or the nobles? The people. Who attend the meetings in behalf of Poland? the aristocracy?—some two or three of them, indeed, for the vanity of uttering orations; but it is the people who fill the assembly. The people may be right, or they may be wrong, in their zeal for either cause, but it is at least the zeal of generosity.

Poverty,—crime itself,—does not blunt this noble characteristic. In some of the work-houses the overseers devised a method to punish the refractory paupers by taking away from them the comforts permitted to the rest; the rest, out of their own slender pittance, supplied their companions! In his work upon prisons, Mr. Buxton informs us, that in the jail of Bristol the allowances of bread to criminals was below the ordinary modicum necessary for subsistence; to the debtor *no* allowance, however, was made, their friends, or the charity of strangers, supported them: there have been times when these resources have failed, and some of the debtors would have literally perished for want, but that they were delivered—how? by the generosity of the criminals themselves, who voluntarily shared with them at once the food and the distress!

In the last election I remember to have heard a tory orator, opposed to the emancipation of the West Indian slaves, take advantage of the popular cry for economy, and impatience under taxation, and assure his audience, all composed of the labouring part of the population, that to attempt to release the slaves would be to increase the army, and consequently, the national burdens: the orator on the other side of the question, instead of refuting this assertion, was contented to grant it. "Be it so," he said; "suppose that your burdens are augmented—suppose that another shilling is monthly or weekly, wrung from your hard earnings—suppose all this, and I yet put it to you, whether, crippled and bowed down as you are by taxation, you would not cheerfully contribute your mite to the overthrow of slavery, though in so distant a clime— though borne by men of a different colour from yourselves, rather than even escape your burdens, grievous though they be, and know that that human suffering still exists, which you, by a self-sacrifice of your own, had the power to prevent?" The meeting rang with applause; the appeal was to generous emotions: had the generosity not been there, the appeal would have been unavailing.

It is, indeed, in popular elections, that a foreigner can alone fully learn the generous character of the English people—what threats they brave, what custom they lose, what profits they surrender, in order to act up to a motive of conscience, or a principle of honour. Could you be made aware of the frequent moral exaltation of the Constituent, your Excellency would be astonished to see the Representative so often an apostate.

Thus, then, generosity is the character of the nation; but the character rather of the people than the nobles; and while a certain school of theorists maintain that the chief good of an aristocracy is to foster that noble quality, they advance an argument which is so easily refuted as to endanger the cause it would support.

Your Excellency, if I mistake not, is tolerably well acquainted with the weaker side of Madame de Staël, and have, doubtless, in your experience of the courtly circles of England, seen whether their "moral air" be entitled to all the panegyrics it received from that ingenious Architect on Hypotheses. A regard for character is a quality on which we value ourselves justly; yet it scarcely, perhaps, produces those excellent effects on morality which ought to be its offspring. The reason is possibly this: we defer, it is true, to what we consider to be a good character; but it very often happens that our notions of the elements of a good character are any thing but just. We sometimes venerate a Saint where your Excellency would recognise a Mawworm. In the first place, as regards public character, that character has usually been considered the best, which adopts the principles most *à la mode*. Now the aristocracy influence the mode, and the best character, therefore, has been usually given to the strongest supporter of the aristocrats: the people not being educated, at least politically, and judging not for themselves, have formed their opinion from the very classes interested against them, maligned their friends, and wept tears of gratitude for the consistency of their foes. Mr. Thelwall advocated reform; and Mr. Canning informs us, that he was pelted as he went:—[1]

Another fault in our judgment of public men has been, that we have confounded too often a private sobriety of life with political respectability. If a gentleman walked betimes in the park, with his seven children and a very ugly wife, the regularity of such conduct would have stamped him as an unexceptionable politician. Your Excellency remembers Lord Mediocre So-So—he was a cabinet minister. He ordained a vast number of taxes, and never passed one popular law; but then he was very domestic, and the same coldness of constitution that denied him genius, preserved him from vice. He was a most pernicious statesman; but he bore the highest of characters. His very frigidity made him considered *'a safe politician';* for we often seem to imagine that the property of the mind resembles the property of sea water, and loses all its deleterious particles when once it is fairly frozen.

Sometimes in those visions of public virtue, which your Excellency knows all men now and then conceive—in their closet; I have fancied that public character should be proportioned only to public benefits; that the statesman should be weighed in a balance, where the laws he has assisted to frame should be thrown into the opposite scale; and that the light of his private amiabil-

1. "Thelwall and ye, that lecture as ye go,/And for your pains get pelted," &c.

ities should, instead of casting into shade his public character, be lost to the general eye in the wide blaze of universal utility.

At present, or at least until very lately,

> Whene'er of statesmen we complain,
>   They cry, 'why raise this vulgar strife so?
> 'Tis true, that tax too hard may strain;
>   But then—his lordship loves his wife so!
> That law, indeed, may gall ye rather;
>   But then—his lordship's such a father!'

I have observed in a former chapter, that the undue regard for wealth produces a false moral standard; that respectability is the favourite word of eulogium with us, as virtue was with the ancients; and that a man may be respectable, without being entitled from his virtues to respect. Hence it follows, that a regard for character may often be nothing but the regard of popular prejudices; and that, though a virtue in itself, it may neither be directed to, or productive of, virtues in others. Still this characteristic is a great and noble superstructure to build upon:—it is those nations who are indifferent to moral distinctions of whom Improvement may despair: a People who respect what they consider good, sooner or later discover in what good really consists. Indifference to moral character is a vice; a misunderstanding of its true components is but an error. Fortunately, the attention of our countrymen is now turned towards themselves; the spirit of *self*-examination is aroused; they laugh at the hyperbolical egotisms in which they formerly indulged; they do not take their opinions of their own excellence from ballad-singers, any more than their sentiments on the goodness of their constitution from the commonplaces of tories. "Imposters," said the acute Shaftesbury, "naturally speak the best of human nature, that they may the easier abuse it." The Imperial Tyrant of the Roman Senate always talked of the virtues of the senators.

But men now think for themselves. That blind submission to teachers, which belongs to the youth of Opinion, is substituted for bold examination in its maturity; and the task of the latter period is too often to unlearn the prejudices acquired in the first. When men begin to think for themselves, they will soon purify in the process of thought the errors they imbibed from others. To the boldness of the once abused and persecuted Paulicians, in judging themselves of the gospel, we owe that spirit which, though it suffered with Huss and Wickliffe, triumphed with Zuinglius and Luther. The scanty congregations of Armenia and Cappadocia were characterized by the desire to think freely—they have been the unacknowledged authors of *this very era* when men begin to think rightly. The agitation of Thought is the beginning of Truth.

If the effect of our regard for character has been a little over-rated, so I apprehend that the diplomatist of a thousand cabinets must sometimes have smiled at the exaggerated estimate which we form of our Common Sense. It is that property upon which we the most value ourselves; and every statesman, whether he propose to pass a bill for English reform or for Irish coercion, always trusts the consequences "to the known good sense of the British community." Let us put on our spectacles and examine this attribute.

The "common sense" of the ancient stoics was the sense of the *common* interest; the common sense of the modern schools is the sense of *one's own!* All traders are very much alive to this peculiar faculty—the Dutch, the Americans, as well as the English; it is, indeed, an inevitable consequence of the habit of making bargains; but, I think, on inquiry, we shall see that it belongs not so much to the whole nation as to the trading part of it.

That common sense, the practice of which is a sober and provident conduct, is, I fear, only visible amongst our middle classes in their domestic relations. It is possessed neither by the aristocracy nor the poor; least of all in *foreign relations* has it hitherto been our characteristic.

Like the nobility of other civilized countries, our own are more remarkable for an extravagant recklessness of money, for an impatient ardour for frivolities, for a headlong passion for the caprices, the debaucheries, the absurdities of the day, than for any of those prudent and considerate virtues which are the offspring of common sense. How few estates that are not deeply mortgaged! The Jews and the merchants have their grasp on more than three parts of the property of the peerage. Does this look like common sense? But these excesses have been carried to a greater height with *our* aristocracy than with any other, partly because of their larger command of wealth, principally because they, being brought like the rest of the world under the control of fashion, have not, like the ancient sieurs of France, or the great names of Germany, drawn sufficient consequence from their own birth to require no further distinctions. Our nobles have had ambition, that last infirmity of noble minds, and they have been accordingly accustomed to vie with each other in those singular phantasies of daring vulgarity with which a head without culture amuses an idleness without dignity. Hence, while we have boasted of our common sense, we have sent our young noblemen over the world to keep up that enviable reputation by the most elaborate eccentricities: and valuing ourselves on our prudence, we have only been known to the continent by our extravagance. Nor is this all: those who might have been pardonable as stray specimens of erratic imbecility, we have formally enrolled as the diplomatic representatives of the nation:—the oligarchical system of choosing all men to high office not according to their fitness for the place, but, according to their connexion with the party uppermost, has made our very ambassadors frequently seem the delegates from our *maisons des fous;* and the envoy of the British nation at the imperial court of Metternich and craft, was no less a person than the present Marquis of Londonderry.[2]

If in society, if abroad, if in our diplomatic relations, our common sense, our exquisite shrewdness, our sterling solidity are not visibly represented by our aristocracy, they are still less represented by them in our political relations. If we look to the progress of the Reform Bill through the Lords, we shall see the most lamentable want of discretion, the most singular absence of common sense. The peers did not think the Reform Bill necessary, accordingly they rejected it. Sensible men never do a bold thing without being prepared for its consequences. Were the peers prepared? No!—they expressed the greatest astonishment at Lord Grey's going out of office, after his declaring repeatedly that he would do so if they rejected his proposition; and the greatest consternation at the resolution of the people to get the Bill, after their expressing that resolution uninterruptedly for nearly two years.

2. This noble lord is only worse because more noisy than his brethren of the *corps diplomatique.* Look over the whole list: how rarely you can by an extraordinary accident discover a man not below par. Sir Frederic Lamb is a superficial man of pleasure, and yet he is the cleverest of all.

Taken by surprise, they therefore received the Bill again, and, after refusing to conciliate the people, voluntarily placed themselves in the condition of being beat by the people. Sensible men make a virtue of necessity. The peers put themselves in the condition of granting the necessity and losing all virtue in the grant. They paraded their weakness up and down—placed it in the most ostentatious situation, and with all the evils of concession, insisted on uniting all the odium of resistance. This might be very fine, but your Excellency need not think twice to allow that it was not very sensible.

Let us now look at our Poor. Where is their common sense. Alas, what imprudence!—Early marriages; many children; poor-rates, and the workhouse—see the history of the agricultural labourers! Of them, indeed, it may be said, in those words, in which an eastern writer asserts that the chronicle of the whole Human Race is found—"They are born; they are wretched; they die." In no foreign country, even of far less civilzation than England, is there the same improvidence: in France, where there is a much greater inclination to pleasure, there is yet a much more vigorous disposition to save. The French peasants never incur the *wicked,* because voluntary, calamity of bringing children into the world whom they cannot feed: the youngest a new robber of the pittance of the eldest; brother the worst foe to brother, and each addition to the natural ties bringing nearer and more near the short and ghastly interval between Penury and Famine, Despair and Crime: nor do they—no, nor the peasants of Spain, of Germany, of Italy, of Holland—squander in the selfish vices of an hour, the produce of a week's toil. The continental peasant is not selfish in his pleasure; he shares his holiday with his family, and not being selfish, he is not improvident: his family make *him* prudent—the same cause often makes the Englishman desperate.

In an account of Manchester, lately published, what a picture of the improvidence of the working classes!

> Instructed in the fatal secret of subsisting on what is barely necessary to life—yielding partly to necessity, and partly to example—the labouring classes have ceased to entertain a laudable pride in furnishing their houses, and in multiplying the decent comforts which minister to happiness. What is superflu-

ous to the mere exigencies of nature, is too often expended at the tavern; and for the provision of old age and infirmity, they too frequently trust either to charity, to the support of their children, or to the protection of the poor-laws. . . .

The artisan too seldom possesses sufficient moral dignity or intellectual or organic strength to resist the seductions of appetite. His wife and children, subjected to the same process, have little power to cheer his remaining moments of leisure. Domestic economy is neglected, domestic comforts are too frequently unknown. A meal of coarse food is hastily prepared, and devoured with precipitation. Home has little other relation to him than that of shelter—few pleasures are there—it chiefly presents to him a scene of physical exhaustion, from which he is glad to escape. His house is ill furnished, uncleanly, often ill ventilated—perhaps damp; his food, from want of forethought and domestic economy, is meagre and innutritious; he generally becomes debilitated and hypochondriacal, and unless supported by principle, falls the victim of dissipation. . . .

Some idea may be formed of the influence of these establishments (gin shops, &c.) on the health and morals of the people, from the following statement; for which we are indebted to Mr. Braidley, the boroughreeve of Manchester. He observed the number of persons entering a gin shop in five minutes, during eight successive Saturday evenings, and at various periods from seven o'clock until ten. *The average result was, 112 men and 163 women, or 275 in forty minutes, which is equal to 412 per hour.*[3]

Whenever a class of the people are inclined to habitual inebriety, it is evidently absurd to attribute to them the characteristic of that clear and unclouded faculty which we call common sense. It may be enough, therefore, of proof that the English poor are *not* distinguished above their equals on the continent for their claim to common sense, to point to the notorious fact, that they *are* so distinguished for their addition to inebriety.

But if this faculty does not characterize the two extremes of society, it certainly characterizes the medium? Granted:—but, even here, I suspect our interested panegyrists have been "praising us that they might the easier impose." In fact, what they meant by common sense was, our general indifference to political the-

3. Kay's *Manchester.*

ories; our quiet and respectable adherence to the things that are. I fear in the eyes of these, our flatterers, we are somewhat fallen of late. But yet this propensity has for centuries assuredly distinguished us: we have been very little alive to all speculative innovations in morals and in politics. Those continental writings that have set the rest of the world in a blaze, have never been widely popular with us. Voltaire, Rousseau, Diderot, have been received with suspicion, and dismissed without examination: they were known to be innovators, and that was enough to revolt

Our sober certainty of waking bliss.

Even Paine, the most plausible and attractive of all popular theorists, was scarcely known to any classes but the lowest, at the moment when the government suddenly thought fit to toss him into celebrity on the horns of a prosecution. Godwin, Harrington, Sidney, how little we know of their writings! A political speculator presents nothing interesting to us, unless we behead him; even then he travels down to posterity, merely on the festive brevity of a toast. We would fight for the cause for which Sidney bled on the scaffold, but we would not for the life and soul of us read a single chapter of the book in which he informs us what the cause *was*. Through a long life the great Bentham struggled against the neglect of the British public—in vain he was consulted by foreign states—in vain he was extolled by philosophers, and pillaged by lawyers. He was an innovator, who wrote against received customs of thinking, and that was sufficient to prevent his being read. Even now, when so many quote his name as if they had his works by heart, how few have ever opened them. The limited sale of the wittiest of all his books, is a melancholy proof of our indifference to theories: and the 'Popular Fallacies' are a proof of the unpopularity of truths.

The indifference to theory is certainly a proof of what is ordinarily termed common sense; but it obviously has its disadvantages. It is customary for writers of a certain school to say that all truths *ought* to make their way slowly: this is praising mankind for their greatest fault, and elevating apathy into virtue. Hence, in this country, that absurd deference to what is called "practical men," that is to say, men who, belonging to some particular calling, are imbued with all the narrow views and selfish interests that belong to it. If you want a reform on the stage, you would be told that the best performers are the most practical men, they have all an interest in the monopoly they enjoy; poor Kean, accordingly said before the Committee of the House of Commons that he heard the voice, and saw the play of countenance, as well at the back of the centre boxes at Covent Garden, as in the side boxes of the Haymarket. Mr. Kean's answer is the type of most answers, on whatsoever point, that you extort from practical men in opposition to thinking men; they reason according to their interests; practical men are prejudiced men; usually knowing the details of their own business well, they are astonished at the presumption of men who think to improve the principle. These are like the writing-master who would not believe Newton was a great mathematician—"He!—pooh!—he is an hour over a sum in the Rule of Three!" This unbeliever was a practical man, who could not understand the theory that mastered worlds and hesitated over the multiplication table.

The Emperor Julian, whose mind was peculiarly adapted to the notions of the present age in all things but his levity in religion, and his solemnity in slovenliness, says very well upon this head, "that a man who derives experience from his own habits, rather than the principles of some great theory is like an empiric, who, by practice, may cure one or two diseases with which he is familiar, but having no system, or theory of art, must necessarily be ignorant of all the innumerable complaints which have not fallen under his personal observation."

The practical man is one who should give you all his facts, and never reason upon them; unfortunately the English take his reasonings even more willingly than his facts, and thus, according to Julian, under the notion of avoiding quackery, they have, in all their legislative changes, been peculiarly the victims of quacks.[4]

I think we shall discover a principal cause of our indifference to violent political speculation, and our content with "the ills that are,"—which qualities are termed common sense,—in that Pecu-

4. Those were practical men who resisted the theory of Mr. Arkwright's machine, under pretence of throwing the poor out of employ;—those were practical men who, being wig-makers, petitioned George III. to cut off his hair and wear a peruke, in order to set the fashion of wigs. Imagine the contemptuous scorn with which the honest wig-makers must have regarded a theorist opposed to wigs.

niary system of Credit, which is so universally carried on among the middle classes of England. People are afraid of every shock of opinion, because it is a shock on their credit. Quiet times are good for all trade, but agitated times are death to a man with a host of alarmed creditors. This makes the middle class, especially in London, a solid and compact body against such changes as seem only experiment, and they are generally pushed on by the working classes, before they stir much themselves in the question of even necessary reforms. It is from the fear of a concussion with persons without property, that people with property hazard voluntarily a change.

The habits of a commercial life, also, drain off the enterprise of the mind by the speculations which belong to commerce; and the first thing a trader asks himself in a change is, "How will this affect my returns?" He is therefore always zealous for a reduction of taxes, but he is not very eager about law taxes, unless he has a suit;—and he is more anxious to cut down the pension list than to ameliorate the criminal code.

The great legislative good of admitting the poor to vote is this: It is from the poorer classes that the evils and the dangers of a state arise; *their* crimes are *our* punishments; therefore it is well, even on selfish principles of government, that they, sensible to their own grievances, should choose those who will work for their redress: As *they* carry an election in a populous town, so they force their opinions relating to their own condition on the middle class, and the middle class on the Representative. Thus the same vote which relieves the Poor protects the state, and the Reform which removes abuses, prevents the Revolution that avenges them.

The favourite accusation with foreigners against the English is their cruelty, and the crowd round a gibbet is the supposed proof of the justice of the charge. It is astonishing how few men deem it necessary to think a little when they are writing much. The English are by no means a cruel people, and their avidity to see an execution is no evidence whatsoever against them. The one fact, that while our laws are the severest in the world, we have not for centuries been able to accustom ourselves to the severity, and our administration of them has been singularly relaxed and gentle;—the one fact that Public Opinion has snatched the sword from the hand of the Law, and that the unaltered barbarism of a code of ages has not sufficed to harden our sympathies, is alone a sufficient proof that the English are not a cruel, but a mild and humane[5] people.

In his *Thoughts upon Secondary Punishments* (p. 30), the distinguished Archbishop of Dublin is pleased to express himself with severity against that "misplaced compassion" for offenders, especially juvenile delinquents, which is a characteristic of the public. This remark is shallow and inconsiderate; the feeling that the punishment is disproportioned to the offense is, generally, the cause of the public sympathy with the offender, especially if young; and this very compassion, misplaced, as Dr. Whately deems it, is a proof of the humanity of the people. In elections, during all the riot and excess which formerly disgraced those septennial saturnalia, when men were heated with drink, passion, and party animosities, it is astonishing how little cruelty or outrage mingled with the uproar and bludgeon-fights which were considered necessary to the deliberate exercise of the reasoning faculty, on one of the most important occasions in which it could be exerted. In no continental people could the passions have been so inflamed and instances of ferocity so miraculously rare. Our armies lay an acknowledged claim to the same character for humanity, which has so unjustly been denied to our people; and neither the French, Prussian, Spaniard, nor any European army, can compare with the humanity with which an English soldiery sack a town and traverse a country; our military outrages are conducted with the mildness of a Duval, and we never commit rape, arson, or murder,—unless *it is absolutely necessary!*

The superficial jest against our partiality to a newspaper tale of murder, of our passion for the *spectacle* of the gibbet, proves exactly the reverse of what it asserts. It is the tender who are the most susceptible to the excitation of terror. It is the women who hang with the deepest interest over a tale or a play of gloomy and tragic interest. Robespierre liked only stories of love. Nero was partial to the mildest airs of music. Ali Pacha abhorred all accounts of

---

5. Another proof of this fact is in the unwillingness of persons to prosecute when they consider the punishment may be too severe. The dearness of a prosecution, to be sure, goes some way towards this forbearance; but in civil causes we readily brave expense for revenge, it is only in criminal causes that we shudder, and draw back from the urging of the passions.

atrocity. The treacherous and bloody tribes of the South Sea islands prefer the calm strains of descriptive poetry, even to those of victory and war. If you observe a ballad-vender hawking his wares, it is the bloodiest murders that the women purchase. It is exactly from our unacquaintance with crime, viz., from the restless and mysterious curiosity it excites, that we feel a dread pleasure in marvelling at its details. This principle will suffice to prove that the avidity with which we purchase accounts of atrocity, is the reverse of a proof of our own cruelty of disposition, and re-torts upon the heads of our shallow assailants. What is true in books is true in sights. What is true on the mimic stage is true on the real; and, if that which I have just said be a legitimate vindi-cation of our love for narratives of terror, it is also a vindication of our tendency to crowd round an execution. But as regards the last, I believe that the vulgar of all nations would be equally dis-posed to gaze at that dread solemnization of death, ever an event so fraught with dark interest to the race that is born to die, if among all nations the gloomy ceremonial were as public as it is with us, and the criminal were rendered as notorious by the com-ments of journals, and the minute details of the session-court and the prison-house.

Another absurd and ancient accusation against us ought, by this time, to be known by our accusers, the French, to be un-founded on fact, viz., our *unequalled* propensity to suicide. That offence is far more frequent among the French themselves than it is with us. In the year 1816 the number of suicides committed in London amounted to seventy-two; in the same year, at Paris, they amounted to one hundred and eight-eight; the population of Paris being some 400,000 less than that of London![6] But suicides, if not unequalled in number by those of other countries, are in-deed frequent with us, and so they always will be in countries where men can be reduced in a day from affluence to beggary. The loss of fortune is the general cause of the voluntary loss of life. Wounded pride,—disappointment,—the schemes of an existence laid in the dust,—the insulting pity of friends,—the humbled de-spair of all our dearest connexions for whom perhaps we toiled and wrought,—the height from which we have fallen,—the im-

---

6. *Not* taking into account the number of those unfortunates exposed at the *Morgue*, one-half at least of whom were probably suicides.

possibility of regaining what we have lost,—the searching curiosity of the public,—the petty annoyance added to the great woe,—all rushing upon a man's mind in the sudden convulsion and turbulence of its elements, what wonder that he welcomes the only escape from the abyss into which he has been hurled!

If the Spaniards rarely commit suicide, it is because they, neither a commercial nor gambling people, are not subject to such reverses. With the French it is mostly the hazard of dice, with the English, the chances of trade, that are the causes of this melancholy crime;—melancholy! for it really deserves that epithet with us. We do not set about it with the mirthful gusto which characterizes the *felo de se* in your Excellency's native land. We have not yet, among our numerous clubs, instituted a club of suicides, all sworn to be the happiest dogs possible, and not to outlive the year! These gentlemen ask you to see them "go off"—as if Death were a place in the *malle poste.*—"Will you dine with me to-morrow, my dear Dubois?"

"With the greatest pleasure;—yet, now I think of it, I am particularly engaged to shoot myself; I am really *au désespoir!*—but one can't get off *such* an engagement, you know."

"I would not ask such a thing, my dear fellow. Adieu!—By the way, if you should ever *come back* to Paris again, I have changed my lodgings, *au plaisir!*"

Exeunt the two friends; the one twirling his mustaches, the other humming an opera tune.

This gaiety of suicidalism, is not the death *à la mode* with us; neither are we so sentimental in these delicate matters, as our neighbours over the water. We do not shoot each other by way of being romantic. Ladies and gentlemen forced to "part company," do not betake themselves "to a retired spot," and tempt the dread unknown, by a brace of pistols, tied up with cherry-coloured ribbons.

In a word, when we shoot ourselves, we consider it no joke; we come to the resolution in sober sadness; we have no inherent predilection for the act; no "hereditary imperfection in the nervous juices" (as Montesquieu, with all the impudence of a philosopher, has gravely asserted) forcing us on to the *"funis, amnis,"*—the gates out of this world into the next. No people destroy themselves with a less lively inclination; and, so generally are sudden reverses of fortune, the propellers to the deed, that with us not one suicide in ten would cease to live, if it were not that he has nothing to live upon. In fact, he does not relinquish life—life relinquishes him.

But if it be true, then, that we are so far from being a suicidal people, that the French have, by *strict* calculations, been computed to kill *their five to our one;* if among no commercial people, has the crime of suicide, perhaps, been not only less frequent, but committed with less levity,—the abhorrent offspring of the most intolerable reverses;—if this be true, what becomes of all those admirable books, witty and profound, which your Excellency's fellow-countrymen have written about our acknowledged propensity to ropes and razors, our inclination to kill ourselves, from the slightest causes, and out of a principle of *ennui?* What becomes of the ingenious systems that have been built upon that "fact"; enlivened by the gaiety of Voltaire;—rendered touching by the sentimentality of de Staël—one writer accounting for it one way, one another; but, all sure to account for what they had forgotten to prove? Your Excellency, may perceive, by their theories, which I think I have now for ever demolished, how necessary it is for an Englishman sometimes to write about England. I say, their theories I have for ever demolished; yet, Heaven knows if I have,—there is a wonderful vigour of constitution in a popular fallacy. When the world has once got hold of a lie, it is astonishing how hard it is to get it out of the world. You beat it about the head, till it seems to have given up the ghost; and, lo, the next day it is as healthy as ever. The best example of the vitality of a fine saying, which has the advantage of being a fallacy, is in the ever-hacknied piece of nonsense attributed to Archimedes; viz., "that he could move the earth, if he had any place at a distance from it, to fix a prop for his lever." Your Excellency knows that this is one of the standard allusions, one of the necessary stock in trade for all orators, poets, and newspaper writers; and persons, whenever they meet with it, take Archimedes for an extraordinary great man, and cry, "Lord, how wonderful!"—Now, *if* Archimedes had found his place, his prop, and his lever, and if he could have moved with the swiftness of a cannon-ball, 480 miles every hour, it would have taken him just 44,963,540,000,000 years to have raised the earth one inch![7] And yet, people will go on quoting absurdity as gospel; wondering at the wisdom of Archimedes, and accounting for the unparalleled suicidalism of the English, till we grow tired of contradiction; for, when you cannot convince the Squire Thornhills of the world, you must incur the mortification of Moses, and be contented to let them out talk you.

I think, however, that I need take no pains to prove the next characteristic of the English people,—a characteristic that I shall but just touch upon; viz., their wonderful Spirit of Industry. This has been the saving principle of the nation, counteracting the errors of our laws, and the imperfections of our constitution. We have been a great people, because we have been always active;—and a moral people, because we have not left ourselves time to be vicious. Industry is, in a word, *the* distinguishing quality of our nation, the pervading genius of our riches, our grandeur and our power!

Every great people has its main principle of greatness, some one quality, the developing and tracing, and feeding and watching of which, has *made* it great. Your Excellency remembers how finely Montesquieu has proved this important truth, in the *Grandeur et Decadence des Romains.* With France, that principle is the love of glory; with America, it is the love of liberty; with England, it is the love of action;—the safest and most comprehensive principle of the three; for it gains glory, without seeking it too madly, and it requires liberty, in order to exist.

Now, I think, that your Excellency (than whom, if no man sees more the folly in a statesman of over-refining, no man also, I apprehend, sees more clearly the necessity of his piercing beyond the surface, and seizing, from the confused History of the Past, some one broad, though metaphysical principle, by which to guide and work out his policy)—I think, I say, that your Excellency will perceive, that when we have once discovered the national quality which has chiefly made a nation great, we cannot too warmly foster, and too largely encourage it; we should break down all barriers that oppose it; foresee, and betimes destroy, all principles that are likely to check or prevent it.

---

7. Ferguson. Critics have said, 'what a fine idea of Archimedes'! but how much finer is the fact that refutes it. One of the sublimest things in the world is, plain truth!

It is the Vestal Fire which daily and nightly we must keep alive; and we should consider all our prosperity to be coupled with its existence. Thus; then, if *industry* be the principle of our power, we cannot too zealously guard it from all obstacle, or too extensively widen the sphere for its exertions; a truth which our statesmen have, to be sure, diligently cultivated, by poor-laws, that encourage idleness; and bounties, prohibitions, and monopolies, that amputate the sinews of action.

From this it would seem, that a policy that would be bad with other countries, has been pre-eminently bad with us.

The last time Micromegas paid us a visit, he was struck by a singular spectacle. He saw an enormous Giant, laid at full length upon the ground, in the midst of a mighty orchard laden with fruit—chains were on his limbs, and weights upon his breast. The Giant kicked most lustily against these restraints, and his struggles so convulsed the ground, that every now and then they shook plenty of fruit from the neighbouring trees; the natives stood round, and seized the fruit as it fell. Nevertheless, there was far from being enough for the whole crowd, and the more hungry amongst them, growled very audibly at the more fortunate and better fed. The compassionate Micromegas approached the throng. "And, who art thou, most unhappy giant?" he asked.

"Alas!" said the Giant, "my name is Industry, and I am the parent of these ungrateful children, who have tied me down, in order that my struggles to get free may shake a few fruits to the ground."

"Bless me," said Micromegas, "what a singular device!—but do you not see my good friends," turning to the crowd, "that your father, if he were free from these shackles, could reach with his mighty arms the boughs of the trees, and give you as much fruit as you wanted. Take this chain for instance from one arm and try."

"That chain!" shouted some hundreds of the crowd; "impious wretch—it is Tithes!"

"Well then, these cords."

"Idiot!—those cords are Bounties; we should be undone if *they* were destroyed."

At this instant up came a whole gang of elderly ladies, with a huge bowl of opium, which they began thrusting down the throat of the miserable giant.

"And what the devil is that for?" said Micromegas.

"We don't like to see our good father make such violent struggles," replied the pious matrons, "we are giving him opium to lie still."

"But that is a drug to induce him to shake down *no* fruit, and then you would be starved—spare him the opium at least."

"Barbarous monster!" cried the ladies, with horror, "would you do away with the Poor-laws?"

"My children," said the poor giant, well-nigh at his last gasp, "I have done my best to maintain you all, there is food enough in the orchard for fifty times your number, but you undo yourselves by the injustice of crippling your father. You mean well by me—you compassionate my struggles—but instead of giving me liberty, these good ladies would set me to sleep. Trust to nature and common sense, and we shall all live happily together, and if these orchards ever fail you, I will plant new."

"Nature and common sense, dear father," cried the children, "oh beware of these new-fangled names—let us trust to experience, not to theory and speculation!"

Here a vast rush was made upon those eating the fruit they had got, by those who in the late scrambles had got no fruit to eat; and Micromegas made away as fast as he could, seeing too plainly, that if the Giant were crippled much longer, those who had laid by the most fruit would stand some chance of being robbed by the hunger and jealousy of the rest.

IV

I have reserved for a separate chapter a few remarks upon one
of our national attributes—viz., Courage; because they will naturally involve the consideration of a certain question that has
lately attracted much attention amongst us, viz., corporal punishments in the army. Your own incomparable La Bruyère
has remarked, "that in France a soldier is brave and a lawyer is
learned; but in Rome (says he) the soldier was learned and the
lawyer was brave—every man was brave." Now I think that
with *us* every man is brave. Courage is more *universally* spread
through the raw material of England than it is among that of any
other people; but I do not think the manufacture is quite so
highly wrought up in individual specimens as it is in France.
I think that an English gentleman, from the fear of a duel,
would eat his words sooner than a Frenchman. You see a proof
of this every day in our newspaper accounts of these "little
affairs." The following is a very fair specimen of duelling
correspondence:

To the Editor of "The Times"

SIR,
    You will oblige us by inserting the following account of
the late affair between Mr. Hum and Lord Haw.

Your obedient servants,
LIONEL VARNISH.
PETER SMOOTHAWAY,
Col. of the ——— Regt.

In the late election for the borough of Spoutit, Mr. Hum being the candidate on the whig side, was reported in the *Spoutit and Froth Chronicle,* to have made use of the following expressions relative to Lord Haw who is supposed to have some interest in the borough: "As for a certain noble lord who lives not very far from Haw Castle, I confess that I cannot sufficiently express my contempt for his unworthy conduct (great applause)—it is mean, base, treacherous, and derogatory in the highest degree, for any nobleman to act in the manner that nobleman has thought proper to do.

On reading this extract, purporting to be from a speech by Mr. Hum, Colonel Smoothaway was deputed to wait on that gentleman by Lord Haw. Mr. Hum appointed Sir Lionel Varnish to meet Colonel Smoothaway upon the matter, the result was the following memorandum:

In applying the words "mean, base, treacherous, and derogatory," to Lord Haw, Mr. Hum did not in the smallest degree mean to reflect upon his lordship's character, or to wound his feelings. With this explanation, Colonel Smoothaway declares, on the part of Lord Haw, that Lord H. is perfectly satisfied.

(Signed)   Lionel Varnish.

Peter Smoothaway.

But this epeapophogy, or word-swallowing, is only on one side in *this* specimen of correspondence. It is usually on *both* sides, and may be currently supposed to run thus:

"Mr. Hum having declared, that in calling Lord Haw 'a rascal,' he meant nothing personal to that nobleman, Lord Haw has no hesitation in saying, that he did not mean to offend Mr. Hum, when he called him 'a rogue' in reply."

Now this sort of shuffling with one's honour, as your Excellency very well knows, is never practised in France: the affront given, out at once go affronter and affrontee; they fight first, and retract afterwards. But the difference in the bilboa appetite of the gentry of the two nations depends, I suspect, rather on the advantage the French possess over the English in animal spirits, than in real courage. With your countrymen, duelling, as well as suicide, is a mere jest—an ebullition of mettlesome humour: with us, it is an affair of serious will-making and religious scruples. Your courage is an impulse; ours must be made a principle. When once our blood is up, it does not descend in the thermometer very readily. The easy lubricity with which our gentlemen glide out of a duel is an understood thing with us; and neither party considers it a disgrace to the other. But if an Englishman has an affair with a foreigner, the case is very different; he is much more tenacious of apology, and ready for the field. A countryman of mine asked me once to officiate for him as second, in a quarrel he had with a Parisian *roué;* the cause was trifling, and the Englishman to blame. I recommended a compromise. "No," said my hero, throwing his chest open, "if my antagonist were an Englishman, I should be too happy to retract a hasty expression; but these d——d French fellows *don't understand generosity.*"

I reminded my friend of his religious scruples. "True," said he; "but how can I think of religion when I know De—— is— an *atheist.*"

There is a doggedness in English courage which makes it more stubborn against adversity, than that of any other people: it has in it more of the spirit of resistance, if less of the spirit of assault.

When we look to the army under Napoleon, and that under the Duke of Wellington, we are astonished at the difference of the system: in the one the utmost conceivable encouragement is given to the soldier to distinguish himself; in the other the least. To rise from the ranks was, in the French army, an occurrence of every day. The commonest soldier could not obey a field-marshal, scarcely his emperor, without seeing the widest scope for personal ambition;—in the obedience that he rendered;—if the risks were immense, so also were the rewards. But in England, a wall, rarely to be surmounted, divides the soldier from all promotion beyond that of the halberd. He is altogether of a different metal, of a different estimate from the Frenchman. He has equal punishments to deter, not equal rewards to encourage: he can scarcely be a captain, but he can be terribly flogged. The two principles of conduct, hope and terror, ought to be united.

The question of flogging in the army, however, is far more important to England, more complicated in itself, than appears at first sight. Whenever it be abolished, the abolition to be safe, should work an entire revolution in the service. I confess I think wonderful ignorance has been shown, both in the popular cry and in the parliamentary debates on that subject. People have not, in the least, perceived the consequences to which the abolition of corporal chastisement must lead. The heads of the army are perfectly right!—If it were abolished, *as a single alteration* in the martial code, one of two consequences would infallibly ensue, viz., the loss of discipline, or the substitute of the punishment of death. You hear men and legislators say, in the plentitude of their ignorance, "Look at the French army and the Prussian army; you see no flogging there; why have flogging in the British army?" The answer to those who have studied the question is easy: in the first place, if there is not flogging in the French army, there is the penalty of death. *For all the offences for which we flog a soldier, the French shoot him.* Nay, they award death to an *incalculably greater* number of offences than meet corporal punishment with us: there are not above four offences for which flogging is inflicted in the greater part of our regiments; and certainly not eight in any: there are thirteen capital offences. *With the French there are above forty offences punishable with death!* Besides these, what a long catalogue in France of military faults, to which are appended the terrible awards, *"Fers* 5, 6, 10 ans." *Boulet,—Travaux Publiques,* for the same periods! The French code does not embrace flogging, but it embraces punishments much more severe, and much more lightly incurred. But the Prussian army? In the first place, the Prussian code *does* sanction corporal punishment to the amount of one hundred lashes, forty of which only can be received at a time, so that the criminal may be brought out twice or thrice to complete his sentence. In the next place, what a superior rank of moral being does a Prussian soldier hold above an English one! How, in that military nation, is he schooled, and trained, and selected from the herd! *Before* he is a soldier how necessarily is he a man of honour! Now this last consideration brings us to the true view of a question far too vitally important to be intrusted to hustings oratory and schoolboy declamation. In no nation in the world is the army so thoroughly selected from the dregs and refuse of the people as it is in England: this is the real reason why flogging has been retained by us so long, and why, as a *single* measure of military reform, it would be dangerous to the last

degree, to take *the power* of inflicting it out of the hands of a
court martial. In France the Conscription raises the army from
respectable classes: in Prussia the military system is even still
more productive than in France of a superior moral soldiery;—
but, in England, we have no conscription, no military schools; the
soldier is culled from the sink of the peasantry; a man who runs
away from a wife for whom he is too lazy to labour, who has had
the misfortune of an illegitimate child; who has taken to poach-
ing instead of to work, and fears the tread-mill; this is the hero
you put into the British army, and about whom the eloquent
Daniel O'Connell talks of chivalry and honour![1]—"But oh!"
cries one of our inconsiderate philanthropists, "if you take away
flogging, you will, in the first place, have a higher class of men
willing to enlist; and, in the second place, you will instil a more
dignified sense of moral feeling into those already enlisted."
Stay a bit; let us consider these arguments. Certainly you will gain
these advantages if the abolition of flogging be made a part of a
general reform (hereafter to be specified); but, as certainly you
will not gain either of these advantages by that abolition alone.
Let us look to the constitution of the army! Suppose a soldier
commits theft, he is given up to the civil authority, he is transported for seven years: he returns a most accomplished rascal,
where then does he go? Why back into the army again. Let a
soldier be ever such a rogue, it is exceedingly difficult for the officer to procure his discharge from the War Office. For what reason? Why, because to discharge a soldier would be considered
a premium to a man to behave ill. An excellent reason; but what
does it prove? It proves that the service is felt to be such a hardship, even by the depraved and imbruted, who at present belong
to it, that a discharge is a blessing, which men would (if encouraged by any hope of success) behave as ill as possible, in order to
procure. Is it flogging alone that makes it a hardship? Pooh, no
—scarcely one man in a whole regiment is flogged in a year. He
who knows any thing of the constitution of Human Nature,
knows that it is not the remote chance of punishment, it is actual
and constant *désagrémens* that make men discontented with their

---

1. Two-thirds of the army, too, are Irish, and the lowest of them:—the dregs
of an Irish populace! What a reflection!

situation.[2] Now, how then can one rationally suppose that if you abolished corporal punishment, "a better class of persons" would voluntarily consent to herd with returned convicts, and rush open armed into a state of existence which even returned convicts would be too happy to get discharged from?—Still less, how can one hope to institute a high sense of honour among men already selected from classes where honour is unknown. Talk of Prussia, indeed! *there* a soldier considers it not the greatest blessing, but the heaviest misfortune to be discharged: *he was trained to think so before he went into the army.* They make the feeling of honour *first,* and *then* they appeal to it.[3] To deprive a Prussian soldier of his cockade, is a grievous humiliation. A certain English colonel, desirous of imitating the Prussians, took away the cockade from a soldier whom he thought seemed more alive to honour than the rest of his comrades; the soldier was exceedingly grateful; it saved him the trouble of keeping it clean! But, in some regiments, flogging has been done away with? Ay, and how has it succeeded? I venture to affirm that those regiments are the most insubordinate in the army.[4] In some the punishment was abolished, and the commanding officer has been compelled to restore it. But am I then the advocate for this horrible punishment?—certainly not; only when we begin to reform the army let us begin at the right end—let us begin with the system of Recruiting. If flogging be continued, we may continue to have a courageous and

2. Thus, among the offences of an English soldier are these instances of "disgraceful conduct":

"In wilfully maiming or injuring himself or another soldier, even at the instance of such soldier, with intent to render himself, or such soldier unfit for the service.

"In tampering with his eyes.

"In absenting himself from hospital whilst under medical care, or other gross violation of the rules of any hospital, thereby wilfully producing or aggravating disease or infirmity, or wilfully delaying his own cure." A pretty alluring sort of condition, in which a man is forbidden to contract diseases and to court blindness for the purpose of getting out of it!

3. Even in the *civil* schools of Prussia there is a law, "That no punishment shall be inflicted which wounds the sentiment of honour."

4. Mr. Hume declares that in those regiments discipline is equally preserved. He has a right to his opinion; but just ask military men: nay the officers of those regiments themselves, in which the experiment was tried: its fruitlessness is notorious in the army.

disciplined army under the present system—if it is to be removed, we must alter the system altogether. As we diminish the motive of fear we must increase the motive of hope; as we diminish the severity of punishment, we must inculcate the sentiment of shame. In the first place we should institute Military Schools for privates, where the principle of honour can be early instilled: in the second place, we ought, as in Prussia, to introduce into the army the system of *degrading*. By this system every man first enlisting, enters into a certain class, and is entitled to certain distinctions of dress; if found, in that class, incorrigible by its ordinary punishments, *then* he is degraded to another class, the distinctions are taken away from him and he is liable to severer penalties. It is only when thus degraded that a Prussian soldier can receive corporal punishment. Amendment restores him to his former rank. In the third place, as the soldier ought at these military schools to receive a much better degree of education than at present, so he ought to be much more capable of rising from the ranks, even to the highest stations.[5] In the fourth place, no soldier should be enlisted without the recommendation of a good character.[6] In the fifth place, the system of adequate pensions after a certain service should be firmly established; nothing can be more injudicious than the recent alterations on that head;[7] but the pension should not depend solely on the date of the service—good conduct should abbreviate, bad conduct prolong it. No soldier once given up to the civil law should be allowed to return to the army. If it be practicable under the present passion for petty economies[8] and niggling reforms to do all this, the power of corporal punishment may be safely denied to court martials, and the abolition of flogging, *coupled* with such amelio-

5. Nor ought promotion to be a matter of purchase.—What custom more discouraging to all worth save that of wealth!

6. A principal cause of the unwillingness of soldiers to serve is, that the profligate dislike restraint, and the orderly dislike companionship with the profligate; you remove both these causes by refusing to receive the profligate.

7. It would be a great source of consolation to a soldier to be sure to receive his discharge after a certain number of years, accompanied with a competence for his old age; by this hope, you would indeed attract a better class of men. The small economists cried out on this system;—they complain that there is too much fear in the military code, and yet they have taken away its most agreeable and reasonable incitement of hope!

8. For such alterations would be evidently attended with expense.

rations, would indeed contribute to produce a higher sense of honour and a more generous spirit of discipline; but if that punishment be abolished, as a *single and unaccompanied* act of reform, I confess that I tremble for the consequences. I see before me an uneducated and reckless soldiery, proverbially addicted before that of all other armies to the temporary insanity of drunkenness, from whom you suddenly take one strong governing motive of fear, without substituting another of hope—from whom you remove restraint, but in whom the whole spirit of your remaining laws forbids you to instil honour. I see that there may be times, as on a march, when all the punishments you would substitute are not at hand; and I know that with a soldier, above all men, punishment to be effectual must be immediate.[9] I fear that, discipline once weakened, not only insubordination, but rapine and licentiousness, the absence of which has hitherto so distinguished our army, would creep in among men to whom a moral education is unknown; I fear yet more, that in any collision with the people of manufacturing towns, who at present are even incensing, by their own animosity, that of the soldiers; the check upon armed retaliation would be found insufficient and feeble;—inhuman restraints on soldiers are a great evil —an unruly soldiery would be a far greater one. Let us hope that if such an evil should arise, it will find its cure: it can do so either in the reforms I have sketched, but which I fear the aristocracy will not propose and the people will not pay for, or in the substitution of the terror of death for that of corporal punishment[10] —this last is the more probable, and though the military code would be thus rendered severer by the abolition of flogging, I doubt if it would not be a more wise and a more honourable severity. It is said by very competent authorities, that if you were

9. Thus on board ship, where, for want of the necessary court martial, a delinquent cannot be immediately punished, all sorts of insubordination frequently prevail. The offender knows that he may be punished when he gets on shore, but in the mean while, he has three or four weeks of impunity. The Duke of Wellington was right if he said, as he is reported to have done, "The English soldier is always a boy."

10. There are several offences not punishable at present, either with death or transportation, but which I fear must become so, if the power of corporal punishment be altogether forbidden. For instance: persuading to desert—drunkenness on duty—spreading false reports in the field—seizing supplies for the army, &c.

to poll the privates, you would find a majority against the entire abolition of the power of inflicting corporal punishment. This for two reasons: first, that when it is removed, all sorts of small and vexatious restraints, to which the soldiers are unaccustomed, are often resorted to by the officer, who, fearing that if Insubordination rose to a certain point, he should lose the power to repress it, is for ever, even to frivolity, guarding against its fancied beginnings:—but the second and more powerful reason is, that many of the soldiers have the sagacity to fear, that the removal of the power to flog them would be followed by a more facile prerogative to shoot.

Observe, in conclusion, that it is to the aristocratic spirit which pervades the organization of our army, a spirit which commands order by suppressing the faculties, not by inciting the ambition;—and which has substituted for a proper system of recruiting and of military schools, the barbarous but effective terror of the scourge—observe, I say, that it is to that spirit we owe the low moral standard of our army, and the consequent difficulty of abolishing corporal punishment. To one good end, our aristocracy have proceeded by the worst of means, and the nobleness of discipline has been wrought by the meanness of fear.

V

Supplementary Illustrations of Character

Sir Harry Hargrave is an excellent gentleman; his conscience is scrupulous to the value of a pin's head; he is benevolent, hospitable, and generous. Sir Harry Hargrave is never dishonest nor inhumane, except for the best possible reasons. He has, for instance, a very worthless younger son; by dint of interest with the Bishop of ———, he got the scapegrace a most beautiful living: the new rector has twenty thousand souls to take care of; and Sir Harry well knows, that so long as pointers and billiard-tables are to be met with, young Hopeful will never bestow even a thought on his own. Sir Harry Hargrave, you say, is an excellent gentleman; yet he moves heaven and earth to get his son a most responsible situation, for which he knows the rogue to be wholly unfit. Exactly so; Sir Harry Hargrave applauds himself for it: he calls it—*taking care of his family*. Sir Harry Hargrave gives away one hundred and two loaves every winter to the poor; it is well to let the labourer have a loaf of bread now and then for nothing: would it not be as well, Sir Harry, to let him have the power always to have bread cheap? Bread cheap! what are you saying? Sir Harry thinks of his rents, and considers you a revolutionist for the question. But Sir Harry Hargrave, you answer, is a humane man, and charitable to the poor. Is this conscientious? My dear sir, to be sure; he considers it his first duty —*to take care of the landed interest*. Sir Harry Hargrave's butler has robbed him; the good gentleman has not the heart to proceed against the rascal; he merely discharges him. What an excel-

lent heart he must have! So he has; yet last year he committed
fifteen poachers to jail. Strange inconsistency! Not at all:—*what
becomes of the country gentleman if his game is not properly
protected?* Sir Harry Hargrave is a man of the strictest integrity;
his word is his bond—he might say with one of the Fathers, "that
he would not tell you a lie to gain heaven by it"; yet Sir Harry
Hargrave has six times in his life paid five thousand pounds to
three hundred electors in Cornwall, whom he knew would all
take the bribery oath, that they had not received a shilling from
him. He would not tell a lie, you say; yet he makes three hundred
men forswear themselves! Precisely so; and when you attempt to
touch this system of perjury, he opposes you to his last gasp:
but he is not to be blamed for this—*he is only attached to the
venerable constitution of his forefathers!* Sir Harry Hargrave is
an accomplished man, and an excellent scholar; yet he is one
of the most ignorant persons you ever met with. His mind is
full of the most obsolete errors; a very Monmouth-street of
threadbare prejudices: if a truth gleam for a moment upon him,
it discomposes all his habits of thought, like a stray sunbeam on a
cave full of bats. He enjoys the highest possible character among
his friends for wisdom and virtue: he is considered the most consistent of human beings: consistent!—yes, to his party!

Tom Whitehead is a very different person; he is cleaver, sharp,
shrewd, and has lived a great deal at Paris. He laughs at antiquity;
he has no poetry in his nature; he does not believe in virtue; with
him "all men are liars." He has been a great gambler in his
youth; he professes the most profligate notions about women; he
has run through half his fortune; he is a liberal politician, and
swears by Lord Grey. His father was a whig before him; and for
the last twenty years he has talked about "the spirit of improvement." He is a favourite at the clubs; an honest fellow, because
he laughs so openly at the honesty of other people. He is half an
atheist, because he thinks it cant to be more than half a believer.
But religion is a good thing for the people; whom, while he talks
of enlightenment, he thinks it the part of a statesman to blind
to every thing beyond the Reform Bill. He is for advancement
to a certain point—till his party come in; he then becomes a conservative—lest his party go out. Having had the shrewdness to
dismiss old prejudices from his mind, he has never taken the

trouble to supply their place with new principles: he fancies himself very enlightened, because he sees the deficiencies of other people; he is very ignorant, because he has never reflected on his own. He is a sort of patriot; but it is for "people of property"; —he has a great horror of the *canaille*. As Robert Hall said of Bishop Watson, "he married Public Virtue in his youth, and has quarrelled with his wife ever since." His party think him the most straightforward fellow in the world; for he never voted against them, and never will.

William Muscle is a powerful man; he is one of the people, radical to the backbone: of the old school of radicals;—he hates the philosophers like poison. He thinks Thistlewood a glorious fellow; and no words can express his hatred of William Pitt. He has got at last into parliament, which he always declared he could convince in a fortnight that he was the sole person in the Universe fit to govern England;—whenever he speaks, he says one word about England, to fifty about America. Presidents with five thousand a year are the visions that float for ever in his brain: he seeth not why the Speaker of the House of Commons should have more than a hundred a year; he knoweth many an honest man among his constituents who would be Speaker for less. He accuses the aristocracy of an absolute and understood combination to cheat the good citizens of his borough. He thinketh that Lord Grey and Sir Robert Peel meet in private, to consult how they may most tax the working-classes. He hateth the Jews because they don't plough. He has no desire that the poor man should be instructed. He considereth the cry against taxes on knowledge as sheer cant. He hath a mortal hatred to Museums, and asketh the utility of insects. His whole thought for the poor is how they shall get bread and bacon: he despiseth the man who preferreth tea to ale. He is thoroughly English; no other land could have produced the bones and gristle of his mind. He writeth a plain, strong style, and uttereth the most monstrous incredibilities, as if they were indisputable. He thinks fine words and good periods utter abomination. He esteemeth himself before all men. He believes that the ministers have consulted several times on the necessity of poisoning him. He is indignant if others pretend to serve the People; they are his property. He is the Incarnation of popular prejudices and natural sense. He is changeable as a

weathercock, because he is all passion. He is the living representation of the old John Bull: when he dies, he will leave no like:
it was the work of centuries to amalgamate so much talent, nonsense, strength, and foibles, into one man of five feet eight: he
is the Old Radical—the great Aboriginal of annual parliamen-
tarilism: he is the landmark of Reform fifty years ago: you may
whitewash and put new characters on him, but he sticketh still
in the same place: he is not to be moved to suit the whims of the
philosophers. He hath done his work: a machine excellent at its
day—coarse, huge, massive, and uncouth; not being easily put
out of order, but never perfectly going right. People have invented new machines, all the better for being less rude, and regulated by a wiser principle, though wrought from a less strong
material.

Samuel Square is of a new school of Radicals; he also is a
Republican. He is not a philosopher, but he philosophizes eternally. He liveth upon "first principles." He cannot move a step
beyond them. He hath put the feet of his mind into boxes, in
order that they may not grow larger, and thinks it a beauty that
they are unfit for every-day walking. Whatever may be said
by any man against his logic, he has but one answer—a first principle. He hath no suppleness in him. He cannot refute an error.
He stateth a truism in reply, that hath no evident connexion
with the matter in dispute. He thinketh men have no passions;
he considereth them mere clockwork, and he taketh out his
eternal first principle, as the only instrument to wind them up by.
He is assured that all men of all classes, trades, and intellects act
by self-interest, and if he telleth them that their interest is so-
and-so, so-and-so will they necessarily act. In vain you show him
that he never yet hath convinced any man, he replieth by a first
principle, to prove in spite of your senses, that he hath. He has
satisfied himself, and demands no further proof. He is of no
earthly utility, though he hath walled himself with a supposed
utilitarianism. He cannot write so as to be read, because he conceives that all agreeable writing is full of danger. He cannot
speak so as to be understood, precisely because he never speaks
but in syllogisms. He hath no pith and succulence in him:—he
is as dry as a bone. He liveth by system:—he never was in love in
his life. He refuseth a cheerful glass; nay, perhaps he dieteth only

upon vegetable food. He hath no human sympathies with you, but is a great philanthropist for the people to be born a thousand years hence. He never relieveth any one: he never caresseth any one: he never feeleth for any one—he only reasoneth with every one—and that on the very smallest inch he can find of mutual agreement. If he was ever married I should suspect him to be the father who, advertising the other day for a runaway daughter, begged her, "if she would *not* return to her disconsolate parents, to send them back the key of the tea-chest." What is most strange about him is, that while he thinks all the rest of the world exceedingly foolish, he yet believes they are only to be governed by reason. You will find him visiting a lunatic asylum, and assuring the madman that it is not rational to be insane. He knoweth not one man from another; they seem to him as sheep or babies seem to us—exactly alike. He thinketh that he ought to have a hand in public affairs—the Almighty forbid! This is a scion from the tree of the new radicals: he hath few brethren: he calleth himself a Philosopher, or sometimes a Benthamite. He resembleth the one or the other as the barber's block resembleth a man.—He *is* a block.

The spirit of coxcombry, as you find it on the continent, would seem to be a perversion of the spirit of benevolence;—it is the desire to please, fantastically expressed. With us it is just the reverse, it seems a perversion of the spirit of malignity;—it is the desire to *dis*please;—there is, however, one species of coxcombry which I shall first describe; passive and harmless, it consists in no desire at all.

Lord Mute *is* an English *élégant*—a dandy. You know not what he *has* been. He seems as if he could never have been a boy: all appearance of nature has departed from him. He is six feet of inanity enveloped in cloth! You cannot believe God made him—Stultz must have been his Frankenstein. He dresseth beautifully—let us allow it—there is nothing *outré* about him: you see not in him the slovenly magnificence of other nations. His characteristic is neatness. His linen—how white! His shirt-buttons—how regularly set in! His colours—how well chosen! His boots are the only things splendid in his whole costume. Lord Mute has certainly excellent taste; it appears in his horses, his livery, his cabriolet. He is great in a school of faultless simplicity.

There can be no doubt that in equipage and dress, Englishmen excel all other Europeans. But Lord Mute never converses. When he is dressed there is an end of him. The clock don't tick as it goes. He and his brethren are quiet as the stars—

> In solemn silence, all
> Move round this dark terrestrial ball.

But I wrong him—he *does* speak, though he does not converse. He has a set of phrases, which he repeats every day:—"he can hum thrice, and buzz as often." He knows nothing of Politics, Literature, Science. He reads the paper—but mechanically; the letters present to him nothing to be remembered. He is a true philosopher: the world is agitated—he knows it not: the roar of the fierce democracy, the changes of states, the crash of thrones, never affect him. He does not even condescend to speak of such trifles. He riseth to his labour, dresseth, goeth out, clubbeth, dineth, speaketh his verbal round, and is at the Opera brilliant and composed as ever,

> The calm of heaven reflected on his face.

He never putteth himself into passions. He laughs not loudly. His brow wrinkles not till extreme old age. He is a spectator of life, from one of the dress boxes. Were a *coup-de-soleil* to consume her Ladyship, he would say with Major Longbow, "Bring clean glasses and sweep away your mistress." *That* would be a long speech for him. Lord Mute is not an unpopular man: he is one of the inoffensive dandies. Lord Mute, indeed, is *not!*—it is his cabriolet and his coat that *are.* How can the most implacable person hate a coat and a cabriolet?

But Sir Paul Snarl is of the offending species—the wasp dandy to the drone dandy. He is a clever*ish* man: he has read books and can quote dates, if need be, to spoil a good joke by proving an anachronism. He drawls when he speaks, and raises his eyebrows superciliously. Sir Paul is a man of secondrate family, and moderate fortune. He has had to make his way in the world—by studying to be amiable?—no:—by studying to be disagreeable. Always doubtful of his own position, he has endeavoured to impose upon you by pretending not to care a farthing about you. He has wished to rise by depreciating others, and to become a great man, by showing that he thinks *you* an exceedingly small one. Strange to say, he has succeeded. He is one, indeed, of the most numerous class of successful dandies; a specimen of a common character. People suppose a man who seems to think so little of them, must be thought a great deal of himself. The honourable mistresses say to their husbands, "We must have that odious Sir Paul to dinner; it is well to conciliate him, he says such ill-natured things; besides, as he is so very fine, he will meet, you know, my dear, the Duke of Haut-ton; and we must have Crack to dress the dinner!" Thus, Sir Paul—clever dog!—is not only asked every where, but absolutely petted and courted, because he is so intolerably unpleasant!

Sir Paul Snarl is one of the dandies, but—mistake not the meaning of the word—dandy does not only signify a man who dresses well; a man may be a sloven, and yet a dandy. A man is called a dandy who lives much with persons *à la mode,* is intimate with *the* dandy *clique,* and being decently well-born and rich, entertains certain correct, general notions about that indefinable thing, "good taste."[1] Sir Paul Snarl dresses like other people. Among very good dressers, he would be called rather ill-dressed; among the *oi polloi,* he would be considered a model. At all events, he is not thorough bred in his appearance; he lacks the *senatorius decor;* you might take him for a duke's valet, without being much to blame for inexperience. Sir Paul and his class are the *cutters* in society. Lord Mute rarely *cuts,* unless you are *very* ill-dressed *indeed;* he knows his own station by instinct; he is not to be destroyed by "Who's your fat friend?" But Sir Paul is on a very different footing; *his* whole position is false— he can't afford to throw away an acquaintance—he knows no "odd people"; if he the least doubts your being *comme il faut,* he cuts you immediately. He is in perpetual fear of people finding out what he is; his existence depends on being thought something *better* than he is—a policy effected by knowing every body higher and nobody lower than himself; that is exactly the

1. Good taste is a very favourite phrase with the English aristocracy; they carry it to the pulpit and the House of Commons—"Such a man preached in very good taste," or "in what excellent taste So-and-so's speech was." Good taste applied to legislation and salvation!—what does the phrase mean? Heaven knows what it means in the pulpit; in the House of Commons it always means flattering the old members, and betraying impudence modestly.

definition of Sir Paul's consequence! Sir Paul's vanity is to throw a damp on the self-love of every body else. If you tell a good story, he takes snuff, and turns to his neighbour with a remark about Almack's; if you fancy you have made a conquest of Miss Blank, he takes an opportunity of telling you, *par parenthèse,* that she says she can't bear you: if you have made a speech in the House of Lords, he accosts you with an exulting laugh, and a "Well, never mind, you'll do better next time": if you have bought a new horse at an extravagant price, and are evidently vain of it, he smiles languidly, and informs you that it was offered to him for half what you gave for it, but he would not have it for nothing: when you speak, he listens with a vacant eye: when you walk, he watches you with a curled lip: if he dines with you, he sends away your best hock with a wry face. His sole aim is to wound you in the sorest place. He is a coxcomb of this age and nation peculiarly; and does that from foppery which others do from malice. There are plenty of Sir Paul Snarls in the London world; men of sense are both their fear and antipathy. They are animals easily slain—by a dose of their own insolence. Their sole rank being fictitious, they have nothing to fall back upon, if you show in public that you despise them.

But who is this elderly gentleman, with a portly figure. Hush! it is Mr. Warm, *"a most respectable man."* His most intimate friend failed in trade, and went to prison. Mr. Warm forswore his acquaintance; *it was not respectable.* Mr. Warm, in early life, seduced a young lady; she lived with him three years; he married, and turned her off without a shilling—the connexion, for a married man, *was not respectable.* Mr. Warm is a most respectable man; he pays his bills regularly—he subscribes to six public charities—he goes to church with all his family on a Sunday—he is in bed at twelve o'clock. Well, well, all that's very proper; but is Mr. Warm a good father, a good friend, an active citizen? or is he not avaricious, does he not love scandal, *is not his heart cold,* is he not vindictive, is he not unjust, is he not unfeeling? Lord, sir, I believe he *may* be all that; but what then? *every body allows Mr. Warm is a most respectable man.*

Such a character and such a reputation are proofs of our regard for Appearances. Aware of that regard, behold a real imitating the metaphorical swindler. See that gentleman, "fashionably dressed," with "a military air," and "a prepossessing exterior"; he calleth himself "Mr. Cavendish Fitzroy"—he taketh lodgings in "a genteel situation"—he ordereth jewels and silks of divers colours to be sent home to him—he elopeth with them by the back way. Mighty and manifold are the cheats he hath thus committed, and great the wailing and gnashing of teeth in Marylebone and St. James's. But, you say, surely by this time tradesmen with a grain of sense would be put on their guard. No, my dear sir, no; in England we are never on our guard against "such *respectable appearances*." In vain are there warnings in the papers and example in the police court. Let a man style himself Mr. Cavendish Fitzroy, and have a *prepossessing exterior,* and he sets suspicion at once to sleep. Why not? is it more foolish to be deceived by respectable appearances in Mr. Fitzroy, than by the respectable appearance of Mr. Warm.

But grandeur, in roguery, at least, has its drawbacks in happiness; the fashionable swindler with us, is not half so merry a dog as your regular thief. There is something melancholy and gentlemanlike about the Fitzroy set, in their fur coats and gold chains; they live alone, not gregariously. I should not be surprised, if they read Lord Byron. They are haunted with the fear of the tread-mill, and cannot bear low company; if they come to be hanged, they die moodily,—and often attempt prussic acid; in short, there is nothing to envy about them, except their good looks; but your regular THIEF,—ah, he is, indeed, a happy fellow! Take him all in all, I doubt if in the present state of English society he is not the lightest hearted personage in it. Taxes afflict him not; he fears no scarcity of work. Rents may go down; labour be dirt-cheap; what cares he?—A fall in the funds affects not his gay good humour; and as to the little mortifications of life,—

> If money grow scarce, and his Susan look cold,
> Ah, the false hearts that we find on the shore!

—why, he changes his quarters, and Molly replaces Susan!

But, above all, he has this great happiness—he can never fall in society; that *terror of descending,* which in our complication of grades, haunts all other men, never affects him; he is equally at home in the tread-mill, the hulks, Hobart's Town, as he is when playing at dominoes at the Cock and Hen, or leading the dance in St. Giles's. You must know, by the way, that the English thief has many more amusements than any other class, save the aristocracy; he has balls, hot suppers, theatres, and *affaires du cœur* all at his command; and he is eminently social—a jolly fellow to the core; if he is hanged, he does not take it to heart like the Fitzroys; he has lived merrily, and he dies game. I apprehend, therefore, that if your Excellency would look for whatever gaiety may exist among the English, you must drop the "Travellers" for a short time, and go among the thieves. You might almost fancy yourself in France, they are so happy. This is perfectly true, and no caricature, as any policeman will bear witness. I know not if the superior hilarity and cheerfulness of thieves be peculiar to England; but possibly, over-taxation (from which *our* thieves are exempted) may produce the effect of lowering the animal spirits of the rest of the Community.

Mr. Bluff is the last character I shall describe in this chapter. He is the sensible, *practical* man. He despises all speculations, but those in which he has a share. He is very intolerant to other people's hobbyhorses; he hates both poets and philosophers. He has a great love of facts; if you could speak to him out of the multiplication table, he would think you a great orator. He does not observe how the facts are applied to the theory; he only wants the facts themselves. If you were to say to him thus, "When abuses arise to a certain pitch, they must be remedied," he would think you a shallow fellow—a theorist; but if you were to say to him, "One thousand pauper children are born in London; in 1823, wheat was forty-nine shillings; hop-grounds let from ten to twelve shillings an acre, and you must, *therefore,* confess that, when abuses arise to a certain pitch, they must be remedied"; Mr. Bluff would nod his wise head, and say of you to his next neighbour, "That's the man for my money, you see what a quantity of facts he puts into his speech!"

Facts, like stones, are nothing in themselves, their value consists in the manner they are put together, and the purpose to which they are applied.

Accordingly, Mr. Bluff is always taken in. Looking only at a fact, he does not see an inch beyond it, and you might draw him into any imprudence, if you were constantly telling him "two and two made four." Mr. Bluff is wonderfully English.

It is by "practical men," that we have ever been seduced into the wildest speculations; and the most preposterous of living theorists, always begins his harangues with—"Now, my friends, let us look *to the facts.*"[2]

2. The reader will perceive, I trust, the spirit of these remarks. Of course every true theory must be founded on facts; but there is a tendency in the country to suppose, that a man who knows how gloves are made, must necessarily know best, by what laws glovemaking should be protected; the two species of knowledge are distinct. A mind habituated to principles can stoop to details, because it seizes and classifies them at a glance: but a mind habituated to detail, is *rarely* capable of extending its grasp to a principle. When a man says he is no orator, he is going to make an oration. When a man says he is a plain practical man, I know he is going, by the fact that one and one make two, to prove the theory that two and two make seven!

Book the Second

Society and Manners

Voilà ce que je sais par une expérience de toutes sortes de livres et de personnes.

Pensées de Pascal

I

Society and Manners

I inscribe to you, my dear ————, this part of my work, which consists of sketches from the various aspects of our SOCIAL SYSTEM; for I know no man who can more readily judge if the likeness be correct. Your large experience of mankind, and the shrewdness of your natural faculties of observation, have furnished you with a store of facts, which the philosophy you have gleaned from no shallow meditation, and no ordinary learning, enables you, most felicitously to apply. Many of the remarks in this part of my work are the result of observations we have made together; and, if now and then some deduction more accurate that the rest should please the reader, I might perhaps say, in recollecting how much my experience has profited by yours, *ce n'est pas moi qui parle, c'est Marc Aurèle.*

As the first impression the foreigner receives on entering England is that of the evidence of wealth, so the first thing that strikes the moral inquirer into our social system is the respect in which wealth is held: in some countries Pleasure is the idol; in others Glory, and the prouder desires of the world; but with us, Money is the mightiest of all deities.

In one of those beautiful visions of Quevedo, that mingle so singularly the grand with the grotesque, Death (very differently habited and painted from the ordinary method of portraying her effigies) conducts the poet through an allegorical journey, in which he beholds three spectres, armed, and of human shape, "so like one another," says the author, "that I could not say which was which; they were engaged in fierce contest with a fearful and misshapen monster:"—

"Knowest thou these?" quoth Death, halting abruptly, and facing me.

"No, indeed," said I;—"and I shall insert in my Litany to be for ever delivered from the honour of their acquaintance."

"Fool," answered Death, "these are already thy old acquaintance; nay, thou hast known scarcely any other since thy birth. They are the capital enemies of thy soul—the World, the Flesh, and the Devil. So much do they resemble each other, that in effect he who hath one hath all. The ambitious man clasps the World to his heart, and lo! it is the Devil; the lecher embraces the *Flesh,* and the Devil is in his arms!"

"But who," said I, "is this enemy against whom they fight?"

"It is the Fiend of Money," answered Death: "a boastful demon, who maintains that he alone is equal to all the three; and that where *he* comes, there is need of *them.*"

"Ah!" said I, "the Fiend of Money hath the better end of the staff."

This fable illustrates our social system. The World, the Flesh, and the Devil, are formidable personages; but Lucre is a match for the all. The Fiend of Money has the better end of the staff.

The word Society is an aristocratic term; and it is the more aristocratic bearings of its spirit which we will first consider. Let us begin with FASHION.

The Middle Classes interest themselves in grave matters: the aggregate of their sentiments is called OPINION. The great interest themselves in frivolities, and the aggregate of *their* sentiments is termed FASHION. The first is the moral representative of the popular mind, the last of the aristocratic.

But the legislative constitutions of a people give a colouring even to their levities: and fashion is a shadow of the national character itself. In France, fashion was gallant under Louis XIV., and severe under the Triumvirate of the Revolution: in Venice it was mercantile: in Prussia it is military: in England its coin has opposite effigies—on one side you see the respect for wealth —on the other side the disdain! The man of titles has generally either sprung from the men of wealth (acknowledging the founder of his rank in the rich merchant, or the successful lawyer), or else he has maintained his station by intermarriages with their order; on the one hand, therefore, he is driven to respect and to seek connexion with the wealthy; but, on the other hand, the natural exclusiveness of titular pride makes him (or rather his wife) desire to preserve some circle of acquaintance-ship sacred from the aspirations even of that class from which he derives either his origin or the amount of his rent-roll. We allow the opulent to possess power, but we deny them fashion: the wheel turns round, and, in the next generation, behold the rich *roturier* has become the titled exclusive! This sustains, at once, the spirit of a ridiculous rivalry among the low-born rich and that of an inconsistent arrogance among the hereditary great. The merchant's family give splendid entertainments in order to prove that they are entitled to match with the nobleman's:—the nobleman is unwilling to be outdone by the banker, and ostentation becomes the order of the day. We do not strive, as should be the object of a court, to banish dulness from society. No! we strive to render dulness magnificent, and the genius of this miserable emulation spreading from one grade to another, each person impoverishes himself from the anxiety not to be considered as poor.

When Lucien Bonaparte was residing in England some years ago, he formed to himself the chimerical hope of retrenchment; he was grievously mistaken! the brother of Napoleon, who, as ambassador in Spain, as minister in France, and as prince in Italy, never maintained any further show than that which belongs to elegance, found himself in England, for the first time, compelled to ostentation. "It was not *respectable* for a man of his rank to be so plain!" Singularly enough, the first blow to the system of pomp was given by a despot. The Emperor of Russia went about London in a hackney-coach, and familiarized the London *grands seigneurs* with the dignity of simplicity.

Fashion in this country, then, is a compound of opposite qualities; it respects the rich and affects to despise them; to-day you wonder at its servility, to-morrow at is arrogance.

A notorious characteristic of English society is the universal marketing of our unmarried women;—a marketing peculiar to ourselves in Europe, and only rivalled by the slave-merchants of the East. We are a matchmaking nation; the lively novels of Mrs.

Gore have given a just and unexaggerated picture of the intrigues, the manœuvres, the plotting and the counterplotting
that make the staple of matronly ambition. We boast that in our
country, young people not being affianced to each other by their
parents, there are more marriages in which the heart is engaged
than there are abroad. Very possibly; but, in good society, the
heart is remarkably prudent, and seldom falls violently in love
without a sufficient settlement: where the heart is, *there* will the
treasure be also! Our young men possessing rather passion than
sentiment, form those *liaisons,* which are the substitute of love;
they may say with Quin to the fair glovemaker, "Madam, I never
make love, I always buy it *readymade.*" We never go into a
ball-room without feeling that we breathe the air of diplomacy.
How many of those gentle *chaperons* would shame even the wisdom of a Talleyrand. What open faces and secret hearts! What
schemes and ambushes in every word. If we look back to that
early period in the history of our manners, when with us, as it is
still in France, parents betrothed their children, and, instead of
bringing them to public sale, effected a private compact of exchange, we shall be surprised to find that marriages were not
less happy nor women less domestic than at present. The custom of open matchmaking is productive of many consequences
not sufficiently noticed; in the first place, it encourages the spirit
of insincerity among all women,—"Mothers and Daughters,"—
a spirit that consists in perpetual scheming, and perpetual hypocrisy; it lowers the chivalric estimate of women, and damps
with eternal suspicion the youthful tendency to lofty and honest
love. In the next place, it assists to render the tone of society dull,
low, and unintellectual; it is not talent, it is not virtue; it is not
even the graces and fascination of manner that are sought by the
fair dispensers of social reputation: no, it is the title and the
rent-roll. You do not lavish your invitations on the most agreeable member of a family, but on the richest. The elder son is
the great attraction. Nay, the more agreeable the man be, if poor
and unmarried, the more dangerous he is considered; you may
admit him to acquaintanceship, but you jealously bar him from
intimacy. Thus society is crowded with the insipid and beset with
the insincere. The women that give the tone to society take the
tone from their favourites. The rich young man is to be flattered

in order that he may be won; to flatter him you seem to approve his pursuits; you talk to him of balls and races; you fear to alarm him by appearing his intellectual superior; you dread lest he should think you a blue; you trust to beauty and a graceful folly to allure him, and you harmonize *your* mind into "gentle dulness," that it may not jar upon his own.

The ambition of women absorbed in these petty intrigues, and debased to this paltry level, possesses but little sympathy with the great objects of a masculine and noble intellect. They have, in general, a frigid conception of public virtue: they affect not to understand politics, and measure a man's genius by his success *in getting on.* With the women of ancient times, a patriot was an object of admiration; with the women of ours, he is an object of horror. Speak against pensions, and they almost deem you disreputable,—become a placeman, and you are a person of consideration. Thus our women seldom exalt the ambition of public life. They are inimitable, however, in their consolation under its reverses.

Mr. Thurston is a man of talent and ambition; he entered parliament some years since, through the medium of a patron and a close borough. He is what you call a Political Adventurer. He got on tolerably well, and managed to provide at least for his family. He professed liberal opinions, and was, perhaps, not insincere in them, as men go. He had advocated always something like Parliamentary Reform. THE BILL came—he was startled; but half-inclined to vote for it. Mrs. Thurston was alarmed out of her senses; she besought, she wheedled, she begged her spouse to remember, that by Parliamentary Reform would fall Government Patronage;—she would say nothing of their other children; but he had a little boy two years old; what was to become of *him?* It was in vain to hope any thing from the whigs; they had too many friends of their own to provide for. This bill, too, could never be passed: the tories would—must—come back again, and then what gratitude for his vote! So argued Mrs. Thurston; and like a very sensible woman; but as one who used no earthly arguments but those addressed to self-interest;—not a word as to what would be best for the nation; it was only, what was best for the family. Mr. Thurston wavered—was seduced—voted against Reform, and is out of parliament for the rest of his life. What makes matters still worse is, that his father, a merchant of moderate fortune, whose heir he was, failed almost immediately after this unfortunate vote. Thurston, with a large family, has become a poor man; he has retired into the country; he can have nothing of course, to expect from Government. Public life is for ever closed for him in the prime of his intellect, and just as he had begun to rise. All this may, perhaps, be borne cheerfully enough by a man who has acted according to his conscience, but the misfortune is, that Thurston was persuaded to vote against it.

But now, however, we must take another view of the picture. If Mrs. Thurston *was* the undoer, she *is* the consoler. In prosperity, vain, extravagant, and somewhat vehement in temper; in adversity she has become a very pattern of prudence, and affectionate forbearance. Go down into the country, and see the contrast in her present, and her past manner; she is not the same woman. This amendment on her part is very beautiful, and very English. But has she been able really to console Thurston? No, he is a gone man; his spirit is broken; he has turned generally peevish; and if you speak to him on politics, you will soon have to look out for a *second*. Mrs. Thurston, however, is far from thinking she was the least in the wrong; all that she can possibly understand about the whole question is, *"that it turned out unlucky."*

A gentleman of good birth and much political promise, had been voting in several divisions with the more Radical Party. A man of authority, and one of the elders, who had been a Minister in his day, expressed his regret at the bad company Mr. ——— had been keeping, to the aunt of that gentleman, a lady of remarkable talents and of great social influence. The aunt repeated the complaint to the member—"And what said you, dear madam, in reply?"

"Oh! I exculpated you most cleverly," replied the aunt. "Leave ——— alone," said I; "nobody plays his cards better; you may be sure that his votes against the Irish Coercion Bill, &c. wo'n't tell against him one of these days. No, no; ——— is not a rash, giddy young man, to be talked over; be sure he has calculated that it will be best for him in the end."

"Good Heavens!" cried the member, "what *you—you* say this?

you insinuated that I am actuated by my own interest! why not have said at once the truth, that I voted according to my conscience?"

The lady looked at her nephew with mingled astonishment and contempt:—"Because—because," replied she, hesitating, *"I really did not think you such a fool."*

Yet this innocent unconsciousness of public virtue is to be found only among the women of the metropolis brought in contact with the Aristocracy;—in the provincial towns, and in humbler life, it is just the reverse. Any man who has gone through a popular election, knows that there it is often by the honesty of the women, that that of the men is preserved. *There* the conjugal advice is always, "Never go back from your word, John."—"Stick true to your colours."—"All the gold in the world should not make you change your coat." How many poor men have we known who would have taken a bribe but for their wives. There is nothing, then, in English women that should prevent their comprehension of the nobleness of political honesty; it is only the great ladies, and their imitators, who think self-interest the sole principle of public conduct. Why is this? because all women are proud; *station* incites their pride. The great man rats, and is greater than ever; but the poor elector who turns his coat loses his station altogether. The higher classes do not imagine there is a public opinion among the poor. In many boroughs a man may be bribed, and no disgrace to him; but, if *after* being bribed, he break his word, he is cut by his friends for ever.

A very handsome girl had refused many better offers for the sake of a young man, a scot and lot voter in a certain borough. Her lover, having promised in her hearing to vote one way, voted the other. She refused to marry him. Could this have happened in the higher classes? Fancy, my dear ————, how the great would laugh; and what a good story it would be at the clubs, if a young lady just going to be married, were to say to her suitor one bright morning,—"No, sir, excuse me; the connexion must be broken off. Your vote in the House of Commons last night was decidedly against your professions to your constituents."

It is a remarkable fact, that with us, a grave and mediative people, Ridicule is more dangerous and powerful in its effects, than it is with our lighter neighbours, the French. With them, at no period has it been the fashion to sneer at lofty and noble motives; they have an instantaneous perception of the Exalted—they carry their sense of it even to bombast—and they only worship the Natural when it appears with a stage effect. The lively demireps of Paris, were charmed with the adoration of virtue professed by Rousseau;—and at an earlier period, even a Dangeau could venerate a Fenelon. At this moment, how ridiculous in our country would be the gallant enthusiasm of Chateaubriand: his ardour, his chivalry, his quixotism, would make him the laughingstock of the whole nation;—in France these very qualities are the sole source of his power. Ridicule, in Paris, attaches itself to the manners; in London, to the emotions: it sneers with us less at a vulgar tone, a bad address, an ill-chosen equipage, than at some mental enthusiasm. A man professing very exalted motives is a very ridiculous animal with us. We do not laugh at vulgar lords half so much as at the generosity of patriots, or the devotion of philosophers. Bentham was thought exceedingly ludicrous because he was a philanthropist; and Byron fell from the admiration of fine ladies when he set out for Greece. It is the great in mind, whom a fine moral sense never suffers to be the object of a paltry wit. Francis I. forbade his courtiers to jest at Ariosto; and Louis XIV. declared a certain general first for high office, because he had evinced the mental littleness of laughing at Racine.

Ridicule is always a more dangerous goddess with a sober and earnest than with a frivolous people. Persons of the former class can *be more easily made ashamed of emotion;* hence the reason why they conceal the sentiments which lighter minds betray. We see this truth every day in actual life—the serious are more deeply moved by ridicule than the gay. A satirist laughed the Spaniards out of chivalry; the French have never to this day been laughed out of any thing more valuable than a wig or a bonnet.

One characteristic of English society is the influence of CLIQUES. Some half a dozen little persons have, God knows how, got into a certain eminence—in some certain line;—they pretend to the power of dispensing all kinds of reputation. Some years ago, there was the Authors' *clique* of Albemarle Street, a circle of gentlemen who professed to weigh out to each man his modicum of fame; they praised each other—were *the* literary class, and thought Stewart Rose a greater man than Wordsworth —peace be with them—they are no more—and fame no longer hangs from the nostrils of Samuel Rogers.[1]

The *clique* of fine ladies and the *clique* of dandies still, however, exist; and these are the donors of social reputation: we may say of them as the Irishman said of the thieves, "They are mighty generous with what does not belong to them,"—being without character themselves, we may judge of the merits which induce them to give a character to others.

Is is rather strange, till we consider the cause, that society in the Provinces is often more polished, intellectual, and urbane, than society in the Metropolis; when some great landed proprietor fills his country halls with a numerous circle of his friends, you see perhaps the most agreeable and charming society which England can afford. You remember (dear ———) Sir Frederick Longueville and his family: you know how disagreeable we used to think them; always so afraid they were not fine enough. Sir Frederick, with his pompous air, asking you when you had last seen your uncle, the earl, and her ladyship, dying to be good-natured, but resolved to keep up her dignity;—the girls out at *every* ball, and telling you invariably as a first remark that they did not see you at Almack's last Wednesday; so ashamed if you caught them at a party the wrong side of Oxford Street, and whispering, "Papa's country connexions, you know!"—You remember, in short that the Longuevilles impressed every one with the idea of being fussy, conceited, second-rate, and wretchedly educated; they *are* all this in town. Will you believe it—they are quite the contrary if you visit them in Sussex? There Sir Frederick is no longer pompous; frank and good-humoured, he rides with you over his farm, speaks to every poor man he meets, forgets

1. This *clique,* while it lasted, made a vast number of small reputations, upon which the owners have lived very comfortably ever since. Theirs was the day of literary jobbing; they created sinecures for the worthless, and time makes them a kind of property, which it seems wrong to take away; yet, whenever we meet any of the surviving possessors of these "unmerited pensions," such as ——— and ——— we cannot help thinking with Gibbon, how often Chance is the dispenser of Reputation; and that the tutelary saint of England, the pattern doubtless of these gentlemen, is called the noble Saint George, though, in reality, he was the worthless George of Cappadocia. O Literature, how many Georges of Cappadocia have you converted into Saint Georges of England!

that you have an uncle an earl, and is the very pattern of a great country gentleman—hospitable and easy, dignified and natural. Lady Longueville you will fancy you have known all your life—so friendly is her nature, and so cordial her manner; and, as for the girls, to your great surprise, you will find them well read and accomplished, affectionate, simple, with a charming spice of romance in them; upon my word I do not exaggerate. What is the cause of the change? Solely this: in London they know not their own station; here it is fixed; at one place they are trying to be something they are not; here they try at nothing; they are contented with what they are.

What an enviable station is that of a great country gentleman in this beautiful garden of England; he may unite all the happiest opposites—indolence and occupation, healthful exercise and literary studies. In London, and in public life, we may improve the world—we may benefit our kind, but we never *see* the effects we produce; we get no gratitude for them; others step in and snatch the rewards; but, in the country, if you exert equal industry and skill, you cannot walk out of your hall but what you see the evidence of your labours: Nature smiles in your face and thanks you! yon trees you planted; yon corn-fields were a common—your capital called them into existence; they feed a thousand mouths, where, ten years ago, they scarce maintained some half a dozen starveling cows. But, above all, as you ride through your village, what satisfaction creeps around your heart. By half that attention to the administration of the Poor-laws which, in London, you gave to your clubs,[2] you have made industry replace sloth, and comfort dethrone pauperism. You, a single individual, have done more for your fellow-creatures than the whole legislature has done in centuries. This is true power; it approaches men to God; but the country gentleman often re-

2. See the recent Evidence on the Poor-laws in proof of the possibility of this fact. Even in the present wretched system, a vigorous and wise management has sufficed to put down pauperism. In Stanford Rivers, Essex, one man, Andrews, a farmer, with the concurrence of the rest of the parishioners, resolved to put down pauperism: in 1825 the money expended on the poor was 834*l.*; by management and energy, in 1828, it was only 196*l.* "All capable of work were employed; the labourers improved in their habits and comforts during the four years this system was in progress; there was not a single commitment for theft, or any other offence." Oh, *if* the country gentleman *would* awake to a sense of what he might be!

fuses to acknowledge this power;—he thinks much more of a certificate for killing partridges!

Clubs form a main feature of the social system of the richer classes of the Metropolis. Formerly they were merely the resort of gamblers, politicians, or *bons vivans*—now they have assumed a more intellectual character; every calling has a peculiar club —from the soldier's to the scholar's. The effect which this multiplicity of clubs has produced is salutary in the extreme; it has begun already to counteract the solitary disposition of the natives; it opens a ready intercourse with our foreign guests, who are usually admitted as honorary members; prejudices are rubbed off, and by an easy and unexpensive process, the most domestic or the most professional learn the views of the citizen of the world. At these resorts the affairs of the public make the common and natural topic of conversation, and nothing furthers the growth of public principle like the discussion of public matters. It is said that clubs render men less domestic. No, they only render them less unsocial; they form a cheap and intellectual relaxation, and (since in *most* of the recent clubs the custom turns to neither gambling nor inebriety) they unbend the mind even while improving it. But these are the least advantages of clubs; they contain the germ of a mighty improvement in the condition of the humbler classes. I foresee that those classes will, sooner or later, adopt institutions so peculiarly favourable to the poor. By this species of co-operation, the man of 200*l.* a year can, at present, command the nobler luxuries of a man of 5000*l.*; airy and capacious apartments, the decent comforts of the table,[3] lights, fires, books, and intellectual society. The same principle on a humbler scale would procure the same advantages for the shopkeeper or the artisan, and the man of 50*l.* a year might obtain the same comforts as the man of 500*l.* If the experiment were made by the middle and lower classes in a provincial town, it could not fail of success; and, among its advantages would be the check to early and imprudent marriages, and the growth of that sense of moral dignity which is ever produced by a perception of the higher comforts of life.

3. At the Athenæum, for instance, the dinner, which at an hotel would cost 7*s.* or 8*s.*, costs about 3*s.*: viz., a joint, vegetables, bread, butter, cheese, &c., and half a pint of wine. I believe in some clubs the price is even less.

Probably, from the success of this experiment, yet newer and more comprehensive results would arise. A gentleman of the name of Morgan, in a letter to the Bishop of London, proposes the scheme of clubs, not for individuals only, but families—a plan which might include education for children and attendance in sickness. Managed by a committee, such clubs would remove the possibility of improvidence and unskilful management in individuals. For professional and literary men, for artists, and the poorer gentry, such a scheme would present the greatest advantages. But the time for its adoption is not come: two great moral checks still exist in our social habits—the aristocratic pride not of *being as well off* as our neighbours, but of *seeming better off,* and that commercial jealousy of appropriation which makes us so proverbially like to have *a home of our own.* If ever these feelings decrease among us, I have little doubt that, from the institution of clubs will be dated a vast social Revolution. But France, rather than England, is the proper arena for the first experiment of Mr. Morgan's system.

II

Conversation and Literary Men

Among the characteristics of English society, there is one, my dear ———, which cannot but have seemed to you as worthy of notice, and that is "the curious felicity" which distinguishes the tone of conversation. In most countries, people of the higher stations, if they do not express their ideas with all the accuracy and formality of a treatise on logic, preserve, at least, with a certain degree of jealousy, the habit of a clear and easy elegance in conversation. In France, to talk the language well is still the indispensable accomplishment of a gentleman. Society preserves the happy diction, and the graceful phrase, which literature has stamped with its authority: And the Court may be considered as the Master of the Ceremonies to the Muses.[1] But in England, people even in the best and most fastidious society, are not remarkable for cultivating the more pure or brilliant order of conversation, as the evidence of *ton,* and the attribute of rank. They reject, it is true, certain vulgarities of accent, provincial phrases, and glaring violations of grammar; nay, over certain words, they now and then exercise the caprices of fashion: James to-day, may be Jeemes to-morrow; Rome may be softened into Room; and cucumber may receive its final exactness of pronunciation from the prosodiacal fiat of my Lord Hertford. But these are trifles: the regular and polished smoothness of conversation, the unpedantic and transparent preciseness of meaning, the happy

1. Nay, to catch the expressions of the courts is, in France, to acquire elegance of style.

choice, unpremeditated, because habitual, of the most graceful phrases and polished idioms which the language affords—these, the natural care and province of a lettered court, are utterly un-heeded by the circles of the English aristocracy. Nor is there any other circle, since literary men with us are so little gregarious, that repairs their inattention; and our rational conversation is for the most part carried on in a series of the most extraordinary and rugged abbreviations—a species of talking shorthand. Hesi-tating, Humming, and Drawling, are the three Graces of our Conversation.

We are at dinner:—a gentleman, "a man about town," is in-forming us of a misfortune that has befallen his friend: "No—I assure you—now err—errr—that—er—it was the most shock-ing accident possible—er—poor Chester was riding in the Park—er—you know that grey—er—(substantive dropped, hand a little flourished instead)—of his—splendid creature!—er—well sir, and by Jove—er—the—er—(no substantive, flourish again)—took fright, and—e—er"—here the gentleman throws up his chin and eyes, sinks back exhausted into his chair, and after a pause adds, "Well, they took him into—the shop—there—you know—with the mahogany sashes—just by the Park—er—and the—er—man there—set his—what d'ye call it—er—collar-bone; *but* he was—er—ter-ri-bly—terribly"—a full stop. The gentleman shakes his head,—and the sentence is suspended to eternity.

Another gentleman takes up the wondrous tale thus logically: "Ah! shocking, shocking!—*but* poor Chester was a very agree-able—er"— full stop!

"Oh! devilish gentlemanlike fellow!—quite shocking!—quite—did you go into the—er—to-day?"

"No, indeed; the day was so *un*—may I take some wine with you?"

The ladies usually resort to some pet phrases, that, after the fashion of shorthand, express as much as possible in a word: "what do you think of Lady ———'s last novel?"

"Oh! they say 'tis not very natural. The characters, to be sure, are a little overdrawn; and then the style—so—so—I don't know what—you understand me—but it's *a dear* book altogether!—Do you know Lady ———?"

"Oh dear yes! *nice* creature she is."
"Very *nice* person indeed."

"What a *dear* little horse that is of poor Lord ———!"
"He is very vicious."
"Is he really?—*nice* little thing."

"Ah! you must not abuse poor Mrs. ———;—to be sure, she is very ill-natured, and they say she's *so* stingy—but then she really is such a *dear*—"

Nice and *dear* are the great To Prepon and To Kalon of feminine conversational moralities.

But, perhaps, the genius of our conversation is most shown in the art of explaining—

"Where you in the House last night?"

"Yes—er—Sir Robert Peel made a splendid speech!"

"Ah! and how did he justify his vote? I've not seen the papers."

"Oh, I can tell you exactly—ehem—he said you see, that he disliked the ministers, and so forth! you understand—but that—er—in these times, and so forth—and with this river of blood—oh! he was very fine *there!*—you must read it—well, sir; and then he was very good against O'Connell, capital—and all this agitation *going on*—and murder, and so forth—and then, sir, he told a capital story, about a man and his wife being murdered, and putting a child in the fireplace—you see—I forget now, but it was capital: and then he wound up with—a—with—a—in his usual way, in short. Oh! he quite justified himself—you understand—in short, you see, he could not do otherwise."

Caricatured as this may seem to others, I need not assure you that it is to the life: the explainer, too, is reckoned a very sensible man; and the listener saw nothing inconclusive in the elucidation.

Women usually form the tone of conversation, having first taken the tone of mind from the men. With us, women associate with the idler portion of society—the dandies, the hangers-on; they are afraid of being thought blue, because then these gentlemen would be afraid of them. They connect literature and wisdom with 'odd persons not in society'; senators and geniuses are little seen amongst them. It is their bore of an uncle who

97

makes long speeches about the malt tax. The best matches are the young men of Melton and Crockford's; (as I have before said) they must please the best matches; they borrow the tone most pleasing to them; the mothers, for the sake of the daughters, the daughters for their own sake—thus, to a slang of mind, they mould a fitting jargon of conversation. Our aristocracy does not even preserve elegance to *ton,* and, with all the affectations, fosters none of the graces, of a court. France owes the hereditary refinement and airiness of conversation, that distinguishes her higher orders, less, however, to the courtiers than to those whom the courtiers have always sought. Men of letters and men of genius have been at Paris invariably drawn towards the upper circles, and have consumed their own dignity of character in brightening the pleasures of the great; but, in London, men of intellectual distinctions are not frequently found in that society which is termed the best; the few who do haunt that gloomy region, are but the scattered witlings of an ancient *clique,* who have survived even the faculty of premeditating good things; they do not belong to this day, but to the past, when Devonshire House and Melbourne House were for a short time and from fortuitous circumstances made the resort of genius, as well as rank; the fashion thus set was brief and evanescent, and expired with the brilliant persons who, seeking to enliven the great world, only interrupted its dulness. They have played off the fireworks, and all is once more dark.

The modern practice of Parliament to hold its discussions at night has a considerable influence in diminishing the intellectual character of general society. The House of Commons naturally drains off many of the ablest and best informed of the English gentlemen: the same cause has its action upon men of letters, whom statesmen usually desire to collect around them; the absence of one conspires to effect the absence of the other: our saloons are left solely to the uncultivated and the idle, and you seek in vain for those nightly reunions of wits and senators which distinguished the reign of Anne, and still give so noble a charm to the assemblies of Paris.

The respect we pay to wealth absorbs the respect we should pay to genius. Literary men have not with us any fixed and settled position *as* men of letters. In the great game of honours, none

fall to their share. We may say truly with a certain political economist, "We pay best, 1st, those who destroy us, generals; 2d,
those who cheat us, politicians and quacks; 3rd, those who amuse
us, singers and musicians; and, least of all, those who instruct us.
It is an important truth noted by Helvetius, that the degree of
public virtue in a state depends exactly on the proper distribu-
tion of public rewards. "I am *nothing* here," said one of the
most eminent men of science this country ever produced, "I am
forced to go abroad sometimes to preserve my self-esteem."

Our English authors thus holding no fixed position in society,
and from their very nature being covetous of reputation, often
fall into one of three classes; the one class seek the fashion they
cannot command, and are proud to know the great; another become irritable and suspicious, afraid that they are never sufficiently esteemed, and painfully vain out of a sense of bashfulness;
the third, of a more lofty nature, stand aloof and disdainful, and
never consummate their capacities, because they will not mix with
a world to which they know themselves superior.

A literary man with us is often forced to be proud of something else than talent—proud of fortune, of connexion, or of
birth—in order not to be looked down upon. Byron would never
have set a coronet over his bed if he had not written poetry;[2] nor
the fastidious Walpole have affected to disdain the author, if he
had not known that with certain circles, authorship was thought
to lower the gentleman. Every one knows the anecdote of a certain
professor of chemistry, who, eulogizing Boyle, thus concluded
his panegyrics: "He was a great man; he was *father* of chemistry,
and— —*brother* to the Earl of Cork!"

You laugh at the simplicity of the professor; after all it was no
bathos in practice;—depend upon it, the majority of the world
thought quite as much of the brother of Lord Cork as they did

2. We blame Lord Byron for this absurd vanity too hastily, and without
considering that he often intended it rather as a reminiscence to his equals
than as an assumption over his inferiors. He was compelled to struggle against
the vulgar feelings of England, that only low people are authors. Every body
knows what you are when you are merely a gentleman, they begin to doubt it
when you become a man of letters. In standing for Lincoln, a small secondrate
country squire was my opponent. One of his friends was extolling his pedigree,
as if to depreciate mine. "Do you not know that Mr. B.'s family is twice as old
as Col. S——'s, if *that* be any merit in a Legislator?" was asked of this gentleman. "Impossible," replied he, "Why, Mr. B—— *is* —*an Author!*"

the father of chemistry. The Professor was only the unconscious echo of the vulgar voice of Esteem.

Observe Mr. Nettleton; he is a poet of celebrity: is that all? marry come up! he is a much greater man than that comes to— *he is on the best possible terms at Holland House.* He values himself much on writing smooth verse; he values himself more on talking with a certain tone of good breeding. He is a wit—a very rare character; yes, but he does not take so much pride in being merely a wit, as *on being a wit at the best houses!* Mr. Nettleton is one of the vainest of men; but it would not please him much to hear you admired him, if he thought you a nobody. He is singularly jealous; but you might make Europe ring with your name, and he would not envy you, unless the *grands seigneurs* ran after you. "Mr. ——— has written a beautiful book; have you seen it Nettleton?"

"No; *who says* it is beautiful?"

"Oh! all the world, I fancy."

"There you are mistaken. We talked over all the new works at Miss Berry's last night, and all the world said nothing about your Mr. What's-his-name, and his book."

"Well, you are a judge of these matters; all I know is, that the Duke of Devonshire is mad to be introduced to him."

Nettleton, turned quite pale, *"The Duke of Devonshire introduced to him!"*

A smaller man than Mr. Nettleton in the literary world, is Mr. Nokes. Mr. Nokes is a prototype of the small gear; not exactly a poet, nor a novelist, nor an historian, but a little of all three; a literary man, in short—*homme des lettres.* In France he would enjoy a very agreeable station, mix with other *hommes des lettres,* have no doubt of his own merit, and be perfectly persuaded of his own consequence. Very different from all this is Mr. Nokes: he has the most singular distrust of himself; he liveth in perpetual suspicion that you mean to affront him. If you are sallying out on the most urgent business, your friend dying, your motion in the House of Commons just ready to come on, your mistress waiting to see you for the last time before she returns your letters, and hopes you may be happy, though she would hate you if you were not miserable to your dying day—if, I say, on some such business you should be hurrying forth, woe to you if you meet Nokes. You pass him with a hasty nod, and a "how are you, dear sir?" Nokes never forgives you, you have hurt his feelings indelibly. He sayeth to himself, "Why was that man so eager to avoid me?" He ruminateth, he museth, he cheweth the cud upon your unmannerly accost. He would have had you stop and speak to him, and ask him after the birth of his new poem, and hope his tale in the Annual was doing as well as could be expected; he is sorely galled at your omission; he pondereth the reason; he looketh at his hat, he looketh at his garments, he is persuaded it is because his habiliments were not new, and you were ashamed to be seen with him in the street. He never hits on the right cause; he never thinketh you may have pressing business; Nokes dreameth of no business save that which to Nokes appertaineth. Nokes is the unhappiest of men; he for ever looks out for cantharides to rub into his sores. If you meet him in a literary party, you must devote the whole evening to him and his projects, or he considers you the most insolent and the most frivolous of mankind; he forgetteth that there are fifty other Nokes's in the room. He boweth to you always with a proud humility, as if to say, "I am a great man, though *you* don't think so." Nokes is, at once, the most modest and the most impudent of our species. He imagines you despise him; yet he is chafed because you do not adore. You are oppressed with incalculable business; a lawyer, perhaps, in full practice; the editor of a daily newspaper; the member of a Reformed Parliament engaged in thirteen committees; yet, on the strength of a bare introduction, he sendeth you in manuscript, the next day—three plays, two novels, and thirty poems, which he bashfully requesteth you first, to read; secondly, to correct; and, thirdly, to interest yourself to get published. Two days after, you receive the following letter:

SIR,

When, on Wednesday last, I sent to your house, my *humble* attempts soliciting your attention in the *most respectful* language; I certainly did expect, in common courtesy, to have received, ere this, a reply. I am conscious that you have many engagements that *you* doubtless think of superior consequence to the task of reading *my* compositions; but there are others, sir, who have thought highly of what you apparently despise. But enough—I beg you will *immediately* send back, by the bearer,

ALL THE PAPERS which, trusting to your *reported* sympathy with men of letters, I had the folly to trouble you with. To *me* at least they are of importance.

I am, sir,
Your obedient servant,
JOHN SAMUEL NOKES.

Send back the papers, by all means: Nokes would be still more offended by any apology for delay, or any excuse for not ultimately prevailing on some bookseller to ruin himself by their publication. Nokes is a vindictive man—though he knoweth it not—nay, he esteemeth himself a very reservoir of the lacteal humanities. You may have served him essentially to-day—to-morrow you may have "wounded his feelings"; and, by next Saturday, be sure of a most virulent anonymous attack on you. But Nokes is to be more pitied than blamed: he is unfit for the world, only because he has no definite position in it.

Look now at a third species of literary man. Perhaps, dear ————, you recollect Mr. Lofty: what a fine creature he is—how full of deep learning, of pure sentiment, of generous romance; how you would like him, if you could but know him—but *that* may never be!—He builds a wall between himself and other men. In the streets he walketh alone; he sitteth alone in the large arm-chair at the Athenæum; he refuseth to converse; he is a ruminative, but not a gregarious animal. His books are admirable; but, somehow or other, they are not popular—he writeth for himself, not mankind: he is not at his ease in society, even with literary men; he will not let out,—his mind is far away. He is tenderly benevolent, but frigidly unsocial: he would rather give you his fortune than take a walk with you. Hence, with all his genius, not knowing how to address mankind and disdainful of the knowledge, he does not a tithe of the benefit that he might: could he learn to co-operate with others, he might reform a world, but he saith with Milton, "The world that I regard is myself." Yet blame affects him sensibly—a hostile review wounds him to the quick: he telleth not his complaint, but it preys within: he knows himself to be undervalued: he is not jealous of lesser men's success, but he chafes at it—it is a proof of injustice to him: he is melancholic and despondent: he pines for the Ideal: he feels society is not made for the nobler aims, and sickens at the littleness of daily life: he has in him all the elements of greatness, but not of triumph: he will die with his best qualities unknown.

These are three specimens of the Literary Man, essentially different in most things, but having something in common, and formed alike by peculiarities in our social system. All three are the growth of England, and I apprehend that they can scarcely be met with elsewhere.

III

From the tone of Society which I have attempted to describe, arises one of the most profound of our national feelings; that listless and vague melancholy which partakes both of the Philosophical and the Poetic; that sad and deep sentiment which is found only in the English and the German character, and is produced in each nation by the same causes; it is the result in both of an eager mind placed in a dull and insipid circle. (For in the small towns of Germany, society, if it possesses more wisdom than in England, does not proffer more charms.) A weariness of spirit creeps over us, and the flatness of the World produces somewhat the same moral result as the vanity of Knowledge. Hence, with the more intellectual of our gentry, that roving and desultory thirst of travel. Unsatisfied desire, which they do not analyze, urges them on to escape from the "stale and unprofitable usages" of their native world. And among the rich of no other people do you so constantly find examples of the DISCONTENTED. This habit of mind, so unfortunate to the possessor, is not unfavourable to poetry; and though derived from the pettiest causes, often gives something of interest and nobleness to the character. But it is chiefly confined to the young; after a certain age we grow out of it; the soul becomes accustomed to the mill, and follows the track mechanically, which it commenced in disgust.

But if there be one sentiment more mournful than another while it lasts, it is that conviction that All is Vanity which springs from the philosophy of Idleness; that craving for a sympathy which we never find, that restlessness of checked affection and crippled intellect, which belong to a circle in which neither affection nor intellect can be exerted. The little desires of petty circles irritate, but cannot absorb the larger capacity of mind. One reason why we, above other nations, cling to the consolations of Religion is, that we have cultivated so sparingly the fascinations of the World.

As mankind only learnt the science of Navigation in proportion as they acquired the knowledge of the stars,—so, in order to steer our course wisely through the Seas of Life, we have fixed our hearts upon the more sublime and distant objects of Heaven.

IV

I breakfasted the other day with M——; you recollect that two years ago he was one of the supereminent of the Dandies; silent, constrained, and insolent: very scrupulous as to the unblemished character of his friends—*for ton;* affecting to call every thing 'a bore,' and, indeed, afraid to laugh, for fear of cracking himself in two. M—— is *now* the last man in the world one could thus describe. He talks, rattles, rubs his hands, affects a certain jollity of manner; wants you to think him a devilish good fellow; dresses, to be sure, as the young and the handsome are prone to dress—*selon les règles;* but you may evidently see that he does so mechanically; his soul is no longer in his clothes. He startled me too, by quoting Bacon. You know we never suspected he had so much learning; but, between you and me, I think the quotation is a motto to one of the newspapers. However that be, M—— is evidently no longer indifferent as to whether you think he has information or not: he is anxious for your good esteem: he is overwhelmingly courteous and complimentary; he, who once extended the tip of his finger to you, now shakes you by both hands; it is not any longer M——'s fault if he is not agreeable; he strives to be so with might and main; and, in fact, he succeeds; it is impossible not to like such a gentlemanlike, good-looking, high-spirited fellow, when he once condescends to wish for your good opinion. His only fault is, that he is *too* elaborately off-hand, too stupendously courteous; he has not yet learnt, like Will Honeycomb, "to laugh easily"; it will take him some little time to be good-natured spontaneously; howbeit, M—— is marvellously improved. After breakfast, we walked down St. James's Street; M—— has lost his old walk entirely; you recollect that he used to carry his eyes and nose in the air, never looking on either side of him, and seeming to drop upon your existence by accident. *Now* he looks round him with a cordial air, casts a frequent glance to the opposite side of the street, and seems mortally afraid lest he should by chance overlook some passing acquaintance. We met two or three plain-dressed, respectable-looking persons, the last people in the world whom M—— (you would say) could by possibility have known; M—— stops short, his face beaming with gratulation, shakes them by the hand, pulls them by the button, whispers them in the ear, and tears himself away at last with a "recollect, my dear sir, I'm entirely at your service."

All this is very strange! what can possibly have wrought such a miracle in M——? I will tell you; M—— HAS NOW GOT CONSTITUENTS.

It is a profound observation in an Italian historian, that the courtesy of nobles is in proportion to the occasions imposed on them by the constitution, of mixing among the people. We do not want to be told that the Roman nobles were polished and urbane; that they practised all the seductions of manners; we ought to know this at once, by reading the method of their elections. M—— was in the House two years ago, when you recollect him; but he had never in his life seen the keeper, the butler, and the steward who returned him to parliament. For the last twelve months M—— has been practising the familiar and the friendly to some three thousand electors in ——shire. The effort to please, at first necessary to him, has grown agreeable. He is getting into the habit of it. He *is in* for a large commercial town; he is the youngest, that is, the active, member; he is compelled to mix with men of all classes; how on earth can he continue to be an Exclusive? Do you not perceive, therefore, dear ——, how much the operations of the Reform Bill will ultimately bear upon the tone of manners? Do you not perceive how much they have done so already? M—— is still the glass of fashion. Sliding, as he has done, into the temper of the times, his set imitate him now as they used to imitate him two years ago. Changed himself, he has inoculated a whole coterie. Thus laws and manners react upon each other.

We may perceive every where, indeed, that "Fashion" has received a material shock. If there is less fine gentlemanship than formerly, so also fine ladies are not quite so powerful as they were; they no longer fill the mouth of the gaping world with tales of triumphant insolence and abashed servility. A graver aspect settles on the face of society. The great events that have taken place have shaken the surface of the Aristocratic Sentiment too roughly, to allow it easily to resume its former state. Fashion cannot for many years be what it has been. In political quiet, the aristocracy are the natural dictators of society, and their sentiments are the most listened to. Now, the sum of their sentiments, as we have seen, is Fashion: in agitated times, the people rise into importance, and their sentiments become the loudest and most obtrusive; the aggregate of *their* sentiments, as we have seen, is Opinion. It is *then,* that unable to lead, the aristocracy unconsciously follow the impulse, and *it becomes the fashion to be popular.* Hence may we date, if we descend to the philosophy of trifles, the innovations even in costume: and the spirit of the French Revolution, which breathed vainly through the massive eloquence of Fox, succeeded at least in sweeping away from our saloons the brocaded waistcoat and the diamond buckles. At the time of the discussions on Reform, our drawing-room gossips affected the tone of Birmingham liberalism; and the *élégans* of Parliament lisped forth sturdy dogmas on the "Rights of the People." Thus, while *social* habits descend from the upper to the lowest class, *political* principles, on the contrary, are reverberations of opinion travelling from the base to the apex of society. The Aristocracy form the Manners of Life, and the People produce the Revolutions of Thought.

This reflection leads us deeper into the subject before us. Let us transport ourselves from the metropolis to a manufacturing town, and see from what cause in the habits of social life the political sentiments of one class are forced on the acceptance of another.

There is this germ of truth in the Owenite principle of co-operation: Co-operation is power; in proportion as people combine, they know their strength; civilization itself is but the effect of combining. If, then, there are two classes, supposed to be antagonists to each other, and the members of the one class combine more than those of another, the former class will be the more powerful; keep this truth in view—we shall apply it presently.

We are now at a manufacturing town; observe those respectable tradesmen—they are the master manufacturers—the aristocracy of the place. Look in that drawing-room, betraying the evidence of a decorous and honourable opulence; there is a little coterie assembled: yon short gentleman in blue is a retired captain in the navy: that portly personage, with the large bunch of seals, is the mayor of the town: yonder is a small proprietor, who has purchased a white house, and a few acres, and become a squire: that knot of confabulators is composed of the richest manufacturers of the place: at the other end of the room are the ladies, wives and daughters of the gentlemen. Enter a visiter in the town—a stray legislator, perhaps, who has come to see the manufactories; or, perhaps, like us, to know the men who work them: the gentlemen gather round him—a conversation ensues—he is anxious for general information—he speaks of the good sense and practical knowledge of a certain manufacturer he has visited that day.

"Ah, a good sort of a man, I believe," says the mayor, "and very clever at elections; but we seldom meet, except at a canvass —our wives don't visit ———.''

There is a patronizing air about the magistrate as he says this —our stranger is surprised—he turns to the rest—he perceives that he is praising somebody whom the company decidedly consider low and ungenteel; not one of their set. He finds, as conversation proceeds, that he is as much among exclusives as if he were at St. James's. The next day he dines with the manufacturer he praised—the household appurtenances are less elegant than those he witnessed the day before—the man-servant at the one house is a footboy at the other. He turns the conversation on his entertainer of the preceding day.

"Ay, a good sort of man," says his host, "but set up, full of prejudice and purse pride."

"Yes," adds the hostess; "yet I recollect his wife's father kept a stall. She now has more airs than the member's lady, who is an earl's daughter."

Our stranger next speaks of a manufacturer of still less wealth and consequence than his entertainer.

"Oh," says his host, "a sharp fellow, but of coarse habits, and his opinions are *so* violent. He behaved very ill to Mr. ———, at the last election."

"And his wife," adds the lady, "is very angry with us, she wanted to go with *us* to the town balls—now you know, Mr. ———, that we must draw *some* distinction."

The conversation at each of these places turns little upon *theories* of politics; the Ministers are talked over; perhaps also the history of the last election; the ladies discuss small scandals, the same as if they were at Almack's; our stranger goes away; he finds these two houses a type of the general divisions of one class; yet, mark—this is one class—the Manufacturers, to which another class—the Operatives, suppose they have an antagonist interest.—

Our visiter now resolves to see something more of the other class—he attends a festive meeting of the Operatives, at the Blue Bear. It is a long room crowded to suffocation. His health is drunk—he makes a vague liberal speech—it is received with applause. An Operative is next called upon; he addresses the meeting—he begins with many apologies for his own incapacity, but gradually becoming assured, he reconciles himself and his audience to the task, by the recollection, that whatever his own deficiencies he is one of *them;* he is strengthened by the unanimity of their cause. "*We* Operatives," he says (and the audience shout forth their sympathy and approbation), "*we* are oppressed with taxes and unjust laws, but let us only be firm to each other, and we shall get redress at last. The people must help themselves— our rulers won't help us—Union is our watchword."

Such are the materials with which the orator works upon the sympathy of the audience; and as he progresses, he applies himself less to the small points than to the startling theories of politics. He touches little on party politics; much upon abstract principles; the necessity of knowledge, and the effects of education. What is the conclusion forced upon our stranger's mind? This: That where the one class was divided by small jealousies into a hundred coteries, the other class is consolidated into a powerful union: that where one class think little of the theories of politics, such speculations are ever present to the other—the staple matter of their meetings—the motive and the end of their association. Thus, fastening our attention to things below the surface, we perceive the true reason why Democratic Opinion must become more and more prevalent;—*its espousers are united!*—at each ensuing election they form a sturdy body, not to be detached from each other by isolated appeals—they must be gained by addressing the whole. If the manufacturers, therefore, desire to return a representative, they must choose a candidate *professing such sentiments* as are generally pleasing to this powerful body, viz., the class below them. Thus, unconsciously to themselves, they adopt the principles of their inferiors, whom they dread, and in returning what they call "their own member," return in reality the supporter of the doctrines of the operatives.[1]

Two causes militate against the compact solidity of this democratic body; corruption is the first. But I apprehend that (even if the ballot be not obtained, which sooner or later it probably will be) with every succeeding election this cause will grow less and less powerful, in proportion as the truth forces itself on the mass, that each individual will gain more by the permanent reduction of taxes than by the temporary emolument of a bribe. By indisputable calculation, it can be shown that every working man is now taxed to the amount of one-third of his weekly wages; supposing the operative to obtain twelve shillings a week, he is taxed, therefore, to the amount of four shillings a week; at the end of six years (the supposed duration of parliament) he will, consequently, have contributed to the revenue, from his poor earnings, the almost incredible sum of 62*l*. 8*s*. What is any bribe that can be offered to him, in comparison to the hope of materially diminishing this mighty and constant expenditure? You may say the hope is vain—perhaps it is so—but he will always cherish and endeavour to realize it.

---

1. It is absurd to suppose (yet it is the commonest of suppositions) that if you keep *only* gentlemen and noblemen's sons in parliament, parliament is therefore less democratic than if alloyed with Plebeians. It is the laws which are made, not the men who make them, that advance the democratic movement. If an earl's son pledge himself to certain measures, which act as a blow to the aristocracy, what could a mechanic do more? Does it signify whether you break down a wall by a plain pickaxe, or one with a coronet carved on the handle? The Romans obtained the power to choose plebeians, they chose patricians;—but the patricians they chose destroyed the aristocracy.

Credula vitam
Spes fovet, et fore cras semper ait melius.

Thus, the distress of the lower orders, hitherto the source of corruption, may become its preventive.

Another cause of division among the operatives, may be that which superficial politicians have considered the most dangerous cementer of their power; viz., "the establishment of Political Unions." If we look to the generality of towns,[2] we shall find that it is a very small proportion of even the ultra liberal party that have enrolled themselves in these Associations. In fact, the Unions are regarded with jealousy; the men who originate them, the boldest and most officious of their class, are often considered by their equals as arrogant pretenders, assuming a dictatorship, which the vanity of the body at large is unwilling to allow. Hence, instead of uniting the mass, they tend to introduce divisions. Another effect they produce is, from their paucity of numbers, to weaken the influence of the operatives, by showing a front of weakness, as well as an evidence of schism. The other classes are apt to judge of the strength of the party, by these its assumed host and army; and to estimate the numbers of persons professing the same opinions as Political Unions, by counting the names that these combinations have enrolled. A party to *be* strong, should always *appear* strong; the show often wins the battle; as the sultans of the east, in order to defeat rebellion, have usually found it sufficient merely to levy an army. I conceive, therefore, however excusable or useful such associations may be in a conflux of fierce and agitated events, they are, in a state of ordinary peace, as prejudicial to the real power and solidity of the more popular party, as they are arrogant interferers with the proper functions of the government.[3] There is only one just,

2. Of course I do not here refer to the Unions in Birmingham and one or two other Towns—*There* they are indeed powerful in point of numbers—but I suspect they will fall by divisions among themselves.

3. Besides these consequences, their natural effect, if successful, would be the establishment of an oligarchy in every town. Two or three, not of the wisest men, but of the most active, and the most oratorical (the last quality is, in all popular assemblies, more dangerous than salutary—it has been ever so in Parliament) will gain possession of the assembly. In fact, these assemblies would operate by making in every town a machine for taking away the power of the many, and gratifying the ambition of the few. The greatest fear in an

natural, and efficacious Political Union—and that is the STATE —a State that shall at once rule and content the People;—never *yielding* to their will, *because* always *providing* for their wants.

---

aristocratic country is, that the opposition of one aristocracy should be but the commencement of another. My principles are so generally known to be in favour of the people, that what I have said on this point will possibly have more weight than if I were a higher authority, but of a different party.

V

The Social Habits of the Population

"Man is born to walk erect, and look upon the heavens." So says the Poet. Man does not always fulfil the object of his birth; he goeth forth to his labour with a bending and despondent frame, and he lifts not his eyes from the soil whose mire hath entered into his soul. The physical condition of the Working Classes in Manufacturing Towns is more wretched than we can bear to consider. It is not that the average of deaths in manufacturing towns is greater than that in the agricultural districts. The labourers in the latter are subject to violent and sudden diseases, proceeding from acute inflammation; medical assistance is remote, and negligently administered; their robust frames feed the disease that attacks them; they are stricken down in the summer of their days, and die in the zenith of vigorous health. Not so with the Mechanic; he has medical aid at hand; acute disorders fall light on the yielding relaxation of his frame; it is not that he *dies sooner* than the labourer; he *lives more painfully;* he knows not what health is; his whole life is that of a man nourished on slow poisons; Disease sits at his heart, and gnaws at its cruel leisure. *Dum vivat, moritur.* The close and mephitic air, the incessant labour—in some manufactories the small deleterious particles that float upon the atmosphere,[1] engender painful and imbittering maladies, and afflict with curses, even more dread than

1. I have held correspondence on this point with some inhabitant or other in most of our manufacturing towns, and it seems that *nearly* all manufactories engender their peculiar disease.

are the heritage of literary application, the Student of the Loom. But it is not only the diseases that he entails upon himself to which the Operative is subject; he bears in the fibre of his nerves and the marrow of his bones the terrible bequeathments of hereditary Affliction. His parents married under age, unfit for the cares, inadequate to the labours which a rash and hasty connexion has forced upon them;—each perhaps having resort to ardent spirits in the short intervals of rest,—the mother engaged in the toil of a factory at the most advanced period of her pregnancy;—every hour she so employs adding the seeds of a new infirmity to her unborn offspring!—

Observe the young mother, how wan and worn her cheek; how squalid her attire; how mean her home; yet her wages and those of her partner are amply sufficient, perhaps, to smooth with decorous comforts the hours of Rest, and to provide for all the sudden necessities of toiling life. A thriftless and slattern waste converts what ought to be competence into poverty, and, amidst cheerless and unloving aspects, the young victim is ushered into light. The early years of the Poor have been drawn by the hand of a master. I quote the description not only as being wholly faithful to truth, but as one of the most touching (yet least generally known) examples of the highest order of pathetic eloquence which Modern Literature has produced.

> The innocent prattle of his children takes out the sting of a man's poverty. But the children of the *very* poor do not prattle! It is none of the least frightful features in that condition, that there is no childishness in its dwellings. Poor people, said a sensible old nurse to us once, do not *bring* up their children; they *drag* them up. The little careless darling of the wealthier nursery, in their hovel is transformed betimes into a premature reflecting person. No one has time to dandle it, no one thinks it worth while to coax it, to soothe it, to toss it up and down, to humour it. There is none to kiss away its tears. If it cries, it can only be beaten. It has been prettily said that "a babe is fed with milk and praise." But the ailment of this poor babe was thin, unnourishing; the return to its little baby-tricks, and efforts to engage attention, bitter ceaseless objurgation. It never had a toy, or knew what a coral meant. It grew up without the lullaby of nurses; it was a stranger to the patient fondle, the hushing caress, the attracting novelty, the costlier plaything, or

the cheaper off-hand contrivance to divert the child; the prattled
nonsense (best sense to it), the wise impertinences, the wholesome lies, the apt story interposed, that puts a stop to present
sufferings, and awakens the passion of young wonder. It was
never sung to—no one ever told to it a tale of the nursery. It was
dragged up, to live or to die as it happened. It had no young
dreams. It broke at once into the iron realities of life. A child
exists not for the very poor as any object of dalliance; it is only
another mouth to be fed, a pair of little hands to be betimes
inured to labour. It is the rival, till it can be the co-operator, for
food with the parent. It is never his mirth, his diversion, his
solace; it never makes him young again, with recalling his young
times. The children of the very poor have *no* young times. It
makes the very heart to bleed to overhear the casual street-talk
between a poor woman and her little girl, a woman of the better
sort of poor, in a condition rather above the squalid beings which
we have been contemplating. It is not of toys, of nursery books,
of summer holidays (fitting that age); of the promised sigh, or
play; of praised sufficiency at school. It is of mangling and clear-
starching, of the price of coals, or of potatoes. The questions of
the child, that should be the very outpourings of curiosity in
idleness, are marked with forecast and melancholy providence.
It has come to be a woman, before it was a child. It has learned
to go to market; it chaffers, it haggles, it envies, it murmurs; it
is knowing, acute, sharpened; it never prattles. Had we not
reason to say, that the home of the very poor is no home?[2]

What homely and passionate pathos! I can do no homage to
that critic who will not allow that I have quoted one of the most
striking masterpieces of English composition.

But if this be the ordinary state of the children of the poor,
how doubly aggravated in the case of the *manufacturing* poor.
What a dark and terrible history of early suffering is developed
in the evidence on the Factory Bill. Let us take an instance:

EVIDENCE OF DAVID BYWATER

Were you afterwards taken to the steaming department?
—Yes.

At what age?—I believe I was turned thirteen then.

Is that a laborious employment?—Yes; we stood on one side
and turned the cloth over, and then we had to go to the other
side and turn the cloth over.

2. *The Last Essays of Elia.* Moxon, 1833.

Were you there some time before you worked long hours?
—Yes; but there was so much work beforehand that we were obliged to start night-work.

At what age were you when you entered upon that night-work?—I was nearly fourteen.

Will you state to this Committee the labour which you endured when you were put upon long hours, and the night-work was added?—I started at one o'clock on Monday morning, and went on till twelve o'clock on Tuesday night.

What intervals had you for food and rest?—We started at one o'clock on Monday morning, and then we went on till five, and stopped for half an hour for refreshment; then we went on again till eight o'clock, at breakfast-time; then we had half an hour, and then we went on till twelve o'clock, and had an hour for dinner: and then we went on again till five o'clock, and had half an hour for drinking; and then we started at half-past five, and if we had a mind we could stop at nine and have half an hour then, but we thought it would be best to have an hour and a half together, which we might have at half-past eleven; so we went on from half-past five, and stopped at half-past eleven for refreshment for an hour and a half at midnight; then we went on from one till five again, and then we stopped for half an hour; then we went on again till breakfast-time, when we had half an hour; and then we went on again till twelve o'clock, at dinner-time, and then we had an hour; and then we stopped at five o'clock again on Tuesday afternoon, for half an hour for drinking; then we went on till half-past eleven, and then we gave over till five o'clock on Wednesday morning. . . .

You say you were taken to be a steamer; are not very stout and healthy youths usually selected for that purpose?—Yes, the overlooker said he thought I should be the strongest.

When did you commence on Wednesday morning?—At five o'clock, and then we worked till eight o'clock, and then we had half an hour again; then we went on to dinner-time, and had an hour at twelve o'clock; and then at one o'clock we went on again till five, and then we had half an hour, and then we went on till half-past eleven again; and then we started again at one o'clock on Thursday morning, and went on till five o'clock; then we had half an hour, and then we went on till eight o'clock; we had half an hour for breakfast, and then we went on till twelve and got our dinner; then at one o'clock we went on till five o'clock, and then we had half an hour; then we went on till half-past eleven, and then we gave over till five o'clock on Friday morning; then we started again at five o'clock, and went on till eight; then we went on till dinner-time at twelve o'clock; then at one o'clock we went on till five; then we had half an hour, and then we went on till half-past eleven; then we started again at one o'clock on Saturday morning, and went on till five; then we had half an hour and went on till eight; then we had half an hour for breakfast and went on till twelve; then we had an hour for dinner, and then went on from one o'clock till seven, or eight, or nine o'clock; we had no drinking-time on Saturday afternoon; we could seldom get to give over on the Saturday afternoon as the other people did. . . .

You said that you was selected as a steamer by the overlooker, on account of your being a stout and healthy boy?—Yes, he said he thought I was the strongest, and so I should go.

Were you perfect in your limbs when you undertook that long and excessive labour?—Yes, I was.

What effect did it produce upon you?—It brought a weakness on me; I felt my knees quite ache.

Had you pain in your limbs and all over your body?—Yes.

Show what effect it had upon your limbs?—It made me very crooked.—[Here the witness showed his knees and legs.]

Are your thighs also bent?—Yes, the bone is quite bent.

How long was it after you had to endure this long labour before your limbs felt in that way?—I was very soon told of it, before I found it out myself.

What did they tell you?—They told me I was getting very crooked in my knees; my mother found it out first.

What did she say about it?—She said I should kill myself with working this long time.

If you had refused to work those long hours, and have wished to have worked a moderate length of time only, should you have been retained in your situation?—I should have had to go home; I should have been turned off directly.

EVIDENCE OF ELDIN HARGRAVE

In attending to this machine, are you not always upon the stretch, and upon the move?—Yes, always.

Do you not use your hand a good deal in stretching it out? —Yes.

What effect had this long labour upon you?—I had a pain across my knee, and I got crooked.

Was it the back of your knee, or the side of your knee?—All round.

Will you show your limbs?—[Here the witness exposes his legs and knees.]

Were your knees ever straight at any time?—*They were straight before I went to Mr. Brown's mill. . . .*

You say that you worked for seventeen hours a day all the year round; did you do that without interruption?—*Yes.*

Could you attend any day or night-school?—No.

Can you write?—No.

Can you read?—I can read a little in a spelling-book.

Where did you learn that; did you go to a Sunday-school?—No, I had not clothes to go in.

EVIDENCE OF Mr. THOMAS DANIEL
Relative to the Boys called Scavengers

You have stated that there is considerable difference in the ages of the children employed; are the younger or older of the children employed those that have to undergo the greatest degree of labour and exertion?—The younger.

Those you call scavengers?—Yes, scavengers and middle-piecers.

Will you state their average age?—The average age of scavengers will not be more than ten years.

Describe to the Committee the employment of those scavengers?—Their work is to keep the machines, while they are going, clean from all kinds of dust and dirt that may be flying about, and they are in all sorts of positions to come at them; I think that their bodily exertion is more than they are able to bear, for they are constantly kept in a state of activity.

Have they not to clean the machines, and to creep under, and run round them, and to change and accommodate their position in every possible manner, in order to keep those machines in proper order?—They are in all sorts of postures that the human body is capable of being put into, to come at the machines.

Are they not peculiarly liable to accidents then?—In many instances they are; but not so much now as they formerly were; spinners take more care and more notice of the children than they formerly did.

Do you think that they are capable of performing that work for the length of time that you have described?—Not without doing them serious injury with respect to their health and their bodily strength.

State the effect that it has upon them, according to your own observation and experience?—*Those children, every moment that they have to spare, will be stretched all their length upon the floor in a state of perspiration, and we are obliged to keep them up to the work by using either a strap or some harsh language, and they are kept continually in a state of agitation; I consider them to be constantly in a state of grief, though some of them cannot shed tears; their condition greatly depresses their spirits.*

They live in a state of constant apprehension, and often in one of terror?—They are always in terror; and I consider that that does them as much injury as their labour, their minds being in a constant state of agitation and fear.

You consider then, upon the whole, their state as one of extreme hardship and misery?—So much so, that I have made up my mind that my children shall never go into a factory, more especially as scavengers and piecers.

What do you mean by saying that those children are always in a state of terror and fear?—The reason of their being in a state of terror and fear is, that we are obliged to have our work done, and we are compelled therefore to use the strap, or some harsh language, which it hurts my feelings often to do, for I think it is heart-breaking to the poor child.

Do not you think that their labour is more aggravating to them at the end of the day?—I do; for we have to be more harsh with them at the latter part of the day than in the middle part of it. The greatest difficulty that we have to contend with in point of making them do their labour, is in the morning, and after four o'clock in the afternoon; the long hours that they have laboured the day before, in my opinion, cause them to be very stupid in the morning.

Have you observed them to be drowsy towards the after part of the day?—Very much so.

I could go on multiplying these examples[3] at random, from every page of this huge calendar of childish sufferings; but

3. But then, cry some pseudo-economists, on the Factory Bill we want farther inquiry. We have instituted farther inquiry—for what? To prove that children can be properly worked above ten hours a day?—No, but to prove that the master manufacturers are slandered. Very well; that is quite another affair. Let us *first* do justice to those whom you *allow* to be overworked, and we will *then* do justice to those whom you *suppose* to be maligned. The great mistake of modern liberalism is, to suppose that a government is never to interfere, except through the medium of the tax-gatherer. A government should represent a parent; with us, it only represents a dun, with the bailiff at his heels!

enough has been said to convince the reader's understanding, and I would fain trust, to open his heart.

Thus prepared and seasoned for the miseries of life, the boy enters upon manhood—aged while yet youthful—and compelled, by premature exhaustion, to the dread relief of artificial stimulus. Gin, not even the pure spirit, but its dire adulteration—opium— narcotic drugs; these are the horrible cements with which he repairs the rents and chasms of a shattered and macerated frame. He marries; and becomes in his turn the reproducer of new sufferers. In afterlife he gets a smattering of political knowledge; legislative theories invite and lull him from himself; and with all the bitter experience of the present system, how can you wonder that he yearns for innovation?

In manufacturing towns, the intercourse between the sexes is usually depraved and gross. The number of illegitimate children is, I allow, proportionally less in a manufacturing, than in an agricultural district, but a most fallacious inference has been drawn from this fact; it has been asserted by some political economists, that sexual licentiousness is therefore less common among the population of the latter than that of the former—a mischievous error—the unchaste are not fruitful. The causes why illegitimate children are less numerous in manufacturing towns are manifold; of these I shall allude but to two (to the Quarterly Reviewers, so severe on Miss Martineau, a third may occur)—the inferior health of the women, and the desperate remedy of destroying the burden prematurely in the womb. The existence of these facts will be acknowledged by any one who has seen, with inquiring eyes, the *actual* state of the Manufacturing Population. The great evil of licentiousness is almost less in its influence on the Principles, than the Affections. When the passions are jaded and exhausted, the kindly feelings, which are their offspring, lie supine. The social charities, the household ties, the fond and endearing relations of wife and husband, mother and child, are not blessings compatible with a life of impure excitement. The Ancients tell us of a Nation of Harlots, who exposed their children:—the story may be false, but he who invented it, and showed how profligacy banished the natural affections, had studied with accuracy the constitution of the human mind.

Amidst these gloomier portraitures of our mechanic population, there are bright reliefs. Many of the Operatives have been warned, and not seduced, by the contagion of example; and of these I could select some who, for liberal knowledge, sound thought, kindly feeling, and true virtue, may rank among the proudest ornaments of the country. It has been my good fortune to correspond with many of the Operative Class, not only, as a member of parliament, upon political affairs, but in my prouder capacity, as a literary man, upon various schemes, which in letters and in science had occurred to their ingenuity. I have not only corresponded with these men, but I have also mixed personally with others of their tribe, and I have ever found that an acuteness of observation was even less the distinction of their character, than a certain noble and disinterested humanity of disposition. Among such persons I would seek, without a lantern, for the true Philanthropist. Deeply acquainted with the ills of their race, their main public thought is to alleviate and relieve them: they have not the jealousy common to men who have risen a little above their kind; they desire more "to raise the wretched than to rise"; their plots and their schemings are not for themselves, but for their class. Their ambition is godlike, for it is the desire to enlighten and to bless. There is a divine and sacred species of Ambition which is but another word for Benevolence. These are they who endeavour to establish Mechanics' Institutes, and Plans of National Education; who clamour against Taxes upon Knowledge; who desire Virtue to be the foundation of Happiness. I know not, indeed, an order of men, more than that of which I speak, interesting our higher sympathies; nor one that addresses more forcibly our sadder emotions, than that wider class which they desire to relieve.

The common characteristic of the Operatives, even amidst all the miseries and excesses frequent amongst them, is that of *desires better than their condition*. They all have the wish for knowledge. They go to the gin-shop, and yet there they discuss the elements of virtue! Apprenticed to the austerest trials of life, they acquire a universal sympathy with oppression. "Their country is the world." You see this tendency in all their political theories; it is from the darkness of their distress, that they send forth the loud shouts which testify Injustice. It is their voice which is heard the earliest, and dies the latest, against Wrong in every corner of the Globe; they make to themselves common cause with spoliated Poland—with Ireland, dragooned into silence—with the slaves of Jamaica—with the human victims of Indostan: wherever there is suffering, their experience unites them to it; and their efforts, unavailing for themselves, often contribute to adjust the balance of the World. As (in the touching Arabian proverb) the barber learns his art on the orphan's face, so Legislation sometimes acquires its wisdom by experiments on Distress.

For the demoralized social state which I have ascribed to a large proportion of the Operatives, there are two cures, the one physical, the other moral. If you bow down the frame by the excess of early labour, the sufferers must have premature recourse to the artificial remedies of infirmity. Opium and gin are the cheapest drugs;[4] these corrupt the mind, and take reward from labour. Of what use are high wages, if they are spent in a single night? Children, therefore, should not be worked at too early an age, nor to too great an extreme. Women in the latter stages of childbearing should not be permitted to attend the toil of the manufactories—they have no right to entail a curse on the Unborn. Legislation must not, it is true, *over* interfere; but she is a guardian, as well as an executioner; she may interfere to prevent, if she interferes to punish.

So much for the physical cure:—the moral cure is Education. National Schools, on a wide and comprehensive plan, embrace more than the elements of knowledge (I shall enlarge upon this point in the next section of my work); they ought to teach social, as well as individual morals; they ought to be adapted to the class to which they are dedicated; they should teach, not so much labour, as *habits* of labour; and bring up the young mind, especially the female mind, to the necessities of domestic economy. Labour schools should be united to Intellectual. So far the Government can provide a cure. Individuals may assist it. The sexes should be, in all manufactories, even at the earliest age, carefully separated; and a master should demand a good moral character with those he employs. This last precaution is too generally neglected; a drunken, disorderly character is no barrier to

---

4. See the account of the number of visiters to a gin-shop, pp. 48–49.

the obtaining work; it is therefore no misfortune—if no misfortune, it is no disgrace. The best cure for demoralization is to establish a moral standard of opinion. To these remedies, add a revision of the Poor-laws for both classes, the manufacturing and the agricultural. After all, the remedies are less difficult than they appear to the superficial. But to a Government, nowadays, every thing has grown difficult,—even the art of taxation.

The mention of the Poor-laws now links my inquiry into the social state of the manufacturing, with that of the agricultural, population. The operation of the Poor-laws is the History of the Poor. It is a singular curse in the records of our race, that the destruction of one evil is often the generation of a thousand others. The Poor-laws were intended to prevent mendicants; they have made mendicancy a legal profession;[5] they were established in the spirit of a noble and sublime provision, which contained all the theory of Virtue; they have produced all the consequences of Vice. Nothing differs so much from the end of institutions as their origin. Rome, the mother of warriors, was founded on a day consecrated to the goddess of shepherds. The Poor-laws, formed to relieve the distressed, have been the archcreator of distress.

Of all popular suppositions, the most common among our philanthropical philosophers is, to believe that in England Poverty is the parent of Crime. This is not exactly the case. *Pauperism* is the parent of crime; but pauperism is not poverty. The distinction is delicate and important.

In the extracts from the information received by his Majesty's Commissioners as to the administration and operation of the Poor-laws, just published, appears the following evidence, from Mr. Wontner, the governor of Newgate; Mr. Chesterton, the

---

5. The shallow politicians of the Senate tell you, with a pompous air, that the abolition of the monasteries was the only cause of Elizabeth's Poor-law. Why, did they ever read the old writers, poets, and chroniclers, before Elizabeth?—Did they ever read *Barclay's Eclogues,* descriptive of the state of the poor?—No, to be sure not. Did they ever read, then, the Acts of Parliament prior to Elizabeth? One Act in Henry the Eighth's time, years before the monasteries were abolished, contains the germ of the Poor-law, by confining the poor to their parishes, on the plea of the great increase of vagabonds and rogues. Did they ever read this?—Not they. Their province is to vote, not read.

governor of the House of Correction for Middlesex; and Mr. Gregory, the treasurer of Spitalfields parish.

Mr. Wontner—"Of the criminals who come under your care, what proportion, so far as your experience will enable you to state, were by the *immediate pressure of want* impelled to the commission of crime? by want is meant, the absence of the means of subsistence, and not the want arising from indolence and an impatience of steady labour? *According to the best of my observation, scarcely one-eighth.* This is my conclusion, not only from my observations in the office of governor of this gaol, where we see more than can be seen in court of the state of each case, but from six years' experience as one of the marshals of the city, having the direction of a large body of police, and seeing more than can be seen by the governor of a prison.

"Of the criminals thus impelled to the commission of crime by the immediate pressure of want, what proportion, according to the best of your experience, were previously reduced to want by heedlessness, indolence, and not by causes beyond the reach of common prudence to avert?—When we inquire into the class of cases to which the last answer refers, we generally find that the criminals have had situations and profitable labour, but have lost them in consequence of indolence, inattention, or dissipation, or habitual drunkenness, or association with bad females. *If we could thoroughly examine the whole of this class of cases, I feel confident that we should find that not one-thirtieth of the whole class of cases brought here are free from imputation of misconduct, or can be said to result entirely from blameless want.* The cases of juvenile offenders from nine to thirteen years of age arise partly from the difficulty of obtaining employment for children of those ages, partly from the want of the power of superintendence of parents, who, being in employment themselves, have not the power to look after their children; and in a far greater proportion from the criminal neglect and example of parents."

Mr. Chesterton states, "I directed a very intelligent yardsman, and one who had never, I believe, wilfully misled me to inquire into the habits and circumstances of all in the yard (sixty prisoners), and *the result was that he could not point out one who appeared to have been urged by want to commit theft.* It appears, that in the house of correction the proportion of prisoners who have been paupers is more numerous than in the other gaols."

Mr. Richard Gregory, the treasurer of Spitalfields parish, who for several years distinguished himself by his successful exertions for the prevention of crime within that district, was asked—

"We understand you have paid great attention to the state and prevention of crime; can you give us any information as to the connexion of crime with pauperism?—I can state, from experience, that they invariably go together.

"But do poverty—meaning unavoidable and irreproachable poverty—and crime invariably go together? That is the material distinction. In the whole course of my experience, which is of twenty-five years, in a very poor neighbourhood, liable to changes subjecting the industrious to very great privations, I remember but one solitary instance of a poor but industrious man out of employment stealing anything. I detected a working man stealing a small piece of bacon;—he burst into tears, and said it was his poverty and not his inclination which prompted him to do this, for he was out of work, and in a state of starvation.

"Then are we to understand, as the result of your experience, that the great mass of crime in your neighbourhood has always arisen from idleness and vice, rather than from the want of employment?—Yes, and this idleness and vicious habits are increased and fostered by pauperism, and by the readiness with which the able-bodied can obtain from parishes allowances and food without labour."

The whole of this valuable document on the Poor-laws generally bears out the evidence adduced above. Idleness and vice, then, are the chief parents of crime and distress; viz., indisposition to work, not the want of work. This is a great truth never to be lost sight of; for, upon a deduction to be drawn from it, depends the only safe principle of Parochial Reform. But how, in so industrious a county, arises the indifference to toil? The answer is obvious—wherever idleness is better remunerated than labour, idleness becomes contagious, and labour hateful. Is this the fact with us? Let us see; the following fable shall instruct us:

"The most benevolent of the angels was Eriel. Accustomed to regard with a pitying eye the condition of Mankind, and knowing (in the generous spirit of angelic philosophy) how much circumstance is connected with crime, he had ever wept over even the sufferings of the felon, and attempted to interfere with the Arch Disposer of events for their mitigation. One day, in walking over the earth, as was his frequent wont, he perceived a poor woman, with a child in her arms, making her way through a tattered and squalid crowd that thronged around the threshold of a certain house in the centre of a large town. Something in the aspect of the woman interested the benevolent angel. He entered the house with her, and heard her apply to the overseers of the parish for relief: she stated her case as one of great hardship; to add to her distress, the infant in her arms was suffering under the fearful visitation of the smallpox. The overseers seemed ready enough to relieve her—all the overseers, save one; *he* sturdily stood out, and declared the woman an impostor.

"This is the fourth child," quoth he, "that has been brought to us this day as suffering under the smallpox; there is not, I am sure, so much disease in the village. Come hither, my good woman, and let us look at your infant."

The mother seemed evidently reluctant to expose the seamed and scarred features of the child—"It is maternal vanity, poor creature!" whispered the kind heart of the angel.

She showed the arm and the leg, and the stamp of the disease was evidently there, *but the face!*—it would disturb the little sufferer—it would shock the good gentleman—it might spread the disease. What was the good of it? The hard overseer was inexorable; he lifted the handkerchief from the child's face—"I thought so!" quoth he, in triumph, "Go, my good woman—*the child is not your own!*"

The woman quailed at the overseer's look; she would have spoken, but she only cried; she slunk into the crowd and disappeared. The fact came out, *the child was a borrowed commodity!* it had been shifted from matron to matron: now its face had been shown, now only its hand; its little pustules had been an India to the paupers. The hard overseer was a very Solomon in his suspicion.

Now, in witnessing this scene, one remarkable occurrence had excited the astonishment of the angel; he perceived standing behind the Parochial Authorities, no less a personage than the celebrated demon Mephistopheles; and, instead of steeling the hearts of the official judges, he remarked that the Fiend whispered charity and humanity to them, whenever any doubt as to the appropriate exercise of those divine virtues arose within their breasts. Struck by this inconsistency in demoniacal traits, when the assembly broke up, Eriel accosted the Fiend, and intimated his surprise and joy at his apparent conversion to the principles of benevolence. Every one knows that Mephistopheles is a devil, so fond of his sneer, that he will even go out of his way to indulge it. He proposed to the angel to take a walk and chat over the sentiments of harmony; Eriel agreed, they walked on, arguing and debating, till they came to a cottage, which struck the ramblers as unusually neat in its appearance; they assumed their spiritual prerogative of invisibility, and, crossing the threshold, they perceived a woman of about thirty years of age, busying herself in household matters, while her husband, a sturdy labourer, was partaking with two children a frugal meal of coarse bread and mouldy cheese. About the cottage and its inmates was a mingled air of respectability and discontent. "My poor boy," quoth the labourer to his son, "you can have no more; we must set the rest by for supper."

"It is very hard, father," grumbled the boy, "we work all day, and are half starved, and Joe Higgins, who is supplied by the parish, works little and is well fed."

"Yes, boy, but thank God we are *not* on the parish yet," said the mother, turning round, with a flush of honest pride.

The father sighed and said nothing.

When the meal was done the peasant lingered behind to speak to his wife.

"It is very true, Jane," said he, "that we have been brought up in a spirit of independence and do not like to go to the parish, but where's the good of it? Jack's perfectly right. There's Higgins does not do half what we do, and see how comfortable he is: and, you know, we are rate-payers, and absolutely pay for *his* indolence. This is very discouraging, Jane; I see it is spoiling my boys for work; depend on't we can't be better than our neighbours; we must come on the parish, as all of them do."

So saying, the father shook his head and walked out.

The poor wife sat down and wept bitterly.

"This is a very, very sad case!" said Eriel; Mephistopheles grinned.

Our wanderers left the cottage and proceeded on their walk; they came to another cottage, of a slatternly and dirty appearance; the inmates, also were at dinner, but they were much better off in point of food, though not in point of cleanliness. "I say, Joe Higgins," quoth the dame of the cottage, "this bacon is not half so good as they get at the workhouse. There's my sister and her two brats does not do no work, and they has beef every Sunday."

"And all the men," interrupted Joe, "has three pints of beer a day; spose we makes a push to get in."

"With all my heart," said the wife, "and the overseers be mighty kind gemmen."

The Immortal Visiters listened no more; they resumed their journey, and they came to the Poor-house: here all was sleek indolence and lazy comfort; the parochial authorities prided themselves on *buying the best of every thing*. The Paupers had vegetables, and beer, and bread; and the children were educated at the parish pauper school. Nevertheless, as our visiters listened and looked on, they found that Discontent could enter into even this asylum of untasked felicity. They overheard a grim and stalwart pauper whispering to some three or four young and eager listeners, "Arter all, you sees we be not so well off as my brother Tom, what is a convict in the hulks yonder. And you sees, if we *do* do that ere job what I spoke to you about, we should only be sent to the hulks, and be then as well fed and as easy as brother Tom himself."

The three lads looked at each other, and the Immortals perceived by the glance, that the "job" would be soon done.

"Perhaps now, Mr. Eriel," said Mephistopheles with a sneer, "you see why I strove to soften the hearts of the overseers."

"Alas! yes," replied the Angel sorrowfully, "and I see also that there is no fiend like a mistaken principle of Charity."

This fable is but the illustration of stern fact.

"The following table, drawn chiefly from official returns, will show clearly, and at a glance, the comparative condition of each class, as to food, from the honest and independent labourer, to the convicted and transported felon. For better comparison, the whole of the meat is calculated as cooked."

THE SCALE

I. THE INDEPENDENT AGRICULTURAL LABOURER—
According to the returns of Labourers' Expenditure, they are unable to get, in the shape of
solid food, more than an average allowance of   oz.

    Bread (daily) 17 oz. = per week 119
    Bacon, per week, ... 4 oz.
        Loss in cooking . . . . . . 1 "   Solid Food.
                       —   3—122 oz.

II. THE SOLDIER—
    Bread (daily) 16 oz. = per week . . . 112
    Meat . . . 12 . . . . . . 84 oz.
        Loss in cooking . . . . 28 "
                  —   56—168

III. THE ABLE-BODIED PAUPER—
    Bread . . . . per week 98
    Meat . . . . 31 oz.
        Loss in cooking . . . . . 10 "
                —   21
    Cheese 16
    Pudding . . . . 16—151
In addition to the above, which is an average
allowance, the inmates of most workhouses
have,
    Vegetables . . . . . . 48 oz.
    Soup . . . . 3 quarts.
    Milk Porridge 3   "
    Table Beer 7   "
and many other comforts.

IV. THE SUSPECTED THIEF—
    (See the Gaol Returns from Lancaster.)
    Bread . . . . .per week 112
    Meat . . . . 24 oz.
        Loss in cooking . . . . . . 8 "
                —   16
    Oatmeal 40
    Rice 5
    Pease 4
    Cheese . . . . 4—181

Winchester.
```
Bread   . . . . . . . .   per week   192
Meat    . . . . . . . . . 16 oz.
     Loss in cooking . . . . . . 5  "
                            —        11—203
```

V. THE CONVICTED THIEF—
```
Bread   . . . . . . . .   per week   140
Meat    . . . . . . . . . 56 oz.
     Loss in cooking . . . . . . 18 "
                            —        38
Scotch Barley . . . . . . . .       28
Oatmeal   . . . . . . . . . .       21
Cheese . . . . . . . . . . .        12—239
```

VI. THE TRANSPORTED THIEF—
```
10½ lbs. meat per week = . . .   168 oz.
     Loss in cooking . . . . . . 56  "
                            —        112
10½ lbs. flour, which will increase, ⎫
    when made into bread          ⎬ . . . 218—330
                                  ⎭
```

"So that the industrious labourer has less than the pauper, the pauper less than the suspected thief, the suspected thief less than the convicted, the convicted less than the transported, and by the time you reach the end of the gradation, you find that the transported thief has nearly three times the allowance of the honest labourer!"

What effect then must those laws produce upon our social system, which make the labourer rise by his own degradation, which bid him be ambitious to be a pauper and aspire to be a convict!

Perhaps, however, you console yourself with the notion, that at all events our Poor-laws provide well and comfortably for the decline of life, that whatever we throw away upon the sturdy and robust pauper, we afford, at least, in the spirit of the original law, a much better provision for the aged and infirm. Alas! it is just the reverse; *it is the aged and infirm who are the worst off*. Here is one parallel, among many, between the two classes; Joseph Coster, aged thirty-four, and Anne Chapman, a widow, aged seventy-five, are of the same parish. Joseph Coster, in the prime of life, receives from the parish no less than 49*l*. 11*s*. 8*d*. per year, or 16*s*. 8*d*. per week; Anne Chapman, the *decrepit widow,* 1*s*. 6*d. a week, or* 3*l*. 18*s. a year!* So much for the assistance really afforded to the aged.

And why does the sturdy young man obtain more than the aged and helpless?—1st, Because he may be violent; he can clamour, he can threaten, he can break machines, and he can burn ricks. The magistrates are afraid of *him;* but the old and helpless are past fearing. 2dly, Because *he* has been reckless and improvident, he has brought children into the world without the means of maintaining them, and it is well to encourage private improvidence by public pay. 3dly, Because *he* is paid his wages out of the poor-rates—the consequence of which, vitiating his industry itself, takes from labour its independence, and degrades all poverty into pauperism. It often happens that employment is given rather to the pauper than the independent labourer, because it eases the parish; and *labourers* have absolutely reduced themselves to pauperism in order to be employed.

Do not let us flatter ourselves with the notion that these laws bind the poor to the rich; that the poor consider parish relief as charity.—No, they consider it as a right,—a right which they can obtain, not by desert, but worthlessness; not by thrift, but extravagance; not by real distress, but by plausible falsehood. A shoemaker at Lambeth swore he could only earn thirteen shillings a week—he applied for parish relief—an overseer discovered that he made thirty shillings a week, and the supply was refused. "It is a d——d hard case," quoth the shoemaker, "it was as good to me as a freehold—I've had it these seven years!"

And now it is my duty to point out to the reader one important truth. How far may it safely be left to individuals to administer and provide individual remedies? If ever—you would imagine at first—if ever there was an Aristocracy, which by its position ought to remedy the evils existent among the poorer population in the provinces, it is ours:—unlike the *noblesse* of other countries, they are not congregated only at the Capital, they live much in the provinces; their grades of rank are numerous, from the peer to the squire; they spread throughout the whole state; they come in contact with all classes; they are involved in all country business; they have great wealth; they can easily obtain practical experience—would you not say they are the very men who would most naturally, and could most successfully, struggle against the abuses that, while they demoralize the poor, menace the rich? Alas! it is exactly the reverse: the influence of the Aristocracy, in respect to those within the operation of the Poor-laws, has only been not pernicious, where it has been supine and negative. Among the great gentry, it is mostly the latter—their influence is neglect; among the smaller gentry, it is the former—their influence has been destruction!

I take an instance of this fact in the parish of Calne. Its neighbour and main proprietor is the Marquis of Lansdowne, a man rich to excess; intelligent, able—a political economist—his example, activity, and influence, might *have done* much—his interest was *to do* much—to correct the pauperism of his neighbourhood, and to enlighten the surrounding magistrates and overseers. Well, the parish of Calne is most wretchedly, most *ignorantly,* administered; it is one of the strongest instances of abuse and mental darkness in the Evidence of the Poor-law Commissioners.

So much for the influence of your great noble. Now see, in the same borough, the far more pernicious influence of your magistrate. The magistrates have established the scale system; viz., have insisted on paying the wages of labour out of the parish; the evil effects of this we have already seen. The assistant overseer, and the other parish officers of Calne, allowed that no attention whatever was paid to character; to the most notorious drunkards, swearers, and thieves, the magistrates equally insisted on the application of their blessed scale:—the demands on the parish were made with insolence and threats. The Commissioner inquires if the parish officers never took these men to the bench for punishment. "Yes, they had, but had been so often reprimanded and triumphed over, that they had given it up."

"Thus," adds the Commissioner, "with the appearance of no appeal to the magistrates, the magisterial (viz. the aristocratic) influence is unbounded, complete, and, *by tacit consent, always in exercise, and ever producing evils of the greatest magnitude, and the worst description.*[6]

Wherever the magistrates interfere, the interference is always fatal;—they support, out of an ungenerous fear, or a foolish pride of authority, or at best a weak and ignorant charity, the worst and most vicious characters, in opposition to the remonstrances of the parochial officers—they appoint the scale of allowance by which they pauperize whole districts—afraid of the vengeance of the rickburner, they dare not refuse (even if they wish it) allowance to the pauper. Wherever they interfere rates rise as by a miracle, and the parish falls into decay. It is they who, to aid a temporary policy in Pitt's time, persuaded the poor that it was no disgrace to apply to the parish—it is they who engendered and support the payment of wages from rates—the allowance of relief to the able-bodied—in other words, it is they who, in these two abuses, have produced the disease we are now called upon to cure. Wherever they do not interfere the malady is comparatively slight.

Stratford-upon-Avon, says Mr. Villiers, is the only place in the division not subject to the jurisdiction of the county magistrates, and the only one where it is said that the rate-payers are not dissatisfied. In Poole, a large and populous town, magisterial influence is unknown—all that relates to the government of the poor is excellent.[7] Moore Critchell, Devizes, Marlborough, are similar examples.

Enough of these facts.—I have made out my case. Individual and local influence has been usually pernicious, and it follows,

---

6. "The district of Sturminster Newton is the worst regulated as to poor concerns, with the highest proportionate rates in the county;—in no district is there so much magisterial interference."—*Mr. Okeden's Report.* I might accumulate a thousand instances in support of this general fact, but it is notorious.

7. Some faint, though unsuccessful, attempt has been made to throw suspicion upon the Report of these Commissioners. It may be possible that the Commissioners have been mistaken in one or two details or calculations; even so, the *principles* they have established would be still untouched. *In truth,* the Commissioners have not made a single discovery, they have only classified and enforced the discoveries we had already made. I quote *illustrations* from their Report, as being the most recent work on the subject—the facts will remain notorious, however you may wrangle with the illustrations.

therefore, that in any reform of the Poor-laws, the first principle will be to leave nothing to the *discretion* of that Influence.

Before I pass on to another view of my subject, let me pause one moment to do justice to a body of men, whom, in these days of party spirit, it requires some courage in a legislator professing liberal opinions to vindicate, and whom, in the progress of this work it will be again my duty and my pleasure to vindicate from many ignorant aspersions—I mean the Clergy of the Establishment. I exempt them in general, from the censure to be passed on the magistrates. A certain jealousy between the parson and the squire has often prevented the latter from profiting by the experience of the former, and led to combinations on the bench to thwart the superior enlightenment of the Clerical influence. We shall find various instances in which an active and intelligent minister has been the main reformer of his parish, and the chief corrector of the obstinacy of the magistrate and the sloth of the overseer. But in very few of these instances shall we find the clergyman a scion of the Aristocracy.

A book lies open before me, which ascribes to our Aristocracy many of our Public Charities. What impudence!—most of them have been founded by persons sprung from the people. The author rejoices over the fine names in the list of patrons to such institutions.—Let him!—One thing is perfectly clear, that Public Charities may be administered and regulated with greater sagacity than they are. Let us take a survey of these Institutions—it will perhaps interest, and certainly instruct us.

The system of Public Charities, however honourable to the humanity of a nation, requires the wisest legislative provisions not to conspire with the Poor-laws to be destructive to its morals. Nothing so nurtures virtue as the spirit of independence. The poor should be assisted undoubtedly—but in what—*in providing for themselves*. Hence the wisdom of the Institution of Savings Banks. Taught to lean upon others, they are only a burden upon industry. The Reverend Mr. Stone has illustrated this principle in a vein of just and felicitous humour. He supposes a young weaver of twenty-two marrying a servant-girl of nineteen. Are they provident against the prospects of a family—do they economise—toil—retrench?—No: they live in Spitalfields, and rely upon *the Charitable Institutions*. The wife gets a ticket for the

"Royal Maternity Society,"—she is delivered for nothing—she wants baby-linen—the Benevolent Society supply her. The child must be vaccinated—he goes to the Hospital for Vaccination. He is eighteen months old, "he must be got out of the way;"— he goes to the Infant School;—from thence he proceeds, being "distressed," to the Educational Clothing Society, and the Sunday Schools.—Thence he attains to the Clothing Charity Schools. He remains five years—he is apprenticed gratis to a weaver—he becomes a journeyman—the example of his parents is before his eyes—he marries a girl of his own age—his child passes the ancestral round of charities—his own work becomes precarious —but his father's family was for years in the same circumstances, and was always saved by charity; to charity, then, he again has recourse. Parish gifts of coals, and parish gifts of bread are at his disposal. Spitalfields Associations, Soup Societies, Benevolent Societies, Pension Societies—all fostering the comfortable luxury of living gratuitously—he comes at length to the more fixed income of parish relief—"he *begs* an extract from the parish register, proves his settlement by the *charity-school indenture of apprenticeship,* and quarters his family on the parish, with an allowance of five shillings a week. In this uniform alternation of voluntary and compulsory relief he draws towards the close of his mendicant existence. Before leaving the world, he might, perhaps, return thanks to the public. He has been *born for nothing*—he has been *nursed for nothing*—he has been *clothed for nothing*—he has been *educated for nothing*—he has been *put out in the world for nothing*—he has had *medicine and medical attendance for nothing;* and he has had his children also *born, nursed, clothed, fed, educated, established, and physicked—for nothing!*

"There is but one good office more for which he can stand indebted to society, and *that* is his Burial! He dies a parish pauper, and, at the expense of the parish, he is provided with shroud, coffin, pall, and burial-ground; a party of paupers from the workhouse bear his body to the grave, and a party of paupers are his mourners."[8]

8. "I wish it to be particularly understood," Mr. Stone then adds, "that in thus describing the operation of charity in my district, I have been giving an *ordinary,* and not an *extra*ordinary, instance. I might have included many

Thus we find, that Public Charities are too often merely a bonus to public indolence and vice. What a dark lesson of the fallacy of human wisdom does this knowledge strike into the heart! What a waste of the materials of kindly sympathies! What a perversion individual mistakes can cause, even in the virtues of a nation! Charity is a feeling dear to the pride of the human heart—it is an aristocratic emotion! Mahomet testified his deep knowledge of his kind when he allowed the vice hardest to control,—sexual licentiousness; and encouraged the virtue easiest to practise,—charity. The effect of the last is, in the East, productive of most of the worst legislative evils in that quarter of the globe; it encourages the dependant self-reconciliation to slavery, and fosters the most withering of theological fallacies—predestination.

The effects of the Poor-laws on the social system are then briefly these;—they encourage improvidence, for they provide for its wants; they engender sexual intemperance, for they rear its offspring; by a necessary reaction, the benefits conferred on the vicious pauper, become a curse on the honest labourer.[9] They widen the breach between the wealthy and the poor, for compulsory benevolence is received with discontent;—they deaden the social affections of the labourer, for his children become to him a matter of mercantile speculation. "An instance," says Mr. Villiers, speaking from his experience in the county of Gloucester, "was mentioned, of a man who had lately lost all his children, saying publicly, that it was a sad thing for him, for he had lost his parish pay, *and that his children lived he should have been well to do.*"

Another instance of their operation, not on paternal, but filial affection, is recorded by Dr. Chalmers, in his work on Civic Economy. "At Bury, in Lancashire," saith he, "some very old

---

other details; some of them of far more aggravated and offensive nature. I have contented myself, however, with describing the state of the district as regards charitable relief, and the extent to which that relief *may be,* and actually *is* made to minister to *improvidence and dependence.*"

9. The merit of the origin of Public Hospitals has been inconsiderately ascribed to Christianity. It was the Druids who founded hospitals—they also sacrificed human flesh! Charities, as at present administered, must be partially included in the same censure.

out-pensioners, who had been admitted as inmates to the *poor-house,* with the families of their own children, often preferred the workhouse, because, on purpose to get altogether *quit of them, their children made them uncomfortable.*"

"I have been frequently at vestry-meetings," said Mr. Clarkson, some years ago, "where I have told the father, *'Your* children are *yours.'* The answer has always been, *'No, they belong to the parish!'* No one can beat it into their heads, that their own children belong to them, not to the parish."—The parish is mightily obliged to them!

If the Poor-laws operate thus on the social ties, they are equally prejudicial to the sexual moralities. In the rural districts, a peasant-girl has a child first, and a husband afterwards. One woman in Swaffham, Norfolk, had seven illegitimate children; she received, 2*s.* a-head for each: had she been a widow, with seven legitimate children, she would have received 4*s.* or 5*s.* less. An illegitimate child is thus 25 per cent. more valuable to a parent than a legitimate one. It is considered a very good speculation to marry a lady with a fortune of one or two pledges of love.

"I requested," says Mr. Brereton, of Norfolk, in an excellent pamphlet, published some time ago, on the Administration of the Poor-laws—"I requested the governor of a neighbouring hundred house to furnish me with the number of children born within a certain period, distinguishing the legitimate from the illegitimate. The account was 77 children born:—23 legitimate, 54 *il*legitimate": viz., the illegitimate children were more than double the number of the legitimate.

The Poor-laws, administered as at present through the southern parts of the Island, poison morality, independence, and exertion;—the encouragers, the propagators, and the rewarders of Pauperism. To these evils we must add those incurred by the Laws of Settlement.[10] At present, if there is no labour in one parish, instead of transferring the labourer to another, you chain him to the soil as a pauper. Nor must we forget the mischievous

10. See an excellent exposition of these absurd laws in an able letter to Lord Brougham on the Poor-laws, by Mr. Richardson, of Norfolk. In one parish, cited by him, the expense of trying the settlement of one pauper amounted to 71*l.* 2*s.* 4*d.*

and contagious example of the itinerant vagabonds from Ireland. These Hibernian adventurers, worthy successors of the fierce colonisers of old, are transported in myriads by the blessed contrivance of steam, into a country where "to relieve the wretched is our pride": with much greater capacities for omnipossession than the English labourer, whom the laws of settlement chain to his parish—they spread themselves over the whole country; and wherever they are settled at last, they establish a dread example of thriftless, riotous, unimprovable habits of pauperism. They remind us of the story of a runaway couple, who were married at Gretna Green. The smith demanded five guineas for his services. "How is this," said the bridegroom, "the gentleman you last married assured me that he only gave you a guinea."

"True," said the smith, "but *he* was an Irishman. I have married him six times. *He is a customer. You* I may never see again."

The parish overseers adopt the principle of the smith, and are mighty lenient to the Irishman, who walks the world at his pleasure, and laughs at the parish labourer. He goes to a thousand parishes—he is relieved in all—*he is a customer.*

But what are the remedies for these growing evils? Every one allows the mischief of the present Poor-laws; puts his hands in his pockets, and says, "But what are we to do?" This is ever the case; men suffer evils to surround them, and then quarrel with every cure. There is an impatient cowardice in the spirit of Modern Legislation, which, seeing difficulties on all sides, thinks only of the difficulty of removing them. But, in fact, by a vigorous and speedy reform, the worst consequences of the Poor-laws may be arrested—the remedies are not so difficult as they seem. This truth is evident, from numerous instances in which the energy of select vestries—or even the skilful exertions of an individual—by sturdily refusing relief to able-bodied labourers, without work, by a severely regulated workhouse, which no inmate might leave without an order; and by a general rejection of out-of-door relief;—have succeeded in redeeming whole parishes from pauperism; in reducing the rates in an incredibly short time, to a third of their former amount; and in raising the prostrate character of the pauper to the moral standard of the industrious and independent labourer. This is an undeniable proof then, that remedies are neither very difficult, nor even very slow, in their operation. But—mark this—the remedies depended on the *rare* qualities of great judgment, great firmness, and great ability, of individuals.

No wise government will trust remedies so imperiously demanded to the *rare* qualities of individuals. There is a general inertness in all parochial bodies, I may add in all communities that share an evil disguised under plausible names. In some places the magistrate will not part with power, in other places the farmer deems it a convenience to pay wages from the poor-rates; in some districts the sturdy insolence and overgrown number of paupers intimidate reform, in others the well-meant charity of Lady Bountifuls perpetuates immorality under the title of benevolence. Were the evil to be left to parishes to cure, it would go on for half a century longer, and we should be startled from it at last by the fierce cries of a Servile War.[11] The principle of legislation in this country has long been that merely of punishing—the proper principle is prevention. A good government is a *directive government.* It should be in advance of the people— it should pass laws *for* them, not receive all law *from* them. At present we go on in abuses until a clamour is made against them, and the government gives way; a fatal policy, which makes a weak legislature and a turbulent people. *A government should never give way*—it should never place itself in a condition to give way[12]—it should provide for changes ere they are fiercely demanded, and by timely diversions of the channels of opinion

11. The slow growth of each individual and unassisted reform, is visible by comparing the instances mentioned by Dr. Chalmers seven years ago, with the recent ones specified in the Report of the Poor-law Commissioners; the proportion of reforms appears even to have decreased. A curious proof of general supineness may be found in Cookham parish. By a change of system, that parish has most materially improved its condition. *It is surrounded by other parishes suffering all the agonies of the old system; yet not one of them has followed so near and unequivocal an example!*—I allow, however, that we must not suppose the whole kingdom to be in the same situation as the districts visited by the Poor-law Commissioners. In the north of the island, the worst abuses of the system are not found.–But if those abuses *did* exist every where, it would be no use *writing* against them—cure would be impracticable—it is precisely *because* the evil is as yet partial, that we should legislate for it in earnest; because now we can legislate with effect.

12. "Nothing destroyeth authority so much as the unequal and untimely interchange of power pressed too far and relaxed too much."—*Bacon on Empire.*

prevent the possibility of an overflow. When a government acts thus, it is ever strong—it never comes in contact with the people —it is a directive government not a conceding one, and procures the blessings of a free constitution by the vigour of a despotic one.

The Government then should now take the sole management of the Poor into its own hands. That the present laws of settlement must be simplified and reduced, every one grants; the next step should be the appointment of a Board intrusted with great discretionary powers, for in every parish has been adopted, perhaps, a different system requiring a different treatment—the same laws cannot be applicable to every parish. The number of commissioners cannot be too small, because the less the number the less the expense, and the greater the responsibility;—the greater the responsibility the more vigorous the energy.[13]

These commissioners should of course be paid—gratuitous work is bad work, and the smallness of their number would make the whole expense of so simple a machinery extremely small.

Those parishes too limited in size to provide work for all the able-bodied, and in which consequently pauperism is flagrant and advancing, should be merged into larger districts. For my own part, unless (which I do not believe) a violent opposition were made to the proposal, I should incline to a general enlargement and consolidation of all parishes throughout the kingdom.

The principal machinery of reform should lie in the discipline of the workhouse. It is a fact at present, that where the comforts at a workhouse exceed those of the independent labourer, pauperism increases; but where the comforts at the workhouse have been reduced below those of the independent labourer, pauperism has invariably and most rapidly diminished. On this principle all reform must mainly rest. A workhouse *must be a house of work, requiring severer labour and giving less remuneration than can be obtained by honest competition elsewhere.*

The asylums for the aged and the infirm, should on the con-

13. They might have power to obtain assistant commissioners subordinate to them if necessary. In a conversation I have had with an eminent authority on this head, it was suggested that these assistant commissioners should be itinerant. They would thus be freed from the local prejudices of the magistrates, and enabled to compare the various modes of management in each district.

trary be rendered sufficiently commodious to content, though not so luxurious as to tempt, the poor. There may well be a distinction between the house for labour to the idle, and that of rest for the exhausted.

The Board shall make and publish an Annual Report; this Report will be the best mirror of the condition of the Poor we can obtain, and the publication of their proceedings will prevent abuse and stimulate improvement. The Board, by the aid of its assistant commissioners, would supersede the expensive necessity of many special Parliamentary commissions, and would be always at hand to afford to the Government or to parliament any information relative to the labouring classes.

That such a Board may finally be made subservient to more general purposes, is evident.[14] Its appointment would be popular with all classes, save, perhaps, the Paupers themselves—it would save the country immense sums—it would raise once more in England the pride of honest toil.

It is time that a Government so largely paid by the people should do something in their behalf. "The Poor shall be with you always," are the pathetic words of the Messiah; and that some

---

14. I mention *Recruiting* as one. At present, we have before seen, nothing in the army requires so much reform as the system of recruiting it. A Central Board with its branch commissioners, with its command over the able-bodied applicants for work, might be a very simple and efficacious machine for supplying our army—not, as now, from the dregs of the people—but from men of honesty and character. The expense of our present system of recruiting is enormous—it might in a great measure be saved by a Central Board. Emigration is, of course, another purpose to which it might be applied. Is it true that population presses on capital? In this country it assuredly does, the area of support is undeniably confined—meanwhile the population *increases*. Very well, we know exactly how many to remove. Mr. Wakefield has settled this point in an admirable pamphlet. He takes the British population at twenty millions; he supposes that their utmost power of increase would move at the rate of four per cent. per annum, the constant yearly removal of the percentage, viz., 800,000, would prevent any domestic increase. But of these 800,000 you need to select only those young couples from whom the increase of population will proceed —these amount to 400,000 individuals—the expense of removing them at 10*l.* a head, is four millions a year. *We now therefore know exactly what it will cost to prevent too great a pressure of the population on the means of subsistence!* But what individual emigration-companies can either preserve the balance or persuade the people to accede to it? Is not this clearly the affair of the state, as in all ancient polity it invariably was? See the evidence before the Emigration Committee of 1827, and the intelligent testimony of Mr. Northhouse.

men must be poor and some rich, is a dispensation, with which, according to the lights of our present experience, no human wisdom can interfere. But if legislation cannot prevent the inequalities of poverty and wealth it is bound to prevent the legislative *abuse* of each;—the abuse of riches is tyranny; the corruption of poverty is recklessness. Wherever either of these largely exist, talk not of the blessings of free Institutions, *there* is the very principle that makes servitude a curse. Something is, indeed, wrong in that system in which we see "Age going to the workhouse, and Youth to the gallows." But with us the evil hath arisen, not from the malice of Oppression, but the mistake of Charity. Occupied with the struggles of a splendid ambition, our rulers have legislated for the poor in the genius not of a desire to oppress, but of an impatience to examine. At length there has dawned forth from the dark apathy of Ages a light, which has revealed to the two ranks of our social world the elements and the nature of their several conditions. That light has the properties of a more fiery material. Prudence may make it the most useful of our servants; neglect may suffer it to become the most ruthless of our destroyers. It is difficult, however, to arouse the great to a full conception of the times in which we live: the higher classes are the last to hear the note of danger. The same principle pervades the inequalities of Social Life, as that so remarkable in the laws of Physical Science: they who stand on the lofty eminence,—the high places of the world,—are deafened by the atmosphere itself, and can scarcely hear the sound of the explosion which alarms the quiet of the plains!

Book the Third

Survey of the State of Education, Aristocratic and Popular, and of the General Influences of Morality and Religion in England

INSCRIBED TO

THOMAS CHALMERS, D.D.,

PROFESSOR OF MORAL PHILOSOPHY IN THE
UNIVERSITY OF ST. ANDREW'S

Men generally need knowledge to overpower their passions and master their prejudice; and therefore to see your brother in ignorance is to see him unfurnished to all good works: and every master is to cause his family to be instructed; every governor is to instruct his charge, every man his brother, by all possible and just provisions. For if the people die for want of knowledge, they who are set over them shall also die for want of charity.

BISHOP JEREMY TAYLOR

O curvæ in terras animæ et celestium inanes?

PERSIUS

I

The Education of the Higher Classes

Sir,

No man, in these days of trite materialism, and the discordant
jealousies of rival sects, has been more deeply imbued than yourself with the desire of extending knowledge, and the spirit of a
large and generous Christianity. It is to you that I most respect-
fully, and with all the reverence of political gratitude, dedicate
this Survey of the present state of our Education, coupled with
that of our Religion. In Prussia, that country in which, throughout the whole world, education is the most admirably administered, the authority over the Public Worship of the State is
united with that over the Public Instruction. The minister of
the one is minister also of the other. In the Duchy of Saxe Weimar, which has seemed as the focus of a brilliant philosophy to
the eyes of abashed Europe, in which liberty of thought and piety
of conduct have gone hand in hand, the whole administration of
the instruction of the people may be said to be intrusted to the
clergy,[1] and the light which has beamed over men has been
kindled at the altars of their God. A noble example for our own
clergy, and which may be considered a proof, that as virtue is
the sole end both of true religion and of true knowledge—so,
to unite the means, is only to facilitate the object.

I shall consider then in one and the same section of my work,

---

1. A member of the Laity has, indeed, been added to the Ecclesiastical Commissioners of Saxe Weimar; but he unites entirely with them in the ecclesiastical spirit. That ecclesiastical spirit in Saxe Weimar is benevolence.

as subjects legitimately conjoined, the state of Education in England, and the state of Religion.

And, first, I shall treat of the general education given to the higher classes. In this, sir, I must beseech your indulgence while I wrestle with the social prejudices which constitute our chief obstacle in obtaining, for the youth of the wealthier orders, a more practical and a nobler system of education than exists at present. If my argument at first seems to militate against those venerable Endowments which you so eloquently have defended, you will discover, I think, before I have completed it, that I am exactly friendly to their principle, *because* I am hostile to their abuses. Be it their task to reform themselves, it is for us to point out the necessity of that reform.

"Pour water hastily into a vessel of a narrow neck, little enters; pour it gradually, and by small quantities—and the vessel is filled!" Such is the simile employed by Quintilian to show the folly of teaching children too much at a time. But Quintilian did not mean that we should pour the water into the vase drop by drop, and cease suddenly and for ever the moment the liquid begins to conceal the surface of the bottom. Such, however, is the mode in which we affect to fill the human vessel at the present day. It can be only that people have never seriously reflected on the present academical association for the prevention of knowledge, that the association still exists. The unprejudiced reasoning of a moment is sufficient to prove the monstrous absurdities incorporated in the orthodox education of a gentleman.

Let us suppose an honest tradesman about to bind his son apprentice to some calling—that, for instance, of a jeweller, or a glovemaker. Would not two questions be instantly suggested by common sense to his mind?—1st. Will it be useful for my son to know only jewellery or glovemaking? 2d. And if so, will he learn *how* to set jewels, or make gloves, by being bound an apprentice to Neighbor So-and-so, since it is likely that if Neighbour So-and-so does not teach him that, he will teach him nothing else?

Why do not these plain questions force themselves into the mind of a gentleman sending his son to Eton? Why does he not ask himself—1st. Will it be useful for my son to know only Latin and Greek? and secondly, If it be, will he *learn* Latin and Greek by being sent to Dr. K——, for it is not likely that Dr. K—— will teach him any thing else?

If every gentleman asked himself those two questions previous to sending his sons to Eton, one might suspect that the head-mastership would soon be a sinecure. But before I come to examine the answers to be returned to these questions, let us dispose of some subtle and unacknowledged reasons in favour of the public school, which actuate the parent in consenting to sacrifice the intellectual improvement of his son. Writers in favour of an academical reform have not sufficiently touched upon the points I am about to refer to, for they have taken it for granted that men would allow education alone was to be the end of scholastic discipline; but a great proportion of those who send their children to school secretly meditate other advantages besides those of intellectual improvement.

In the first place the larger portion of the boys at a public school are the sons of what may be termed the minor aristocracy —of country gentlemen—of rich merchants—of opulent lawyers—of men belonging to the "untitled property" of the country: the smaller portion are the sons of statesmen and of nobles. Now each parent of the former class thinks in his heart of the advantages of acquaintance and connexion that his son will obtain, by mixing with the children of the latter class. He looks beyond the benefits of education—to the chances of getting on in the world. "Young Howard's father has ten livings—young Johnson may become intimate with young Howard, and obtain one of the ten livings." So thinks old Johnson when he pays for the Greek which his son will never know. "Young Cavendish is the son of a minister—if young Smith distinguishes himself what a connexion he may form!" So says old Smith when he finds his son making excellent Latin verses, although incapable of translating Lucan without a dictionary! Less confined, but equally aristocratic, are the views of the mother.—"My son is very intimate with little Lord John: he will get, when of age, into the best society!—who knows but that one of these days he may marry little Lady Mary!"

It is with these notions that shrewd and worldly parents combat their conviction that their sons are better cricketers than scholars; and so long as such advantages allure them, it is in vain that we reason and philosophize on education—we are proving only what with them is the minor part of the question, nay, which they may be willing to allow. *We* speak of educating the boy, *they* think already of advancing the man: *we* speak of the necessity of knowledge, but the Smiths and the Johnsons think of the necessity of connexions.

Now here I pause for one moment, that the reader may mark a fresh proof of the universal influence which our aristocracy obtain over every institution—every grade of our social life—from the cradle to the grave. Thus insensibly they act on the wheels of that mighty machine—the education of our youth—by which the knowledge, the morals, and the welfare of a state are wrought; and it becomes, as it were, of less consequence to be wise, than to form a connexion with the great.

But calmly considered, we shall find that even this advantage of connexion is not obtained by the education of a public school. And knowing that this prevailing notion must be answered, before the generality of parents will dispassionately take a larger view of this important subject, I shall proceed to its brief examination.

Boys at a public school are on an equality. Let us suppose any boy, plebeian or patrician,—those of his contemporaries whose pursuits are most congenial to his become naturally his closest friends. Boarders, perhaps, at the same house, custom and accident bring such as wish to be intimate constantly together, and a similarity of habits produces a stronger alliance than even a similarity of dispositions.

Howard, the peer's eldest, and Johnson, the commoner's younger son, leave school at the same age—they are intimate friends—we will suppose them even going up to the same University. But Howard is entered as a nobleman at Trinity, and Johnson goes a pensioner to Emanuel; their sets of acquaintance become instantly and widely different. Howard may now and then take milk punch with Johnson, and Johnson may now and then "wine" with Howard, but they have no circle in common—they are not commonly brought together. Custom no longer favours their intercourse—a similarity of pursuits no longer persuades them that they have a similarity of dispositions. For the first time, too, the difference of rank becomes markedly visible.

At no place are the demarcations of birth and fortune so faintly traced as at a School—nowhere are they so broad and deep as at an University. The young noble is suddenly removed from the side of the young commoner: when he walks he is indued in a distinguishing costume: when he dines he is placed at a higher table along with the heads of his college: at chapel he addresses his Maker, or reads the Racing Calendar, in a privileged pew. At *most* colleges[2] the discipline to which *he* is subjected is, comparatively speaking, relaxed and lenient. Punctuality in lectures and prayers is of no vital importance to a "young man of such expectations." As regards the first, hereditary legislators have no necessity for instruction; and as to the last, the religion of a college has no damnation for a lord. Nay, at Cambridge, to such an extent are the demarcations of ranks observed, that the eldest son of one baronet assumes a peculiarity in costume to distinguish him from the younger son of another, and is probably a greater man at college than he ever is during the rest of his life. Nor does this superstitious observance of the social grades bound itself to titular rank: it is at college that an eldest son suddenly leaps into that consequence —that elevation above his brothers—which he afterwards retains through life. It usually happens that the eldest son of a gentleman of some five thousands a year, goes up as *a Fellow*[3] *Commoner,* and his brothers as *Pensioners.* A marked distinction in dress, dinners, luxuries, and, in some colleges, discipline, shows betimes the value attached to wealth—and wealth only; and the younger son learns, to the full extent of the lesson, that he is *worth* so many thousands less than his elder brother. It is obvious that these distinctions, so sudden and so marked, must occasion an embarrassment and coldness, in the continuance at college, of friendships formed at school. The young are commonly both shy and proud—our pensioner Johnson, chilled and struck by the new position of our nobleman Howard, is a little diffident in pressing his acquaintance on him; and our nobleman Howard—though not desirous, we will suppose, to cut his old friend—yet amidst new occupations and new faces

2. Chiefly, however, at the smaller colleges, and less at Oxford than at Cambridge.

3. *Fellow* Commoners at Cambridge; *Gentleman* Commoners at Oxford.

—amidst all the schemes and amusements of the incipient man, and the self-engrossed complacency of the budding lord for the first time awakened to his station, naturally and excusably reconciles himself to the chances that so seldom bring him in contact with his early ally, and by insensible but not slow degrees he passes from the first stage of missing his friendship to the last of forgetting it. This is the common history of scholastic "connexions" where there is a disparity in station. It is the vulgar subject of wonder at the University, that "fellows the best friends in the world at Eton are never brought together at college." And thus vanish into smoke all the hopes of the parental Johnsons!—all 'the advantages of early friendship!' —all the dreams for which the shrewd father consented to sacrifice, for "little Latin and *no* Greek," the precious—the irrevocable season—of "the sowing of good seed," of pliant memories and ductile dispositions—the lost, the golden opportunity, of instilling into his son the elements of real wisdom and true morality—the knowledge that adorns life, and the principles that should guide it!

But suppose this friendship *does* pass the ordeal; suppose that Howard and Johnson do preserve the desired connexion; suppose that together they have broken lamps and passed the 'little-go,' together they have "crammed" Euclid and visited Barnwell; suppose that their pursuits still remain congenial, and they enter the great world *"mutuis animis amanter"*—how little likely is it that the 'connexion' will continue through the different scenes in which the lot of each will probably be cast. Ball-rooms and hells, Newmarket and Crockford's, are the natural element of the one, but scarcely so of the other. We will not suppose our young noble plunging into excesses, but merely mingling in the habitual pleasures belonging to his station; we imagine him not depraved, but dissipated; not wicked, but extravagant; not mad, but thoughtless. Now mark—does he continue his connexion with Johnson or not; the answer is plain— if Johnson's pursuits remain congenial—yes! if otherwise—not! How can he be intimate with one whom he never meets? How can he associate with one whom society does not throw in his way? If then Johnson continue to share his friendship, he must continue to share his occupations; the same ball-rooms and the same hells must bring them into contact, and the common love of pleasure cement their sympathy for each other. But is this exactly what the prudent father contemplated in the advantages of connexion; was it to be a connexion in profusion and in vice? Was it to impair the fortunes of his son, and not to improve them? This question points to no exaggerated or uncommon picture. Look round the gay world and say if loss, and not gain, be not the ordinary result of such friendships between the peer's elder son and the gentleman's younger one as survive the trials of school and college—the latter was to profit by the former— but the temptations of society thwart the scheme; the poor man follows the example the rich; dresses—hunts—intrigues— games—runs in debt, and is beggared through the very connexion which the father desired, and by the very circles of society which the mother sighed that he should enter. I do not deny that there are some young adventurers more wary and more prudent, who contrive to get from their early friend, the schemed-for living or the dreamt-of place, but these instances are singularly rare, and, to speculate upon such a hazard, as a probable good, is incalculably more mad than to have bought your son a ticket in the lottery, by way of providing for his fortune.

The idea then of acquiring at public schools a profitable connexion, or an advantageous friendship, is utterly vain. 1st, Because few school connexions continue through college; 2d, Because, if so continued, few college connexions continue through the world; 3d, Because, even if they do, experience proves that a friendship between the richer man and the poorer, is more likely to ruin the last by the perpetual example of extravagance, than to enrich him by the uncommon accident of generosity. Add to these all the usual casualties of worldly life, the chances of a quarrel and a rupture, the chances that the expected living must be sold to pay a debt, the promised office transferred to keep a vote, the delays, the humiliations, the mischances, the uncertainties, and ask yourself if whatever be the advantages of public education, a connexion with the great is not the very last to be counted upon?

"But, perhaps, my boy may distinguish himself," says the ambitious father, "he is very clever. Distinction at Eton lasts through life; he may get into parliament; he may be a great man; why not a second Canning?"

Alas!—granted that your son be clever, and granted that he distinguish himself, how few of those who are remarkable at Eton are ever heard of in the world; their reputation "dies and makes no sign." And this, for two reasons: first, because the distinctions of a public school are no evidence of real talent; learning by heart and the composition of Latin or Greek verse are the usual proofs to which the boy's intellect is put; the one is a mere exertion of memory—the other, a mere felicity of imitation;—and I doubt if the schoolboy's comprehensive expression of "knack" be not the just phrase to be applied to the faculty both of repeating other men's words, and stringing imitations of other men's verses. Knack! an ingenious faculty indeed, but no indisputable test of genius, and affording no undeniable promise of a brilliant career! But success, in these studies, is not only no sign of future superiority of mind; the studies themselves scarcely tend to adapt the mind to those solid pursuits by which distinction is ordinarily won. Look at the arenas for the author or the senator; the spheres for active or for literary distinction; is there any thing in the half idle, and desultory, and superficial course of education pursued at public schools, which tends to secure future eminence in either. It is a great benefit if boys learn something solid, but it is a far greater benefit if they contract the desire and the habit of acquiring solid information. But how few ever leave school with the intention and the energies to continue intellectual studies. We are not to be told of the few great men who have been distinguished as senators, or as authors, and who have been educated at public schools. The intention of general education is to form the many, and not the few; if the many are ignorant, it is in vain you assert that the few are wise—we have —even supposing their wisdom originated in your system, a right to consider them exceptions, and not as examples. But how much vainer is it to recite the names of these honoured few when it is far more than doubtful even whether they owed any thing to your scholastic instruction; when it is more than doubtful whether their talents did not rise in *spite* of your education, and *not because* of it; whether their manhood was illustrious, not because their genius was formed by the studies of youth, but because it could not be crushed by them. All professions and all ranks have their Shakspeare and their Burns, men who are superior to the adverse influences by which inferior intellects are chilled into inaction. And this supposition is rendered far more probable when we find how few of *these* few were noted *at school* for any portion of the mental power they afterwards developed; or, in other words, when we observe how much *the academical process stifled and repressed their genius,* so that if their future life had been (as more or less ought to be the aim of scholars) a continuation of the same pursuits and objects as those which were presented to their youth, they would actually have lived without developing their genius, and died without obtaining a name. But Chance is more merciful than men's systems, and the eternal task of Nature is that of counteracting our efforts to deteriorate ourselves.

But you think that your son shall be distinguished at Eton, and that the distinction shall continue through life; we see then that the chances are against him—they are rendered every day more difficult—because, formerly the higher classes only were educated. Bad as the public schools might be, nothing better perhaps existed; superficial knowledge was pardoned, because it was more useful than no knowledge.

But now the people are wakened; education, not yet general, is at least extended; a desire for the Solid and the Useful circulates throughout mankind. Grant that your son obtains all the academical honours; grant, even, that he enters parliament through the distinction he has obtained,—have those honours taught him the principles of jurisprudence, the business of legislation, the details of finance, the magnificent mysteries of commerce;—perhaps, even, they have not taught him the mere and vulgar art of public speaking! How few of the young men thus brought forward ever rise into fame!

A mediocre man, trained to the habits of discerning what is true knowledge, and the application to pursue it, will rise in any public capacity to far higher celebrity than the genius of a public school, who has learnt nothing it is necessary to the public utility to know. As, then, the hope of acquiring connexions was a chimera, so that of obtaining permanent distinction for your son, in the usual process of public education, is a dream. What

millions of 'promising men,' unknown, undone, have counter-
balanced the success of a single Canning!

I may here observe, that the abolition of close boroughs is
likely to produce a very powerful effect upon the numbers sent
to a public school. As speculation is the darling passion of mankind, many, doubtless, were the embryo adventurers sent to Eton,
in the hope that Eton honours would unlock the gates of a
Gatton or Old Sarum. Thus, in one of Miss Edgeworth's tales,
the clever Westminster boy without fortune, receives even at
school, the intimation of a future political career as an encouragement to his ambition, and the Rotten Borough closes the vista
of Academical Rewards. This hope is over; men who would
cheer on their narrow fortunes by the hope of parliamentary
advancement, must now appeal to the people, who have little
sympathy with the successful imitator of Alcæan measures, or the
honoured adept in 'longs and shorts.' And consequently, to
those parents who choose the public school as a possible opening
to public life, one great inducement is no more, and a new course
of study will appear necessary to obtain the new goals of political advancement.

I have thus sought to remove the current impression that
public schools are desirable, as affording opportunities for advantageous connexion and permanent distinction. And the ambitious father (what father is not ambitious for his son?) may
therefore look dispassionately at the true ends of education and
ask himself if, at a public school, those ends are accomplished?
This part of the question has been so frequently and fully examined, and the faults of our academical system are so generally allowed, that a very few words will suffice to dispose
of it. The only branches of learning really attempted to be
taught at our public schools are the dead languages.[4] Assuredly
there are other items in the bills—French and arithmetic, geography and the use of the globes. But these, it is well known,

4. Formerly a nobleman, or rich gentleman, in sending his son to school
sent with him a private tutor, whose individual tuition was intended to supply
the deficiencies of the public course of study. This custom has almost expired,
and aristocratic education, therefore, instead of improving, is still more superficial than it was.

are merely nominal instructions: the utmost acquired in geography is the art of colouring a few maps; and geography itself is only a noble and a practical science when associated with the history, the commerce, and the productions of the country or the cities, whose mere position it indicates. What matters it that a boy can tell us that Povoa is on one side the river Douro, and Pivasende on the other; that the dusky inhabitant of Benguela looks over the South Atlantic, or that the waters of Terek exhaust themselves in the Caspian sea? Useful, indeed, is this knowledge, combined with other branches of statistics;—useless by itself,—another specimen of the waste of memory and the frivolity of imitation. But even this how few learn, and how few of the learners remember?

Arithmetic and its pretended acquisitions, is, of all scholastic delusions, the most remarkable. What sixth-form ornament of Harrow or Eton has any knowledge of figures? Of all parts of education, this the most useful is, at aristocratic schools, the most neglected. As to French, at the end of eight years the pupil leaves Eton, and does not know so much as his sister has acquired from her governess in three months. Latin and Greek, then, alone remain as the branches of human wisdom to which serious attention has been paid.

I am not one of those who attach but trifling importance to the study of the Classics; myself a devoted, though a humble student, I have not so long carried the thyrsus but that I must believe in the God. And he would indeed be the sorriest of pedants who should affect to despise the knowledge of those great works, which, at their first appearance, enlightened one age, and in their after restoration, broke the darkness of another! Surely one part of the long season of youth can scarcely be more profitably employed than in examining the claims of those who have exercised so vast and durable an influence over the human mind.

But it is obvious that even thoroughly to master the Greek and Latin tongues, would be but to comprehend a very small part of a practical education. Formerly it was obviously wise to pay more *exclusive* attention to their acquisition than at present, for formerly they contained *all* the literary treasurers of the world, and now they contain only a part. The literature of France, Germany, England, are at least as necessary for a man born in the nineteenth century, as that of Rome and Athens.

But, it is said, the season of childhood is more requisite for mastering a skill in the dead languages than it is for the living? Even if this assertion were true there would be no reason why the dead languages *alone* should be learnt; if the early youth of the mind be *necessary* for the acquisition of the one, it is at least a desirable period for the acquisition of the other. But the fact is, that the season of youth is at least as essential for the learning the living languages as it is for acquiring the dead; because it is necessary to speak the one and it is not necessary to speak the other: and the facile and pliant organs of childhood are indeed almost requisite for the mastery of the tones and accents in a spoken language, although the more mature understanding of future years is equally able to grasp the roots and construction of a written one.

As the sole business of life is not literature; so education ought not to be only literary. Yet what can you, the father of the boy you are about to send to a public school, what, I ask, can you think of a system which, devoting the whole period of youth to literature, not only excludes from consideration the knowledge of all continental languages—the languages of Montesquieu and Schiller, but also totally neglects any knowledge of the authors of your own country, and even the element of that native tongue in which all the business of life must be carried on? Not in Latin, nor in Greek, but in his English tongue your son must write, in that tongue, if you desire him to become great, he is to be an orator, an historian, a poet, or a philosopher. And this language is above all others the most utterly neglected, its authors never studied, even its grammar never taught. To know Latin and Greek is a great intellectual luxury, but to know one's own language is almost an intellectual necessity.

But literature alone does not suffice for education; the aim of that grave and noble process is large and catholic, it would not be enough to make a man learned; a pedant is proverbially a useless fool. The aim of education is to make a man wise and good. Ask yourself what there is in modern education that will fulfil this end? Not a single doctrine of moral science is taught—

not a single moral principle inculcated.[5] Even in the dead languages it is the poets and the more poetical of the historians the pupil mostly learns, rarely the philosopher and the moralist. It was, justly, I think, objected to the London University, that religion was not to be taught in its schools; but is religion taught at any of our public institutions; previous at least, to a course of Paley at the University. Attendance at church or chapel is not religion! the life, the guidance, the strength of religion, where are these? Look round every corner of the fabric of education, still Latin and Greek and Greek and Latin are all that you can descry,

> Mixtaque ridenti fundet colocasia acantho.

But the father hesitates. I see, sir, you yet think Greek and Latin are excellent things, are worth the sacrifice of all else. Well, then, on this ground let us meet you. Your boy will go to Eton to learn Greek and Latin; he will stay there eight years (having previously spent four at a preparatory school), he will come away, at the end of his probation, but what Latin and Greek will he bring with him? Are you a scholar yourself, ex-

---

5. The only moral principle at a public school is that which the boys themselves tacitly inculcate and acknowledge; it is impossible to turn a large number of human beings loose upon each other, but what one of the first consequences will be the formation of a public opinion, and public opinion instantly creates a silent but omnipotent code of laws. Thus, among boys there is always a vague sense of honour and of justice, which *is the only morality* that belongs to schools. It is this vague and conventional sense to which the master trusts, and with which he seldom interferes. But *how* vague it is, how confused, how erring! What cruelty, tyranny, duplicity, are compatible with it! it is no disgrace to insult the weak and to lie to the strong, to torment the fag and to deceive the master. These principles grow up with the boy, insensibly they form the matured man. Look abroad in the world, what is the most common character?—that which is at once arrogant and servile. It is this early initiation into the vices of men, which with some parents is an inducement to send their son to public school. How often you hear the careful father say, "Tom goes to Eton to *learn the world.*" One word on this argument: Your boy does *not* accomplish your object: he learns the *vices of the world*, it is true, but not the caution which should accompany them. Who so extravagant or so thoughtless as the young man escaped from a public school;—who so easily duped,—who so fair a prey to the trading sharper and the sharping tradesman—who runs up such bills with tailors and horsedealers—who so notoriously the greenhorn and the bubble? Is this his boasted knowledge of the world? You may have made your boy vicious, but you will find that that is *not* making him wise.

amine then the average of young men of eighteen; open a page of some author they have *not* read, have not parrot-like got by heart; open a page in the dialogues of Lucian, in the Thebaid of Statius. Ask the youth, you have selected from the herd, to construe it as you would ask your daughter to construe a page of some French author she has never seen before, a poem of Regnier, or an exposition in the *Esprit des Lois*. Does he not pause, does he not blush, does he not hesitate, does not his eye wander abroad in search of the accustomed "Crib," does he not falter out something about lexicons and grammars, and at last throw down the book and tell you he has never learnt *that*, but as for Virgil or Herodotus, *there* he is your man! At the end then of eight years, without counting the previous four, your son has not learnt Greek and Latin, and he has learnt nothing else to atone for it. Here then we come to the result of our two inquiries.—1st. Is it necessary to learn something else besides Latin and Greek?—It is! But even if not necessary, are Greek and Latin well taught at a public school? —They are not. With these conclusions I end this part of my inquiry.

Mr. Bentham in his *Chrestomathia* has drawn up a programme of what he considered might be fairly taught and easily acquired in the process of a complete education. There is something formidable in the list of studies, it is so vast and various, that it seems almost visionary; the leap from the 'learn nothing' to 'the learn all' is too wide and startling. But without going to an extent which would leave no branch of human knowledge excluded, it is perfectly clear that the education of our youth may be conveniently widened to a circle immeasurably more comprehensive than any which has yet been drawn.

It is probable that the System of Hamilton may be wrong; probable that there is a certain quackery in the System of Pestalozzi; possible that the Lancasterian System may be overrated; but let any dispassionate man compare the progress of a pupil under an able tutor in any one of these systems with the advances made at an ordinary public school.[6] What I complain of,

6. The Monitorial System was applied with eminent success by Mr. Pillans, at the High School, Edinburgh, to the teaching of Latin, Greek, and Ancient Geography. He applied it for several years to a class of boys not less in number

and what you, sir, to whom I address these pages, must complain of also, is this: that these schools—in which our hereditary legislators are brought up—in which those who are born to frame and remodel the mighty Mechanism of Law, and wield the Moral Powers of Custom, receive the ineffaceable impressions of youth—at these schools, I say, Religion is not taught—Morals are not taught—Philosophy is not taught—the light of the purer and less material Sciences never breaks upon the gaze. The intellect of the men so formed is to guide our world, and that intellect is uncultured!

In various parts of the Continent there are admirable schools for teachers, on the principle that those who teach, should themselves be taught. Still more important is it in an aristocratic constitution, that those who are to *govern* us, should be at least enlightened. Are you who now read these pages, a parent? Come—note the following sentence. Ages have rolled since it was written, but they have not dimmed the brightness of the maxim: "Intellect is more excellent than science, and a life according to intellect preferable to a life according to science." So said that ancient philosopher, whose spirit approached the nearest to the genius of Christianity. What then is that preparation to life which professes to teach learning and neglects the intellect, which loads the memory, which forgets the soul. Beautifully proceedeth Plato:—"A life according to Intellect is alone free from the vulgar errors of our race, it is that mystic

---

than 230 (ages varying from 12 to 16), without any assistance in the teaching of the above branches of learning, save what he derived from the boys themselves. Of this most important experiment of applying to the higher branches of learning a principle thitherto limited to the lower, Mr. Pillans speaks thus, in an able letter, with which he was kind enough to honour me: "When I compare the effect of the Monitorial System with my own experience of that class, both when I was a pupil of it myself under Dr. Adam, and during the first two years after I succeeded him, I have no hesitation in saying, that it multiplied incalculably the means and resources of the teacher, both as regarded the progress of the pupils in good learning, and the forming of their minds, manners, and moral habits. Not long after he became professor of Humanity, Mr. Pillans adopted the Monitorial System, first in his junior, next in his senior class. He thus speaks of its success: "I believe this is the only instance of the Monitorial principle being acted on within the walls of a college. In the limited application I make of it there, it has succeeded even beyond the expectations I had formed. Of this I may be tempted to say more hereafter."

port of the soul, that sacred Ithaca, into which Homer conducts Ulysses after the education of life." But far different is the Port into which the modern education conducts her votaries and the Haven of Prejudice is the only receptacle to the Ship of Fools.[7]

It is the errors that have thus grafted themselves on the system of our educational endowments, which have led the recent philosophy to attack with no measured violence, the principle of endowments themselves—an attack pregnant with much mischief, and which, if successful, would be nearly fatal to all the loftier and abstruser sciences in England. I desire to see preserved—I desire to see strengthened—I desire to see beloved and regenerated the principle of literary endowments, though I quarrel with the abuses of endowments that at present exist. You yourself, sir, have placed the necessity of endowments in a right and unanswerable point of view. Mankind must be invited to knowledge—the public are *not* sufficient patrons of the abstruse sciences—no dogma has been more popular, none more fallacious; there is no appetence in a commercial and bustling country to a learning which does not make money—to a philosophy, which does not rise to the Woolsack, or sway the Mansion-house. The herd must be courted to knowledge. You found colleges and professorships, and you place Knowledge before their eyes—*then* they are allured to it. You clothe it with dignity, you gift it with rewards—*then* they are unconsciously disposed to venerate it, Public opinion follows what is honoured; honour knowledge, and you chain to it that opinion. Endowments at a University beget emulation in subordinate institutions; if they are nobly filled, they produce in the latter the desire of rivalry; if inadequately, the ambition to excel. They present amidst the shifts and caprices of unsettled learning a constant landmark and a steadfast example. The public will not patronize the higher sciences. Lacroix, as stated, sir, in your work, gave lessons in

7. If I have dwelt only on Public Schools, it is because the private schools are for the most part modelled on the same plan. Home tuition is rare. The private tutor, viz., the gentleman who takes some five or six pupils to prepare for the University, is often the best teacher our youth receive. Whatever they learn thoroughly they learn with him; but unhappily this knowledge stints itself to the classics and the physical sciences required at college;—they prepare the pupil for college and not for wisdom. At many of these, however, religious instruction is perhaps for the first time in the pupil's life, a little insisted upon.

the higher mathematics,—to *eight* pupils! But the higher sciences *ought* to be cultivated, hence another necessity for endowments. Wherever endowments are the most flourishing, thither learning is the most attracted. Thus, you have rightly observed, and Adam Smith before you, that in whatever country the colleges are more affluent than the church, colleges exhibit the most brilliant examples of learning. Wherever, on the other hand, the church is more richly endowed than the college, the pulpit absorbs the learning of the chair. Hence in England, the learning of the clergy; and in Scotland, that of the professors.[8] Let me add to this, the example of Germany, where there is scarce a professor who does not enjoy a well-earned celebrity— the example of France, where, in Voltaire's time, when the church was so wealthy, he could only find one professor of any literary merit (and he but of mediocre claims), and where, in the present time, when the church is impoverished, the most remarkable efforts of Christian philosophy have emanated from the chairs of the professional lecturer.[9]

I have said that the public will not so reward the professor of the higher sciences as to sanction the idea, that we may safely leave him to their mercy. Let us suppose, however, that the public are more covetous of lofty knowledge than we imagine. Let us suppose that the professor of philosophy *can* obtain sufficient pupils to maintain him, but that by *pupils alone* he is maintained, what would be the probable result? Why, that he would naturally seek to enlarge the circle of his pupils—that in order to enlarge it, he would stoop from the starred and abstruse sphere of his research—that he would dwell on the more familiar and less toilsome elements of science—that he would fear to lose his pupils by soaring beyond the average capacity —that he would be, in one word, a teacher of the rudiments of science, not an investigator of its difficult results. Thus we should have, wherever we turned, nothing but elementary

8. "Half the distinguished authorship of Scotland has been professional." —*Chalmers on Endowments.*

9. If in the mediated reform of the church the average revenues of the clergy be more equalized, the Professorships would gain something in learning while the Church would still be so affluent as to lose nothing. The chair and the pulpit should be tolerably equalized in endowments in order to prevent the one subtracting from the intellectual acquirements of the other.

knowledge and facts made easy—thus we should contract the eagle wing of philosophy to a circle of male Mrs. Marcets—ever dwelling on the threshold of Knowledge and trembling to penetrate the temple.

Endowments raise (as the philosopher *should* be raised) the lofty and investigating scholar above the necessity of humbling his intellect in order to earn his bread—they give him up to the serene meditation from which he distils the essence of the diviner—nay, even the more useful, but hitherto undiscovered—wisdom. If from their shade has emanated the vast philosophy of Kant, which dwarfs into littleness the confined materialism of preceding schools, so also from amidst the shelter they afford broke forth the first great regenerator of practical politics, and the origin of the *Wealth of Nations,* was founded in the industrious tranquillity of a professorship at Glasgow.[10]

Let us then eschew all that false and mercantile liberalism of the day which would destroy the high seats and shelters of Learning, and would leave what is above the public comprehension to the chances of the public sympathy. It is possible that endowments favour many drones—granted—but if they produce one great philosopher, whose mind would otherwise have been bowed to lower spheres, that advantage counterbalances a thousand drones. How many sluggards will counterpoise an Adam Smith! "If you form but a handful of wise men," said the great Julian, "you do more for the world than many kings can do." And if it be true that he who has planted a blade of corn in the spot which was barren before is a benefactor to his species; what shall we not pardon to a system by which a nobler labourer is enabled to plant in the human mind an idea which was unknown to it till then?

But if ever endowments for the cultivators of the higher letters were required it is now. As education is popularized, its tone grows more familiar but its research less deep—the demand for the elements of knowledge vulgarizes scholarship to the necessity of the times—there is an impatience of that austere and vigorous toil by which alone men can extend the knowledge

---

10. Dr. Chalmers eloquently complains, that they made Dr. Smith a commissioner of customs, and thereby lost to the public his projected work on Jurisprudence.

already in the world. As you diffuse the stream, guard well the fountains. But it is in vain for us—it is in vain, sir, even for you, how influential soever your virtues and your genius, to exert yourself in behalf of our Educational Endowments, if they themselves very long continue unadapted to the growing knowledge of the world. Even the superior classes are awakened to a sense of the insufficiency of fashionable education—of the vast expense and the little profit of the system pursued at existing schools and universities.

One great advantage of diffusing knowledge among the lower classes is the necessity thus imposed on the higher of increasing knowledge among themselves. I suspect that the new modes and systems of education which succeed the most among the people will ultimately be adopted by the gentry. Seeing around them the mighty cities of a new Education—the education of the nineteenth century—they will no longer be contented to give their children the education of three hundred years ago. One of two consequences will happen: either public schools will embrace improved modes and additional branches of learning, or it will cease to be the fashion to support them. The more aristocratic families who have no interest in their foundations will desert them, and they will gradually be left as monastic reservoirs to college institutions.[11]

Let us hope to avert this misfortune while we may, and, by exciting among the teachers of education a wholesome and legitimate spirit of alarm, arouse in them the consequent spirit of reform. Let us interest the higher classes in the preservation of their own power: let them, while encouraging schools for the

11. For one source of advantage in the public schools will remain unchoked —they will continue to be the foundation on which certain University Emoluments are built. College scholarships, college fellowships, and college livings, will still present to the poorer gentry and clergy an honourable inducement to send their sons to the public schools; and these will, therefore, still remain a desirable mode of *disposing* of children, despite of their incapacities to *improve* them. If we could reform the conditions on which University Endowments are bestowed on individuals, a proportionate reform in the scholars ambitious to obtain them, would be a necessary consequence. This may be difficult to do with the old endowments, and the readiest mode would be to found new endowments on a better principle and under better patronage, as a counterpoise to the abuses of the old. Thus not by destroying old endowments, but by creating new, shall we best serve the purposes of the loftier knowledge.

children of the poor, improve, by their natural influence, the schools adapted for their own; the same influence that now supports a superficial education, would as easily expedite the progress of a sound one, and it would become the fashion to be educated well, as it is now the fashion to be educated ill. Will they refuse or dally with this necessity?—they cannot know its importance to themselves. If the aristocracy would remain the most powerful class, they must continue to be the most intelligent. The art of printing was explained to a savage king, the Napoleon of his tribes. "A magnificent concept," said he, after a pause; but it can never be introduced into my domains; it would make knowledge equal, and I should fall. How can I govern my subjects, except by being wiser than they?"—Profound reflection, which contains the germ of all legislative control! When knowledge was confined to the cloister, the monks were the most powerful part of the community, gradually it extended to the nobles, and gradually the nobles supplanted the priests: the shadow of the orb has advanced—it is resting over the people —it is for you, who, for centuries, have drunk vigour from the beams—it is for you to say if the light shall merely extend to a more distant circle, or if it shall darken from your own. It is only by diverting the bed of the Mighty River, that your city can be taken, and your kingdom can pass away!

II

State of Education among the Middling Classes

A very few words will dismiss this part of my subject. The middle classes, by which I mean chiefly shopkeepers and others engaged in trade, naturally enjoy a more average and even education, than either those above or below them;—it continues a shorter time than the education of the aristocracy—it embraces fewer objects—its discipline is usually more strict: it includes Latin, but not too much of it; and arithmetic and caligraphy, merely nominal with the aristocratic teachers, are the main matters considered, where the pupils are intended for trade. English themes usually make a part of their education, instead of Latin Sapphics; but as critical lectures do not enlighten and elevate the lesson, the utmost acquired is a style tolerably grammatic. Religion is more attended to: and explanations of the Bible are sometimes a weekly lesson. Different schools give, of course, more or less into religious knowledge; but, generally speaking, all schools intended to form the trader, pay more attention to religion than those that rear the gentleman. Religion may not be minutely explained, but it is much that its spirit is attended to; and the pupil carries a reverence for it in the abstract, throughout life, even though, in the hurry of commercial pursuits, he may neglect its principles. Hence the middle classes, with us, have a greater veneration than others for religion; hence their disposition, often erroneous, to charity, in their situation of overseers and parochial officers; hence the desire (weak in the other classes) with them so strong, of keeping holy the Sabbath-day;

hence their enthusiasm for diffusing religious knowledge among the negroes; hence their easy proselytism to the stricter creeds of Dissenting Sects.

But if the spirit of religion is more maintained in their education, *the science* of morals, in its larger or abstruser principles, is equally neglected. Moral works, by which I mean the philosophy of morals, make no part of their general instruction: they are not taught, like the youth of Germany, to think—to reflect—so that goodness may sink, as it were, into their minds and pervade their actions, as well as command their vague respect. Hence, they are often narrow and insulated in their moral views, and fall easily, in afterlife, into their great characteristic error, of considering Appearances as the substance of Virtues.

The great experiment of the day for the promotion of Education among the middle classes, has been the foundation of the London University and King's College. The first is intended for all religions, and therefore all religion is banished from it!— a main cause of the difficulties with which it has had to contend, and of the jealousy with which it has been regarded. Its real capital was 158,882*l.* 10*s.*, but this vast sum has not sufficed to set the University clear from the most grievous embarrassments. In its February report of this year, it gives a view of its financial state, by which it calculates, that in October next, there will be a total balance against it of 3715*l.* The council are charmed with every thing in the progress of the University— except the financies; they call on the proprietors to advance a further sum, or else they drily declare, they may be "under the necessity of giving notice, that the Institution cannot be reopened upon its present footing." And what is the sum they require?— what sum will preserve the University?—what sum will establish this Great Fountain of Intelligence, in the heart of the richest and vastest Metropolis in the world, and for the benefit of the most respectable bodies of dissent in the Christian community. One additional thousand a year!—It is for this paltry pittance that the Council are disquieted, and proprietors are appealed to. —See now the want of a paternal and providing State! In any other country, the Government would at once supply the deficiency. King's College, with a more lordly and extensive patronage, is equally mournful, when it turns to the pounds and pence part of the prospect; it has a necessity of completing "the River Front"; it calls upon the proprietors for an additional loan of ten per cent., and for their influence to obtain new subscriptions—the sum required is about 8000*l*. As they demand it merely as a loan, and promise speedy repayment, a State that watched over Education would be no less serviceable to King's College than to the London University.

At both these Universities the Medicine Class is the most numerous. At King's College the proportions are as follows (April 1833).

Regular Students for the prescribed
Course of Education 109
Occasional ditto in *various* departments of Science and Literature 196
                                      305

Medical Department
Regular Students for the whole
Course of Medical Education .. 77
Occasional ditto in various branches
of Medical Science 233
                     310—Total 615.

I am informed, too, that of the general Lectures, those upon Chemistry are the most numerously attended.

At the London University, February 1833, the proportions are in favour of Medical Science.

Faculties of Arts and Law 148
———— of Medicine 283
                                    431

The Medical Students have increased in number progressively.

At the London University there is a just complaint of the indifference to that class of sciences, the knowledge of which is not profitable to the possessor in a pecuniary point of view, but which exert a great influence on the "wellbeing of society," viz., Moral Philosophy—Political Economy and Jurisprudence. "It was in order," say the Council, "to afford opportunities for the study of these sciences, and to confer on this country the facilities given by foreign universities, that this university was mainly founded and supported. The advantage of these studies, being rather felt by their gradual operation upon society, than by any specific benefit to the possessor, *the taste for them must be created by pointing out the nature of these advantages to the public and to the student:* in other words, the study must be produced by teaching them."

This, sir, is in the spirit of your own incontrovertible argument for endowments—viz., that the higher and less worldly studies must be *obtruded* upon men—they will not seek them of themselves. This obtrusion ought not to be left to individuals —it is the proper province of the State.

At King's College there is no professorship of Moral Philosophy, that study is held to be synonymous with Divinity. In my survey of the State of Morality, I think I shall be able to show, that no doctrine can be more mischievous to accurate morals and to uncorrupted religion.

To both these Universities schools are attached, and these I apprehend will prove much more immediately successful than the Colleges.

At the school attached to King's College, there are already (April 1833) 319 pupils.

At that belonging to the London University (February 1833) 249.

Viz., at the latter a number about equal to the number of boys at the ancient establishment of Westminster.

At King's College School, the business of each day commences with prayers and the reading of the scriptures; the ordinary educational system of the great public schools is adopted.

At the London University School there is a great, though perhaps a prudent, timidity in trying new educational systems; but there is less *learning by heart* than at other schools, and the wise and common result of all new systems, viz., the plan of a close and frequent questioning is carefully adopted.

At both Schools (and this is a marked feature in their system) there is strict abstinence from corporal punishment.

In both these Universities the Schools answer better than the Colleges, and have immeasurably outstripped the latter in the numeral progression of students, because the majority of pupils are intended for commercial pursuits, and their education ceases at sixteen; viz., the age at which the instruction of the College commences. If this should continue, and the progressing School supplant the decaying College, the larger experiment in both Universities will have failed and the two Colleges be merely additional cheap schools pursuing the old system, and speedily falling into the old vices of tuition.

Be it observed, that the terms at neither of these Universities, (or rather at the schools attached to them, for Universities, now-adays, can scarcely be intended for the poor, viz., the working poor,)[1] are low enough to admit the humble, and are, therefore, solely calculated to comprehend the children of the middling, orders.

1. The school tuition, at King's College, is for boys, nominated by a pro-prietor, 15*l*. 15*s*. per annum. To boys not so nominated, 18*l*. 11*s*. per annum. The school tuition for those at the London University is 15*l*. a year.

III

Popular Education

I shall not enter into any general proofs of the advantage of general education: I shall take that advantage for granted. In my mind, the necessity of instruction was settled by one aphorism centuries ago: "Vice we can learn of ourselves; but virtue and wisdom require a tutor."[1] If this principle be disrupted, the question yet rests upon another: "We are not debating now whether or not the people shall be instructed—that has been determined long ago—but whether they shall be *well* or *ill* taught."[2]

With these two sentences I shall rest this part of my case, anxious to avoid all superflous exordium and to come at once to the pith and marrow of the subject.[3]

1. Seneca.
2. Lord Brougham.
3. Persons who contend that *individuals* may not be the better for Education, as an argument against *general* Instruction, forget that, like Christianity and civilization, it is upon the wholesale character of large masses, that it is its nature to *act*. Thus Livingstone, the American statesman, informs us, such success has attended the Schools at Boston, "that though they have been in operation more than ten years, and on an average more than 3000 have been educated at them every year, *not one of those* educated there has been ever committed for a crime. In New York, a similar effect has been observed. Of the thousands educated in the public schools of that city, taken generally from the *poorest* classes, but one, it has been asserted, has ever been committed, and that for a trifling offence."—Livingstone's *Introductory Report to the Code of Prison Discipline for Louisiana*. Now, just as a curiosity, read the following account of a certain people many years ago: "At country-weddings, markets, burials, and other the like public occasions, both men and women are to be seen per-

If ever, sir—a hope which I will not too sanguinely form—if ever the people of this country shall be convinced that a government should be strong, not feeble—that it should be a providing government and not a yielding one—that it should foresee distant emergencies and not remedy sudden evils (sudden! a word that ought not to exist for a great legislator—for nothing in the slow development of events is sudden—all incidents are the effects of causes, and the causes should be regulated, not the effects repaired);—if ever we should establish, as our political creed, that a STATE should never be taken by surprise, nor the minds of its administrators be occupied in hasty shifts, in temporary expedients, in the petty policies and bolsterings up and empirical alteratives of the Hour; if ever we should learn to legislate afar off, and upon a great system—preparing the Public Mind and not obeying—masters of the vast machine and not its tools; if ever that day should arrive, I apprehend that one of the first axioms we shall establish will be this: Whatever is meant for the benefit of the people shall not be left to chance operation, but shall be administered by the guardians of the nation. Then, sir, we shall have indeed, as Prussia and Holland already enjoy—as France is about to possess—A NATIONAL EDUCATION. Without incessant watchfulness—without one unsleeping eye for ever over Public Institutions—they become like wastes and commons, open apparently to all, productive of benefits to none.

Never was this truth more clearly displayed than in the state of our popular education. Behold our numberless charities, sown throughout the land.—Where is their fruit?—What better meant, or what more abused? In no country has the education of the poor been more largely endowed by individuals—it fails —and why? Because in no country has it been less regarded by the government. Look at those voluminous Reports, the result of Lord Brougham's inquiry into Charities, some thirteen years ago. What a profusion of Endowments! What a mass of in-

---

petually *drunk, cursing, blaspheming,* and *fighting* together." What people is it, thus described?—*The Scotch!* The moral, sober, orderly Scotch people—such as they were in the time of Fletcher of Saltoun, whose words these are! Is this a picture of existing Scotland? No! Existing Scotland is educated!

iquities! Let me once more evoke from the ill-merited oblivion into which it hath fallen, the desolate and spectral instance of Pocklington School! Instance much canvassed, but never controverted! This school is largely endowed; it has passed into decay; its master possessed an income of 900*l.* a year! How many boys do you think were taught upon that stipend?—*One!* —positively one! Where is the school itself?—The school, sir! it is a saw-pit! Where is the schoolmaster?—Lord bless you, sir, he is hiding himself from his creditors! Good Heavens! and is there no one to see to these crying abuses?—To be sure, sir, the Visiters of the school are the Master and Fellows of St. John's Cambridge.[4] Now then, just take a drive to Berkhamstead; that school is very richly endowed; the schoolmaster teaches one pupil, and the usher resides in Hampshire!

These are but two out of a mass of facts that prove how idle are endowments where the nation does not appoint one general system of vigilant *surveillance*—how easily they are abused— with what lubricity they glide from neglect into decay!

But if the poor have been thus cheated of one class of schools, they have been ousted from another. Our ancestors founded certain great schools (that now rear the nobles, the gentry, and the merchants) for the benefit of the poor. The Charter-house —Winchester—King's College, were all founded "pro pauperes et indigentes scholares," for poor and indigent scholars. In 1562, 141 sons of the inhabitants of Shrewsbury were at that ancient school, 125 of whom were below the ranks of squires or bailiffs. From the neighbouring district there came 148 boys, of whom 123 were below the rank of squire, *so that out of 289 boys, 248 were of the lower or middle class! Our* age has no conception of the manner in which education spread and wavered; now advancing, now receding, among the people of the *former* age. And, reverently be it said, the novels of Scott have helped to

4. It seems, however, by a letter (imputed to Dr. Ireland, Vicar of Croydon) to Sir William Scott, that the omission of the worthy Master and Fellows of St. John's in exercising their visitorial powers, originated in the uncertainty of their right rather than any neglect of duty. But uncertainty of a right, where such revenues, such public benefits were concerned! Can there be a greater evidence of abuse? What long neglect must have produced that uncertainty! Is not this a proof that educational endowment cannot be left to the inspection of distant Visiters, however respectable and honest as individuals.

foster the most erroneous notions of the ignorance of our ancestors—a tolerable antiquarian in ballads, the great author was
a most incorrect one in facts.[5] At that crisis of our history, a
crisis, indeed, of the history of Europe, which never yet has been
profoundly analyzed, I mean the reign of Richard II., the nobles
wished to enact a law to repress the desire of knowledge that
had begun to diffuse itself throughout the lower orders. The
statute of Henry VIII. prohibits reading the Bible privately—to
whom? To lords and squires?—No!—to husbandmen and labourers, artificers or servants of yeomen. A law that could
scarcely have occurred to the legislators of the day, if husbandmen, labourers, artificers, or servants of yeomen, had been *unable
to read at all!* The common investigator ponders over the history
of our great Church Reform; he marvels at the readiness of the
people to assist the king in the destruction of those charitable
superstitions; he is amazed at the power of the king—at the
rapidity of the revolution. He does not see how little it was the
work of the king, and how much the work of the people; he
does not see that the growth of popular education had as much
to do with that Reform as the will of the grasping Tudor. Let
me whisper to him a fact: Within thirty years prior to that Reformation, more grammar-schools had been established than had
been known for 200 years before! Who, ignorant of that fact
shall profess to instruct us in the history of that day? The blaze
is in Reform, but the train was laid in Education. As the nobles
grew less warlike, they felt more the necessity of intelligence for
themselves;[6] the court of the schoolmaster replaced that of the
baron; their sons went to the schools originally intended for the
humbler classes, the gentry followed their example, and as the
school was fed from a distance, the abashed and humiliated
pupils of the town diminished. Another proof how Custom

5. "*Equally* distinguished," said Lord Salisbury of Sir Walter Scott, at a
meeting at the Mansion-house in aid of the Abbotsford subscription—"*equally*
distinguished as a poet, an historian, and an antiquarian."—That was not
saying much for him as a poet! God defend our great men in future from the
panegyrics of a marquis!

6. Latimer complains with great bitterness, "that there are none now but
great men's sons at college"; and that "the devil hath got himself to the university, and causeth great men and esquires to send their sons thither, and put
out *poor scholars* that should be divines."

weans institutions from their original purpose;—how, if left to the mercy of events, the rich, by a necessary law of social nature, encroach upon the poor;—how necessary it is for the education of the people, that a government should watch over its endowments, and compel their adherence to their original object.

A great progress in popular education was made fifty years ago, by the establishment of Sunday Schools, and the efforts of the benevolent Raikes, of Gloucestershire; a still greater by the Bell and Lancaster Systems in 1797 and 1798. The last gave an impetus to education throughout the country. And here, sir, let us do justice to the clergy of our established church. No men have been more honourably zealous in their endeavours to educate the poor. They have not, perhaps, been sufficiently eager to enlighten the poor *man;* but they have cheerfully subscribed to educate the poor *boy.* I find them supporters of the Sunday and Infant Schools, of the School Societies, &c.; but I never see them the encouragers of Mechanics' Institutes, nor the petitioners against the Taxes upon Knowledge. Why is this? the object in both is the same. Education closes not with the boy—education is the work of a life. Let us, however, be slow to blame them; it may be that, accused by indiscriminate champions of knowledge, they have not considered the natural effects of the diffusion of knowledge itself. They may imagine, that knowledge, unless chained solely to religious instruction, is hostile to religion. But, for the poor, religion must be alway; they want its consolations; they solace themselves with its balm. Revelation is their Millennium—their great Emancipation. Thus in America,[7] knowledge

---

7. In an oration delivered at Philadelphia by Mr. Ingersoll, in 1832, the following fine passage occurs. Speaking of the religious spirit so rife throughout the States, the orator insists on religion as a necessary result of popular power. "Even Robespierre," saith he, "in his remarkable discourse on the restoration of public worship, denounced atheism as inconsistent with equality, and a *crime of the aristocracy;* and asserted the existence of a Supreme Being, who protects the poor, and rewards the just, as a popular consolation, without which the people would despair. *If there were no God,"* said he, *"we should be obliged to invent one."* This fine sentiment bespeaks truly the sympathies of Republican governments with that faith which the author of Christianity brought into the world; laying its foundations on the corner-stones of equality, peace, good will —*it would contradict all philosophy if this country were irreligious."* But Mr. Ingersoll errs in attributing that noble sentiment to Robespierre—it is a quotation from Voltaire; the thought runs thus, and is perhaps the finest Voltaire ever put into words: "Si Dieu n'existoit pas il faudroit l'inventer."

is the most diffused, and Religion is the most fondly, and enthusiastically beloved. There you may often complain of its excess, but rarely of its absence. To America I add the instances of Holland, of Germany, and of Scotland.

I take pleasure in rendering due homage to the zeal of our country's clergy. One-third part of all the children educated in England are educated under their care; and in vindicating them, let us vindicate, from a vulgar and ignorant aspersion, a great truth: The Christian clergy throughout the world have been the great advancers and apostles of education. And even in the darker ages, when priestcraft was to be overthrown, it received its first assaults from the courageous enlightenment of priests.

A far greater proportion of the English population are now sent to school than is usually supposed, and currently stated. I see before me at this moment, a statistical work, which declares the proportion to be only one in 17 for England, one in 20 for Wales. What is the fact? Why, that our population for England and Wales amounts nearly to 14 millions, and that the number of children receiving elementary education in 1828 are, by the returns, 1,500,000. An additional 500,000 being supposed, not without reason, to be educated at independent schools, not calculated in the return. Thus, out of a population of 14 millions, we have no less than two millions of children receiving elementary education at schools.

In the number of schools and of pupils, our account, on the whole, is extremely satisfactory. Where then do we fail? Not in the schools, but in the instruction that is given there: a great proportion of the poorer children attend only Sunday-schools, and the education of once a week is not very valuable; but generally throughout the primary schools, nothing is taught but a little spelling, a very little reading—still less writing—the Catechism —the Lord's Prayer, and an unexplained unelucidated chapter or two in the Bible;—add to these the nasal mastery of a Hymn, and an undecided conquest over the rule of Addition, and you behold a very finished education for the poor. The schoolmaster and the schoolmistress, in these academies, know little themselves beyond the bald and meagre knowledge that they teach; and are much more fit to go to school than to give instructions. Now the object of education is to make a reflective, moral, prudent, loyal, and healthy people. A little reading and writing of themselves contribute very doubtfully to that end. Look to Ireland: does not the Archbishop of Cashel tell us, that a greater proportion of the peasantry in Ireland, yes, even in Tipperary, can read and write, than can be found amidst a similar amount of population in England? I have been favoured with some unpublished portions of the recent evidence on the Poor-laws. Just hear what Mr. Hickson, a most intelligent witness, says on this head:

Query. "Are you of opinion that an efficient system of National Education would materially improve the condition of the labouring classes?"

Answer. "Undoubtedly; but I must beg leave to observe, that something more than the mere teaching to read and write is necessary for the poorer classes. Where books and newspapers[8] are inaccessible, the knowledge of the art of reading avails nothing; I have met with adults who, after having been taught to read and write when young, have almost entirely forgotten those arts for want of opportunities to exercise them."

"At the Sunday-schools," observes Mr. Hickson, afterwards, "of most Dissenters, nothing is taught generally—I except rare instances—but reading the Bible and repeating Hymns."

While we have so many schools organized, and while so little is taught there, just let me lead your attention to the four common class-books taught at all the popular schools of Saxe Weimar.

The first class-book is destined for the youngest children; it contains, in regular gradations, the alphabet, the composition of syllables, punctuation, elementary formation of language, slight stories, sentences or proverbs of one verse upwards, divers selections, sketches, &c. "The sentences," says Mr. Cousin, "struck

8. I am happy to find in this witness a practical evidence of the advantage of repealing the stamp duty on newspapers, an object which I have so zealously laboured to effect.—"I believe," says he, in his answer to the Commissioners, "that the Penny Magazines will work usefully, but cheap newspapers would do much more good. I have found it difficult to create an interest in the mind of an ignorant man on matters of mere general literature; but his attention is easily enlisted by a narrative of the stirring events of the day, or local intelligence. . . . The dearness of newspapers in this country is an insurmountable obstacle to the education of the poor. I could name twenty villages within a circuit of a few miles, in which a newspaper is never seen from one year's end to the other."—"Evidence of Mr. Hickson" (unpublished).

me particularly—they contain, in the most agreeable shapes, the most valuable lessons, which the author classes under systematic titles—such as our duties to ourselves, our duties to men, our duties to God—and the knowledge of His divine attributes, —so that in the germ of Literature, the infant receives also the germ of Morals, and of Religion!"

The second book for the use of children from eight to ten is not only composed of amusing sketches—the author touches upon matters of general utility. He proceeds on the just idea that the knowledge of the faculties of the soul ought a little to precede the more profound explanations of religion;—under the head of dialogue between a father and his children; the Book treats first, of man and his physical qualities; secondly, of the nature of the soul and of its faculties, with some notions of our powers of progressive improvement and our heritage of immortality; and, thirdly, it contains the earliest and simplest elements of natural history, botany, minerality, &c.

The third work contains two parts, each divided into two chapters: the first part is an examination of man as a rational animal—it resolves these questions: What am I? What am I able to do? What *ought* I to do? It teaches the distinction between men and brutes—instinct and reason—it endeavours to render the great moral foundations of truth clear and simple by familiar images and the most intelligible terms.

As the first chapter of this portion exercises the more reflective faculties, so the second does not neglect the more acute, and compromises songs, enigmas, fables, aphorisms, &c.

The second part of the third work contains first, the elements of natural history in all its subdivisions—notions of geography —of the natural rights of man—of his civil rights—with some lessons of general history. An Appendix comprises the geography and especial history of Saxe Weimar. The fourth book, not adapted solely for Saxe Weimar, is in great request throughout all Germany, it addresses itself to the more advanced pupils— it resembles a little the work last described, but is more extensive on some points; it is equally various, but it treats in especial more minutely on the rights and duties of subjects—it proceeds to conduct the boy, already made rational as a being, to his duties as a citizen. Such are the four class-books in the popular schools of Saxe Weimar, such are the foundation of that united, intellectual, and lofty spirit which marks the subjects of that principality.[9]

Pardon me if I detain you, sir, somewhat longer on the important comparison of England with other states. Pardon me, if from the petty duchy of Saxe Weimar, which to the captious may seem so easy to regulate, I turn to the kingdom of Prussia, containing a population almost similar to our own; and like our own also broken up into a variety of religious sects. There, universal education is made a necessary, pervading, paramount, principle of the state. Let us see what is there taught at the popular schools, established in every district, town, and village, throughout the kingdom.

The Prussian law, established in 1819, distinguishes two degrees in popular education, *les écoles élémentaires, et les écoles bourgeoises.*

What is the object of these two schools—the law thus nobly explains:

> To develop the faculties of the soul, the reason, the senses, and the physical frame. It shall embrace religion and morals, the knowledge of size and numbers, of nature, and of man, the exercises of the body, vocal music, drawing, and writing.
>
> Every elementary school includes necessarily the following objects:
>
> Religious instruction for the formation of Morality, according to the positive truths of Christianity.
>
> The Language of the Country.
>
> The Elements of Geometry and the general principles of Drawing.
>
> Practical Arithmetic.
>
> The Elements of Physical Philosophy, of Geography, of general History; but especially of the history of the pupil's own country. These branches of knowledge [to be sparingly and drily taught? *No!* the law adds] to be taught and retaught as often as possible, by the opportunities afforded in learning to read and write, independently of the particular and special lessons given upon those subjects.
>
> The Art of Song—to develop the voice of children—*to elevate*

9. I know nothing we more want in this country than good class-books for the use of popular schools; books that shall exercise the judgment and teach children to *reflect*. Such works should be written by a person of philosophical mind, practised in education, and linked to no *exclusive system,* the curse of knowledge in this country.

their minds—to improve and ennoble both popular and sacred melodies.

Writing and the gymnastic exercises, which fortify our senses, especially that of sight.

The more simple of the manual arts, and some instructions upon agricultural labours.

Such is the programme of the education of elementary schools in Prussia; an education that exercises the reason, enlightens the morals, fortifies the body, and founds the disposition to labour and independence. Compare with that programme our Sunday-schools, our dame-schools, all our thrifty and meagre reservoirs of miserly education! But what, sir, you will admire in the Prussian system is not the laws of education only, but the spirit that framed and pervades the laws—the full appreciation of the dignity and objects of men—of the duties of citizens—of the powers, and equality, and inheritance of the human soul. And yet in that country the people are said to be less *free* than in ours!—how immeasurably more the people are *regarded!*

At the more advanced school—(*L'Ecole Bourgeoise*)—are taught,

Religion and Morals.

The National tongue; Reading, composition, exercises of style and of the invention; the study of the National Classics.

Latin is taught to all children, under certain limitation, *in order to exercise their understanding;*[10]—even whether or no they are destined to advance to the higher schools, or to proceed at once to their professions or trades.

The Elements of Mathematics, and an accurate and searching study of practical Arithmetic.

Physical Philosophy, so far as the more important phenomena of Nature are concerned.

Geography and History combined; so as to give the pupil a knowledge of the divisions of the Earth, and the History of the World.—Prussia, its History, Laws, Constitution, shall be the object of especial study.

The principles of Drawing, at all occasions.

Writing, Singing, and Gymnastic Exercises.

10. This is the great object of other studies, that may seem at first super-fluous; such as the elements of geography or mathematics. It is not for themselves that they are useful—it is for the manner in which they task and exercise the faculties: the knowledge, comparatively speaking, is nothing—the *process* of acquiring it is every thing.

This is the education given by Prussia to all her children. Observe, here is no theory—no programme of untried experiments:—this is the actual education, actually given, and actually received. It is computed that thirteen out of fifteen children from the age of seven to that of fourteen are at the public schools: the remaining two are probably at the private schools, or educated at home; so that the *whole* are educated—and *thus* educated! Observe, this is no small and petty state easily managed and controlled—it is a country that spreads over large tracks—various tribes—different languages—multiform religions:—the energy of good government has conquered all these difficulties. Observe, the account I give is taken from no old—no doubtful—no incompetent authority: it is from the work just published—not of a native, but a foreigner;—not of a credulous tourist—not of a shallow bookmaker, but of an eyewitness—of an investigator;—of a man accustomed to observe, to reflect, to educate others; in a word—of one of the profoundest and most eminent men in France—of a counsellor of state—of a professor of philosophy —of a Member of the Royal Counsel of Public Instruction—of a man who brings to examination the acutest sagacity—who pledges to its accuracy the authority of the highest name—it is the report of Victor Cousin! He undertakes the investigation— he publishes the account—at the request of a French minister, and to assist in the formation of a similar system in France. I have introduced some part of his evidence, for the first time, to the notice of English readers, that they may know what *can* be done by seeing what *is* done—that they may resent and arouse the languor of their own government by a comparison with the vivifying energy of government elsewhere. I know that in so doing I have already kindled a spark that shall not die. In the phrase of Cousin himself, with the exception of one word, "It is of Prussia that I write, but it is of *England* that I think!"

As this subject is one of immense importance, (though somewhat dry, perhaps, for the ordinary reader,) I have pursued it further in detail, and those interested in the question will find in the Appendix A the result of my observations.—I have therein suggested the outline of a practical system of Universal Education—I have advocated the necessity of making religion a vital component of instruction—I have shewn in what manner (by adopting the wise example of Prussia) we can obviate the obstacles of hostile sects, and unite them in a plan of education which shall comprehend religion, yet respect all religious differences. In giving the heads of a national education, I have shewn also in what manner the expenses may be defrayed.

Before I conclude, I must make one reflection. Whatever education be established, the peace and tranquility of social order require that in its main principles it *should be tolerably equal,* and that it should penetrate every where. We may observe (and this is a most important and startling truth) that nearly all social excesses arise, not from intelligence, but from *inequalities* of intelligence. When Civilization makes her efforts by starts and convulsions, her progess may be great, but it is marked by terror and disaster;—when some men possess a far better education than others of the same rank, the first are necessarily impelled to an unquiet Ambition, and the last easily misled into becoming its instruments and tools: Then vague discontents and dangerous rivalries prevail—then is the moment when demagogues are dangerous, and visionaries have power. Such is the Spirit of Revolutions, in which mankind only pass to wisdom through a terrible interval of disorder. But where Intelligence is equalized —and flows harmonious and harmonizing throughout all society —then one man can possess no blinding and dangerous power over the mind of another—then demagogues are harmless and theories safe. It is this equality of knowledge, producing unity of feeling, which, if we look around, characterizes whatever nations seem to us the most safe in the present ferment of the world —no matter what their more material form of constitution— whether absolute Monarchy or unqualified Republicanism. If you see safety, patriotism, and order in the loud democracy of America, you behold it equally in the despotism of Denmark, and in the subordination of Prussia. Denmark has even refused a free constitution, because in the freedom of a common knowledge she hath found content. It is with the streams that refresh and vivify the Moral World as with those in the Material Earth— *they tend and struggle to their level!* Interrupt or tamper with this great law, and city and cottage, tower and temple, may be swept away. Preserve unchecked its vast but simple operation, and the waters will glide on in fertilizing and majestic serenity, to the illimitable ocean of Human Perfectibility.

IV

View of the State of Religion

It is an acute, though fanciful observation of Gibbon's, that "in the profession of Christianity, the variety of national characters may be clearly distinguished. The natives of Syria and Egypt abandoned their lives to lazy and contemplative devotion: Rome again aspired to the dominion of the world, and the wit of the lively and loquacious Greeks was consumed in the disputes of metaphysical theology." If we apply the notion to existing times, we may suppose also that we trace in the religion of the Germans their contemplative repose, and household tenderness of sentiment; in that of the Americans, their impatience of control, and passion for novel speculations; that the vain and warlike French stamp on their rites their passion for the solemnities of show, and the graces of stage effect; while the commercial and decorous inhabitants of England manifest in their religion, their attachment to the decency of forms, and the respectability of appearances. Assuredly, at least amongst us, the outward and visible sign is esteemed the best, perhaps the only, token of the inward and spiritual grace. We extend the speculations of this world to our faith in another, and give credit to our neighbour in proportion to his external respectabilities.

There is, sir, in this country, and in this age, a certain spirit of rationalism, the result of that material philosophy which I shall hereafter contend we have too blindly worshipped; a certain desire to be logical in all things; to define the illimitable, and demonstrate the undemonstrable, that is at variance with the glowing and ardent devotion, which Religion, demanding eternal sacrifice of self interests and human passions, must appear to a larger wisdom necessarily to demand. A light and depreciating habit of wit, taught the people of France the desire of moderating belief by reason, till with them belief, deprived of its very essence, has almost ceased to exist at all. In England, that soberizing love of what is termed common sense, that commercial aversion from the Poetical and Imaginative, save in the fictitious alone, which characterizes this nation, tends greatly to the same result. The one people would make religion the subject of wit, the other, more reverent, but not more wise, would reduce it to a matter of business. But if we profess religion at all, if we once convince ourselves of its nobler and more exalting uses, of its powers to elevate the virtues, as well as to check the crimes, of our kind, we must be careful how we tear it from the support of the emotions, and divorce from its allegiance the empire of the heart.

To comprehend the effects, to sustain the penalties, to be imbued with the ardour of religion, we must call up far more trustful and enterprising faculties than reason alone; we must enlist in its cause all the sentiment, and all the poetry of our nature. To the great work of God we must apply the same order of criticism we apply to the masterpieces of men. We do not examine the designs of Raffaelle, or the soaring genius of Milton, with mathematical analogies. We do not externally ask, with the small intellect of the logician, "What do they prove?" We endeavour to scan them by the same imagining powers from which they themselves were wrought. We imbue our notions with the grandeur of what we survey, and we derive from, not bring to, that examination alone, the large faith of that ideal and immaterial philosophy, which we reject alone when we examine what still more demand its exercise—the works of God.

Ambition—Glory—Love—exercise so vast an influence over the affairs of earth, because they do not rest upon the calculations of reason alone; because they are supported by all that constitutes the Ideal of Life, and drink their youth and vigour from the inspiring Fountains of the Heart. If Religion is to be equally powerful in its effects—if it is to be a fair competitor with more worldly rivals—if its office is indeed to combat and counterbalance the Titan passions which, for ever touching earth, for ever take from earth new and gigantic life—if it is to

Allure to brighter worlds, and lead the way,

—it must call around itself all the power we can raise; to defeat the passions, the passions must feed it; it can be no lukewarm and dormant principle, hedged in, and crippled by that reason which, in our actions, fetters nothing else. It has nothing to do with rationalism; it must be a sentiment, an emotion, for ever present with us—pervading, colouring and exalting all. Sensible of this, the elder propagators of all creeds endeavour to connect them, equally as love and glory, with the poetry of life. Religion wanes from a nation, as poetry vanishes from religion. The creeds of states, like their constitutions, to renew their youth, must return to their first principles. It is necessary for us at this time to consider deeply on their truths; for many amongst us, most anxious, perhaps to preserve religion, are for ever attempting to attenuate its powers. Rationality and Religion are as much contradictions in terms as Rationality and Love. Religion is but love with a sacred name, and for a sacred object—it is the love of God. Philosophy has no middle choice; it can decide only between scepticism and ardent faith.

There is a sort of semi-liberalism, common to the aristocracies of all nations, and remarkable in the Whig portion of the aristocracy in this, which is favourable neither to pure religion nor to high morality; it is the result of a confined knowledge of the world, the knowledge of circles and coteries. Men who run a course of indolence and pleasure, acquire in the career an experience of the small and more debasing motives of their kind; they apply that experience universally. They imagine that all professions are hollow, from their conviction of the hypocrisies common with the great. With them, indeed, virtue is but a name; they believe in sober earnest, the truth of Fielding's ironical definitions:

> Patriot—A candidate for place.
> Politics—The art of getting one.
> Knowledge—Knowledge of the Town.
> Love—A word properly applied to our delight in particular kinds of food; sometimes *metaphorically* spoken of the favourite objects of our appetites.

Virtue ⎱
Vice ⎰ Subjects of discourse.

Worth—Power, rank, wealth.

Wisdom—The art of acquiring all three.[1]

This code they propagate through the means of the influence which we call Fashion; and morality becomes undermined by a disbelief in its existence. Mignet has observed profoundly that "in revolutions a man soon becomes what he is believed." In ordinary times, a whole people may become what they are constantly asserted to be. The Romans preserved a species of rude and gigantic virtue, so long as they were told it was natural to Romans. The patrician *roués* preceding Cæsar's time, set the fashion of asserting the corruptibility of all men, till what was declared to be common ceased to be a disgrace.

When we once ridicule the high and the generous, the effect extends to our legislation and our religion. In Parliament, the tone is borrowed from the profligates of a club. Few venture ever to address the nobler opinions, or appeal to the purer sentiments; and the favourite cast or oratory settles into attacks upon persons, and insinuations against the purity of parties.

A fellow-member of the present House of Commons—a man of great knowledge, and imbued with all the high philosophy we acquire in our closets, from deep meditation over settled principles, and a conviction that law-making ought to be the science of happiness—expressed to me very eloquently the disgustful surprise with which he found that the great characteristic of that assembly was the constant appeal to the lowest passions, and the incredulous ridicule that attached to all who professed the higher ones. It is not so with other popular assemblies; but it *is* so with the members of the National one: meeting every morning at clubs, and knowing intimately the motives of each other—they catch the sort of cleverness that characterized the friends of the Regent Orleans—a cleverness that depreciates and suspects—they write upon their minds the motto, 'No cant!' and what they do not comprehend they believe to be insincere,—as if there were a species of honesty which consisted in denying honesty itself!

1. *Covent-Garden Journal*, no. 3.

This habit of mind vulgarises the tone of eloquence, and we may trace its effect from the senate to the pulpit. A love for decencies, and decencies alone—a conclusion that all is vice which dispenses with them, and all hypocrisy which would step beyond them—damps the zeal of the established clergy: it is something disreputable to be too eloquent; the aristocratic world does not like either clergymen, or women, to make too much noise. A *very* popular preacher, who should, in the pulpit, be carried away by his fervour for the souls of his flock, who should use an extemporaneous figure of speech, or too vehement a gesticulation, would be considered as betraying the dignity of his profession.—Bossuet would have lost his character with us, and St. Paul have run the danger of being laughed at as a mountebank.

Walk into that sacred and well-filled edifice,—it is a fashionable church: you observe how well cleaned and well painted it is; how fresh the brass nails and the red cloth seem in the gentlefolks' pews; how respectable the clerk looks—the curate, too, is considered a very gentlemanlike young man.—The rector is going to begin the sermon: he is a very learned man, people say he will be a bishop one of these days, for he edited a Greek play, and was private tutor to Lord Glitter.—Now observe him—his voice, how monotonous!—his manner, how cold!—his face, how composed! yet what are his words?—"Fly the wrath that is to come.—Think, of your immortal souls. Remember, oh, remember! how terrible is the responsibility of life!—how strict the account!—how suddenly it may be demanded!" Are *these* his words; they are certainly of passionate import, and they are doled forth in the tone of a lazy man saying, "John, how long is it to dinner?" Why, if the calmest man in the world were to ask a gamekeeper not to shoot his favourite dog, he would speak with a thousand times more energy; and yet this preacher is endeavouring to save the souls of a whole parish—of all his acquaintance—all his friends—all his relations—his wife (the lady in the purple bonnet, whose sins no man doubtless knows better) and his six children, whose immortal welfare must be still dearer to him than their temporal advancement; and yet what a wonderful command over his emotions! I never saw a man so cool in my life! "But, my dear sir," says the fashionable purist, "that coolness is decorum; it is the proper characteristic of a clergyman of the established church."

Alas! Dr. Young did not think so, when finding he could not impress his audience sufficiently, he stopped short, and burst into tears.

Sir, Dr. Young was a great poet; but he was very well known not to be entirely orthodox.

This singular coldness—this absence of eloquence, almost of the appearance of human sympathy, which characterize the addresses of the Established Church, are the result of the Aristocratic Influences, which setting up Ridicule as the criminal code, produce what is termed *good taste* as the rule of conduct. The members of the Aristocracy naturally give the tone to the members of the Established Church, and thus the regard for the conventional quiet of good breeding destroys the enthusiasm that should belong to the Preacher of Religion. A certain bishop, a prelate of remarkable sense and power of mind, is so sensible of the evils that may result to religion itself from this almost ludicrous lukewarmness of manner in its pastor, that he is actually accustomed to send such young clergymen as he is acquainted with to take lessons in delivery from Mr. Jones, the celebrated actor, in order that they may learn to be warm and study to be in earnest.

The critical axiom "to make me feel, you must seem yourself to feel," is as applicable to the pulpit as to the rostrum—to the sermon as the drama.

The eloquent Channing has insisted forcibly upon this point. He proposes, even in his discourse on *"Increasing the Means of Theological Education,"* a professorship that shall embrace for its object *sacred eloquence* and instruction in pastoral duty. "It should be designed," saith he, "to instruct candidates for the ministry in the composition and delivery of sermons, and in the best methods of impressing the human mind and to awaken an enlightened zeal and ardour in the performance of all the offices of ministerial life. What serious and reflective man is not often reminded on the Sabbath, of the painful truth, that some institution is needed to train our ministers for the impressive and effectual discharge of their duty."

It often happens, when we compare the largeness of the living with the apathy of the preacher, that we cannot but exclaim with the Prince of Conti, "Alas! our good God is but very ill served for his money."

The influence of the higher classes upon religion is frequently pernicious in this—the livings of the Church are chiefly the property of the Aristocracy; and the patron of a benefice naturally and pardonably, perhaps, bestows it in general, on his own relations or intimate acquaintances. Thus the preaching of salvation really becomes a family office, and the wildest rakes of a college are often especially devoted to the hereditary cure of souls. Any one who has received an university education, knows well how common it is to see among the noisiest and wildest students (student *a non-studendo*) the future possessor of the most tempting specimens of preferment. Let me be just, however, and confess that the consequences are not so flagrantly bad as they would seem to a mere theoretical observer—the rake once made a clergyman, usually alters prodigiously in external seeming—you see very few clergymen in the English Church of known licentious habits, or notoriously prone to excesses. The decorum which numbs the generous fervour of virtue restrains the irregular tendencies to vice—the moral air chills and controls the young pastor suddenly transplanted to it, and he puts on with his snowy surplice a correspondent external of decent life. But though the neophyte ceases to be a *bad* man, I doubt exceedingly if he can be said to become a *good* one.[2] He enters into the com-

2. Burnet observes, that "in his time, our clergy had less authority and were under more contempt, than those of any other church in Europe, for they were much the most remiss in their labours and the least severe in their lives— *it was not that their lives were scandalous; he entirely acquitted them of any such imputation, but they were not as exemplary as it became them to be.*"— *Southey's Wesley,* p. 324.

Mr. Southey himself allows the cause for the past complaint, though he would start from conceding it in the present, viz.—that the ecclesiastics, owing to individual Lay patronage, are not enough taken from the people and too much from the gentry. Just observe the truth and logical soundness of the following passage: "Under the Reformed as well as under the Romish establishment, the clerical profession offered an easy and honourable provision for the younger sons of the *gentry;* but the Church of Rome had provided stations for them, where, if they were not qualified for active service, their sins of omission would be of a very trivial kind. The Monasteries had always a large proportion of such persons—they went through the ceremonies of their respective rules, &c.—their lack of ability or learning brought no disgrace to themselves, for they were not in a situation where either was required, and their inefficiency was not injurious to the great establishment of which though an inert, they were in no wise an inconvenient body. *But when such persons, instead of entering the convents which their ancestors had endowed, were settled upon family livings as parochial clergy, then indeed a serious evil was*

mon moralities of social existence; visits, feasts, plays a rubber, and reads the *John Bull,* according to the appointed orbit of hebdomandary pursuits. But where that continued self-sacrifice —where that exalted charity—where that intimate familiarity with the poor—that unwearied exertion for their comfort, their education, their improvement—that household sympathy with their wants—that tender control over their conduct, which Goldsmith might paint, but which Oberlin practised?—you find these virtues in many of our clergy, but not in that class to which I now refer. There is a wide chasm between the flock and the shepherd—the orbit of the preacher may be regular, but it throws little light or warmth upon the habitations of the poor.

It will be easily seen that this separation between the clergyman and the humbler portion of his charge, and which is so peculiar to England, is the result of the same influence, visible throughout the whole workings of the social system. The aristocratic doctrine which makes it so imperiously necessary for clergymen to be "gentlemen"—which makes the pastor a member of an aristocratic profession—renders him subject to all the notions of the aristocracy; it makes him passionless in the pulpit, but decorous in his habits, and it fits him rather, not to shock the prejudices of the drawing-room, than to win the sympathies of the cottage. Grant him the best intentions, his situation scarcely allows him to execute them; if he be rich, or well endowed, he must keep up his dignity, or his parish is too large to go all over it himself. He gives soup and coals, and ministers to public charities, but he does not make himself a household name in every poor man's hearth.[3] He is respected, not influential from the very distance at which he is respected. He is a good man, but he is

<hr />

done to the character of the church, and to the religious feelings of the nation —their want of aptitude or inclination for the important office into which they had been thrust, then became a fearful thing for themselves and a miserable calamity for the people committed to their charge."

The evil cause still exists. Believe me, Mr. Southey, that the emulation to which Wesley excited the establishment, produced but a momentary cure of the evil effect.

3. The Bishop of London says truly, in his evidence before Sir A. Agnews's Committee, that *"Mere sermons from the pulpit, with reference to the lower classes, will seldom effectually inculcate any religious duty if the clergyman does not follow up his instruction by private conversations."* How rare are such conversations!

too great a man. You may say of his tribe as Bacon says of the philosophers. "They are as the stars, which give little light because they are so high." Now, take the poor curate, these are not the dignified difficulties of situation which surround him, but he has his own. He is poor, but he is a gentleman; he is proud, he knows his birth and station, he cannot let himself down. *He has his very poverty to keep up.* He can preach to the boor, he can pity him, nay he will pinch himself to relieve, but he can scarcely visit him very often. Thus a certain pride attends the established preachers of humility, and feudal distinctions exist in religion while they vanish from politics. Charity ceases to be sympathy and becomes condescension. In order to see this more closely, let me here (first reminding the reader that we have remarked how much the aristocratic influences must pervade the clergy who on the aristocracy depend) state a fact which may be found in the Evidence in the Parliamentary Committee on the better Observance of the Sabbath. My Lord Bishop of London, permit me to address you, you whose clear judgment and wise piety adorn, and will, I trust, contribute to reform the Establishment. You assert in your evidence before the Committee that you are frustrated in your benevolent desire, that in the new churches the seats of the poor should be distributed among those of the rich, in order that the former might be so enabled to hear better the common word of God;—you assert that you are frustrated by what?—*the refusal of the rich whose contributions sustain the churches,* to allow so undignified an admixture! What an exemplification of the religion of the aristocracy, they subscribe to build churches, but on condition of retaining there the distinctions which out of church separate them from the poor! This principle undermines the safety of the establishment, and operates on the clergymen who are their younger sons, or were brought up at college with themselves. We unhappily direct that "The gorgeous palaces, and the solemn temples" shall stand in the same street, be lit by the same lamps and guarded by the same watchmen!

But while many of the established preachers are thus apart from the poor, the dissenters are *amongst* them, are *of* them: vehement in the pulpit, they address the passions of their flock; —familiar at their hearths, they secure their sympathies. Thus the poor choose some dissenting, instead of the established sect, much on the same principle as in the Tonga Islands it is customary for the inhabitants to choose a foster-mother even during the life of their natural parent, "with a view," says Mariner, "of being better provided with all necessaries and comforts." The mother church is indolent in dispensing spiritual consolation, in visiting intimately, in comforting, in cheering the poor; the foster-mother is sedulous and unwearied in these duties, for without such care she would receive no attachment in return. And she thus gradually weans from the first parent the love that she attracts towards herself.

There is another cause of weakness in the Established Church proceeding from that aristocratic composition which appears a part of its very strength. Its members never harmonize with the people in political opinion; they often take a severe and active course in direct opposition to the wishes of the Popular Heart. As a body, they are and profess themselves to be, wound up with the anti-popular and patrician party; whereas, the greater part of the dissenting sects are, more or less, favourers of the popular side; the latter thus acquire power by consulting opinion, and become the rulers of the poor by affecting to be their friends. Even where, in the case of the loyal and subordinate Wesleyan, the politics generally may incline to the powers that be, some individual point, some isolated but stirring question—to-day the Slavery Question, to-morrow the Factory Bill, occurs, on which the Wesleyan, no less than the bold and generous "Independent," is united with the most popular opinions. For I know not how it is, sir, but it seems to me, that wherever a man is very active on some point of humanity, he always finds himself suddenly surrounded by the great body of English People.

Let me not, however, be misconceived; I would not desire the preachers of a serene and passionless Religion to mix themselves ostentatiously with the politics of the day, or to be seen amidst the roar and tumult of democratic action; but surely, if they ought not to be active in support of the people, it is like laying a mine of gunpowder beneath their spiritual efficiency and their temporal power, to be distinguished in activity *against* them. Every unpopular vote of the bishops is a blow on the foundation of the church. Religion is the empire over the human heart;

alienate the heart, the empire necessarily departs. But if, sir, the composition of the church establishment were less exclusively aristocratic; if its members, as in its days of power and of purity, sprang more generally from the midst of the great multitudes they are to rule,[4] I apprehend that while they would be equally on the side of order and of strong government, their principles would be less exposed than at present to suspicion, and would seem to the people dictated rather by the sacred spirit of peace, than by the oligarchical and worldly influence of temporal connexions. And thus, sir, by a far-sighted and prophetic sagacity, thought the early patriarchs, and mighty men, of the Reformation. It is they who complained that general zeal and diffused learning would cease to be the characteristics of the clergy, exactly in proportion as the church should become more an established provision for the younger sons of the great. It is they who predicted that when the people saw none of their own order officiating in the ministry, the divine sympathy between flock and preacher would decay, and the multitude would seek that sympathy elsewhere, in schisms and sects. The lethargy of the Established Church is the life of Dissent.

But if the true benefit and natural influence of our Establishment be thus thwarted and diminished, let us seek to remedy,

---

4. The vulgar notion that "clergymen must be gentlemen born," is both an upstart and an insular opinion. Not so have thought the great founders of all powerful sects; not in so poor and small a policy has experience taught us that ecclesiastical influence is created. Look over the history of the world. Look how the mighty Papacy grew and spread. Her great men were chosen from the people, and so they connected and mingled themselves with the people's prejudices and love. Look (to take a lesser view of the question), look at the great divines, who are the light and galaxy of our own church. From what descent came the bold virtue of Latimer? What hereditary blood animated that unfaltering tongue which preached chastity to the Eighth Henry, and was eloquent with courage at the stake. Latimer was a yeoman's son! From whom came the studious thought, and the serene charity, and the copious *verve* of Barrow? Barrow was the son of a London trader. What progenitor claimed the subtile mind of Clarke, the champion of God himself?—A plain citizen of Norwich. To the middle class belonged the origin of the sturdy Warburton; of the venerable Hooker; of the gentle Tillotson, once the standard of all pulpit persuasion. From amongst the ranks of the people rose Taylor, the Milton of the church, whose power and pathos, and "and purple grandeur" of eloquence, beautified even piety itself. In fact the births of our great divines may be said to illustrate the principle of every powerful church which draws its vigour from the multitude and languishes only when confining its social influences to a court.

and not destroy it. It is a singular circumstance, that the two ablest defenders of an ecclesiastical Establishment have been a Dissenter and a Deist; the first, yourself; the second, David Hume;—a fact that may induce the philosophers of the day to be less intolerant in their accusations of those who support the expediency of an endowed church. Hume's aphorism, that where the support of the ecclesiastic depends wholly upon the people, he stimulates their zeal by all the quackeries of fanaticism, is, to my mind, amply borne out by the experience of America; it is not that religion is lost for want of an Establishment, but that it splits into a thousand forms, each vying with the other in heated and perverting extravagance. For the people never abandon a faith that flatters and consoles them; they are too apt, on the contrary, to carry it to excess. A mild and tolerant Establishment presents to the eye a certain standard of sober sense; and sectarianism thus rather forsakes the old abuses, than wanders with any wide success into new. I hold, that an abolition of our ecclesiastical establishment would, in this country, be followed up by a darkening and gloomy austerity. For nearly all sectarianism with us is indisposed to the arts, and the amusements that grace and brighten existence; and were the church no more, one sect vying with the other in religious zeal, the result would be an emulation of severities, and of mutual interference with the sunny pleasures of life. So that exactly the disposition we ought the most to discourage (in England especially, too prone to it already), we should the most strengthen and unite. The Church, with all failings it inherits from a too violent and therefore incomplete Reform at first, and a too rigid resistance to Reform subsequently, has still, in England, been a gentle, yet unceasing, counterpoise to any undue spirit of fanatical hypochondria. With all its aristocratic faults, too, we may observe, that in the rural districts it has often helped to resist the aristocratic ignorance of the country gentry. More enlightened than the mere squire, you will find the clerical magistrate possessing a far clearer notion of the duties of his office than the lay one; and nine times out of ten, wherever the Poor-laws have been well administered by a neighbouring magistrate, that magistrate is a clergyman. I leave, sir, your admirable argument untouched. I leave the reader to recall to his remembrance how wisely you have defended the establishment of churches, upon the same broad principle as that on which we defend the establishment of schools, viz., that mankind do not feel the *necessity* of religion and of knowledge so pressingly as they feel that of clothing and food; and the laws that regulate the physical supply and demand are not, therefore, applicable to those that regulate the moral; that we ought to leave men to *seek* the one, but we ought to *obtrude* upon them the other. What I insist upon is this—that an established church and sectarianism operate beneficially on each other; that a tolerated, instructed sect, incites the zeal of the establishment; and where *that* lies oppressed beneath abuses, it directs the Christian public to those abuses themselves: that, on the other hand, the sober and quiet dignity of an Establishment operates as a pressure upon the ebullitions of sectarian extravagance. Every man sees the errors of our Establishment, but few calculate the advantage of an Establishment itself. Few perceive how it carries through the heart of the nation, not only the light of the Gospel, but a certain light also of education—how it operates in founding schools for the poor, and exciting dissenters to a rivalry in the same noble benevolence—how, by emulation, it urges on the sectarian to instruct himself as well as others—how, by an habitual decorum of life in its members, it holds forth to all dissenters a steadfast example, from which they rarely swerve—and how a perpetual competition in good works tends to a perpetual action of energy and life in their execution. If this be the principle of an ecclesiastical establishment, we have only to preserve, by purifying, the principle. And if I have rightly argued, that it is from too unmixed an aristocratic composition, owing to individual patronage, that most of the present failings of the Establishment arise, we have only to transfer, as far as we safely and prudently can, the patronage of the Establishment from individuals to the state. In a free state, ever amenable to publicity, the patronage of the state, rightly administered will become the patronage of the people; but free from the danger that would exist were it dependent on the people alone. Public opinion would watch over the appointments; they would cease to be *family concerns;* they would cease to be exclusively aristocratic. A more wise and harmonious mixture of all classes, from the higher to the lower, would ensue; and the greater openness of general honour to merit, would encourage zeal, but not the zeal of fanaticism. Pastors would cease to be brought in wrangling and hostile collision with their flock; and, with a more rooted sympathy with the people than exists at present, the clergy would combine the sway of a serener dignity. In the church, as with education, and with the Poor-laws, the most efficacious administration of a complicated machinery, is the energy of a Free State.

V

The Sabbath

The keeping holy the sabbath-day is a question which does not seem to me to have been placed upon fair and legislative grounds of consideration. That the Sunday of the Christian is not the Sabbath of the Jews is perfectly clear; that in the early ages of the church, it was set apart as a day of recreation, as well as of rest, is equally indisputable; the first reformers of our English church continued to regard it in this light, and upon that cheerful day games were permitted to the poor, and tournaments to the rich. The spirit of puritanism distinguished from that of the established church was mainly this—the former drew its tenets and character principally from the *Old* testament, the latter from the New. The puritans, therefore, by a gross theological error, adopted the rigid ceremonial of the Hebrew sabbath, which our Saviour in fact had abolished, and for which, all His earlier followers had substituted a milder institution. The consequence of overstraining the ceremonial has, in England, invariably been this—as one order of persons became more rigid, another class became more relaxed in their observance of church rites and worship. When it was a matter of general understanding that the fore part of the day was set apart for worship, and the latter part for recreation, if every body indulged in the latter, every body also observed the former. But when one class devoted the whole day to ritual exaction and formal restraint, and this too with an ostentatious pedantry of sanctification—by a necessary reaction, and from an unavoidable result of ridicule, the other class fell into an opposite extreme. Political animosities favoured the sectarian difference, and to this day, there are two classes of reasoners on the sabbath, one asking for too much, and the other conceding too little. Perhaps nothing has more marred the proper respect that all classes should pay to the sabbath, than the absurd and monstrous propositions of Sir Andrew Agnew.

But, putting aside the religious views of the question, the spirit of good legislation requires that if any gross and evident cause of demoralization exists, we should attempt to remove it.

It appears (and this is highly satisfactory) by the evidence on Sir A. Agnew's committee, that the sabbath is generally observed by all orders except the poorest,[1] that churches are filled as soon as built, and that even those seats reserved for the working classes are usually thronged. The poorer part of the working classes are in large towns alone lax in their attendance—we inquire the cause, and we find it nearly always in the effects of habitual intemperance. Now having got to the root of the evil, for that only ought we to legislate. There are two causes that favour intoxication on the Sunday; these we may endeavour to remedy, not only because they injure the holiness of the sabbath, but because they taint the morality of the state.

There are two causes: the first is the custom of paying wages on a Saturday night;—a day of entire idleness ensuing, the idler and more dissipated mechanic especially in the metropolis, goes at once to the gin-shop on the Saturday night, returns there on the Sunday morning, forgets his wife and his family, and spends on his own vices, the week's earnings that should have supported his family. Now if he were paid on Friday night, and went to work on Saturday morning, he would have an imperious inducement not to disable himself from work; the temptation of money just received, would not be strengthened by a prospect of being drunk with impunity, because he would have the indolent next day to recover the effects. The money would probably come into

1. The greater part of the more "respectable" metropolitan tradesmen of Sunday trading, are anxious for an effectual prohibition by law, but I suspect not so much from piety as from a jealousy of the smaller shopkeepers, who by serving customers on Sunday, either lure away the customers on Monday also (supposing the greater tradesmen rigidly decline "to oblige" on the sabbath), or by compelling the "more respectable" to do business also, prevent their running down to their country villas and driving *their own gigs.*

the hands of his wife, and be properly spent in the maintenance of the family. He who knows any thing of the mind of the uneducated poor man, knows that it is only in the first moment of receiving money that he is tempted to spend it indiscreetly— and if he received it on Friday, by Sunday morning the novelty would be a little worn off. This alteration would be attended, I am convinced with the most beneficial results, and where it has been tried already it has met with very general success.

The law indeed ought to legislate for Saturday rather than Sunday; for all the police agree, (and this is a singular fact) that there are more excesses committed on a Saturday night than any night in the week, and fewer excesses of a *Sunday* night!

The second course that favours intemperance as connected with the sabbath, is the opening of gin-shops to a late hour on Saturday, and till eleven on Sunday morning: not only the temptation to excess, but the abandoned characters that throng the resort, make the gin-shop the most fatal and certain curse that can befall the poor. The husband goes to drink, the wife goes to bring him out, and the result is, that she takes a glass to keep him company or to console herself for his faults. Thus the vice spreads to both sexes, and falls betimes on their children. These resorts might, especially in the Metropolis, be imperatively shut up on Sunday, and at an early hour on Saturday. Beyond these two attempts to remedy the main causes of demoralization on the sabbath, I do not think that it would be possible to legislate with success.

But so far from shutting up whatever places of amusement are now open, it is clear, that all those which do not favour drunkenness, are so many temptations to a poor man not to get drunk. Thus, tea-gardens a little removed from towns (if *not* licensed on Sunday to sell any kind of spirits, for here the law might go to the verge of severity) would be highly beneficial to the morals of the working orders. They are so even now. We have the evidence of the police, that instances of excess or disorder at these places of recreation are very rare; and the great advantage of them is this, a poor man can take his wife and daughters to the tea-garden though he cannot to the gin-shop; selfishness (the drunkard's vice) is counteracted, the domestic ties and affections are strengthened, and the presence of his family imposes an invisible and agreeable restraint upon himself. I consider that it is to the prevalence of amusements in France which the peasant or artisan can share with his family, that we are to ascribe the fact that he does not seek amusement *alone,* and the innocent attractions of the *guinguette* triumph over the imbruting excesses of the *cabaret.*

Riding through Normandy one beautiful Sunday evening, I overheard a French peasant decline the convivial invitation of his companion. "Why—no thank you," said he, "I must go to the *guinguette* for the sake of my wife and the young people, dear souls!"

The next Sunday I was in Sussex, and as my horse ambled by a cottage, I heard a sturdy boor, who had apparently just left it, grumble forth to a big boy swinging on a gate, "You sees to the sow, Jim, there's a good un, I be's jist a gooing to the Blue Lion *to get rid o' my missus and the brats, rot e'm!*"

We see by a comparison with continental nations, that it is by making the sabbath dull that we make it dangerous. Idleness must have amusement or it falls at once into vice; and the absence of entertainments produces the necessity of excess. So few are the harmless pleasures with us on the sabbath, that a French writer, puzzled to discover any, has called the English Sunday, with a most felicitous *naïveté, "jour qu'on distingue par un* POUDING!" Save a pudding he can find no pleasurable distinction for the Holy Day of the week!

But while, sir, I think that innocent and social pleasures are the first step toward an amelioration of the consequences produced by a day of idleness to the poor, I am perfectly prepared to concede a more lofty view of the moral reform that we may effect in the maintenance of that day. Serious contemplation and instructive reading improve the mind even more than the gentle cheerfulness of recreation. Man has high aims and immortal destinies before him; it is well that he should sometimes ponder upon them, "commune with his own heart and be still." But this we cannot enforce by law; we can promote it, however, by education. In proportion as the poor are enlightened, they will have higher and purer resources than mere amusement to preserve them from drunkenness and vice; and even in pursuing amusement they will not fall readily into its occasional temptations.

Give opportunities of innocence to the idle, and give opportunities of preventing idleness itself, by the resources of instruction.

In short, with the lower orders, as education advances, it will be as with the higher,—the more intellectual of whom do not indulge generally in frivolous amusements, solely because *it amuses them less* than intellectual pursuits.

"Why do you never amuse yourself?" said the rope-dancer to the philosopher.—"That is exactly the question," answered the philosopher, astonished, "that I was going to ask *you!*"

But, sir, there is one very remarkable deduction, to which nearly all the witnesses on the evidence for a sabbath reform have arrived, and which, as nobody yet has remarked, I cannot conclude this chapter without touching upon. I pass over the extraordinary interrogatories which the legislative wisdom deemed advisable to institute, of which two may be considered a sufficient sample. Some sapient investigator asks what class of persons were in the habit of attending the beer-shops, to which the unlooked-for answer is, "The lower classes." This seems to surprise the interrogator, for he asks immediately afterwards *if the better classes don't resort there as well?*

Again, the Committee summons before it a Mr. M'Kechney, agent to a flour-factor, and on the principle, I suppose, that you should question a man on those points with which his previous habits have made him acquainted, some gentlemen appear to have discovered a mysterious connexion between a knowledge of flour and a knowledge of beards. This witness is accordingly examined, touching the expediency of Saturday shaving. His answer is bluff, and decided:—"It is MY OWN OPINION," quoth he, "that a poor man can get shaved on a Saturday night; and *that he would have as good an appearance on Sunday morning*"! —A startling affirmation, it must be allowed, and one evincing a deep knowledge of the chins of the poor.

I pass over, however, these specimens of Phil-Agnewian acuteness, tempting and numerous as they are, and I come to the deduction I referred to. The whole of the evidence, then, is a most powerful attack upon the influence of the aristocracy—to their example is imputed all the crime of England: for first, all crime is traced to sabbath-breaking; and, secondly, sabbath-breaking is imputed to the aristocratic influences of evil. Mr. Rowland, of Liverpool, affirms that divers reports of metropolitan evil-doings on the sabbath, perpetrated by the great, travel down to that distant town, and are the common excuse to the poor for sabbath-breaking. Mr. Ruell, chaplain of the Clerkenwell prison, after deposing, that he did not know "a single case of capital offence, where the party has not been a sabbath-breaker," is asked, whether the prisoners of the different prisons he has known, when reproved for their misdemeanors, have made any observations on the habits of the higher classes of society. Mark his answer—it is very amusing. "Frequently," saith he; "and it would be difficult for me to describe the shrewdness with which their remarks are often made. Some have been so pointed in reference to persons in the higher ranks, *as to call forth my reproof.*"—Wickedly proceedeth Mr. Ruell to observe, that "they take a peculiar pleasure in referring to any remarkable departure from the principles of religion or morality among the great, as affording a sort of sanction to their own evil conduct." This he calls "the great barrier he has found in his ministry to impressing the minds of the lower orders with a sense of religion and moral order." But more anti-aristocratic than all, is the evidence of the philosophical and enlightened Bishop of London. "It is difficult," says he, with deliberate authoritativeness, "to estimate the degree in which the labours of the Christian ministry are impeded, especially in towns, by the evil example of the rich!" That most able prelate, insisting afterwards on the necessity of "legislating very tenderly for the poor" on offences shared with impunity by their betters, contends that "the influence of the higher classes, were their example generally exemplary, would prevent the necessity of any religious legislation for the poor." He confesses, however, "that he entertains no hope of such a state of things being speedily brought to pass."

Now, sir, observe first, that while all the evidence thus summoned imputes the fault to the great, all the legislative enactments we have been and shall be called upon to pass, are to impose coercion solely upon the poor; and observe, secondly, I pray you, the great vindication I here adduce in favour of certain tenets which I have boldly advanced. If it be true that the negligent or evil example of the aristocracy be thus powerfully pernicious (not, we will acknowledge, from a design on their part, but [we will take the mildest supposition] from a want of attention—from a want of being thoroughly aroused to the nature and extent of their own influence),—if this be true, how necessary, how called for have been the expositions of this work, how successfully have I followed out the bearings of Truth in proving that whatever moral evil has flowed downward among the people has, not according to the disciples of a rash and inconsiderate radicalism, emanated from the vices of a Monarchy or of an Established Church, but from the peculiar form and fashion of our aristocratic combinations, from the moral tone they have engendered, and the all-penetrating influence they have acquired! In so doing, without advancing a single violent doctrine, without insisting on a single levelling innovation, but rather, in the teeth of the vulgar policy, advocating an energetic State and a providing Government, I have helped to correct the mischief of a peculiar power, by summoning it to the bar of that Public Opinion, by whose verdict power exists. This is the true legislative benefit of an investigating research. Exhibit the faults of any description of moral influence, and it is impossible to calculate how far you have impaired its capacities of mischief.

VI

State of Morality

There are many persons who desire that we should never learn Morality as a separate science—they would confine it solely to theological expositions, and make ecclesiastics its only lecturers and professors—this is a common error in English opinion, it proceeds from the best intentions—it produces very dangerous consequences both to morality, and to religion itself. These reasoners imagine and contend that religion and morality have the same origin, that they are inseparable. Right notions on this head are very important, let us see the origin of the two, I fancy we shall find by one minute's inquiry that nothing can be more distinctly separate—we shall see the mode by which they became connected, and the inquiry will prove the vital expedience of cultivating morality as a science in itself.

When men first witness the greater or the less accustomed phenomena of Nature, they tremble, they admire, they feel the workings of a superior power, and they acknowledge a God! Behold the origin of all Religion save that of Revelation!

When men herd together, when they appoint a chief, or build a hut, or individualize property in a bow or a canoe, they feel the necessity of obligation and restraint —they form laws—they term it a duty to obey them.[1] In

1. If we adopt the metaphysics of certain schools, we may suppose the origin both of religion and of morality to be in inherent principles of the mind; but even so, it might be easily shown that they are the result either of different principles or of utterly distinct operations of the same principle.

that duty (the result of utility), behold the origin of Morality![2]

But the Deity whom they have bodied forth from their wonder and their awe, men are naturally desirous to propitiate—they seek to guess what will the most please or the most offend their unknown Divinity. They invest Him with their own human attributes, carried only to a greater extent; by those attributes they judge him: naturally, therefore, they imagine that such violations of morality as interrupt the harmony of their own state must be displeasing to the Deity who presides over them. To the terror of the Law they add that of the anger of God. Hence the origin of the connexion between Religion and Morality.

These two great principles of social order were originally distinct, the result of utterly different operations of mind. Man, alone in the desert, would have equally conceived Religion; it is only when he mixes with others, that he conceives Morality.[3]

But men anxious to please the Deity—to comprehend the laws by which He acts upon the physical and the mental nature—beginning first to adore, proceed shortly to examine. Behold the origin of Philosophy!—Survey the early tribes of the world. Philosophy is invariably the offspring of Religion. From the Theocracy of the East came the young Sciences, and Reason commenced her progress amidst the clouds and darkness gathered round the mystic creeds of Egypt, of Persia, and of Ind. But inquiring into the nature of the Creator, and the consequent duties of man, Philosophy, if the *result* of religion, becomes necessarily the *science* of morals. Examining the first, it elucidated the last; and as human wisdom is more felicitous in its dealings with the Known and Seen than with the Unexperienced and the Invisible, so the only redeemer of the ancient extravagance in religion, has been the ancient exposition of morals. The creeds are dead—the morals survive—and to this very day make the main part of our own principles, and (kneaded up with the Christian code) are the imperishable heritage that we must transmit (but that we ought also to *augment*) to our posterity.

Thus then have I briefly shown the distinctive origin of Re-

2. Thus, the origin of law and morals is simultaneous, but not exactly similar. The necessity of *framing* a law originates law, the utility of *obeying* law originates morality.

3. A flash of lightning may strike upon the mind the sense of a Superior Being; but man must be in fear of man before he learns the utility of moral restraint.

ligion and of Morals; how Philosophy naturally born from the first, enlightens the last, and how fortunate it hath been for the world that philosophy, not confining its speculations to theology, has cultivated also morality as a science.

How, in an artificial society, is it possible to look to religion *alone* for our *entire* comprehension of *all* morals? Religion is founded in one age, and one country; it is transmitted, with its body of laws, to another age and country, in which vast and complicated relations have grown up with time, which those laws are no longer sufficient to embrace. As society has augmented its machinery, it is more than ever necessary, to preserve Morality as the science that is to guide its innumerable wheels. Hence the necessity of not taking our moral knowledge only from the ecclesiastics; or, in pondering over truths which the religion of a different age and time transmits to us, disdain the truths which religion has necessarily omitted; for religion could not be embraced by every tribe, if it had prescribed the minutiæ necessary only to one. Consequently, we find in history, that in those ages have existed the most flagrant abuses and misconceptions in morality, wherein Religion Tuition has been the *only* elucidator of its code. Why refer you to the more distant periods of the world— to those of Egyptian and Indian, and Celtic and Gothic, priest-crafts—take only the earlier Papacy and the Middle Ages—Philosophy banished to the puerilities grafted upon an emasculated Aristotelism, inquiring "whether stars were animals; and, in that case, whether they were blest with an appetite, and enjoyed the luxuries of the table"—left Morality the sole appanage and monopoly of the priests. Hence, as the Priests were but human, they prostituted the science to human purposes; they made religious wars, and donations to the church, the great Shibboleth of Virtue; and the monopoly of Morality became the corruption of Religion.

It is right, therefore, that the science of moral philosophy should be pursued and cultivated in all its freedom and boldness, as the means, not to supplant, but to corroborate—to furnish and follow out—to purify and to enlarge the sphere of—religious instruction. Even such of its expounders as have militated against revealed religion, and have wandered into the Material and the Sceptical, have only tended in a twofold degree to support the life and energies of religion. For in the first place, arousing the ability, and stimulating the learning of the Church, they have called forth that great army of its defenders which constitute its pride; and without its maligners, and its foes, we should not have been enabled at this day, to boast of the high names which are its ornaments, and its bulwark. In the second place, the vigilance of philosophy operates as a guardian over the purity of religion, and preserves it free from its two corruptions—the ferocity of fanaticism, and the lethargy of superstition. So that as Rome was said to preserve its virtue by the constant energy and exercise to which it was compelled by the active power of Carthage, the vigour of religion is preserved by the free and perpetual energy of philosophical science.[4]

It is, sir, I think partly owing to some unconsidered prejudices in regard to this truth, some ignorant fear for religion, if morality should be elucidated as a distinct and individual science, that we see a fatal supineness in this country towards the exercise of metaphysical pursuits, that we feel an obstacle to the correction of public errors in the apathy of public opinion, and that at this moment we are so immeasurably behind either Germany or France in the progress of ethical science. Not so in that country which your birth and labours have adorned. While for more than a century we have remained cabined and confined in the unennobling materialism of Locke, Scotland has at least advanced some steps towards a larger and brighter principle of science; the effect of the study of philosophy has been visible in the maintenance of religion. I firmly believe that Scotland would not at this moment be so religious and reverent a community but for the thousand invisible and latent channels which have diffused through its heart the passion for moral investigation. And the love for analytical discussion that commenced with Hutcheson has produced the dematerializing philosophy of Reid.

Whenever I look around on the state of morality in this country, I see the want of the cultivation of moral science. A thousand of the most shallow and jejune observations upon every point of morality that occurs, are put forth by the press, and listened to by the legislature. Laws are made, and opinions

4. Dr. Reid has said with great beauty of language, "I consider the sceptical writers to be a set of men whose business it is to pick holes in the fabric of knowledge wherever it is weak and faulty, and when those places are properly repaired the whole building becomes more firm and solid than it was formerly."

formed, and institutions recommended upon the most erroneous views of human nature, and the necessary operations of the mind. A chasm has taken place between private and public virtue; they are supposed to be separable qualities; and a man may be called a most rascally politician, with an assurance from his asperser "that he does not mean the smallest disrespect to his *private character!*" Propping morality merely on decorums, we suffer a low and vulgar standard of opinion to establish itself amongst us; and the levelling habits of a commercial life are wholly unrelieved and unelevated by the more spiritual and lofty notions, that a well-cultivated philosophy ever diffuses throughout a people.

I have heard an anecdote of a gentleman advertising for a governess for his daughters—an opera-dancer applied for the situation; the father demurred at the offer: "What!" cries the lady, "am I not fit for the office? Can I not teach dancing, and music, and French, and manners?"—"Very possibly—but still—an opera-dancer—just consider!"—"Oh! if that be all," said the would-be governess, *"I can change my name!"* I admire the *naïveté* of the dancer less than her sagacity; she knew that nine times out of ten, when the English ask for virtues, they look only to the name!

By a blind and narrow folly, we suppose in England that the abstract and the practical knowledge are at variance. Yet just consider: every new law that will not apply itself to the people,—that fails,—that becomes a dead letter,—is a proof that the legislature were ignorant either of the spirit of law or the mind of the people upon whom it was to operate,—is a proof that the Law was not practical from the deficiency of its framers in abstract experience. In no country are so many ineffectual laws passed; and we might ask for no other proof to show that, in no country is there greater ignorance of the science of moral legislation—a branch of moral philosophy.

From this want of cultivating ethical investigation we judge of morals by inapplicable religious rules. Bishop, the murderer, was considered by the newspapers to have made his peace with God, and to be entitled to a cheerful slumber, because he did— what? Why, because he confessed to the ordinary of Newgate the method in which he had murdered his victim! Public Charities, as we have seen, so fatal in their results upon the morality of a people, unless most carefully administered, are considered admirable *in themselves;* the turbulence and riot, and bribery and vice of elections are deemed *necessary* components of liberty. Some men adhere to the past without comprehending its moral; others rush forward to experiments in the future, without a single principle for their guide. Would-be-improvers know not what they desire, and popular principles become the mere pander to popular delusions.

When religion is unaided by moral science there is ever a danger, that too much shall be left to the principle of *fear.* "To preach long and loud damnation," says the shrewd Selden, "is the way to be cried up. We love a man who damns us, and we run after him again to save us." This common principle in theology is transferred to education and laws. We train our children[5] by the rod. We govern our poor by coercion. We perpetually strive to debase our kind by terror instead of regulating them by reason. Yet not thus would the grand soul of Bossuet have instructed us, when in that noble sermon, *"Pour la Profession de Madame de la Valliere,"* the great preacher seeks to elevate the soul to heaven. He speaks not then of terror and of punishment, but of celestial tenderness, of the absence of all dread under the Almighty wings. "What," he cries, "is the sole way by which we approach God and are made perfect?—It is by love alone." A profound truth, which in teaching us a nobler spirit of religion, instructs us also in the three principles of education, of morals, and of laws. But Bossuet's address is not of the fashion established amongst us!

I trace the same want of moral knowledge in our fiscal impositions. Some taxes are laid on which must necessarily engender vice; some taken off as if necessarily to increase it. We have taxed the diffusion of knowledge just a hundred per cent.; the consequence is, the prevention of legal knowledge, and the diffusion of smuggled instruction by the most pernicious teachers. We have taken off the duty upon gin, and from that day commenced a most terrible epoch of natural demoralization. "For-

5. So Wesley, who often concluded his sermon with "I am about to put on the condemning cap—I am about to pass sentence upon you: 'Depart from me ye accursed into everlasting fire,' " advises also the repeated flogging of children, and insists upon the necessity of "breaking their spirit."—See Southey's *Life of Wesley.*

merly," says the wise prelate I have so often quoted, "when I first came to London, I never saw a female coming out of a gin-shop; I have since repeatedly seen females with infants in their arms, to whom they appear to be giving some part of their liquor."

Our greatest national stain is the intemperance of the poor; to that intemperance our legislators give the greatest encouragement;—they forbid knowledge; they interfere with amusement; they are favourable only to intoxication.

For want, too, of extending our researches into morality, the light breaks only the darkness immediately round us, and embraces no ample and catholic circumference. Thus, next to our general regard for appearance, we consider morality only as operating on the connexions between the sexes. Morality, strictly translated with us, means the absence of licentiousness—it is another word for one of its properties—chastity; as the word profligacy bears only the construction of sexual intemperance. I do not deny that this virtue is one of immense importance. Wherever it is disregarded, a general looseness of all other principles usually ensues. Men rise by the prostitution of their dearest ties, and indifference to marriage becomes a means of the corruption of the state. But as the strongest eyes cannot look perpetually to one object without squinting at last, so to regard but one point of morals however valuable, distorts our general vision for the rest. And what is very remarkable among us, out of the exclusiveness of our regard to chastity, arises the fearful amount of prostitution which exists throughout England, and for which no remedy is ever contemplated. Our extreme regard for the chaste induces a contemptuous apathy to the *un*chaste. We care not how many there are, what they suffer—or how far they descend into the lower abysses of crime. Thus in many of the agricultural districts, nothing can equal the shameless abandonment of the female peasantry. Laws favouring bastardy promote licentiousness—and, as I have before shewn, the pauper marries the mother of illegitimate children, in order to have a better claim on the parish. In our large towns an equally systematic contempt of the unfortunate victims, less, perhaps, of sin than of ignorance and of poverty, produces consequences equally prejudicial. No regard, as in other countries, by a rigid police order, is paid to their health, or condition; the average of their career on earth is limited to *four years*. Their houses are unvisited—their haunts unwatched—and thus is engendered a fearful mass of disease, of intemperance, and of theft. Too great a contempt for one vice, rots it, as it were, into a hundred other vices yet more abandoned. And thus, by a false or partial notion of morality, we have defeated our own object, and the exclusive intolerance to the unchaste, has cursed the country with an untended and unmedicated leprosy of prostitution.

To the want, too, of a cultivation of morality as a science, all its rules are with us vague, vacillating, and uncertain: they partake of the nature of personal partiality, or of personal persecution. One person is proscribed by society for some offence which another person commits with impunity. One woman elopes, and is "the abandoned creature"; another does the same, and is only "the unfortunate lady."—Miss ———— is received with respect by the same audience that drove Kean to America. Lady ———— is an object of interest, for the same crime as that which makes Lady ———— an object of hatred. Lord ———— ill uses and separates from his wife—nobody blames him. Lord Byron is discarded by his wife, and is cut by society. ———— is a notorious gambler, and takes in all his acquaintance—every body courts him—he is a man of fashion. Mr. ———— imitates him, and is shunned like a pestilence—*he* is a pitiful knave. In vain would we attempt to discover any clue to these distinctions—all is arbitrary and capricious; often the result of a vague and unmerited personal popularity—often a sudden and fortuitous reaction in the public mind that, feeling it has been too harsh to its last victim, is too lenient to its next. Hence, from a lack of that continuous stream of ethical meditation and instruction, which, though pursued but by a few, and on high and solitary places, flows downward, and, through invisible crevices and channels, saturates the moral soil,—Morality with us has no vigour and no fertile and organized system. It acts by starts and fits—it adheres to mere forms and names—now to a respect for appearances— now to a respect for property:—clinging solely with any enduring strength, to one material and worldly belief which the commercial and aristocratic spirits have engendered, viz., in the value of station and the worth of wealth.

VII

What Ought to Be the Aim of English Moralists in This Age

It seems, then, that owing to the natural tendencies of trade and of an imperfect and unelevating description of aristocracy, the low and the mercantile creep over the national character, and the more spiritual and noble faculties are little encouraged and lightly esteemed. It is the property of moral philosophy to keep alive the refining and unworldly springs of thought and action; a counter attraction to the mire and clay of earth, and drawing us insensibly upward to a higher and purer air of Intellectual Being. Civilized life with its bustle and action, the momentary and minute objects in which it engages and frets the soul, requires a perpetual stimulus to larger views and higher emotions; and where these are scant and feeble, the standard of opinion settles down to a petty and sordid level.

In metaphysical knowledge, England has not advanced since Locke. A few amongst us may have migrated to the Scotch school —a few more may have followed forth the principles of Locke into the theories of Helvetius—a very few indeed, adventuring into the mighty and mooned sea of the Kantian Philosophy, may steer their solitary and unnoticed barks along its majestic deeps; but these are mere stragglers from the great and congregated herd.[1] The philosophy of Locke is still the *system* of the English, and all their new additions to his morality are saturated with his spirit. The beauty and daring, and integrity of his character—the

1. Kant too, has been only introduced to *us* just as Germany has got beyond him.

association of his name with a great epoch in the Liberties of Thought, contribute to maintain his ascendancy in the English heart; and his known belief in our immortality has blinded us to the materialism of his doctrines.

Few, sir, know or conjecture the influence which one mighty mind insensibly wields over those masses of men, and that succession of time which appear to the superficial altogether out of the circle of his control. I think it is to our exclusive attention to Locke, that I can trace much of the unspiritual and material form which our philosophy has since rigidly preserved, and which, so far from counteracting the *levelling influences of a worldly cast has strengthened and consolidated them.* Locke, doubtless, was not aware of the results to be drawn from his theories, but the man who has declared that the soul may be material[2]—that by revelation only can we be certain that it is not so—who leaves the Spiritual and the Immortal undefended by philosophy, and protected solely by theology, may well, you must allow, be the founder of a school of Materialists, and the ready oracle of those who refuse an appeal to Theology and are sceptical of Revelation: And therefore it seems to me a most remarkable error in the educational system of Cambridge, that Locke should be *the sole* metaphysician professedly studied—and that while we are obliged to pore over, and digest, and nourish ourselves with, the arguments that have led schools so powerful and scholars so numerous to pure materialism, we study *none* of those writings which have replied to his errors and elevated his system.

It is even yet more remarkable, that while Locke should be the great metaphysician of a clerical University, so Paley should be its tutelary moralist. Of all the systems of unalloyed and unveiled selfishness which human ingenuity ever devised, Paley's is, perhaps, the grossest and most sordid. Well did Mackintosh observe that his definition of Virtue, alone is an unanswerable illustration of the debasing vulgarity of his code. "Virtue is the doing good to mankind, in obedience to the will of God, and *for the sake of everlasting happiness.*" So that any act of good to man in obedience to God, if it arise from any motive but *a desire of the reward which he will bestow*—if it spring from pure grati-

2. Essay on the Human Understanding, bk. 4, chap. 3.

tude for past mercies, from affectionate veneration to a protecting Being—does not come under the head of virtue; nay, if, influenced solely by such purer motives, if the mind altogether escape from the mercenary desire of rewards—its act would violate the definition of virtue, and, according to Paley, would become a vice![3] Alas for an university, that adopts materialism for its metaphysical code, and selfishness for its moral!

Philosophy ought to be the voice of a certain intellectual want in every age. Men, in one period, require toleration and liberty; their common thoughts demand an expounder and enforcer. Such was the want which Locke satisfied—such his service to mankind! In our time we require but few new theories on these points already established. Our intellectual want is to enlarge and spiritualize the liberty of thought we have acquired—the philosophy of one age advances by incorporating the good, but correcting the error of the last. This new want, no great philosopher has appeared amongst us to fulfil.[4]

But there are those who feel the want they cannot supply; if the lesser Spirits and Powers of the age are unable to furnish forth that philosophy, they can expedite its appearance: and this by endeavouring to dematerialize and exalt the standard of opinion—to purify the physical and worldly influences—to decrust from the wings of Contemplation the dust that, sullying her plumes, impedes her flight—to labour in elevating the genius of action, as exhibited in the more practical world of politics and laws—to refine the coarse, and to ennoble the low; this, sir, it seems to me, is the true moral which the infirmities of this present time the most demand, and which the English writer and

3. See Mackintosh's Dissertation in the Supplement to the *Encyclopædia Britannica*.

4. What I principally mean to insist upon is this—Philosophy ought to counteract whatever may be the prevalent error of the Popular opinion of the time—if the error were that of a fanatical and stilted excess of the chivalric principle.—Philosophy might do most good by insisting on the counteracting principles of sobriety and common sense—but if the error be that of a prevalent disposition to the sordid and worldly influences—Philosophy may be most beneficial by going even to extremes in establishing the more generous and unselfish motives of action. Hence one reason why no individual School of Philosophy can be permanent. Each age requires a new representative of its character and a new corrector of its opinions. A material and cold philosophy may be most excellent at one period, and the very extravagance of an idealizing philosophy may be most useful at another.

the English legislator, studying to benefit his country, ought to place unceasingly before him. Rejecting the petty and isolated points, the saws and maxims, which a vulgar comprehension would deem to be morals where they are only truisms, his great aim for England shall be to exalt and purify the current channels of her opinion. To effect this for others, he shall watch narrowly over himself, discarding, as far as the contaminations of custom and the drawbacks of human feebleness will allow, the selfish and grosser motives that he sees operating around him; weaning himself, as a politician, from the ambition of the adventurer, and the low desire of wealth and power; seeking, as a writer, in despite, now of the popular, now of the lordly clamour, to inculcate a venerating enthusiasm for the true and ethereal springs of Greatness and of Virtue; and breathing thus through the physical action and outward form of Freedom, the noble aspirations that belong in states as in men to the diviner excitation of the soul!

Such seems to me the spirit of that moral teaching which we now require, and such the end and destiny that the moralists of our age and nation should deem their own!

Appendix A
Popular Education

In my remarks upon Popular Education, I endeavoured to show that it was not enough to found schools without prescribing also the outline of a real education—that a constant vigilance was necessary to preserve schools to the object of their endowment—to protect them from the abusive influences of Time, and to raise the tone and quality of education to that level on which alone it can be considered the producer of knowledge and of virtue. By the parallel of Prussia I attempted to convey a notion of the immense difference of education in that country, which makes education a *state* affair, and this country, in which, with equal zeal, and larger capital, it is left to the mercy of *individuals*. If then we are to have a general—an universal—education, let it be an education over which the government shall preside. I demand a Minister of Public Instruction, who shall be at the head of the department;—I demand this, 1st, Because such an appointment will give a moral weight and dignity to education itself; 2dly, Because we require to concentre the responsibility in one person who shall be amenable to Parliament and the Public. He shall have a Council to assist him, and his and their constant vigilance and attention shall be devoted to the system over which they preside.

It is indeed true that we cannot transfer to this country the wholesale education of Prussia; in the latter it is compulsory on parents to send their children to school, or to prove that they educate them at home. A compulsory obligation of that nature would, at this time, be too stern for England; we must trust rather to moral than legislative compulsion. Fortunately so great a desire for education is springing up among all classes, that the government has only to prepare the machine in order to procure the supply. Every where the feeling is in favour of education, and only two apprehensions are enlisted against it; both of these apprehensions we must conciliate. The first is, lest in general instruction religion should be neglected; the second, lest in teaching the poor to think we should forget that they are born to labour. I say we ought to conciliate both these classes of the timid.

I am perfectly persuaded, that nothing has been more unfortunate for popular education in this country than the pertinacity with which one class have insisted on coupling it *solely* with the *Established* religion, and the alarming expedient of the other class in excluding religion altogether. With respect to the last, I shall not here pause to enter into a theological discussion; I shall not speak of the advantage or the disadvantage of strengthening moral ties by religious hopes; or of establishing one fixed and certain standard of morals, which, containing all the broader principles, need not forbid the more complicated;—a standard which shall keep us from wandering very far into the multiform theories and schisms in which the vagaries of mere speculative moralists have so often misled morality. On these advantages, if such they be, I will not now descant. I am writing as a legislator, desirous of obtaining a certain end and I am searching for the means to obtain it. I wish then to establish an Universal Education. I look round; I see the desire for it; I see also the materials, but so scattered, so disorganized are those materials; so many difficulties of action are in the way of the desire, that I am naturally covetous of all the assistance I can obtain.[1]

1. I am happy in this opinion to fortify myself by the expression of a similar sentiment in M. Cousin, in which it is difficult to say whether we should admire most the eloquence or the sagacity, or the common sense. I subjoin some extracts:

"The popular schools of a nation," he says, in recommending the outline of a general education for France to M. Montalivet, "ought to be penetrated with the religious spirit of that nation. Is Christianity, or is it not, the religion of the people of France? We must allow that it is. Then, I ask, shall we respect the religion of the people, or shall we destroy it? If we undertake the destruction of Christianity, then, I own, we must take care not to teach it. But if we do not propose to ourselves that end, we must teach our children the faith

I see a vast, wealthy, and munificent clergy, not bent against education, but already anxious to diffuse it, already founding schools, already educating nearly 800,000 pupils;—I look not only to them, but to the influence they command among their friends and flock; I consider and balance the weight of their names and wealth, and the grave sanction of their evangelical authority. Shall I have these men and this power with me or against me? That is the question? On the one hand, if I can enlist them, I obtain a most efficient alliance; on the other hand, if I enlist them, what are the disadvantages? If indeed they tell me that they will teach religion only, and that, but by the mere mechanical learning of certain lessons in the Bible—if they refuse to extend and strengthen a more general knowledge applicable to the daily purposes of life—such as I have described in the popular education of Prussia—*then,* indeed, I might be contented to dispense with their assistance. But *is* this the case? I do not believe it. I have conversed, I have corresponded with many of the clergy, who are attached to the cause of religious education, and no men have expressed themselves more anxious to combine with it all the secular and citizen instruction that we can desire. What is it then that they demand? What is the sacrifice I must make in order to obtain their assistance? They demand that the Christian religion be constituted the foundation of instruction in a Christian country. You, the Philosopher, say, "I do not wish to prevent religion being taught; but to prevent

which has civilized their parents, and the liberal spirit of which has prepared and sustains our great modern institutions. . . . Religion, in my eyes, is the best base of popular instruction. I know a little of Europe; nowhere have I seen good schools for the people where the Christian charity was *not*. . . . In human societies there are some things for the accomplishment of which Virtue is necessary; or, when speaking of the great masses, Religion! Were you to lavish the treasures of the state, to tax parish and district, still you could not dispense with Christian charity; or with that spirit of humbleness and self-restraint, of courageous resignation and modest dignity, which Christianity, well understood and well taught, can alone give to the instruction of the poor. . . . It would be necessary to call Religion to our aid, were it only a matter of finance."

If M. Cousin, a philosopher, once persecuted by the priesthood, thus feels the practical necessity of enlisting religion on the side of education in France; the necessity is far greater in England. For here Christianity is far more deeply rooted in the land; here the church is a more wealthy friend or a more powerful foe; here, too, the church is ready to befriend education—there, to resist it.

the jar, and discord, and hindrance of religious differences, I wish to embrace all sects in one general plan of civil instruction; let religious instruction be given by the parents or guardians of the children according to their several persuasions."

I believe nothing can be more honest than the intentions of the philosopher; I know many most excellent Christians of the same way of thinking. But, how sir—I address the philosopher again —how can you for a moment accuse the clergy of the Established Church of intolerance in refusing to listen to your suggestion? How, in common duty, and common conscience, can they act otherwise? Reverse the case. Suppose the churchmen said, "We will found a system for the education of the whole people, we will teach nothing but Religion in it, not one word of man's civil duties; not that we wish to prevent the pupil acquiring civil knowledge, but because we wish to avoid meddling with the jarring opinions as to what form of it shall be taught. Whatever civil knowledge the children shall possess, let their parents and guardians teach them out of school, according to their several theories."

Would the philosopher agree to this? No, indeed, nor I neither. Why then should we ask a greater complaisance from the ecclesiastic; he cannot think, unless he be indeed a mercenary and a hypocrite, the very Swiss of religion—that religious knowledge is less necessary than civil instruction. He cannot believe that the understanding alone should be cultivated, and the soul forgotten. But in fact, if we were to attempt to found a wholesale national education, in which religious instruction were not a necessary and pervading principle, I doubt very much if public opinion would allow it to be established; and I am perfectly persuaded, that it could not be rendered permanent and complete. In the first place, the clergy would be justly alarmed; they would redouble their own efforts to diffuse their own education. In a highly Christian country, they would obtain a marked preference for their establishments; *a certain taint and disrepute would be cast on the national system;* people would be *afraid* to send their children to the National Schools; the ecclesiastical schools would draw to themselves a vast proportion—I believe a vast majority —of children; and thus in effect the philosopher, by trying to sow unity would reap division; by trying to establish his own plan, he would weaken its best principle; and the care of education, instead of being *shared* by the clergy, would fall *almost entirely into their hands*. An education *purely* ecclesiastical would be in all probability bigoted, and deficient in civil and general instruction; the two orders ought to harmonize with, and watch over, and blend into, each other. Another consequence of the separation in schools which would be effected by banishing Christian instruction from some, in order to give a monopoly of ecclesiastical instruction to others, would probably be not only to throw a taint upon the former schools, but also upon whatever *improvements* in *education* they might introduce. Civil instruction would be confused with *ir*religious instruction, and amended systems be regarded with fear and suspicion. For all these reasons, even on the ground and for the reasons of the philosopher, I insist on the necessity of making instruction in religion the harmonizing and uniting principle of all scholastic education.

But, how are we to escape from the great difficulty in the unity of education produced by differing sects? In answer to this question, just observe how the government of Prussia, under similar circumstances, emancipates itself from the dilemma. "The difference of religion," says the Prussian law, "is not to be an obstacle in the form of a school society; but in forming such a society, you must have regard to the numerical proportion of the inhabitants of each faith; and, as far as it can possibly be done, you shall conjoin with the principal master professing the religion of the majority—a second master of the faith of the minority."

Again: "The difference of religion in Christian schools, necessarily produces differences in religious instruction. That instruction shall be always appropriate to the doctrines and spirit of the creed for which the schools shall be ordained. But as in every school of a Christian state, the dominant spirit, and the one common to all sects, is a pious and deep veneration for God: so every school may be allowed to receive children of every Christian sect. The masters shall watch with the greatest care that no constraint and no undue proselytism be exercised. *Private* and especial masters, of whatever sect the pupil belongs to, shall be charged with his religious education. If, indeed, there be some places where it is *impossible* for the School Committee to procure an especial instructor for every sect; *then,* parents, if they are unwilling their children shall adopt the lessons of the prevailing creed of the school, are entreated themselves to undertake the task of affording them lessons in their own persuasion."

Such is the method by which the Prussian State harmonizes her system of Universal Education among various sects. That which Prussia can effect in this respect, why should not England? Let us accomplish our great task of Common Instruction, not by banishing all religion, but by *procuring* for every pupil instruction in his own. And in this large and catholic harmony of toleration, I do believe the great proportion of our divines and of our dissenters might, by a prudent Government,[2] be induced cheerfully to concur. For both are persuaded of the necessity of education, both are willing to sacrifice a few minor considerations to a common end, and under the wide canopy of Christian faith, to secure, each to each, the maintenance of individual doctrines. I propose then, that *the State* shall establish Universal Education. I propose that it shall be founded on, and combined with, religious instruction. I remove, by the suggestion I have made, the apprehension of contending sects;—I proceed now to remove the apprehension of those who think that the children of the poor, if taught to be rational may not be disposed to be industrious. I propose that to all popular schools for intellectual instruction, labour, or industry schools should be appended, or rather, that each school shall unite both objects. I propose, that at the schools for girls, (for in the system I recommend, both sexes shall be instructed), the various branches and arts of female employment shall make a principal part of instruction; above all, that those habits of domestic management and activity in which (by all our Parliamentary Reports) the poorer females of the manufacturing towns are grossly deficient, shall be carefully formed and inculcated.[3]

2. One of the greatest benefits we derive from an intelligent and discreet government is in its power of conciliating opposing interests upon matters of detail or of *secondary* principles. Where a government cannot do this, depend upon it the ministers are bunglers.

3. Schools for girls in the poorer classes are equally important as those for boys. Note in Kay's account of Manchester, the slovenly improvidence of females in a manufacturing town; note in the Evidence on the poor-laws, the idleness, the open want of chastity, the vicious ignorance of a vast class of females every where. Mothers have often a greater moral effect upon children than the fathers; if the child is to be moral, provide for the morals of the mother.

I propose (and this also is the case in Prussia) that every boy educated at the popular schools shall learn the simpler elements of agricultural and manual science, that he shall acquire the habit, the love, and the aptitude of work; that the first lesson in his moral code shall be that which teaches him to prize independence, and that he shall practically obey the rule of his catechism, and learn to get his own living.

Thus then, briefly to sum up, the heads of the National Education I would propose for England are these:

1st, It shall be the business of the state, confided to a Minister and a subordinate Board, who shall form in our various counties and parishes, committees with whom they shall keep a vigilant eye on the general working, who shall not interfere vexatiously with peculiar details.—The different circumstances in different localities must be consulted, and local committees are the best judges as to the mode. I propose that the education be founded on religion; that one or more ministers of the Gospel be in every committee; that every sectarian pupil shall receive religious instruction from a priest of his own persuasion.

I propose that at every school for the poor, the art and habit of an industrious calling make a *necessary* part of education.

A report of the working, numbers, progress, &c. of the various schools in each county should be yearly published, so emulation is excited, and abuse prevented.

If the state prescribe a certain form of education, it need not prescribe the books or the system by which it shall be acquired.

To avoid alike the rashness of theories, and the unimprovable and lethargic adherence to blind custom, each schoolmaster desirous of teaching certain books, or of following peculiar systems such as those of Hamilton, Pestalozzi, &c., shall state his wish to the committee of the county, and obtain their consent to the experiment; they shall visit the school and observe its success: if it fail, they can have the right to prohibit; if it work well, they can have the power to recommend it. So will time, publicity, and experience have fair and wide scope in their natural result, viz., the progress to perfection.

But, above all things, to obtain a full and complete plan of education, there should be schools for teachers. The success of a school depends upon the talent of the master; the best system is lifeless if the soul of the preceptor fail. Each county, therefore, should establish its school for preceptors to the pupils, a preference shall be given to the preceptors chosen from them at any vacancies that occur in the popular schools for children. Here, they shall not only learn to know, but also learn to teach, two very distinct branches of instruction. Nothing so rare at present as competent teachers. Seminaries of this nature have been founded in most countries where the education of the people has become of importance.[4] In America, in Switzerland, lately in France, and especially in Germany, their success has everywhere been eminent and rapid. In Prussia M. Cousin devoted to the principal schools of this character, the most minute personal attention. He gives of them a detailed and highly interesting description. He depicts the rigid and high morality[5] of conduct which makes a necessary and fundamental part of the education of those who are designed to educate others; and the elaborate manner in which they are taught the *practical* science of teaching. On quitting the school they undergo an examination both on religious and general knowledge; the examination is conducted by two clergymen of the faith of the pupil, and two laymen. If he pass the ordeal, the pupil receives a certificate, not only vouching for the capabilities and character of the destined teacher and his skill in practical tuition, but, annexing also an account of the *exact* course of studies he has undergone.

An institution of this nature cannot be too strongly insisted upon.[6] In vain shall we build schools if we lack competent tutors. Let me summon Mr. Cook, the clerk of St. Clement's, in a portion of the evidence of the Poor-laws, which as yet is *unpub-*

4. In England, also, certain *private* associations have tacitly confessed the expediency of such institutions.

5. The law even enjoins careful selection as to the town or neighbourhood in which the seminaries for teachers shall be placed; so that the pupils may not easily acquire from the inhabitants any habits contrary to the spirit of the moral and simple life for which they are intended.

6. Insisted upon for the sake of religion as well as of knowledge. Hear the enlightened Cousin again: "The destined teachers of popular schools, without being at all Theologians, ought to have a clear and precise knowledge of Christianity, its history, its doctrines, and above all, its morals; without this, they might enter on their mission without being able to give any other religious instruction than the recitation of the catechism, *a most insufficient lecture*";— Perhaps the only, certainly the best, one our poor children receive. People seem, with us, to think the catechism every thing; they might as well say, the accidence was every thing! the catechism is at most the accidence of religion!

lished. It gives an admirable picture of a schoolmaster for the poor.

> One master was employed in keeping an account of the beer, and it was found that he had not only got liquors supplied to himself by various publicans, and charged an equivalent amount of beer to the parish, but had received *money* regularly, and charged it under the head of beer. *It was believed that his scholars had been made agents in the negotiation of these matters!*

So, in fact, the only thing the Pupils learnt from this excellent pedagogue was the rudiments of swindling!

The order of schools established should be:

1. Infant Schools. These are already numerous in England, but immeasurably below the number required. In Westminster alone, there are nearly 9000 children from two to six years old, fit for infant schools—there are only about 1000 provided with these institutions. Their advantage is not so much in actual education (vulgarly so called) as in withdrawing the children of the poor from bad example, obscene language, the neglect of parents who are busy, the contamination of those who are idle;—lastly, in economy.[7]

2. Primary or Universal Schools, to which Labour Schools should be attached, or which should rather combine the principle of both.

These schools might, as in Prussia, be divided into two classes,

7. On this head, read the following extract from the unpublished evidence of Mr. Smart of Bishopsgate: "Do you find the Infant Schools serviceable in enabling the mothers of the working class to work more, and maintain themselves better?

"That is my opinion. They are enabled to go out and work, when, if there were no such schools, they would be compelled to attend to their children, and would more frequently apply to the parish. I conclude this to be the case from the constant declarations of those mothers who have children, and are not able to send them to school. They say they must have assistance from the parish, on account of having to attend to their children. There are many of the families who reside out of the parish, at too great a distance for their infant children to come to their parish school.

"From the whole of your observations, do you consider the general establishment of infant and other schools a matter of economy, viewing their operation only with relation to the parish rules, and the progress of pauperism?

"I have no doubt whatever of it, viz., that their effects are immediately economical merely in a pounds, shillings, and pence point of view, for I am convinced, that great as the account of pauperism now is, the claims upon the parish funds would be much greater, but for the operation of these schools. Ultimately their effects will be more considerable preventing the extension of pauperism."

of a higher and lower grade of education; but at the onset, I think one compendious and common class of school would be amply sufficient, and more easily organized throughout the country.

3. Sunday Schools. Of these, almost a sufficient number are already established.

And, 4. Schools for teachers.

But how are such schools to be paid and supported? That difficulty seems to be obviated much more easily than our statesmen are pleased to suppose. In the first place, there are 450 endowed grammar-schools throughout England and Wales. The greater part of these, with large funds, are utterly useless to the public. I say at once and openly, that these schools, intended for the education of the people, ought to be applied to the education of the people—they are the moral property of the State, according to the broad intention of the founders. Some have endeavoured to create embarrassments in adapting these schools to use, by insisting on a strict adherence to the exact line and mode of instruction specified by the endowers. A right and sound argument if the *principle* of the endower had been preserved. But *is* the principle preserved?—*is* knowledge taught?—If not, shall we suffer the principle to be lost, because we insist on rigidly preserving the details. Wherever time has introduced such abuses as have eat and rusted away the use itself of the establishment, we have before us this option: Shall we preserve, or shall we disregard the main intention of the Donor—Education. If it be our duty to regard *that* before all things, it is a very minor consideration whether we shall preserve the exact details by which he desired his principle to be acted upon. Wherever these details are inapplicable, we are called upon to remodel them[8]—if this be our duty to the memory of the individual, what is our duty to the State? Are we to suffer the want of an omniscient provi-

8. The absurd injustice of those who insist on an exact adherence to the original form and stipulation of endowments when they prejudice the poor, is grossly apparent in their defence of a departure from, not only the form and detail, but even the spirit and principle of an endowment, where the rich are made the gainers. These gentlemen are they who defend the departure from the express law of schools that, like the Winchester and Charter-house foundations, were originated *solely* for the benefit of "poor and indigent scholars,"—a law so obviously clear in some foundations, that it imposes upon the scholar an actual oath that he does not possess in the world more than some petty sum— I forget the exact amount—but it is under six pounds. The scholar thus limited,

dence in founders of Institutions two or three hundred years old to bind generation after generation to abused and vitiated systems? Is the laudable desire of a remote ancestor to perpetuate knowledge, to be made subservient to continuing ignorance? Supposing the Inquisition had existed in this country, if a man, believing in the necessity of supporting Religion, had left an endowment to the Inquisition, ought we rigidly to continue endowments to the Inquisition, by which Religion itself in the after age suffered instead of prospering? The answer is clear—are there not Inquisitions in knowledge as in religion—are we to be chained to the errors of the middle ages? No—both to the state and to the endowment, our first duty is to preserve the end—knowledge. Our second duty, the result of the first, is, on the evidence of flagrant abuse, to adapt the means to the end.

The greater part of these grammar-schools may then be consolidated into the state system of education, and their funds, which I believe the vigilance of the state would double, appropriated to that end. Here is one source of revenue, and one great store of materials. In the next place, I believe that if religion were made a necessary part of education, the managers of the various schools now established by the zeal and piety of individuals would cheerfully consent to co-operate with the general spirit and system of the State Board of Education. In the third place, the impetus, and fashion, and moral principle of education once made general, it would not lack individual donations and endowments. M. Cousin complains that in France the clergy are hostile to popular education; happily with us we have no such ground of complaint. Fourthly, No schools should be entirely gratuitous—the spirit of independence cannot be too largely fostered throughout the country—the best charity is that which puts blessings within the reach of labour—the worst is that which affects to grant them without the necessity of labour at all. The rate of education should be as low as possible, but as a general system *something* should be paid by the parents.[9] Whatever

---

probably now enjoys at least some two or three hundred a year! If we insisted upon preserving the exact spirit of *this* law,—the original intention of the founders,—these gentlemen would be the first to raise a clamour at our injustice!

9. The system in the case of actual paupers might be departed from, but with great caution; and masters should be charged to take especial care that

deficit might remain it seems to me perfectly clear that the sources of revenue I have just specified would be more than amply sufficient to cover. Look at the schools already established in England —upon what a foundation we commence!

The only schools which it might be found necessary to maintain at the public charge, either by a small county rate, or by a parliamentary grant *yearly* afforded,[10] would be those for Teachers: the expense would be exceedingly trifling. One word more: the expense of education well administered is wonderfully small in comparison to its objects.

About 1,500,000 children are educated at the Sunday-schools in Great Britain *at an expense of 2s. each,* per annum. In the Lancasterian system—the cheapest of all—(but if the experiment of applying it to the higher branches of education be successful, it may come to be the most general)—it is calculated that 1000 boys are educated at an expense not exceeding 300*l.* a year. Now suppose there are four millions of children in England and Wales to be educated (which, I apprehend, is about the proportion), the whole expense on that system would be only 1,200,000*l.* a year. I strongly suspect that if the funds of the various endowed grammar-schools were inquired into, they alone would exceed that sum: to say nothing of the funds of all our other schools—to say nothing of the sums paid by the parents to the schools.

So much for the state of popular education—for its improvement—for the outline of a general plan—for the removal of sectarian obstacles—for the provision of the necessary expenses. I do not apologize to the public, for the length to which I have gone on this vast and important subject—the most solemn—the most interesting that can occupy the mind of the patriot, the legislator, and the Christian. In the facts which I have been the instrument of adducing from the tried and practical system of Prussia—I think I do not flatter myself in hoping that I have added some of the most useful and instructive data to our present desire, and our present experience, of Practical Education.

---

the children of paupers shall be taught the *habits* and *customs* of industry, as well as the advantages of independence.

10. This might be advisable, for the sake of maintaining parliamentary vigilance, and attracting public opinion.

Book the Fourth

View of the Intellectual Spirit of the Time

INSCRIBED TO

I. D'ISRAELI, ESQ.

AUTHOR OF *The Curiosities of Literature,* AND
The Literary Character, ETC.

——Inter sylvas Academi quærere verum.

HOR. EP.

I

Permit me, my dear sir, to honour with your name that section of my various undertaking, which involves an inquiry into the Intellectual Spirit of the Time. I believe that you employ the hours of a serene and dignified leisure in the composition of a work that, when completed, will fill no inconsiderable vacuum in English Literature; namely, the History of English Literature itself. Of the arrival of that work, you wish us to consider those classical and most charming essays you have already given to the world, merely as precursors—specimens of a great whole—which ought, in justice to your present reputation, to add a permanent glory to the letters of your country. It will therefore, perhaps, afford to you a pleasurable interest, to survey the literary aspect of these times, into which your chronicle must merge, and to wander, even with an erring guide, beside those Rivers of Light, which you have tracked to their distant source, with all the perseverance of the antiquarian, and all the enthusiasm of the scholar.

Before, however, I can invite you to the more attractive part of my subject;—before we can rove at will among the gardens of Poesy, or the not less delightful mazes of that Philosophy, which to see is to adore; before the domains of Science and of Art can receive our exploring footsteps, we must pause awhile to examine the condition of that mighty, though ambiguous, Power by which the time receives its more vivid impressions, and conveys its more noisy opinions. As a preliminary to our criticisms

on the productions of the Press, we will survey the nature of its
influence;—and propitiate with due reverence the sibyl who too
often commits

> Her prophetic mind
> To fluttering leaves, the sport of every wind,

ere we can gain admittance to the happy souls,

> In groves who live, and lie on mossy beds,
> By crystal streams that murmur through the meads;

> ————————Choro pæana canentes
> Inter odoratum lauri nemus.

Hitherto I have traced, in the various branches of my inquiry,
the latent and pervading influence of an aristocracy. I am now
about to examine the nature of that antagonist power which is
the only formidable check that our moral relations have yet opposed to it. Much has been said in a desultory manner respecting
the influence of the Press; but I am not aware of any essay on
the subject which seems written with a view rather to examine
than declaim. "Vous l'allez comprendre, j'espère, si vous
m'écoutez,—il est fête, et nous avons le temps de causer."—I
shall go at once to the heart of the question, and with your per-
mission, we will not throw away our time by talking much on
the minor considerations.

It is the habit of some persons more ardent than profound,
to lavish indiscriminate praises on the press, and to term its influence, the influence of Knowledge—it is rather the influence
of Opinion. Large classes of men entertain certain views on matters of policy, trade, or morals. A newspaper supports itself by
addressing those classes; it brings to light all the knowledge
requisite to enforce or illustrate the views of its supporters; it
embodies also the prejudice, the passion, and the sectarian bigotry
that belong to one body of men engaged in active opposition to
another. It is therefore the organ of opinion; expressing at once
the truths and the errors, the good and the bad of the prevalent
opinion it represents.

Thus it is impossible to expect the newspaper you consider
right in regard to sentiments to be fair in regard to persons. Sup-

posing it expresses the *facts* which belong to knowledge, they are never stated with the *impartiality* that belongs to knowledge. —"Heavens! my dear sir! have you heard the report? The Duke of Wellington's horse has run over a poor boy!" A whig paper seizes on the lamentable story—magnifies, enlarges on it—the Duke of Wellington is admonished—indifference to human life is insinuated. The tory paper replies: it grants the fact, but interprets it differently: the fool of a boy was decidedly in the way —the brute of a horse had a mouth notoriously as hard as a brickbat—the rider himself was not to blame—what unheard of malignity, to impute as a reproach to the Duke of Wellington, a misfortune only to be attributed to the eyes of the boy, and the jaw-bone of the horse. But bless me! a new report has arisen:—it was not the Duke of Wellington's horse that ran over the boy; it was Lord Palmerston's. It is now the tory journal's opportunity to triumph. What perversion in the lying whig paper!—and what atrocity in Lord Palmerston! All the insinuations that were so shameful against the duke are now profusely directed against the viscount. The very same interpretations that the tory paper so magisterially condemned, are now by the tory paper unreservedly applied. The offence of distortion is equally continued—it is only transferred from one person to another. This is a type of the power of the press: its very enforcement of opinions prevents its being just as to persons. Facts, indeed, are stated, but the interpretation of facts is always a matter of dispute. And thus to the last chapter, it is easier to obtain a just criticism of the merits of the drama, than of the qualities of the actors. Long after the public mind has decided unanimously with respect to measures, it remains doubtful and divided with regard to the characters of men. In this the press is still the faithful record of Opinion, and the ephemeral Journal is the type of the everlasting History!

Newspapers being thus the organ of several opinions, the result is, the influence of opinion, because, that newspaper sells the best which addresses itself to the largest class; it becomes influential in proportion to its sale, and thus, the most popular opinion grows, at last, into the greatest power.

But from this arises a profound consideration, not hitherto sufficiently enforced. The newspaper represents opinion; but the opinion of whom?—*those persons among whom it chiefly circulates.* What follows?—why, that the price of the newspaper must have a considerable influence on the expression of opinion: because, according to the price would be the extent of its circulation; and, according to the opinion of the majority of its supporters, would be the current opinion of the paper.

Supposing it were possible to raise the price of all the daily newspapers to two shillings each, what would be the consequence?—that a vast number of the poorer subscribers would desert the journal, that the circle of its supporters would become limited to those who could afford its price. It would then be to the opinions and interests of this small and wealthy class, that it could alone address itself; if it did not meet their approbation, it could not exist; their opinion would be alone represented, the opinion of the mass would be disregarded; and a newspaper, instead of being the organ of the *public,* would be the expression of the *oligarchical* sentiment. Although the aggregate of property in England is, perhaps, equally divided among the whigs and tories, the *greater number* of reading persons, possessing property, is alleged to be tory. Supposing the calculation to be correct, the influence of the press would, by our supposed increase of price, be at once transferred to the tories; and *The Standard* and *The Albion* would be the most widely circulated of the daily journals.

If this principle be true, with respect to an increased price, the converse must be true if the price were lowered. If the sevenpenny paper were therefore to sell for twopence, what again would be the result? Why, the sale being extended from those who can afford sevenpence to those who can afford twopence, a new majority must be consulted, the sentiments and desires of poorer men than at present must be addressed; and thus, a new influence of opinion would be brought to bear on our social relations and our legislative enactments.

As the extension of the electoral franchise gave power to the middle classes, so the extended circulation of the press will give power to the operative. To those who uphold the principle, that government is instituted for the good of the greatest number, it is, of course, a matter of triumph, that the interests of the greatest number should thus force themselves into a more immediate voice.[1]

It is manifest, that when the eyes of the people are taught steadily to regard their own interests, the class of writing most pleasing to them, will not be that of demagogues; it is probable indeed, that the cheapest papers will seem to the indolent reader of the higher ranks, the most dry and abstruse. For a knowledge of the principles of trade, and of the truths of political economy, is of so vital an importance to the Poor, that those principles and truths will be the main staple of the journals chiefly dedicated to their use. Not engaged in the career of mere amusement that belongs to the wealthy—frivolity, scandal, and the unsatisfying pleasure derived from mere declamation, are not attractive to them. All the great principles of state morals and state policy are derived from one foundation, the *true direction of labour;*— what theme so interesting and so inexhaustible to those "who by labour live?" We may perceive already, by *The Penny Magazine,* what will be the probable character of cheap newspapers addressed to the working classes. The operative finds *The Penny Magazine* amusing; to the rich man it is the most wearisome of periodicals.

So much for the proud cry of the aristocrat, that the papers to please the rabble must descend to pander the vulgar passions. No! this is the vice of the aristocratic journals, that are sup-

---

1. In removing the stamp duties, which check one part of the influence of the press, it would however be conservative policy to let new sources of enlightenment commence with the new sources of power. At present, what are called the taxes on knowledge are in reality, as we have seen before, taxes on opinion. To make opinion knowledge, its foundation must be laid in instruction. The act which opens the press should be immediately followed by an act to organize National Education; and while the people are yet warm with gratitude for the new boon, and full of confidence to those who give it, care should be taken to secure for the first teachers of political morals, honest and enlightened men;—men too, who, having the competent knowledge, will have the art to express it popularly; not mere grinders of saws and aphorisms, the pedants of a system. By this precaution, the appealers to passion will be met by appealers to interest; and the people will be instructed as well as warmed. Meanwhile, the system of education once begun, proceeds with wonderful rapidity; and, ere the Operative has lost his confidence in the wise government that has granted him the boon of sifting the thoughts of others, his children will have learned the art of thinking for themselves.

ported alone by the excrescences of aristocracy, by gambling-houses, demireps, and valets. The industrious poor are not the purchasers of the *Age*.

A nobleman's valet entertained on a visit his brother, who was a mechanic from Sheffield. The nobleman, walking one Sunday by a newspaper office in the Strand, perceived the two brothers gazing on the inviting announcements on the shopboard, that proclaimed the contents of the several journals; the crowd on the spot delayed him for a moment, and he overheard the following dialogue:

"Why, Tom," said the valet, "see what lots of news there is in this paper!—'Crim. con. extraordinary between a lord and a parson's wife—Jack ——s (Jack is one of our men of fashion, you know, Tom), 'Adventure with the widow—Scene at Crocky's.' Oh, what fun! Tom, have you got sevenpence? I've nothing but gold about *me;* let's buy this here."

"Lots of news!" said Tom, surlily, "D'ye call that news? What do I care for your lords and your men of fashion? Crocky! What the devil is Crocky to me? There's much more for my money in this here big sheet: 'Advice to the Operatives—Full report of the debate on the Property Tax—Letter from an emigrant in New South Wales.' That's what I calls news."

"Stuff!" cried the valet, astonished.

My lord walked on, somewhat edified by what he had heard.

The scandal of the saloon is news in the pantry; but it is the acts of the legislature that constitute news at the loom.

But, while the main characteristic of the influence of the press is to *represent* opinion, it is not to be denied that it possesses also the nobler prerogative of *originating* it. When we consider all the great names which shed honour upon periodical literature; when we consider, that scarcely a single one of our eminent writers has not been actively engaged in one or other of our journals:—when we remember what Scott, Southey, Brougham, Mackintosh, Bentham, Mill, Macculloch, Campbell, Moore, Fonblanque (and I may add Mr. Southern, a principal writer in the excellent *Spectator,* whose writings obtain a reputation, which, thanks to the custom of the anonymous, is diverted from the writer himself,) have, year after year, been pouring forth in periodical publications, the rich hoard of their thoughts and knowledge; it is impossible not to perceive that the press, which they thus adorned, only represented in one part of its power the opinions originated in another.

But it is in very rare instances that a daily paper has done more than represent political opinion; it is the Reviews, quarterly or monthly (and, in two instances, weekly journals) which have aspired to *create* it. And this for an obvious reason: the daily paper looks only to sale for its influence; the capital risked is so enormous, the fame acquired by contributions to it so small and evanescent, that it is mostly regarded as a mere mercantile speculation. Now *new* opinions are not popular ones; to swim with the tide, is the necessary motto of opinions that desire to sell: while the majority can see in your journal the daily mirror of themselves, their prejudices and their passions, as well as their sober sense and their true interests, they will run to look upon the reflection. Hence it follows, that the journal which most represents, least originates opinion, that the two tasks are performed by two separate agents, and that the more new doctrines a journal promulgates, the less promiscuously it circulates among the public.

In this the moral light resembles the physical, and while we gaze with pleasure on the objects which reflect the light, the eye shrinks in pain from the orb which creates it.

A type of that truth in the history of letters, which declares that the popularity of a writer consists not in proportion to his superiority over the public, but in proportion to their sympathy with his sentiments, may be found in the story of Dante and the Buffoon; both were entertained at the court of the pedantic Scaliger, the fool sumptuously, the poet sparely.—"When will you be as well off as I am?" asked the fool triumphantly.— "Whenever," was Dante's caustic reply, "I shall find a patron who resembles *me* as much as Prince Scaliger resembles you."

An originator of opinion precedes the time; you cannot both precede and reflect it. Thus, the most popular journals are Plagiarists of the Past; they live on the ideas which their more far-sighted contemporaries propagated ten years before. What then was Philosophy, is now Opinion.

A great characteristic of English periodicals is the generally strict preservation of secrecy as to the names of the writers. The principal advantages alleged in favour of this regard to the anonymous are three: First, that you can speak of public men with less reserve; secondly, that you can review books with more attention to their real merits, and without any mixture of the personal feelings that, if you were known to the author, might bias the judgment of impartial criticism; thirdly, that many opinions you yourself consider it desirable that the public should know, peculiar circumstances of situations, or private checks of timidity and caution, might induce you to withhold, if your name were necessarily attached to their publication. I suspect that these advantages are greatly exaggerated on the one hand, and that their counterbalancing evils, have been greatly overlooked on the other.

In regard to the first of these advantages, it is clear that if you can speak of public men with less reserve, you may speak of them also with less regard to truth. In a despotic country, where chains are the reward of free sentiments, the use of the anonymous may be a necessary precaution; but what in this country should make a public writer shrink from the open discharge of his duty? If his writings be within the pale of the laws, he has nothing to fear from an avowal of his name; if without the law, the use of the anonymous does not skreen him. But were your name acknowledged, you could not speak of public men with the same vehement acerbity; you could not repeat charges and propagate reports with the same headlong indifference to accuracy or error. There is more shame in being an open slanderer than a concealed one: you would not, therefore, were your name on the newspaper, insert fragments of *"news"* about persons without ascertaining their foundation in truth: you would not, day after day, like to circulate the stories, which, day after day, you would have the ludicrous task of contradicting.

All this I grant; but, between you and me, dear sir, where is the harm of it? It is well to speak boldly of public men; but to speak what boldly?—not falsehood, but the truth. If the political writer ordinarily affixed his name to his lucubration, he would be brought under the wholesome influence of the same public opinion that he affects to influence or to reflect; he would be more consistent in his opinions,[2] and more cautious in examination. Papers would cease to be proverbial for giving easy access to the current slander and the diurnal lie; and the boldness of their tone would not be the less, because it would be also honest. I have said, to make power safe and constitutional, it must be made responsible; but anonymous power is irresponsible power.

And now, with regard to the second advantage alleged to belong to the use of the anonymous—the advantage in literary criticism: You say that being anonymous, you can review the work more impartially than if the author, perhaps your friend, were to know you to be his critic. Of all arguments in favour of the anonymous, this is the most popular and the most fallacious. Ask any man once let behind the curtain of periodical criticism, and you will find that the very partiality and *respect* to *persons,* which the custom of the anonymous was to prevent, the anonymous especially shields and ensures. Nearly all criticism at this day is the public effect of private acquaintance. When a work has been generally praised in the reviews, even if deservedly, nine times out of ten the author has secured a large connexion with the press. Good heavens! what machinery do we not see exerted to get a book tenderly nursed into vigour. I do not say that the critic is dishonest in this partiality; perhaps he may be actuated by feelings that, judged by the test of private sentiments, would be considered fair and praiseworthy.

"Ah, poor So-and-so's book; well, it is no great things; but so-and-so is a good fellow, I must give him a helping hand."

"C—— has sent me his book to review; that's a bore, as it's devilish bad; but as he knows I shall be his critic—I must be civil."

"What, D.'s poems? it would be d——d unhandsome to abuse them, after all his kindness to me—after dining at his house yesterday."

Such, and a variety of similar, private feelings, which it may be easy to censure, and which the critic himself will laughingly

2. Many of the political writers, skreened by the anonymous, shift and turn from all opinions, with every popular breath. The *paper* may be abused for it, but the paper is insensate; no one abuses the *unseen writer* of the paper. Thus, there is no shame, because there is no exposure; where there is no shame, there is no honesty.

allow you to blame, colour the tone of the great mass of reviews. This veil, so complete to the world, is no veil to the book writing friends of the person who uses it. *They* know the hand which deals the blow, or lends the help; and the critic willingly does a kind thing by his friend, because it is never known that in so doing he has done an unjust one by the public. The anonymous, to effect the object which it pretends, must be thoroughly sustained. But in how few cases is this possible! We have but one Junius in the world. At the present day there is not a journal existing in which, while the contributors are concealed indeed from the world at large, they are not known to a tolerably wide circle of publishing friends. Thus, then, in a critical point of view, the advantages supposed to spring from the anonymous vanish into smoke. The mask is worn, not to protect from the petitions of private partialities, but *to deceive the public as to the extent to which partiality is carried;* and the very evils which secrecy was to prevent, it not only produces, but conceals, and *by* concealment defrauds of a remedy. It is clear, on more than a superficial consideration, that the bias of private feelings would be far less strong upon the tenour of criticism, if the name of the critic were known; in the first place, because the check of public opinion would operate as a preventive to any reviewer of acknowledged reputation from tampering with his own honesty; in the second place, because there are many persons in the literary world, who would at once detect and make known to the public the chain of undue motive that binds the praise or censure of the critic to the book. Thus you would indeed, by the publication of the reviewer's name, obtain either that freedom from private bias, or that counterbalance to its exercise, of which, by withholding the name, the public have been so grossly defrauded. Were a sudden revelation of the mysteries of the craft now to be made, what—oh what would be the rage, the astonishment, of the public![3] What men of straw in the rostra, pronouncing fiats

3. The influence of certain booksellers upon certain Reviews, is a cry that has been much raised by Reviews in which *those* booksellers had no share. The accusation is as old as Voltaire's time. He complains that booksellers in France and Holland guided the tone of the periodical Reviews: with us, at present, however, the abuse is one so easily detected that I suspect it has been somewhat exaggerated. I know one instance of an influential weekly journal, which was accused, by certain of its rivals, of favouring a bookseller who had a share in its

on the immortal writings of the age; what guessers at the difference between a straight line and a curve, deciding upon the
highest questions of art; what stop-watch gazers lecturing on
the drama; what disappointed novelists, writhing poets, sale-
less historians, senseless essayists, wreaking their wrath on a

---

property; yet, accident bringing me in contact with that bookseller, I discovered
that it was a matter of the most rankling complaint in his mind, that the editor
of the journal, (who had an equal share himself in the journal, and could not
be removed,) was so anxious not to deserve the reproach as to be unduly harsh
to the books he was accused of unduly favouring: and on looking over the
Review, with my curiosity excited to see which party was right, I certainly
calculated that a greater proportion of books belonging to the bookseller in
question had been severely treated than was consistent with the ratio of praise
and censure accorded to the works appertaining to any other publisher. In
fact, the moment a journal becomes influential, its annual profits are so considerable, that it would be rarely worth while in any bookseller who may possess
a share in it to endanger its sale by a suspicion of dishonesty. The circumstance
of his having that share in it is so well known, and the suspicion to which it
exposes him so obvious, that I imagine the necessary vigilance of public
opinion a sufficient preventive of the influence complained of. The danger to
which the public are exposed is more latent; the influence of acquaintance is far
greater and more difficult to guard against than that of booksellers. On looking
over certain Reviews, we shall find instances in which they have puffed most
unduly; but it is more frequently the work of a contributor than the publication
of the bookseller who promulges the Review. The job is of a more secret character than that which a title-page can betray. It is surprising indeed to see how
readily the slightest and most inferior works of a contributor to one of the
Quarterlies obtains a review, while those of a stranger, however important or
popular, are either entirely overlooked or unnoticed, until the favour of the
public absolutely forces them on the reluctant journal. It often happens that a
successful writer has been most elaborately reviewed in all the other periodicals
of the civilized world, and his name has become familiar to the ears of literary
men throughout the globe, before the Quarterly Reviews of this country bestow
the slightest notice upon him, or condescend even to acknowledge an acquaintance with his very existence. This is a wretched effect of influence, for it
attempts to create a monopoly of literature; nor is that all—it makes the
judges and the judged one body, and a Quarterly Review a mere confederacy of
writers united for the purpose of praising each other at all opportunities, and
glancing indifferently towards the public when the greater duties of self-
applause allow them leisure for the exertion. Great men contribute to these
journals, and are praised—nothing more just!—but *little* men contribute also:
and the jackal has his share of the bones as well as the lion. It is obvious, that
if Reviews were not written anonymously, the public could not be thus cheated.
If contributors put their names to their articles, they could not go on scratch-
ing each other at so indecent a rate; there would be an end to the antic system
of these literary *simiæ,* who, sitting aloft on the tree of criticism, first take care
to stuff themselves with the best of the fruit, and then, with the languid justice
of satiety, chuck the refuse on the gazers below!

lucky rival; what Damons heaping impartial eulogia on their scribbling Pythias; what presumption, what falsehood, what ignorance, what deceit! what malice in censure, what dishonesty in praise! Such a revelation would be worthy a Quevedo to describe!

But this would not be the sole benefit the public would derive from the authority of divulged names. They would not only know the motives of reviewers, but their capacities also; they would see if the critic were able to judge honestly, as well as willing. And this upon many intricate matters; some relating to the arts, others to the sciences; on which the public in general cannot judge for themselves, but may be easily misled by superficial notions, and think that the unknown author must be a great authority;—this, I say, in such cases would be an incalculable advantage, and would take the public at once out of the hands of a thousand invisible pretenders and impostors.

An argument has been adduced in favour of anonymous criticism so truly absurd, that it would not be worth alluding to, were it not so often alleged, and so often suffered to escape unridiculed. It is this: that the critic can thus take certain liberties with the author with impunity; that he may be witty or severe, without the penalty of being shot. Now, of what nature is that criticism which would draw down the author's cartel of war upon the critic?—it is not an age for duels on light offences and vague grounds. An author would be laughed at from one end of the kingdom to the other, for calling out a man for merely abusing his book; for saying that he wrote bad grammar, and was a wretched poet: if the author *were* such a fool as, on mere literary ground, to challenge a critic, the critic would scarcely be such a fool as to go out with him. "Ay," says the critic, "if I only abuse his book; but what if I abuse his person? I may censure his work safely—but supposing I want to insinuate something against his character?" True, now we understand each other; that is indeed the question. I turn round at once from you, sir, the critic— I appeal to the public. I ask them where is the benefit, what the advantage of attacking a man's person, not his book—his character, not his composition? Is criticism to be the act of personal vituperation? then, in God's name, let us send to Billingsgate for our reviewers, and have something racy and idiomatic at least in the way of slang. What purpose salutary to literature is served by hearing that Hazlitt had pimples on his face? How are poor Byron's errors amended, by filthily groping among the details of his private life—by the insinuations and the misconstructions—by the muttered slanders—by the broad falsehoods, which filled the anonymous channels of the press? Was it not this system of espionage more than any other cause which darkened with gloomy suspicion that mind, originally so noble? Was not the stinging of the lip the result of the stung heart? Slandered by others, his irritable mind retaliated by slander in return; the openness visible in his early character hardened into insincerity, the constant product of suspicion; and instead of correcting the author, this species of criticism contributed to deprave the man.

What did the public gain by this result of the convenience of open speaking from invisible tongues?—nothing. But why, my dear sir, (you who have studied the literary character so deeply, and portrayed so well the calamities of authors, can perhaps tell me)—why is the poor author to be singled out from the herd of men (whom he seeks to delight or to instruct) for the sole purpose of torture? Is his nature so much less sensitive and gentle than that of others, that the utmost ingenuity is necessary to wound him? Or why is a system to be invented and encouraged, for the sole sake of persecuting him with the bitterest rancour and the most perfect impunity? Why are the rancour and the impunity to be modestly alleged as the main advantages of the system? Why are all the checks and decencies which moderate the severity of the world's censure upon its other victims, to be removed from censure upon him? Why is he to be thrust out of the pale of ordinary self-defence?—and the decorum and the fear of consequences which make the intercourse of mankind urbane and humanized, to be denied to one, whose very vanity can only be fed—whose very interests can only be promoted, by increasing the pleasures of the society which exiles him from its commonest protection—yes! by furthering the civilization which rejects him from its safeguards?

It is not very easy, perhaps, to answer these questions; and I think, sir, that even your ingenuity can hardly discover the justice of an invention which visits with all the most elaborate and recondite severities that could be exercised against the enemy of his kind, the unfortunate victim who aspires to be their friend. Shakspeare has spoken of detraction as less excusable than theft: but there is a yet nobler fancy among certain uncivilized tribes, viz., that slander is a greater moral offence than even murder itself; for, say they, with an admirable shrewdness of distinction, "when you take a man's life, you take only what he *must,* at one time or the other, have lost; but when you take a man's reputation, you take that which he might otherwise have retained for ever: nay, what is yet more important, your offence in the one is bounded and definite. Murder cannot travel beyond the grave— the deed imposes at once a boundary to its own effects; but in slander, the tomb itself does not limit the malice of your wrong: your lie may pass onward to posterity, and continue, generation after generation, to blacken the memory of your victim."

The people of the Sandwich Islands murdered Captain Cook, but they pay his memory the highest honours which their customs acknowledge; they retain his bones (those returned were supposititious) which are considered sacred, and the priest thanks the gods for having sent them so great a man. Are you surprised at this seeming inconsistency? Alas! it is the manner in which we treat the great! We murder them by the weapons of calumny and persecution, and then we declare the relics of our victim to be sacred!

But there is a third ground for deeming the preservation of the anonymous advantageous in periodicals; namely, that there may be opinions you wish to give to the world upon public events or public characters, which private checks of circumstance or timidity may induce you to withhold from the world, if the publication of your name be indispensably linked with that of your opinions.

Now if, from what I have said, it is plain the anonymous *system* is wrong; then the utmost use you can make of this argument would only prove that there are occasional exceptions to the justness of this rule; and this I grant readily and at once. He is but a quack who pretends that a general rule excludes all exceptions, and how few are the exceptions to *this* rule; how few the persons upon whom the checks alluded to legitimately operate! I leave to them the right of availing themselves of the skreen they consider necessary;—there will always be channels and opportunities enough for them to consult the anonymous, supposing that it were accordant with the *general* system of periodicals to give the public the names of their contributors.[4]

I have elsewhere, but more cursorily, put forth my opinions with regard to the customary use of the anonymous in periodicals: they have met with but little favour from periodical writers, who have continued to reiterate the old arguments which I had already answered rather than attacked my replies. In fact, journalists, misled by some vague notions of the convenience of a plan so long adopted and so seldom questioned, contend against a change which would be of the most incalculable advantage to themselves and their profession. It is in vain to hope that you can make the press so noble a profession as it ought to be in the eyes of men, as long as it can be associated in the public mind with every species of political apostasy and personal slander; it is in vain to hope that the many honourable exceptions will do more than win favour for themselves; they cannot exalt the character of the class. Interested as the aristocracy are against the moral authority of the press, and jealous as they are of its power, they at present endeavour to render odious the general effects of the machine, by sneering down far below their legitimate grade, the station and respectability of the operatives. It is in vain to deny that a newspaper-writer, who, by his talents and the channel to which they are applied, exerts a far greater influence on public affairs than almost any peer in the realm, is only of importance so long as he is in the back parlour of the printing-house; in society he not only runs the risk of being confounded

---

4. It is also obvious that the arguments I have adduced in favour of the latter plan, do not apply to authors publishing separate works, more especially fiction, as in the instance of Sir Walter Scott and his novels: there, no one is injured by the affectation of concealment—there is no third party (no party attacked or defended) between the author and the public: I speak solely of the periodical press, which is the most influential department of the press, and how it may be the most honest and most efficient towards the real interests of the community.

Consequently the reader will remark in any reply that may be put forth to these opinions, first—that it will be no answer to the justice of the rule I assert, to enumerate the exceptions I allow: secondly—that it will be no answer to my proposition relating to the periodical press to revert to the advantages of the anonymous to authors whose writings do not come under that department. With this I leave it to the People, deeply interested in the matter, to see that I am answered, not misinterpreted.

with all the misdemeanours past and present, of the journal he has contributed to purify or exalt, but he is associated with the general fear of *espionage* and feeling of insecurity which the custom of anonymous writing necessarily produces: men cannot avoid looking upon him as one who has the power of stabbing them in the dark—and the libels—the lies—the base and filthy turpitude of certain of the Sunday papers, have an effect of casting upon all newspaper writers a suspicion, from which not only the honourable, but the able[5] among them are utterly free —as at Venice, every member of the secret council, however humane and noble, received some portion of the odium and the fear which attached to the practice of unwitnessed punishment and mysterious assassination. In short, the unhappy practice of the anonymous, is the only reason why the man of political power is not also the man of social rank. It is a practice which favours the ignorant at the expense of the wise, and skreens the malignant by confounding them with the honest; a practice by which talent is made obscure, that folly may not be detected, and the disgrace of vice may be hidden beneath the customs which degrade honour.

In a Spanish novel, a cavalier and a swindler meet one another.

"Pray, sir, may I ask, why you walk with a cloak?" says the swindler.

"Because I do not wish to be known for what I am," answers the gentleman. "Let me ask you the same question."

"Because I wish to be taken for *you*," answered the swindler drily.

The custom of honest men is often the shelter of rogues.

It is quite clear that if every able writer affixed his name to his

---

5. For to the honour of literature be it said, that the libellous Sunday papers are rarely supported by any literary men; they are conducted chiefly by broken down sharpers, *ci-devant* markers at gambling-houses, and the very worst description of uneducated blackguards. The only way, by the by, to check these gentlemen in their career of slander, is to be found in the first convenient opportunity of inflicting upon them that personal chastisement which is the perquisite of bullies.—Pooh! you say, they are not worthy of punishment. Pardon me, they are not worth the denying ourselves the luxury of inflicting it. You should wait, but never miss, the convenient opportunity. In the spirit of Dr. Johnson's criticism on the Hebrides, "they are worth seeing," (said he,) "but not worth going to see," these gentlemen are worth kicking, but not worth *going* to kick.

contributions to newspapers, the importance of his influence would soon attach to himself—

———————— Nec Phœbo gratior ulla est
Quàm sibi quæ Vari præscripsit pagina nomen.

He would no longer be confused with a herd—he would become marked and individualized—a public man as well as a public writer: he would exalt his profession as himself—the consideration accorded to him would, if he produced the same effect on his age, be the same as to a poet, philosopher, or a statesman, and now when an entrance into public life may be the result of popular esteem, it may be the readiest way of rendering men of principle and information personally known to the country, and of transferring the knowledge, which in order to be efficient public writers they must possess on public affairs, to that active career in which it may be the most serviceable to the country, and the most tempting to men of great acquirements and genius. Thus the profession of the Press would naturally attract the higher order of intellect—power would become infinitely better directed, and its agents immeasurably more honoured. These considerations sooner or later must have their due weight with those from whom alone the necessary reform can spring—the journalists themselves. It is not a point in which the legislature can interfere, it must be left to a moral agency, which is the result of conviction. I am firmly persuaded, however opposed I may be now, that I shall live to see (and to feel that I have contributed to effect) the change.

Such is my hope for the future; meanwhile let me tell you an adventure that happened the other day to an acquaintance of mine.

D—— is a sharp clever man, fond of studying character, and always thrusting his nose into other people's affairs. He has wonderful curiosity, which he dignifies by the more respectable name of "a talent for observation." A little time ago D—— made an excursion of pleasure to Calais. During his short but interesting voyage, he amused himself by reconnoitering the passengers whom Providence had placed in the same boat with himself. Scarcely had his eye scanned the deck before it was irresistibly attracted towards the figure of a stranger, who sat alone, wrapped in his cloak, and his meditations. My friend's curiosity was instantly aroused: there was an inscrutable dignity in the air of the stranger; something mysterious, moodful, and majestic. He resolved to adventure upon satisfying the hungry appetite for knowledge that had sprung up in his breast: he approached the stranger, and, by way of commencing with civility, offered him the newspaper. The stranger glanced at him for a moment, and shook his head. "I thank you, sir, I have seen its contents already." *The contents*—he did not say *the paper,* thought D——, shrewdly, the words were not much, but the air! The stranger was evidently a great man; perhaps a diplomatist. My friend made another attempt at a better acquaintance; but about this time the motion of the steam-vessel began to affect the stranger—

And his soul sickened o'er the heaving wave.

Maladies of this sort are not favourable to the ripening of acquaintance. My friend, baffled and disappointed, shrunk into himself; and soon afterwards, amidst the tumult of landing, he lost sight of his fellow-passenger. Following his portmanteau with a jealous eye, as it rolled along in a foreign wheelbarrow, D—— came at last into the court-yard of M. Dessein's hotel, and there, sauntering leisurely to and fro, he beheld the mysterious stranger. The day was warm; it was delightful to bask in the open air. D—— took a chair by the kitchen door, and employed himself on the very same newspaper that he had offered to the stranger, and which the cursed sea winds had prevented his reading on the deck at that ease with which our national sense of comfort tells us that a newspaper ought to be read. Ever and anon, he took his eyes from the page and beheld the stranger still sauntering to and fro, stopping at times to gaze on a green britska with that paternal look of fondness which declared it to be an appropriation of his own.

The stranger was visibly impatient:—now he pulled out his watch—now he looked up to the heavens—now he whistled a tune—and now he muttered, "Those d——d Frenchmen!" A gentleman with a mincing air, and a quick gait, entered the yard. You saw at once that he was a Frenchman. The eyes of the two gentlemen met; they recognised each other. You might tell that the Englishman had been waiting for the new comer, the *"Bon jour mon cher"* of the Frenchman, the "How do you do" of the Englishman, were exchanged; and D—— had the happiness of overhearing the following conversation:

French Gentleman. "I am ravished to congratulate you on the distinguished station you hold in Europe."

English Gentleman (bowing and blushing). "Let me rather congratulate you on your accession to the peerage."

French Gentleman. "A bagatelle, sir, a mere bagatelle; a natural compliment to my influence with the people. By the way, you of course will be a peer in the new batch that *must* be made shortly."

English Gentleman (with a constrained smile, a little in contempt and more in mortification). "No, Monsieur, no; *we* don't make peers quite so easily."

French Gentleman. "Easily! why have they not made Sir George ———— and M. W—— peers? the one a mere *elegant,* the other a mere *gentilhomme de province.* You don't compare their claims with your great power and influence in Europe!"

English Gentleman. "Hum—hi—hum; they were men of great birth and landed property."

French Gentleman (taking snuff). "Ah! I thought you English were getting better of your aristocratic prejudices: *Virtus est sola nobilitas."*

English Gentleman. "Perhaps those prejudices are *respectable.* By the way, to speak frankly, we were a little surprised in England at *your* elevation to the peerage."

French Gentleman. "Surprised;—*diable!*—why?"

English Gentleman. "Hum—really—the editor of a newspaper—ehum!—hem!"

French Gentleman. "Editor of a newspaper! why, who *should* get political rank, but those who wield political power? Your newspaper, for instance, is more formidable to a minister than any duke. Now you know, with us M. de Lalot, M. Thier,—de Villele,—Chateaubriand, and, in short, nearly all the great men you can name, write for the newspapers."

English Gentleman. "Aha! but do they *own* it?"

French Gentleman. "Own it, to be sure; they are too proud to do so: how else do they get their reputation?"

English Gentleman. "Why, with us, if a member of parliament sends us an article, it is under a pledge of the strictest secrecy. As for Lord Brougham, the bitterest accusation ever made against him was, that he wrote for a certain newspaper."

French Gentleman. "And *did* Lord Brougham write for that newspaper?"

English Gentleman. "Sir; that is a delicate question."

French Gentleman. "Why so reserved? In France the writers of our journals are as much known as if they put their names to their articles; which indeed, they very often do."

English Gentleman. "But supposing a great man is known to write an article in my paper, all the other papers fall foul on him for demeaning himself: even *I,* while I write every day for it, should be very angry if the coxcombs of the clubs accused me of it to my face."

French Gentleman (laying his finger to his nose.) "I see, I see, you have not a pride of class with you, as we have. The nobleman with us, is proud of showing that he has power with those who address the people; the plebeian writer is willing to receive a certain respectability from the assistance of the nobleman: thus each class gives consequence to the other. But you all write under a veil; and such a number of blackguards take advantage of the concealment that the respectable man covets concealment as a skreen for himself. This is the reason that you have not, pardon me, Monsieur, as high a station as you ought to have; and why you astonish me, by thinking it odd that I, who, vanity apart, can sway the minds of thousands every morning, should receive" (spoken with dignified disdain) "the trumpery honour of a peerage!"

"*Messieurs,* the dinner is served," said the *garçon;* and the two gentlemen walked into the salon, leaving D—— in a fever of agitation.

"*Garçon, garçon,*" said he, under his breath, and beckoning to the waiter, "who is that English Gentleman?"

"Meestare ———, the—vat you call him, le redacteur of— de editor od de—paper."

"Ha! and the French gentleman?"

"Monsieur Bertin de V——, pair de France, and editor of de *Journal des Debats.*"

"Bless me!" said D——, "what a *rencontre!*"

Such is the account my friend D—— has given me of a dialogue between two great men. It is very likely that D——'s talents for observation may be eclipsed by his talent of invention; I do not, therefore, give it you as a true anecdote. Look upon it, if you please, as an imaginary conversation, and tell me whether, supposing it *had* taken place, it would not have been exceedingly natural. You must class it among the instances of the *vraisemblable,* if you reject it from those of the *vrai.*

But the custom of the anonymous would never have so long sustained itself with us, had it not been sanctioned by the writers of the aristocracy—it is among the other benefits literature owes to them. It is a cloak more convenient to a man moving in a large society, than to the scholar, who is mostly centred in a small circle. The rich man has no power to gain by a happy criticism, but he may have much malice to gratify by a piquant assault. Thus the aristocratic contributors to a journal have the most insisted upon secrecy, and have used it to write the bitterest sallies on their friends. The unfortunate Lord Dudley dies, and we learn that one of his best compositions was a most truculent attack, in a Quarterly Review, upon his intimate companion—of course he was anxious not to be known! There are only two classes of men to whom the anonymous is really desirable. The perfidious gentleman who fears to be cut by the friends he injures, and the lying blackguard who dreads to be horsewhipped by the man he maligns.

With one more consideration I shall conclude this chapter. I intimated at the commencement of it, that the influence of the press was the great antagonist principle to that of the aristocracy. This is a hacknied assertion, yet it is pregnant with many novel speculations.

The influence of the press is the influence of opinion; yet, until very lately, the current opinion was decidedly aristocratic:—the class mostly addressed by the press, is the middle class; yet, as we have seen before, it is among the middle class that the influence of the English aristocracy has spread some of its most stubborn roots.

How then has the press become the antagonist principle of the aristocratic power? In the first place, that portion of the press which *originates* opinion, has been mostly anti-aristocratic, and its reasonings, unpopular at first, have slowly gained ground. In the second place, the anonymous system which favours all personal slander, and which, to feed the public taste, must slander distinguished, and not obscure, station, has forwarded the progress of opinion against the aristocratic body by the most distorted exaggeration of the individual vices or foibles of its members. By the mere details of vulgar gossip, a great wholesale principle of indignation at the privileged order has been at work; just as in ripening the feelings that led to the first French revolution, the tittle-tattle of antechambers did more than the works of philosophers. The frivolity and vices of the court provoked a bitterer contempt and resentment by well-coloured anecdotes of individual courtiers, than the elaborate logic of Diderot, or the polished sarcasms of Voltaire. And wandering for one moment from the periodical press to our lighter fictions, it is undeniable that the novels which of late have been so eagerly read, and which profess to give a description of the life of the higher circles, have, in our own day, nauseated the public mind with the description of men without hearts, women without chastity, polish without dignity, and existence without use.

A third reason for the hostility of the political press to the aristocracy is to be found in the circumstances of those who write for it. They live more separated from sympathy with aristocratic influences than any other class: belonging, chiefly, to the middle order, they do not, like the middle order in general, have any dependence on the custom and favour of the great; literary men, they are not, like authors in general, courted as lions, who, mixing familiarly with their superiors, are either softened by unmeaning courtesies, or imbibe the veneration which rank and wealth personally approached, instil into the human mind, as circumstances at present form it. They mostly regard the great aloof and at a distance; they see their vices which are always published, and rarely the virtues or the amenities which are not known beyond the threshold. The system strikes them, unrelieved by any affection for its component parts. I have observed, with much amusement, the effect often produced on a periodical writer by being merely brought into contact with a man of considerable rank. He is charmed with his urbanity—astonished at his want of visible pride—he no longer sees the pensioned and titled apostate, but the agreeable man; and his next article becomes warped from its severity in despite of himself. One of the bitterest assailants of Lord Eldon, having occasion to wait on that nobleman, was so impressed with the mild and kindly bearing of the man he had been attacking, that he laid it down as a rule never afterwards to say a syllable against him. So shackled do men become in great duties by the smallest conventional incidents.

But the ordinary mass of newspaper writers being thus a peculiar and separate body, untouched by the influence which they examine, and often galled themselves by the necessary effects of the anonymous system, have been therefore willing to cooperate to a certain and limited extent with the originators of opinion. And thus, in those crises which constantly occur in political affairs, when the popular mind, as yet undetermined, follows the first adviser in whom it has been accustomed to confide—when, in its wavering confusion, either of two opinions may be reflected, the representative portion of the press has usually taken that opinion which is the least aristocratic; pushing the more popular, not to its full extent, but to as great an extent as was compatible with its own interest in representing rather than originating opinion. There are certain moments in all changes and transits of political power, when it makes all the difference *which* of the unsettled doubts in the public mind is expressed the first, and hastened into decision.

To these causes of the anti-aristocratic influence of the press, we must add another, broader and deeper than all. The newspaper not only discusses questions, but it gives in its varied pages, the results of systems;—proceedings at law—convictions before magistrates—abuses in institutions—unfairness in taxation—all come before the public eye; thus, though many see not how grievances are to be redressed, all allow that the grievances exist. It is in vain to deny that the grievance is mostly on the side of the Underprivileged. No preponderating power in a state can exist for many years, without (unconsciously, perhaps,) favouring itself. We have not had an aristocratic government, without having had laws passed to its own advantage—without seeing the spirit of the presiding influence enter into our taxation, bias our legislature, and fix its fangs into our pension-lists; the last, though least really grievous of all—yet the most openly obnoxious to a commercial and over-burdened people. Nor must it be forgotten, that while the abuses of any system are thus made evident and glaring, the reasons for supporting that system in spite of abuses, are always philosophical and abstruse: so that the evil is glaring, the good unseen. This, then, is the strongest principle by which the press works against the aristocracy—the principle most constantly and most powerfully enforced. A plain recital affects more than reasoning, and seems more free from passion; and the Press, by revealing facts, exerts a far more irresistible, though less noisy sway, than by insisting on theories: —in the first it is the witness, in the last, the counsel.

And yet this spirit of Revelation is the greatest of all the blessings which the liberty of the press confers; it is of this which philosophers speak when they grow warm upon its praises— when wisdom loses its measured tone of approval, and reasoning itself assumes the language of declamation. As the nature of evidence is the comparison of facts, so to tell us all things on all sides is the sole process by which we arrive at truth. From the moment an abuse is published, sooner or later we are certain the abuse will be cured. In the sublime language of a great moralist, "Errors cease to be dangerous when it is permitted to contradict them; they are soon known to be errors; they sink into the Abyss of Forgetfulness, and Truth alone swims over the vast extent of Ages." This publicity is man's nearest approach to the omniscience of his great Creator; it is the largest result of union yet known, for it is the expression of the Universal Mind. Thus are we enabled, knowing what *is* to be effected, to effect according to our knowledge—for to knowledge power is proportioned. Omnipotence is the necessary consequence of omniscience. Nor can we contemplate without a deep emotion, what may be the result of that great measure, which must sooner or later be granted by the legislature, and which, by the destruction of the stamp duty on political periodicals will extend to so unbounded a circle this sublime prerogative of publicity—of conveying principles—of expressing opinion—of promulging fact. So soon as the first confusion that attends the sudden opening of a long monopoly is cleared away—when it is open to every man, rich or poor, to express the knowledge he has hoarded in his closet, or even at his loom; when the stamp no longer confines to a few the power of legitimate instruction; when all may pour their acquirements into the vast commonwealth of knowledge—it is impossible to calculate the ultimate results to human science, and the advancement of our race. Some faint conjecture may be made from a single glance at the crowded reports of a parliamentary committee; works containing a vast hoard of practical knowledge, of inestimable detail, often collected from witnesses who otherwise would have been dumb for ever; works now unread, scarce known, confined to those who want them least, by them not rendered profitable: when we recollect that in popular and familiar shapes that knowledge and those details will ultimately find a natural vent, we may form some slight groundwork of no irrational guesses towards the future; when the means of knowledge shall be open to all who read, and its expression to all who think. Nor must we forget, that from the mechanic, the mechanic will more easily learn; as it has been discovered in the Lancaster schools, that by boys, boys can be best instructed. Half the success of the pupil depends on his familiarity and sympathy with the master. Reflections thus opened to us, expand into hopes, not vague, not unfounded, but which no dreams of imaginary optimism have yet excelled. What triumph for him, who, in that divine spirit of prophecy which foresees in future happiness the result of present legislation, has been a disciple—a worker for the saving truth, that enlightenment furthers amelioration—who has built the port and launched the ship, and suffered the obstacles of nature and the boundaries of the world to be the only bar and limit to the commerce of the mind: he may look forward into time, and see his own name graven upon a thousand landmarks of the progress of the human intellect. Such men are, to *all* wisdom, what Bacon was only to a part of it. It is better to allow philosophy to be universal, than to become a philosopher. The wreath that belongs to a fame of this order will be woven from the best affections of mankind: its glory will be the accumulated gratitude of generations. It is said, that in the Indian plain of Dahia, the Creator drew forth from the loins of Adam his whole posterity: assembled together in the size and semblance of small ants, these pre-existent nations acknowledged God, and confessed their origin in his power. Even so in some great and living project for the welfare of mankind—the progenitor of benefits, uncounted and unborn—we may trace the seeds of its offspring even to the confines of eternity; we may pass before us, though in a dwarfed and inglorious shape, the mighty and multiplied blessings to which it shall give birth, all springing from one principle, all honouring Him, who of that principle was the Vivifier and the Maker!

II

Literature

"This is a great literary epoch with your nation," said a German to me the other day, "You have magnificent *writers* amongst you at this day, their names are known all over Europe; but (putting the poets out of the question) where, to ask a simple question, are their writings?—which are the great prose works of your contemporaries that you recommend me to read? What, especially, are the recent masterpieces in criticism and the *belles lettres?*"

This question, and the lame answer that I confess I gave to it, set me upon considering why we had undoubtedly at this day many great writers in the Humane Letters, and yet very few great books. For the last twenty years the intellectual faculties have been in full foliage, but have borne no fruit, save on one tree alone; the remarkable fertility of which forcibly contrasts the barrenness of the rest, and may be considered among the most startling of the literary phenomena of the times—I mean the faculty of the Imagination. I am asked for the great books we have produced during the last twenty years, and my memory instantly reverts to the *chef-d'œuvres* of poets and writers of fiction. The works of Byron, Wordsworth, Scott, Moore, Shelley, Campbell, rush at once to my tongue: nay, I should refer to later writers in imaginative literature, whose celebrity is, as yet, un-mellowed, and whose influence limited, long ere the contemporary works of a graver nature would force themselves on my recollection: debar me the imaginative writings, and I could more easily close my catalogue of great works than begin it.

In imaginative literature, then, we are peculiarly rich, in the graver letters we are as singularly barren.

In History we have surely not even secondary names; we have commentators on history, rather than historians: and the general dimness of the atmosphere may be at once acknowledged, when we point as luminaries to a ———— and a ————.[1]

In Moral Philosophy, a subject which I shall reserve for a separate chapter, the reputation of one or two high names does not detract from the general sterility. Few indeed are the works in this noble department of knowledge, that have been, if published, *made known to the public* for a period inconceivably long, when we consider that we live in an age when the jargon of moral philosophy is so popularly affected.

In that part of political literature which does not embrace political economy, we are also without any great works: but yet, singularly enough, not without many perhaps unequalled writers—Southey, Wilson, Cobbett, Sydney Smith, the profound and vigorous editor of the *Examiner*, the original and humorous author of the *Corn Law Catechism*, and many others whom I can name, (but that almost every influential Journal betrays the eminent talent that supports it), are men who have developed some of the highest powers of composition, in a series of writings intended only for the hour. In miscellaneous literature, or what is commonly termed the *belles lettres*, we have not very remarkably enriched the collection bequeathed to us by the Johnsonian era. The name of one writer I cannot, however, help singling from the rest, as that of the most elegant gossip upon the learned letters, not only of his time, but, perhaps, his country; and I select it the more gladly, because popular as he is, I do not think he has ever obtained from criticism a fair acknowledgment of the eminent station he is entitled to claim. The reader has already discovered that I speak of yourself, the author of *The Curiosities of Literature, The Calamities of Authors,* and, above

1. But if we cannot boast of men capable of grasping the events of past ages, we have, at least, one, who in the spirit of ancient history has painted with classic colours the scenes in which he himself was an actor; and has left to posterity the records of a great war, written with the philosophy of Polybius, and more than the eloquence, if less than the simplicity, of Cæsar. I need scarcely add, that I refer to the *History of the Peninsular War,* by Colonel Napier.

all, the *Essay upon the Literary Character.* In the two first of these works you have seemed to me to be to literature what Horace Walpole was to a court;—drawing from minutiæ, which you are too wise to deem frivolities, the most novel deductions, and the most graceful truths; and seeming to gossip, where in reality you philosophize. But you have that which Horace Walpole never possessed—that which is necessary to the court of Letters, but forbidden to the Court of Kings: a deep and tender vein of sentiment runs, at no unfrequent times, through your charming lucubrations; and I might instance, as one of the most touching, yet unexaggerated conceptions of human character, that even a novelist ever formed, the beautiful *Essay upon Shenstone.* That, indeed, which particularly distinguishes your writings, is your marvellous and keen sympathy with the literary character in all its intricate mazes and multiplied varieties of colour. You identify yourself wholly with the persons on whom you speculate; you enter into their heart, their mind, their caprices, their habits, and their eccentricities; and this quality, so rare even in a dramatist, is entirely new in an essayist. I know of no other lucubrator who possesses it: with a subtile versatility you glide from one character to another, and by examination re-create;—drawing from research all those new views and bold deductions which the poet borrows from imagination. The gallant and crafty Raleigh, the melancholy Shenstone, the antiquarian Oldys—each how different, each how profoundly analyzed, each how peculiarly the author's own! Even of the least and lowest, you say something new. Your art is like that which Fontaine would attribute to a more vulgar mastery:

> —— Un roi, prudent et sage,
> De ces moindres sujets fait tirer quelque usage.

But the finest of all your works, to my mind, is the *Essay on the Literary Character;* a book, which he who has once read, ever recurs to with delight: it is one of those rare works, in which every part is adorned, yet subordinate to the whole—in which every page displays a beauty, and none an impertinence.

You recollect the vigorous assault made at one time against a peculiar school of writers; years have passed, and on looking back over the additions those years have brought to our *belles lettres,* the authors of that calumniated school immediately occur to us. The first of these writers is Mr. Hazlitt, a man of a nervous and original mind, of great powers of expression, of a cool reason, of a warm imagination, of imperfect learning, and of capricious and unsettled taste. The chief fault of his essays is, that they are vague and desultory; they leave no clear conclusion on the mind; they are a series of brilliant observations, without a result. If you are wiser when you have concluded one of them, it seems as if you were made so by accident: some aphorism, half an impertinence, in the middle of the essay, has struck on the truth, which the peroration, probably, will again carefully wrap in obscurity. He has aspired to be the universal critic; he has commented on art and letters, philosophy, manners, and men: in regard to the last, for my own part, I would esteem him a far more questionable authority than upon the rest; for he is more occupied in saying shrewd things of character, than in giving you the character itself. He wanted, perhaps, a various and actual experience of mankind in all its grades; and if he had the sympathy which compensates for experience, it was not a catholic sympathy, it was bestowed on particular tenets and their professors, and was erring, because it was sectarian. But in letters and in art, prejudice blinds less than it does in character; and in these the metaphysical bias of his mind renders him often profound, and always ingenious; while the constant play of his fancy redeems and brightens even the occasional inaccuracy of his taste.

Mr. Leigh Hunt's Indicator contains some of the most delicate and subtle criticisms in the language. His kindly and cheerful sympathy with Nature—his perception of the minuter and more latent sources of the beautiful—spread an irresistible charm over his compositions,—but he has not as yet done full justice to himself in his prose writings, and must rest his main reputation upon those exquisite poems which the age is beginning to appreciate.

The Essays of Elia, in considering the recent additions to our *belles lettres,* cannot be passed over in silence. Their beauty is in their delicacy of sentiment. Since Addison, no writer has displayed an equal refinement of humour: and if no single one of Mr. Lamb's conceptions equals the elaborate painting of Sir Roger de Coverley, yet his range of character is more extensive than Addison's, and in his humour there is a deeper pathos. His compositions are so perfectly elaborate, and so minutely finished, that they partake rather of the character of poetry than of prose; they are as perfect in their way as the Odes of Horace, and at times, as when commencing his invocation to "the Shade of Elliston" he breaks forth with

> Joyousest of once-embodied spirits, whither at length hast thou flown?

&c. we might almost fancy that he had set Horace before him as a model.

But the most various, scholastic, and accomplished of such of our literary contemporaries as have written works as well as articles, and prose as well as poetry—is, incontestably, Dr. Southey. "The Life of Nelson" is acknowledged to be the best biography of the day. "The Life of Wesley" and "The Book of the Church," however adulterated by certain prepossessions and prejudices, are, as mere compositions, characterized by an equal simplicity and richness of style,—an equal dignity and an equal ease. No writer blends more happily the academical graces of the style of last century, with the popular vigour of that which distinguishes the present. His Colloquies are, we suspect, the work on which he chiefly prides himself, but they do not seem to me to contain the best characteristics of his genius. The work is overloaded with quotation and allusion, and, like Tarpeia, seems crushed beneath the weight of its ornaments; it wants the great charm of that simple verve which is so peculiarly Southeian. Were I to do justice to Southey's cast of mind—to analyse its properties and explain its apparent contradictions, I should fill the two volumes of this work with Southey alone. Suffice it *now* (another occasion to do him ampler justice may occur elsewhere,) to make two remarks in answer to the common charges against this accomplished writer. He is alleged to be grossly inconsistent in politics, and wholly unphilosophical in morals. I hold both these charges to spring from the coarse injustice of party. If ever a man wrote a complete vindication of himself—that vindication is to be found in Southey's celebrated Letter to a certain Member of Parliament; the triumphant dignity with which he puts aside each successive aspersion—the clearness with which, in that Letter, his bright integrity shines out through all the mists amidst which it voluntarily passes, no dispassionate man can mark and not admire. But he is not philosophical?—No,—rather say he is not logical; his philosophy is large and learned, but it is all founded on hypothesis, and is poetical not metaphysical. What I shall afterwards say of Wordsworth would be equally applicable to Southey had the last been less passionate and less of a political partisan.

It would be no unpleasant task to pursue yet farther the line of individual criticism; but in a work of this nature, single instances of literary merit are only cited as illustrations of a particular state of letters; and the mention of authors must be regarded merely in the same light as quotations from books, in which some compliment is indeed rendered to the passage quoted, but assuredly without disrespect to those which do not recur so easily to our memory, or which seem less apposite to our purpose.

Still recurring to my first remark, we cannot but feel impressed, while adducing some names in the non-inventive classes of literature, with the paucity of those who remain. It is a great literary age—we have great literary men—but where are their works? a moment's reflection gives us a reply to the question; we must seek them not in detached and avowed and standard publications, but in periodical miscellanies. It is in these journals that the most eminent of our recent men of letters, have chiefly obtained their renown—it is here that we find the sparkling and sarcastic Jeffrey—the incomparable humour and transparent logic of Sydney Smith—the rich and glowing criticism of Wilson—the nervous vigour and brilliant imagination of Macaulay, (who, if he had not been among the greatest of English orators, would have been among the most commanding of English authors;) it is in periodicals that many of the most beautiful evidences of Southey's rich taste and antique stateliness of mind are to be sought, and that the admirable editor of *The Examiner* has embodied the benevolence of Bentham in the wit of Courier. Nay, even a main portion of the essays, which, now collected in a separate shape,[2] have become a permanent addition to our literature, first appeared amidst a crowd of articles of fugitive interest in

2. Elia, many of the Essays of Hazlitt, &c.

the journals of the day, and owe to the accident of republication their claims to the attention of posterity. From this singular circumstance, as the fittest fact whereon to build our deductions, we may commence our survey of the general Intellectual Spirit of the Time.

The revolution that has been effected by Periodical Literature, is, like all revolutions, the result of no immediate causes; it commenced so far back as the reign of Anne. The success of the *Tatler* and *Spectator* opened a new field to the emulation of literary men,[3] and in the natural sympathy between literature and politics, the same channels into which the one was directed afforded equal temptation to the other; men of the highest intellect and rank were delighted to resort to a constant and frequent means of addressing the public; the political opinions of Addison, Steele, Swift, Bolingbroke, and the fitful ambition of Wharton himself, found vent in periodical composition. The fashion once set, its advantages were too obvious for it not to continue; and thus the examples of Chesterfield and Pulteney, of Johnson, Goldsmith, and Mackenzie, sustained the dignity of this species of writing so unpretending in its outward appearance, and demanding therefore so much excellence to preserve its importance. The fame acquired by periodical essays gave consequence and weight to periodical miscellanies—criticism became a vocation as books multiplied. The *Journal des Sçavans* of the French begat imitators in England; similar journals rose and increased in number and influence, and the reviewers soon grew a corporate body and a formidable tribunal. The abuses consequent, as we have shown, on an anonymous system, began to be early apparent in these periodicals, which were generally feeble in proportion to their bulk, and of the less value according to their greater ostentation. The public sickened of *The Monthly Review,* and the *Edinburgh Quarterly* arose. From the appearance of this latter work, which was the crown and apex of periodical reviews, commences the deterioration of our standard literature; —and the dimness and scantiness of isolated works on politics,

3. The "Review" of De Foe, commencing in 1704 and continued till 1713, embraced not only matters on politics and trade, but also what he termed a *scandal club,* which treating on poetry, criticism, &c. contained the probable germ of the *Tatler* and *Spectator.*

criticism, and the *belles lettres,* may be found exactly in proportion to the brilliancy of this new focus, and the rapidity with which it attracted to itself the talent and knowledge of the time. The effect which this work produced, its showy and philosophical tone of criticism, the mystery that attached to it, the excellence of its composition, soon made it an honour to be ranked among its contributors. The length of time intervening between the publication of its numbers was favourable to the habits and taste of the more elaborate and scholastic order of writers; what otherwise they would have published in a volume, they willingly condensed into an essay; and found for the first time in miscellaneous writings, that with a less risk of failure than in an isolated publication, they obtained, for the hour at least, an equal reputation. They enjoyed indeed a double sort of fame, for the article not only obtained praise for its own merit, but caught no feeble reflection from the general esteem conferred upon the Miscellany itself; add to this the high terms of pecuniary remuneration, till then unknown in periodicals, so tempting to the immediate wants of the younger order of writers, by which an author was sure of obtaining for an essay in the *belles lettres* a sum almost equal to that which he would have gleaned from a respectable degree of success if the essay had been separately given to the world; and this by a mode of publication which saved him from all the chances of loss, and the dread of responsibility;—the certain anxiety, the probable mortification. In a few years the *Quarterly Review* divided the public with the *Edinburgh,* and the opportunities afforded to the best writers of the day to express, periodically, their opinions, were thus doubled. The consequence was unavoidable; instead of writing volumes authors began pretty generally to write articles, and a literary excrescence monopolized the nourishment that should have extended to the whole body: hence talent, however great; taste, however exquisite; knowledge, however enlarged, were directed to fugitive purposes. Literary works, in the magnificent thought of Bacon, are the Ships of Time; precious was the cargo wasted upon vessels which sunk for ever in a three-months' voyage! What might not Jeffrey and Sydney Smith, in the vigour of their age, have produced as authors if they had been less industrious as reviewers. The evil increased by degrees; the profoundest writers began to perceive that the period allotted to the duration of an article was scarcely sufficient inducement to extensive and exhausting labour; (even in a quarterly review the brilliant article dazzled more than the deep: for true wisdom requires time for appreciation,) and, though still continuing the mode of publication which proffered so many conveniences, they became less elaborate in their reasonings and less accurate in their facts.

Thus, by a natural reaction, a temporary form of publication produced a bias to a superficial order of composition; and, while intellectual labour was still attracted towards one quarter, it was deteriorated, as monopolies are wont to be, by the effects of monopoly itself. But, happily, there was one faculty of genius which these miscellanies could not materially attract, and that was the IMAGINATIVE. The poet and the novelist had no temptation to fritter away their conceptions in the grave and scholastic pages of the Quarterly Journals; they were still compelled, if they exceeded the slender limits allotted to them in magazines, to put forth separate works; to incur individual responsibility; to appeal to Time, as their tribunal; to meditate—to prepare—to perfect. Hence one principal reason, among others, why the Imaginative Literature of the day has been so much more widely and successfully cultivated than any other branch of intellectual exertion. The best writers in other branches write the reviews, and leave only the inferior ones to write the books.

The Imaginative Faculty thus left to its natural and matured tendencies, we may conceive that the spirit and agitation of the age exercised upon the efforts it produced the most direct and permanent influence. And it is in the poetry and the poetic prose of our time that we are chiefly to seek for that sympathy which always exists between the intellectual and the social changes in the prevalent character and sentiment of a People.

There is a certain period of civilization, ere yet men have begun to disconnect the principles to be applied to future changes from a vague reference to former precedents; when amendment is not orthodox, if considered a novelty; and an improvement is only imagined a return to some ancient and dormant excellence. At that period all are willing to listen with reverential interest to every detail of the Past; the customs of their ancestors have for them a superstitious attraction, and even the spirit of innovation is content to feed itself from the devotion to antiquity. It was at this precise period that the genius of Walter Scott brought into vivid portraiture the very images to which Inquiry was willing to recur, satisfied the half unconscious desire of the age and represented its scarcely expressed opinion. At that period, too, a distaste to the literature immediately preceding the time had grown up; a vague feeling that our poetry, become frigid and tame by echoed gallicisms, required some return to the national and more primitive tone. Percy's *Ballads* had produced a latent suspicion of the value of re-working forgotten mines: and, above all, perhaps purer and deeper notions of Shakspeare had succeeded the vulgar criticism that had long depreciated his greatest merits; he had become studied, as well as admired; an affection had grown up not only for the creations of his poetry, but the stately and antique language in which they were clothed. These feelings in the popular mind, which was in that state when both Poetry and Philosophy were disposed to look favourably on any able and deliberate recurrence to the manners and the spirit of a past age, Sir Walter Scott was the first vividly and popularly to represent; and, therefore, it is to his pages that the wise historian will look not only for an epoch in poetical literature, but the reflection of the moral sentiment of an age. The prose of that great author is but a continuation of the effect produced by his verse, only cast in a more familiar mould, and adapted to a wider range;—a reverberation of the same tone, carrying the sound to a greater distance.

A yet more deep and enduring sentiment of the time was a few years afterwards embodied by the dark and meditative genius of Byron; but I apprehend that Criticism, amidst all the inquiries it directed towards the causes of the sensation produced by that poet, did not give sufficient importance to those in reality the most effective.[4]

Let us consider:—

4. I do not here stop to trace the manner in which the genius of Scott or Byron was formed by the writings of less popular authors: Wordsworth and Coleridge assisted greatly towards the ripening of those feelings which produced the Lay of the Last Minstrel and Childe Harold:—my present object is, however, merely to show the sentiment of the age as embodied in the most *popular* and acknowledged shapes. If my limits allowed me to go somewhat more backward in the critical history of our literature, I could trace the first origin, or rather revival of our (modern) romantic poetry to an earlier founder than Coleridge, who is usually considered its parent.

In the earlier portion of this work, in attempting to trace the causes operating on the National Character of the English, I ascribed to the peculiar tone and cast of our aristocracy much of that reserved and unsocial spirit which proverbially pervades all classes of our countrymen. To the same causes, combined with the ostentation of commerce, I ascribed also much of that hollowness and glitter which belong to the occupations of the great world, and that fretfulness and pride, that uneasy and dissatisfied temper, which are engendered by a variety of small social distinctions, and the eternal *vying,* and consequent mortification, which those distinctions produce. These feelings, the slow growth of centuries, became more and more developed as the effects of civilization and wealth rendered the aristocratic influences more general upon the subordinate classes. In the indolent luxuries of a court, what more natural than satiety among the great, and a proud discontent among their emulators? The peace just concluded, and the pause in continental excitement, allowed these pampered, yet not unpoetical springs of sentiment, to be more deeply and sensibly felt; and the public, no longer compelled by War and the mighty career of Napoleon to turn their attention to the action of life, could give their sympathies undivided to the first who should represent their thoughts. And these very thoughts, these very sources of sentiment—this very satiety—this very discontent—this profound and melancholy temperament, the result of certain social systems—the first two cantos of *Childe Harold* suddenly appeared to represent. They touched the most sensitive chord in the public heart—they expressed what every one felt. The position of the author once attracting curiosity, was found singularly correspondent with the sentiment he embodied. His rank, his supposed melancholy, even his reputed beauty, added a natural interest to his genius. He became the Type, the Ideal of the state of mind he represented, and the world willingly associated his person with his works, because they thus seemed actually to incorporate, and in no undignified or ungraceful shape, the principle of their own long-nursed sentiments and most common emotions. Sir Philip Sidney represented the popular sentiment in Elizabeth's day—Byron that in our own. Each became the poetry of a particular age put into action—each, incorporated with the feelings he addressed, attracted towards himself an enthusiasm which his genius alone did not deserve. It is in vain, therefore, that we would now coolly criticise the merits of the first Cantos of *Childe Harold,* or those Eastern Tales by which they were succeeded, and in which another sentiment of the age was addressed, namely, that craving for adventure and wild incident which the habit of watching for many years the events of a portentous War, and the meteoric career of the modern Alexander, naturally engendered. We may wonder, when we now return to those poems, at our early admiration at their supposed philosophy of tone and grandeur of thought. In order to judge them fairly, we must recall the feelings they addressed. With nations, as with individuals, it is necessary to return to past emotions in order to judge of the merits of past appeals to them. We attributed truth and depth to Lord Byron's poetry in proportion as it expressed our own thoughts; just as in the affairs of life, or in the speeches of orators, we esteem those men the most sensible who agree the most with ourselves—embellishing and exalting only (not controverting) our own impressions. And in tracing the career of this remarkable poet, we may find that he became less and less popular in proportion, not as his genius waned, but as he addressed more feebly the prevalent sentiment of his times: for I suspect that future critics will agree that there is in his tragedies, which were never popular, a far higher order of genius than in his Eastern Tales or the *first* two cantos of *Childe Harold.* The highest order of poetical genius is usually evinced by the conception rather than the execution; and this often makes the main difference between Melodrame and Tragedy. There is in the early poems of Lord Byron scarcely any clear conception at all; there is no harmonious plan, comprising one great, consistent, systematic whole; no epic of events artfully wrought, progressing through a rich variety of character, and through the struggles of contending passions, to one mighty and inevitable end. If we take the most elaborate and most admired of his tales, *The Corsair,* we shall recognize in its conception an evident want of elevation. A pirate taken prisoner—released by a favourite of the harem—escaping— and finding his mistress dead; there is surely nothing beyond melodrame in the design of this story, nor do the incidents evince any great fertility of invention to counterbalance the want of greatness in the conception. In this too, as in all his tales, though full of passion—and this is worth considering, since it is for his delineations of passion that the vulgar laud him—we may observe that he describes a passion, not the *struggles* of passions. But it is in this last that a master is displayed: it is contending emotions, not the prevalence of one emotion, that call forth all the subtle comprehension, or deep research, or giant grasp of man's intricate nature, in which consists the highest order of that poetic genius which works out its result by character and fiction. Thus the struggles of Medea are more dread than the determination; the conflicting passions of Dido evince the most triumphant effect of Virgil's skill;—to describe a murder is the daily task of the melodramatist—the irresolution, the horror, the *struggle* of Macbeth, belong to Shakspeare alone. When Byron's heroes commit a crime, they march at once to it: we see not the pause—the self-counsel—the agony settling into resolve; he enters not into that delicate and subtile analysis of human motives which excites so absorbing a dread, and demands so exquisite a skill. Had Shakspeare conceived a Gulnare, he would probably have presented to us in terrible detail her pause over the couch of her sleeping lord: we should have seen the woman's weakness contesting with the bloody purpose; she would have remembered, though even with loathing, that on the breast she was about to strike, her head had been pillowed;—she would have turned aside—shrunk from her design—again raised the dagger: you would have heard the sleeping man breathe—she would quailed —and, quailing, struck! But the death-chamber—that would have been the scene in which, above all others, Shakspeare would have displayed himself—is barred and locked to Byron. He gives us the crime, and not all the wild and fearful preparation to it. So again in Parisina:—from what opportunities of exercising his art does the poet carefully exclude himself! With what minute, and yet stern analysis, would Sophocles have exhibited the contest in the breast of the adultress!—the love—the honour—the grief—the dread—the horror of the incest, and the violence of the passion!—but Byron proceeds at once to the guilty meeting, and the tragic history is, as much as can be compatible with the materials, merged into the amorous fragment. If Byron had, in his early poems, conceived the history of Othello, he would have given us the murder of Desdemona, but never the interviews with Iago. Thus, neither in the conception of the plot, nor the fertile invention of incident, nor, above all, in the dissection of passions, can the early poems of Lord Byron rank with the higher masterpieces of Poetical Art.

But at a later period of his life more exalted and thoughtful notions of his calling were revealed to him, and I imagine that his acquaintance with Shelley induced him to devote his meditative and brooding mind to those metaphysical inquiries into the motives and actions of men which lead to deep and hidden sources of character, and a more entire comprehension of the science of poetical analysis.

Hence his tragedies evince a much higher order of conception, and a much greater mastery in art than his more celebrated poems. What more pure or more lofty than his character of Angiolina, in *The Doge of Venice!* I know not in the circle of Shakspeare's women, one more true, not only to nature—that is a slight merit —but to the highest and rarest order of nature. Let us pause here for one moment—we are in no hacknied ground. The character has never yet been fully understood. An insulting libel on the virtue of Angiolina, by Steno, a young patrician, is inscribed on the ducal throne; the Doge demands the head of the libeller; —the Tribunal of the Forty award a month's imprisonment. What are Angiolina's feelings on the first insult—let her speak for herself:

I heed it not
For the rash scorner's falsehood in itself,
But for the effect, the deadly deep impression
Which it has made upon Faliero's soul.

MARIANNA.
Assuredly
The Doge can not suspect you?
ANGIOLINA.
Suspect me!—
Why Steno dared not.—

MARIANNA.
'Twere fit
He should be punish'd grievously.
ANGIOLINA.
He is so.

MARIANNA.
What! is the sentence pass'd?—is he condemn'd?
ANGIOLINA.
I know not that—*but he has been detected.*

MARIANNA.
Some sacrifice is due to slander'd virtue.
ANGIOLINA.
Why, what is virtue if it needs a victim?
Or if it must depend upon men's words?
The dying Roman said, " 'twas but a name:"
It were indeed no more, if human breath
Could make or mar it.—

What deep comprehension of the dignity of virtue! Angiolina will not even conceive that she *can* be suspected; or, that an insult upon her should need other justice than the indignation of opinion! Marianna subsequently asks, if, when Angiolina gave her hand to the doge,

With this strange disproportion in your years,
And, let me add, disparity of tempers,

she yet loved her father's friend—her spouse: If,

—Previous to this marriage, had your heart
Ne'er beat for any of the noble youth,
Such as in years had been more meet to match
Beauty like yours? or since have you ne'er seen
One, who, if your fair hand were still to give,
Might now pretend to Loredano's daughter?
ANGIOLINA.
I answer'd your *first* question when I said
I married.
MARIANNA.
And the second?
ANGIOLINA.
Needs no answer!

Is not this conception even equal to that of "the gentle lady wedded to the Moor?" The same pure, serene, tender, yet scarce impassioned heart, that loves the abstract, not the actual; that, like Plato, incorporates virtue in a visible shape, and then allows it no rival;—yet this lofty and proud woman has no sternness in her nature; she forgives Steno, not from the calm haughtiness of her high chastity alone.

"Had," she says to the angry Doge,

> Oh! had this false and flippant libeller
> Shed his young blood for his absurd lampoon,
> Ne'er from that moment could this breast have known
> A joyous hour, or dreamless slumber more.

Here the reader will note with how delicate an art the sex's tenderness and charity relieve and warm the snowy coldness of her ethereal superiority. What a union of woman's best qualities! the pride that disdains reproach, the meekness that forgives it! Nothing can be more simply grand than the whole of this character, and the history which it exalts. The old man of eighty years, wedded to the young wife; her heart never wandering, no episode of love disturbing its serene orbit, no impure or dishonouring jealousy casting its shadow upon her bright name; she moves through the dread scene, all angelic in her qualities, yet all human in the guise they assume. In his earlier years Byron would, as he intimates, have lowered and hacknied the antique dignity of this Ideal, by an imitation of the Moor's jealousy: nay, *in yet earlier years* he would, I believe, have made Angiolina guilty; he would have mingled, perhaps, more passionate interest with the stern pathos of the story; but interest of how much less elevated a cast! Who can compare the ideal of Parisina with that of Angiolina? I content myself with merely pointing out the majesty and truth with which the character of the Doge himself is conceived; his fiery and headlong wrath against the libeller, frozen at once by the paltry sentence on his crime; and transferred to the tribunal that adjudged it; his ire at the insult of the libel, merged in a deeper passion at that of the punishment; his patrician self-scorn at his new fellowship with plebeian conspirators; his paternal and patriarchal tenderness for Angiolina— devoid of all uxoriousness and doting; the tragic decorum with which his love is invested; and the consummate and even sublime skill, which, allowing equal scope for passion with that manifested in Othello, makes the passion yet more lofty and refined; for in the Moor, the human and the sexual are, perhaps, too strongly marked—in the doge, they seem utterly merged.

Again, what beautiful conception in the tale of the *Foscari!* how original, how tender, the love of soil in Jacopo—Greek in its outline, but Ausonian in its colouring: you see the very patriotism natural to the sweet south—the heart

> Which never beat
> For Venice, but with such a yearning as
> The dove has for her distant nest—

the conception of this peculiar patriotism, which is for the air, the breath of Venice; which makes a bodily and visible mistress of the sea-girt city; which courts torture, death, dishonour, for one hour alone of her presence—all this is at once thoroughly original and deeply tragic. In vain they give him life—he asks for liberty: in vain they give him liberty, he asks for Venice—he cannot dissociate the two:

> I could endure my dungeon, for 'twas Venice;
> I could support the torture, there was something
> In my native air that buoy'd my spirits up—

> *but afar—*
> *My very soul seem'd mouldering in my bosom.*

In vain, Marina, the brave, the passionate wife, exclaims

> This love of thine
> For an ungrateful and tyrannic soil
> Is passion, and not patriotism—

In this truth is the originality and Euripidean pathos of the conception. In vain she reminds him of the "lot of millions"

> The hereditary exiles that have been.

He answers,

> Who can number
> The hearts which broke in silence of that parting,
> Or after that departure; of that malady
> Which calls up green and native fields to view
> From the rough deep?

> ——You call this weakness! It is strength,

> I say,—the parent of all honest feeling.
> He who loves not his country, can love nothing.

In vain again, with seemingly unanswerable logic, Marina replies,

> Obey her, then; 'tis *she* that puts thee forth.

With what sudden sinking of the heart he replies,

> Ay, there it is: 'tis like a mother's curse
> Upon my soul.

Mark, too, how wonderfully the character of the austere old father, hardened and marbled by the peculiar and unnatural systems of Venetian policy, contrasts that of the son: in both patriotism is the ruling passion; yet how differently developed!

> First at the board in this unhappy process
> Against his last and only son!—

But what glimpses reveal to you the anguish of the father! With what skill your sympathy is enlisted in his behalf; and repugnance at his severity converted into admiration of his devotion!

> MARINA.
> What shall I say
> To Foscari from his father?
> DOGE.
> That he obey
> The laws.
> MARINA.
> And nothing more? Will you not see him
> Ere he depart? It may be the last time.

> DOGE.
> The last!—my boy!—the last time I shall see
> My last of children! *Tell him I will come.*

The same deep and accurate knowledge of the purest sources of effect which taught the great poet to relieve the sternness of the father, makes him also elevate the weakness of the son. Jacopo hath no cowardice, save in leaving Venice. Torture appals him not; he smiles at death. And how tragic *is* the death!

Enter an Officer and Guards.

Signor! the boat is at the shore—the wind
Is rising—we are ready to attend you.
                              JACOPO FOSCARI.
And I to be attended. Once more, father,
Your hand!

                    DOGE.
                              Take it. Alas! how thine own trembles!
                    JACOPO FOSCARI.
No—you mistake; 'tis yours that shakes, my father.
Farewell!

                    DOGE.
                    Is there aught else?
                    JACOPO FOSCARI.
                              No—nothing.
Lend me your arm, good signor. (*To the officer.*)
                    OFFICER.
                              You turn pale,
Let me support you—paler—ho! some aid there!
Some water!

                    MARINA.
                    Ah, he is dying!
                    JACOPO FOSCARI.
                              Now, I'm ready—
My eyes swim strangely—where's the door?
                    MARINA.
                              Away!
Let *me* support him—my best love! Oh, God!
How faintly beats this heart—this pulse!
                    JACOPO FOSCARI.
                              The light!
Is it the light?—I am faint.
                    [*Officer presents him with water.*
                    OFFICER.
                              He will be better,
Perhaps, in the air.
                    JACOPO FOSCARI.
                    I doubt not. Father—wife—
Your hands!
                    MARINA.
                    There's death in that damp clammy clasp.
Oh, God!—My Foscari, how fare you?
                    JACOPO FOSCARI.
                              Well! [*He dies.*

He dies; but where? In Venice—in the light of that beloved sky—in the air of that delicious climate! He dies; but when? At the moment he is about to leave that climate, that sky, for ever! He might have said with another and a less glorious patriot of a later age, "Il mio cadavere almeno non cadrà fra braccia straniere; . . . e le mie ossa poseranno su la terra de' miei padri." Mark now, how the pathos augments by the agency of the bereft survivors.

OFFICER.

He's gone!

DOGE.

He's free.

MARINA.

No—no, he is not dead;
There must be life in that heart—he could not
Thus leave me.

DOGE.

Daughter!

MARINA.

Hold thy peace, old man!
I am no daughter now—thou hast no son.
Oh, Foscari! . . .

And how dreadly the whole force of the catastrophe is summed up, a few lines afterwards, when, amidst the wailings of the widowed mother, the old Doge breaks forth—

My unhappy children!

MARINA.

What!

You feel it then at last—*you!*—Where is now
The Stoic of the State?

How you thrill at the savage yet natural taunt!—how visibly you see the start of the wife!—how audibly you hear the wild laugh and the bitter words—

What!
————————Where is now
The Stoic of the State?

And how entirely the character of the Doge is revealed; how utter and dread becomes the anguish of the scene in the next *one* word:

DOGE (*throwing himself down by the body*).
HERE!

And at that word I doubt if the tragedy should not have been concluded. The vengeance of Loredano—the completion of which makes the catastrophe—is not so grand a termination as the broken heart of the patriot exile, and the broken pride of the patriot judge.

The same high notions of art which characterize these great dramas, are equally evinced in the *Cain* and the *Sardanapalus:* the first, which has more of the early stamp of Byron's mind, is, for that reason perhaps, so well known, and its merit so universally allowed, that I shall not delay the reader by praising the Hercules none have blamed. One word only on the *Sardanapalus.*

The genius developed in this tragedy is more gorgeous and varied than in any other of Byron's works: the magnificent effeminacy, the unsettled courage, the regal generosity of Sardanapalus; the bold and hardy fervour of Arbaces the soldier, and the hoary craft of Beleses the priest, exhibit more extensive knowledge, and afford more glowing contrasts, than even the classic stateliness of Marino Faliero, or the deep pathos of the Foscari: And this drama, above all the rest of Byron's plays, is fitted for representation on the stage: the pomp of scene, the vitality and action of the plot, would, I am confident, secure it success among the multitude, who are more attracted by the external than the latent and less vivid sources of interest. But the chief beauty of this play is in the conception of Myrrha's character. This Greek girl, at once brave and tender, enamoured of her lord, yet yearning to be free; worshipping alike her distant land and the soft barbarian:—what new, and what dramatic combinations of feeling! It is in this *struggle* of emotions, as I have said before, that the master-hand paints with the happiest triumph.

"Why," says Myrrha, reasoning with herself—

> Why do I love this man? My country's daughters
> Love none but heroes. *But I have no country!*
> The slave hath lost all save her bonds. I love him;
> And that's the heaviest link of the long chain—
> To love whom we esteem not. . . .
>
> He loves me, and I love him; the slave loves
> Her master, and would free him from his vices.

> If not, I have a means of freedom still,
> And if I cannot teach him how to reign,
> May show him how alone a king can leave
> His throne.

The heroism of this fair Ionian is never above nature, yet always on its highest verge. The proud melancholy that mingles with her character, recalling her father-land—her warm and generous love, "without self-love"—her passionate and Greek desire to elevate the nature of Sardanapalus, that she may the better justify her own devotion—the grave and yet sweet sternness that pervades her gentler qualities, exhibiting itself in fidelity without fear, and enabling her to hold with a steady hand the torch that shall consume on the pyre (made sacred to her religion by the memory of its own Alcides) both the Assyrian and the Greek; all these combinations are the result of the purest sentiment and the noblest art. Her last words at the pyre sustain the great conception of her character. With the natural yearning of the Achaian, her thoughts in that moment revert to her distant clime, recalled, however, at once to her perishing lord beside her, and uniting, almost in one breath, the two contending affections.

> Farewell, thou earth!
> And loveliest spot of earth! farewell, Ionia!
> Be thou still free and beautiful, and far
> Aloof from desolation! My last prayer
> Was for thee, my last thoughts, save *one*, were of thee!
> SARDANAPALUS.
> And that?
> MYRRHA.
> *Is yours.*

The plot of the drama is worthy the creation of its heroine. The fall of a mighty Empire; the vivid incarnation of a dark and remote time; the primeval craft of the priest conspiring with the rough ambition of the soldier, (main origin of great changes in the world's earlier years;) the splendid and august catastrophe; the most magnificent suicide the earth ever knew!— what a field for genius! what a conception worthy of its toils!

Nothing has been more constantly asserted of Byron than his want of variety in character. Every criticism tells us that he never paints but one person, in whatever costume; that the dress may vary, but the lay figure remains the same. Never was any popular fallacy more absurd! It is true that the dogma holds good with the early poems, but is entirely contradicted in the later plays. Where, in the whole range of fiction, are there any characters more strongly contrasted, more essentially various and dissimilar, than Sardanapalus, the Assyrian king, and Marino Faliero, the Venetian Doge;—than Beleses, the rugged priest, cut out of the marble of nature; and Jacopo Foscari, moulded from the kindliest of the southern elements;—than the passionate Marina, the delicate and queenly Angiolina, the heroic Myrrha—the beautiful incarnation of her own mythology? To name these is sufficient to refute an assertion hitherto so credulously believed, and which may serve as an illustration of the philosophy of popular criticism. From the first works of an author the standard is drawn by which he is compared; and in no instance are the sins of the parents more unfortunately visited on the children.

Yet why, since the tragedies evince so matured and profound a genius, are they so incalculably less popular than the early poems? It may be said, that the dramatic form itself is an obstacle to popularity; yet scarcely so, for I am just old enough distinctly to remember the intense and universal curiosity with which the public awaited the appearance of *The Doge of Venice;* the eagerness with which it was read, and the disappointment which it occasioned. Had the dramatic form been the cause of its unpopularity, it would have occasioned for it at the first a cool and lukewarm reception: the welcome which greeted its announcement is a proof that the disappointment was occasioned by the materials of the play, and not *because* it was a play. Besides, *Manfred,* one of the most admired of all Byron's works, was cast in the dramatic mould. One cause of the comparative unpopularity of the plays is, perhaps, that the *style* is less rich and musical than that of the poems; but the principal cause is *in that very versatility, that very coming out from self, the want of which has been so superficially complained of.* The characters were beautifully conceived; but they represented not that character which we expected, and yearned to see. That mystic and idealized shape, in which we beheld ourselves, had receded from the scene—we missed that touching egotism which was the expression of the Universal Heart—across the enchanted mirror new shadows passed, but it was our own likeness that we desired —the likeness of those deep and cherished feelings with which the poet had identified himself! True, that he still held the glass to human nature; but it was no longer to that aspect of nature which we most coveted to behold, and to which custom had not yet brought satiety. This was the true cause of our disappointment. Byron now addressed the passion, and the sentiment, and the thought, common to *all* time, but no longer those peculiar to the temper of the age—

> Our friend was to the dead,
> *To us he died when first he parted from us.*

> He stood beside us, like our youth,
> Transform'd for us the real to a dream,
> Clothing the palpable and the familiar
> With golden exhalations of the dawn.[5]

The disappointment we experienced when Byron departed from the one ideal image, in which alone our egotism loved to view him, is made yet more visible in examining his character than in analyzing his works. We grow indignant against him in proportion, not as we find him unworthy as a man, but departing from the attributes in which our imagination had clothed him. He was to the Public as a lover to his mistress, who forgives a crime more easily than a foible, and in whom the judgment becomes acute only in proportion as the imagination is undeceived. Had the lives, the sketches, the details, which have appeared subsequently to his early and poetical death, but sustained our own illusions—had they preserved "the shadow and the majesty" with which we had enveloped him, they might have represented him as far more erring than he appears to have been, and we should have forgiven whatever crimes were consistent with the dark but lofty nature we ascribed to him. But weakness, insincerity, the petty caprice, the womanish passion, the vulgar pride, or even the coarse habit—these we forgave not, for they shocked and mocked our own self-love; they were as sardonic reproaches on the blind fallacy of our own judgment;

5. Coleridge's *Wallenstein.*

they lowered the ideal in our own breasts; they humbled the vanity of our own nature; we had associated the poet with ourselves; we had felt *his* emotions as the refining, the exalted expression of *ours,* and whatever debased our likeness, debased ourselves! through his foibles our self-love was wounded: he was the great Representative of the Poetry of our own hearts; and, wherever he seemed unfaithful to his trust, we resented it as a treason to the majesty of our common cause.

But perhaps the hour in which we most deeply felt how entirely we had wound and wrapt our own poetry in himself, was that in which the news of his death reached this country. Never shall I forget the singular, the stunning sensation, which the intelligence produced. I was exactly at that age, half man and half boy, in which the poetical sympathies are most keen —among the youth of that day a growing diversion from Byron to Shelley and Wordsworth had just commenced—but the moment in which we heard he was no more, united him to us at once, without a rival. We could not believe that the bright race was run. So much of us died with him, that the notion of his death had something of the unnatural, of the impossible. It was as if a part of the mechanism of the very world stood still:— that we had ever questioned—that we had ever blamed him, was a thought of absolute remorse, and all our worship of his genius was not half so strongly felt as our love for himself.

When he went down to dust, it was as the abrupt close of some history of deep passion in our actual lives,—the interest—the excitement of years came to a gloomy pause—

> His last sigh
> Dissolved the charm—the disenchanted earth
> Lost all her lustre—Where her glittering towers,
> Her golden mountains, where? all darken'd down
> To naked waste—a dreary vale of years!
> THE GREAT MAGICIAN'S DEAD![6]

Exaggerated as this language may seem to our children, our contemporaries know that all words are feeble to express the universal feeling of England at that lonely death-bed in a foreign land, amidst wild and savage strangers, far from the sister, the

6. Young.

wife, the child, whose names faltered on the lips of the dying man,—closing in desolation in a career of sadness—rendering his latest sigh to the immemorial land which had received his earliest song, and where henceforth and for ever

> Shall Death and Glory a joint sabbath keep.

Even now, at this distance of time, all the feelings that then rushed upon us, melt upon me once more. Dissenting as I now do from much of the vague admiration his more popular works receive, and seeing in himself much that Virtue must lament, and even Wisdom contemn, I cannot but think of him as some early friend, associating with himself all the brightest reminiscences of youth, burying in his grave a poetry of existence that can never be restored, and of whom every harsh sentence, even while not unfaithful to truth, is dishonouring to the fidelity of love—

THE BEAUTIFUL IS VANISHED AND RETURNS NOT.

I have dwelt thus much upon Byron, partly because though the theme is hacknied, it is not exhausted[7]—partly because I perceive an unjust and indiscriminate spirit of depreciation springing up against that great poet (and I hold it the duty of a critic to oppose zealously the caprice and change of mere fashions in opinion)—and principally, because, in reviewing the intellectual spirit of the age, it is necessary to point out at some length the manner in which its most celebrated representative illustrated and identified it with himself.

But while my main task is with the more popular influences of the intellectual spirit of the present day, I must not pass over in silence that deep under-current which in all ages is formed by some writers whose influence floats not on the surface. The sound of their lyres, not loud to the near listener, travels into distance, enduring, deep, and through prolonged vibrations, buoying itself along the immeasurable waves of space. From amidst writers of this class I single out but two, Wordsworth and Shelley. I believe that both these poets have been influential to a degree per-

7. In advancing, too, the new doctrine, that his Dramas are better than his early poems, it was necessary to go somewhat into the conception of those Dramas.

fectly unguessed by those who look only to their popularity; and, above all, I believe that of Wordsworth, especially, to have been an influence of a more noble and purely intellectual character than any writer of our age and nation has exercised. Wordsworth's genius is peculiarly German. This assertion may startle those who have been accustomed to believe the German genius only evinced by extravagant tales, bombastic passion, and mystical *diableries*. Wordsworth is German from his singular householdness of feeling—from the minute and accurate manner with which he follows his ardour for Nature into the smaller links and harmonies which may be considered as her details. He has not, it is true, "the many-sidedness" of Göthe; but he closely resembles a *certain* portion of Göthe's mind, viz. the reverential, contemplative, self-tasking disposition to the study of all things appertaining to THE NATURAL: his ideas, too, fall into that refined and refining *toryism,* the result of a mingled veneration for the past—of a disdain for the pettier cries which float over that vast abyss which we call the public, and of a firm desire for Peace as the best nurse to high and undiurnal thoughts, which so remarkably distinguishes the great artist of Tasso and Wilhelm Meister. This toryism—(I so call it for want of a better name) —is one of which only very high minds are capable; it is the product of a most deep if untrue philosophy: no common Past-worshippers can understand or share it, just as no vulgar sceptics can comprehend the ethereal scepticism of a Spinosa. That Wordsworth's peculiar dogmas should lead him into occasional, and, to my taste, frequent error, is saying of him what we must say of every man of enthusiasm who adopts a system; but, be it observed, it only misleads him in that part of his writings which arrogate "simplicity," and in which, studying to be simple, he becomes often artificial; it never misleads him in his advances to "sublimity": here he is always natural; he rises without effort, and the circumfusing holiness of his mind bathes with a certain religious grandeur the commonest words and the most familiar thoughts. But what temper of the times does Wordsworth represent, and in what is he a teacher? Let us reflect. Whenever there is a fierce contest between opposing parties, it usually happens that to each party there is a small and scarce-calculated band inspired and led by far more spiritualized and refining thoughts than the rest, who share not the passion, nor the feud, nor the human and coarser motives which actuate the noisier herd. Of one of these parties Wordsworth is the representative; of the other, Shelley. Wordsworth is the apostle, the spiritualizer of those who cling to the most idealized part of things that are—Religion and her houses, Loyalty and her monuments—the tokens of the Sanctity which overshadows the Past: these are of him, and he of them. Shelley, on the other hand, in his more impetuous, but equally intellectual and unworldly mind, is the spiritualizer of all who forsake the past and the present, and, with lofty hopes and a bold philanthropy, rush forward into the future, attaching themselves not only to things unborn, but to speculations founded on unborn things. Both are representatives of a class of thought, refined, remote, belonging to the age, but not to the louder wranglers of the age. Scott and Byron are poets representing a philosophy resulting from the passions, or, at least, the action, of life; Shelley and Wordsworth represent that which arises from the intellect, and belongs to the Contemplative or the Ideal. It is natural that the first two should have a large audience, and the two latter a select one; for so far have they (the last) gone into the remoter and more abstract ideas, and wrought poetry from science, that they may be said to appeal to us less as poets than as metaphysicians, and have therefore obtained the homage and the circle which belong to the reasoner rather than the wider worship of the bard; but each appertains emphatically to a time of visible and violent transition—the one preserving all the beauty of the time past, the other with a more youthful genius bodying forth the beauty of a time to be. Each is an equal servitor to knowledge, if we may trust to the truth of Wordsworth's simile, the sublimest in recent poetry—

> Past and Future are the wings
> On whose support harmoniously conjoin'd,
> Moves the great Spirit of Human Knowledge.

But I think, of the two, that Wordsworth has exercised on the present day the more beneficial influence; for it, as I have held, and shall again have occasion to repeat,

> The world is too much with us,

if the vice of the time leans to the Material, and produces a low-born taste and an appetite for coarse excitement,—Wordsworth's

poetry is of all existing in the world the most calculated to refine
—to etherealize—to exalt;—to offer the most correspondent
counterpoise to the scale that inclines to earth. It is for this that I
consider his influence mainly beneficial. His poetry has repaired
to us the want of an immaterial philosophy— it *is* philosophy,
and it is of the immaterial school. No writer more unvulgarizes
the mind. His circle is small—but for that very reason the votaries are more attached. They preserve in the working-day world
the holy sabbath of his muse—and doubtless they will perpetuate that tranquillising worship from generation to generation,
till the devotion of the few shall grow into the custom of the
many.

Shelley, with a more daring and dramatic[8] genius, with greater
mastery of language, and the true Lucretian soul, for ever aspiring *extra flammantia mœnia mundi,* is equally intellectual in his
creations; and despite the young audacity which led him into
denying a God, his poetry is of a remarkably ethereal and spir-
itualizing cast. It is steeped in veneration—it is for ever thirsting
for the Heavenly and the Immortal—and the Deity he questioned avenges Himself only by impressing His image upon all
that the poet undertook. But Shelley at present has subjected
himself to be misunderstood; he has become the apologist
for would-be mystics, and dreamers of foolish dreams,—
for an excellent master may obtain worthless disciples, just as
the young voluptuaries of the Garden imagined vice was sanctioned by Epicurus, and the juvenile casuists of schools have
learned Pyrrhonism from Berkeley. The blinding glitter of his
diction, the confusion produced on an unsteady mind by the rapid
whirl of his dazzling thoughts, have assisted in the formation
of a false school of poetry,—a school of sounding words and unintelligible metaphysics—a school of crude and bewildered jar-
gonists, who talk of "the everlasting heart of things," and the
"genius of the world," and such phrases, which are the terms of a

8. Had Shelley lived, I understand from his friends that he would probably
have devoted himself especially to the drama. The Cençi is the only one of
his writings which contains human interest—and if Shelley's metaphysical
flights had been once tamed down to the actual flesh and blood characters which
the drama exacts, there is little doubt but that as his judgment improved in the
choice of subject and the conception of plot, he would have been our greatest
dramatist since Shakspeare. But "Gemuit sub pondere cymba."

system with Shelley, and are merely fine expressions with his followers. An imitator of Wordsworth must come at once to Nature: he may be puerile, he may be prosaic—but he cannot go far from the Natural. The yearning of Wordsworth's genius is like the patriotism of certain travellers, who in their remotest wanderings carry with them a portion of their native earth. But Shelley's less settled and more presuming faculty deals little with the Seen and Known—it is ever with the spectral images of things, chasing the invisible Echo, and grasping at the bodiless Shadow. Whether he gives language to Pan, to Asia, to Demiurgus, or song to the Cloud, or paints the river love of Alpheus for Arethusa, or follows, through all the gorgeous windings of his most wondrous diction, the spirit of Poesy in Alastor, or that of Liberty in the Revolt of Islaam—he is tasking our interest for things that are not mundane or familiar—things which he alone had power to bind to Nature, and which those who imitate him leave utterly dissevered from her control. They, too, deal with demigods and phantoms—the beautiful Invisibles of creation: but they forget the chain by which the Jupiter of their creed linked each, the highest to the lowest, in one indissoluble connexion, that united even the highest heaven to the bosom of our common earth.

I think, then, that so far as this age is considered, (although for posterity, when true worshippers are substituted for false disciples, it may be otherwise,) Shelley's influence, both poetical and moral, has been far less purifying and salutary than Wordsworth's. But both are men of a purer, perhaps a higher intellectual order than either Byron or Scott, and although not possessing the same mastery over the more daily emotions, and far more limited in their range of power than their rival "Kings of Verse," they have yet been the rulers of more unworldly subjects, and the founders of a more profound and high-wrought dynasty of opinion.

It seems, then, that in each of these four great poets the Imaginative Literature has arrogated the due place of the Philosophical.

In the several characters of their genius, embodying the truth of the times, will the moral investigator search for the expression of those thoughts which make the aspect of an era, and, while they reflect the present age, prepare the next. It is thus that, from time to time, the Imagination assumes the natural office of the Reason, and is the parent of Revolutions, because the organ of Opinion: And to this, the loftiest, moral effect of imaginative literature, many of its superficial decriers have been blind. "The mind," saith the Stagyrite, "has over the body the control which a master exercises over his slave: but the Reason has over the Imagination that control which a magistrate possesses over a freeman"—"who," adds Bacon in his noble comment on the passage, "*may come to rule in his turn.*" At the same time that Lycurgus reformed Sparta, he introduced into Greece the poems of Homer;—which act was the more productive of heroes?— which wrought the more important results upon the standard of legislative morals, or exercised the more permanent influence upon the destiny of states?

I return to the more wide, and popular, and important impression, made upon the times. Göthe has told us, that when he had written *Werther,* he felt like a sinner relieved from the burden of his errors by a general confession; and he became, as it were, inspired with energy to enter on a new existence. The mind of a great writer is the type of the general mind. The public, at certain periods, oppressed with a peculiar weight of passion, or of thought, require to throw it off by expression; once expressed, they rarely return to it again: they pass into a fresh intellectual gradation; they enter with Göthe into a new existence; hence one reason of the ill-success of imitators—they repeat a tone we no longer have a desire to hear. When Byron passed away, the feeling he had represented craved utterance no more. With a sigh we turned to the actual and practical career of life: we awoke from the morbid, the passionate, the dreaming, "the moonlight and the dimness of the mind," and by a natural reaction addressed ourselves to the active and daily objects which lay before us. And this with the more intenseness, because, the death of a great poet invariably produces an indifference to the art itself. We can neither bear to see him imitated, nor yet contrasted; we preserve the impression, but we break the mould. Hence that strong attachment to the Practical, which became so visible a little time after the death of Byron, and which continues (unabated, or rather increased,) to characterize the temper of the time. Insensibly acted upon by the doctrine of the Utilitarians, we desired to see Utility in every branch of intellectual labour. Byron, in his severe comments upon England, and his satire on our social system, had done much that has not yet been observed, in shaking off from the popular mind certain of its strongest national prejudices; and the long Peace, and the pressure of financial difficulties, naturally inclined us to look narrowly at our real state; to examine the laws we had only boasted of, and dissect the constitution we had hitherto deemed it only our duty to admire. We were in the situation of a man who, having run a certain career of dreams and extravagance, begins to be prudent and saving, to calculate his conduct, and to look to his estate. Politics thus gradually and commonly absorbed our attention, and we grew to identify ourselves, our feelings, and our cause, with statesmen and economists, instead of with poets and refiners. Thus, first Canning, and then Brougham, may be said, for a certain time, to have represented, more than any other individuals, the common Intellectual Spirit; and the interest usually devoted to the imaginative, was transferred to the real.

In the mean while the more than natural distaste for poetry that succeeded the death of Byron had increased the appetite for prose fictions; the excitement of the fancy, pampered by the melo-dramatic tales which had become the rage in verse, required food even when verse grew out of fashion. The new career that Walter Scott had commenced tended also somewhat to elevate with the vulgar a class of composition that, with the educated, required no factitious elevation; for, with the latter, what new dignity could be thrown upon a branch of letters that Cervantes, Fielding, Le Sage, Voltaire, and Fenelon had already made only less than Epic? It was not, however, as in former times, the great novel alone, that was read among the more refined circles, but novels of all sorts. Unlike poetry, the name itself was an attraction. In these works, even to the lightest and most ephemeral, something of the moral spirit of the age betrayed itself. The novels of fashionable life illustrate feelings very deeply rooted, and productive of no common revolution. In proportion as the aristocracy had become social, and fashion allowed the members of the more mediocre classes a hope to outstep the boundaries of fortune, and be quasi-aristocrats themselves, people eagerly sought for representations of the manners which they aspired to imitate, and the circles to which it was not impossible to belong. But as with emulation discontent also was mixed, as many hoped to be called and few found themselves chosen, so on a satire on the follies and vices of the great gave additional piquancy to the description of their lives. There was a sort of social fagging established; the fag loathed his master, but not the system by which one day or other he himself might be permitted to fag. What the world would not have dared to gaze upon, had it been gravely exhibited by a philosopher, (so revolting a picture of the aristocracy would it have seemed,) they praised with avidity in the light sketches of a novelist. Hence the three-years' run of the fashionable novels was a shrewd sign of the times; straws they were, but they showed the upgathering of the storm. These novels were the most successful which hit off one or the other of the popular cravings—the desire to dissect fashion, or the wish to convey utility—those which affected to combine both, as the novels of Mr. Ward, were the most successful of all.

Few writers ever produced so great an effect on the political spirit of their generation as some of these novelists, who, without any other merit, unconsciously exposed the falsehood, the hypocrisy, the arrogant and vulgar insolence of patrician life. Read by all classes, in every town, in every village, these works, as I have before stated, could not but engender a mingled indignation and disgust at the parade of frivolity, the ridiculous disdain of truth, nature, and mankind, the self-consequence and absurdity, which, falsely or truly, these novels exhibited as a picture of aristocratic society. The Utilitarians railed against them, and they were effecting with unspeakable rapidity the very purposes the Utilitarians desired.

While these light works were converting the multitude, graver writers were soberly confirming their effect, society itself knew not the change in feeling which had crept over it; till a sudden flash, as it were, revealed the change electrically to itself. Just at the time when with George the Fourth an *old* era expired, the excitement of a popular election at home concurred with the three days of July in France, to give a decisive tone to the *new*. The question of Reform came on, and, to the astonishment of the nation itself, it was hailed at once by the national heart. From that moment, the intellectual spirit hitherto partially directed to, became *wholly* absorbed in, politics; and whatever lighter works have since obtained a warm and general hearing, have either developed the errors of the social system, or the vices of the legislative. Of the first, I refrain from giving an example; of the last, I instance as a sign of the times, the searching fictions of Miss Martineau, and the wide reputation they have acquired.

A description of the mere frivolities of fashion is no longer coveted; for the public mind, once settled towards an examination of the aristocracy, has pierced from the surface to the depth; it has *probed* the wound, and it now desires to *cure*.

It is in this state that the Intellectual Spirit of the age rests, demanding the Useful, but prepared to receive it through familiar shapes: a state at present favourable to ordinary knowledge, to narrow views, or to mediocre genius; but adapted to prepare the way and to found success for the coming triumphs of a bold philosophy, or a profound and subtile imagination. Some cause, indeed, there is of fear, lest the desire for immediate and palpable utility should stint the capacities of genius to the trite and familiar truths. But as Criticism takes a more wide and liberal view of the true and unbounded sphere of the Beneficial, we may trust that this cause of fear will be removed. The passions of men are the most useful field for the metaphysics of the imagination, and yet the grandest and the most inexhaustible. Let us take care that we do not, as in the old Greek fable, cut the wings of our bees and set flowers before them, as the most sensible mode of filling the Hives of Truth!

But the great prevailing characteristic of the present intellectual spirit is one most encouraging to human hopes; it is Benevolence. There has grown up among us a sympathy with the great mass of mankind. For this we are indebted in no small measure to the philosophers (which whom Benevolence is, in all times, the foundation of philosophy); and that more decided and emphatic expression of the sentiment which was common, despite of their errors, to the French moralists of the last century, has been kept alive and applied to immediate legislation by the English moralists of the present. We owe also the popularity of the growing principle to the writings of Miss Edgeworth and of Scott, who sought their characters among the people, and who interested us by a picture of (and not a declamation upon) their life and its humble vicissitudes, their errors and their virtues. We owe it also, though unconsciously, to the gloomy misanthropy of Byron; for proportioned to the intenseness with which we shared that feeling, was the reaction from which we awoke from it; and amongst the more select and poetical of us, we owe it yet more to the dreaming philanthropy of Shelley, and the patriarchal tenderness of Wordsworth. It is this feeling that we should unite to sustain and to develope. It has come to us pure and bright from the ordeal of years—the result of a thousand errors—but born, if we preserve it, as their healer and redemption.

Diodorus Siculus tells us, that the forest of the Pyrenean mountains being set on fire, and the heat penetrating to the soil, a pure stream of silver gushed forth from the earth's bosom, and revealed for the first time the existence of those mines afterwards so celebrated.

It is thus from cause apparently the most remote, and often amidst the fires that convey to us, at their first outbreaking, images only of terror and desolation, that we deduce the most precious effects, and discover the treasures to enrich the generations that are to come!

III

I think, sir, that when our ingenious countryman, Joshua
Barnes, gave us so notable an account of the Pigmies, he must,
in the spirit of prophecy, have intended to allegorize the empire of the Penny Periodicals. For, in the first place, these little
strangers seem, Pigmy-like, of a marvellous ferocity and valour;
they make great head against their foes—they spread themselves incontinently—they possess the land—they live but a
short time, yet are plenteously prolific; they owe much to what
the learned Joshua terms "the royal Lescha," viz. a certain society (evidently the foretype of that lately established under the
patronage of my Lord Brougham)—set up as he sheweth "for
the increase in propagation of experimental knowledge"; above
all, and a most blissful peculiarity it is, *"for taxes, they are
wholly unacquainted with them!"* they make vigilant war against
the cranes, whom I take it are palpably designed for tax-gather-
ers in general, *quocunque gaudentes nomine*—a fact rendered
clear to the plainest understanding by the following description
of these predatory birds:

"The cranes being the only causers of famine in the land, by
reason they are so numerous that they can devour the most plen-
tiful harvest, both by eating the seeds beforehand, and then
picking the ears that remain."

Certes, however, these little gentry seem of a more general
ambition than their Pigmæn types; for the latter confined themselves to a limited territory "from Gadazalia to Elysiana"; but

these, the pigmies of our time, overrun us altogether, and push, with the rude insolence of innovation, our most venerable folios from their stools. The rage for cheap publications is not limited to Penny Periodicals; family libraries of all sorts have been instituted, with the captivating profession of teaching all things useful—bound in cloth, for the sum of five shillings a month! Excellent inventions, which, after showing us the illimitable ingenuity of compilation, have at length fallen the prey of their own numbers, and buried themselves amongst the corpses of the native quartos which they so successfully invaded.

Cheap publications are excellent things in themselves. Whatever increases the reading public, tends necessarily to equalize the knowledge already in the world; but the process by which knowledge is equalized is not altogether that by which the degree of knowledge is heightened. Cheap publications of themselves are sufficient for the *diffusion* of knowledge, but not for its *advancement*. The schoolmaster equalizes information, by giving that which he possesses to others, and for that very reason can devote but little time to increasing his own stock.

Let me make this more familiar by telling you an anecdote of our friend Dr. ———. You know that he is a man of the very highest scientific attainments? You know also that he is not overburdened with those same precious metals on the history of which he can so learnedly descant. He took a book some months ago to a publisher of enterprise and capital: it was full of the profoundest research; the bookseller shook his head, and—

"Pray, sir," said he, musingly, "how many persons in England are acquainted with the ultimate principles by which you come to your result?"

"Not fifty, sir," cried the doctor, with all the enthusiasm of a discoverer.

"And how many can understand the elementary principles which occupy your first chapter?"

"Oh!" said the doctor, with indifference, "*those* principles are merely plain truths in mechanics, which most manufacturers ought to know, and which many literary dandies think it shows learning to allude to; perhaps, therefore, several thousands may be familiar with the contents of the first chapter; but, I assure you, sir, you don't get far before"—

"Pardon me, doctor," interrupted the bookseller, shortly—"if you address the fifty persons, you must publish this work on your own account; if you address the thousands, why it is quite another matter. Here is your MS.; burn all but the first chapter: as a commercial speculation, the rest is mere rubbish; if you will then spin out the first chapter into a volume, and call it *The Elements of ——— Familiarly Explained*—why, I think, sir, with your name, I could afford you three hundred pounds for it."

Necessity knows no law. *The Elements* are published to teach new thousands what other thousands knew before, and the *Discoveries* lie in the doctor's desk, where they will only become lucrative, when some richer man shall invent and propagate them, and the public will call on the poor doctor "to make them familiar."

Now observe a very curious consequence from this story: Suppose a certain science is *only* cultivated by five hundred men, and that they have all cultivated the science to a certain height. A book that should tell them what they knew already, they would naturally not purchase, and a book that told them more than they knew they would eagerly buy; in such a case, the doctor's position would have been reversed, and his *Discoveries* would have been much more lucrative to him than his *Elements*. —Thus we may observe that the tone of knowledge is usually more scholastic in proportion as the circle of readers is confined. When scholars are your audience, you address them after the fashion of a scholar. Hence, formerly, every man thought it necessary, when he wrote a book, to bestow upon its composition the most scrupulous care; to fill its pages with the product of a studious life; to polish its style with the classic file, and to ornament its periods with the academical allusion. He knew that the majority of those who read his work would be able to appreciate labour or to detect neglect; but, as the circle of readers increased, the mind of the writer became less fastidious; the superficial readers had outnumbered the profounder critics. He still addressed the majority, but the taste of the majority was no longer so scrupulous as to the fashion of the address. Since the Revival of Letters itself, the more confined the public, the more laborious the student. Ascham is more scholastic than Raleigh; Raleigh than Addison; and Addison than Scott.

The spirit of a popular assembly can enter into the crowd

you write for, as well as the crowd you address; and a familiar frankness, or a superficial eloquence, charm the assembly when full, which a measured wisdom, and a copious knowledge were necessary to win, when its numbers were scattered and select.

It is natural that writers should be ambitious of creating a sensation: a sensation is produced by gaining the ear, not of the few, but the many; it is natural, therefore, that they should address the many; the style pleasing to the many becomes, of course, the style most frequently aimed at: hence the profusion of amusing, familiar, and superficial writings. People complain of it, as if it were a proof of degeneracy in the knowledge of authors—it is a proof of the increased number of readers. The time is come when nobody will fit out a ship for the intellectual Columbus to discover new worlds, but when everybody will subscribe for his setting up a steam-boat between Calais and Dover. You observe then, sir, (consequences which the fine talkers of the day have wholly overlooked) that the immense superficies of the public operates two ways in deteriorating from the profundity of writers: in the first place, it renders it no longer necessary for an author to make himself profound before he writes; and in the next place, it encourages those authors who *are* profound, by every inducement, not of lucre alone, but of fame, to exchange deep writing for agreeable writing: the voice which animates the man ambitious of wide fame, does not, according to the beautiful line in Rogers, whisper to him "ASPIRE," but "DESCEND." "He stoops to conquer." Thus, if we look abroad, in France, where the reading public is less numerous than in England,[1] a more elevated and refining tone is more fashionable in literature; and in America, where it is infinitely larger, the tone of literature is infinitely more superficial. It is possible, that the high-souled among literary men, desirous rather of truth than fame, or willing to traverse their trial to posterity, are actuated, *unconsciously,* by the spirit of the times; but actuated they necessarily are, just (to return to my former comparison) as the wisest orator, who uttered only philosophy to a thin audience of sages, mechanically abandons his refinements and his reasonings, and expands into a louder tone and more familiar manner as the

1. In France, the proportion of those educated in schools is but one in twenty-eight.

assembly increases;—the temper of the popular meeting is un-avoidably caught by the mind that addresses it.[2]

From these remarks we may perceive then, that in order to increase the height of knowledge, it is not sufficient to diffuse its extent; nay, that in that very diffusion there is a tendency to the superficial, which requires to be counteracted. And this, sir, it seems to me that we can only thoroughly effect by the Endow-ments of which I have before spoken. For since the government of knowledge is like that of states, and instituted not for the power of the few, but the enjoyment of the many, so this *diffu-sion* of information amongst the ignorant is greatly to be com-mended and encouraged, even though it operate unfavourably on the *increase* of information amongst the learned. We ought not, therefore, to resist, even were we able, which we are not, the circulation of intelligence; but by other means we should seek to supply the reservoirs, from which, aloft and remote, the fertilizing waters are supplied. I see not that this can be done by any other means than the establishment of such professorships, and salaries for the cultivators of the highest branches of litera-ture and science, as may be adequate, both in the number and in the income allotted to each, to excite ambition. Thus a tribunal for high endeavour will be established, independent of the court of the larger public, independent indeed, yet each acting upon the other. The main difficulty would be that of appointing fit electors to these offices. I cannot help thinking that there should, for the sake of emulation, and the prevention of corruption or prejudice, be different electoral bodies, that should promote to. vacancies in rotation; and these might be the three branches of the legislature, the different national universities, and, above all, (though the notion may seem extravagant at first sight,) for-eign academies, which being wholly free from sectarian, or party prejudices, would, I am convinced, nine times out of ten, (until at least they had aroused our emulation by exciting our shame,)

2. M. Cousin, speaking of professors who in despair of a serious audience, wish at least for a numerous one, has well illustrated this principle. "Dans ce cas c'en est fait de la science, car on a beau faire, on se proportionne à son auditoire. Il y a dans les grandes foules je ne sais quel ascendant presque magnétique, qui subjugue les ames les plus fermes; et tel qui eût été un pro-fesseur sérieux et instructif pour une centaine d'étudiens attentifs, devient leger et superficiel avec un auditoire superficiel et leger."

choose the most fitting persons: For foreign nations are to the higher efforts of genius, the Representatives of Posterity itself. This, to be sure, is not a scheme ever likely to be realised; neither, I confess, is it wholly free from objections: but unless some such incitement to the loftier branches of knowledge be devised, the increasing demand will only introduce adulteration in the supply. So wide a popularity, and so alluring a remuneration, being given to the superficial, whoever is ambitious, and whoever is poor, will naturally either suit his commodity to the market, or renounce his calling altogether. At present, a popular instructor is very much like a certain master in Italian, who has thriven prodigiously upon a new experiment on his pupils. J—— was a clever fellow, and full of knowledge which nobody wanted to know. After seeing him in rags for some years, I met him the other day most sprucely attired, and with the complacent and sanguine air of a prosperous gentleman:—

"I am glad to see, my dear sir," said I, "that the world wags well with you."

"It does."

"Doubtless, your books sell famously."

"Bah! no bookseller will buy them: no, sir, I hit on a better *metier* than that of writing books—I am giving lessons in Italian."

"Italian! why I thought when I last saw you, that you told me Italian was the very language you knew nothing about?"

"Nor did I, sir; but directly I had procured scholars, I began to teach myself. I bought a dictionary; I learnt that lesson in the morning which I taught my pupils at noon. I found I was more familiar and explanatory, thus *fresh from knowing little,* than if I had been confused and over deep by knowing much. I am a most popular teacher, sir;—and my whole art consists in being just one lesson in advance of my scholars!"

IV

Style

If the observations in my last chapter be correct, and books become less learned in proportion as the reading community becomes more numerous, it is evident that in the same proportion, and for the same cause, style will become less elaborate and polished than when the author, addressing only the scholastic few, found a critic in every reader. Writings addressed to the multitude must be clear and concise: the style of the present day has therefore gained in clearness what it has lost in erudition.

A numerous audience require also, before all things, a natural and frank manner in him who addresses them; they have no toleration for the didascalic affectations in which academicians delight. "Speak out, and like a man!" is their first exclamation to one who seems about to be mincing and pedantic in his accost, or set and prepared in the fashion of his periods. Style, therefore, at the present day, is generally more plain and straightforward than heretofore, and tells its unvarnished tale with little respect to the balanced cadence and the elaborate sentence. It has less of the harmony of the prepared, and more of the vigour of the extempore. At the same time it is to be regretted that the higher and more refining beauties should be neglected—the delicate allusion—the subtle grace. It would be well could we preserve *both* the simplicity and the richness—aiming at an eloquence like that of the Roman orator, which, while seeming to flow most freely, harmonized every accent to an accompanying music.

From the same cause which gives plainness to the modern style, it receives also warmth, and seems entirely to have escaped from the solemn frigidity of Johnson, and the silver fetters that clanked on the graceful movements of Goldsmith, or the measured elegance of Hume. But, on the other hand, this warmth frequently runs into extravagance, and as the orator to a crowd says that with vehemence which to a few he would say with composure, so the main fault of the present style, especially of the younger writers, is often in an exaggerated tone and a superfluous and gratuitous assumption of energy and passion. It is this failing, carried with them to a greater extent than it is with us, which burlesques the romantic French writers of the present day, and from which *we* are only preserved by a more manly and sturdy audience.

As with the increase of the crowd, appeals to passion become more successful, so in the enlargement of the reading public I see one great cause of the unprecedented success of fiction. Some inconsiderate critics prophesy that the taste for novels and romances will wear itself out; it is, on the contrary, more likely to increase as the circle of the public widens. Fiction, with its graphic delineation and appeals to the familiar emotions, is adapted to the crowd—for it is the oratory of literature.

You are acquainted with Mr. Starch. He is a man who professes a vast regard for what he calls *the original purity of the language.* He is bitterly opposed to new words. He hath made two bugbears to his mind—the one hight 'Latinity,' the other 'Gallicism.' He seeth these spectres in every modern composition. He valueth himself upon writing Saxon, and his style walketh about as naked as a Pict. In fact nothing can be more graceless and bald than his compositions, and yet he calls *them* only "the true English." But he is very much mistaken; they are not such English as any English writer, worth reading at least, ever wrote. At what period, sir, would the critics of Starch's order stop the progress of our language? to what elements would they reduce it? The language is like the land,—restore it to what it was for the aboriginals, and you would reduce beauty, pomp, and fertility to a desert. Go beyond a certain point of restitution, and to restore is to destroy. Every great literary age with us has been that in which the language has the most largely borrowed from the spirit of some foreign tongue—a startling proposition, but borne out by facts. The spirit of Ancient Letters passing into our language, as yet virgin of all offspring, begat literature itself. In Elizabeth's day, besides Greek and Latin, we borrowed most largely from the Italian. The genius of that day is Italian poetry transfused, and sublimed by the transition, into a rougher tongue. In the reign of Queen Anne we were equally indebted to the French, and nothing can be more Gallic than the prose of Addison and the verse of Pope. In the day immediately preceding our own, besides returning to our old writers, viz. the borrowers from the Italian and French, we have caught much of the moonlight and dreamy character of romance—much of the mingled chivalry and mysticism that marked the favourite productions of the time, from the masterpieces of Germany.[1] In fact, I suspect that every great writer of a nation a little corrupts its tongue. His knowledge suggests additions and graces from other tongues; his genius applies and makes them popular. Milton was the greatest poet of our country, and there is scarcely an English idiom which he has not violated, or a foreign one which he has not borrowed. Voltaire accuses the simple La Fontaine of having corrupted the language; the same charge was made against Voltaire himself. Rousseau was yet more open to the accusation than Voltaire. Chateaubriand and De Stael are the corruptors of the style of Rousseau, and Courier has grafted new licenses on the liberties arrogated by Voltaire. Nothing could be more simple and unpretending than the style of Scott, yet he is perpetually accused of having tainted the purity of our idioms; so that the language may be said to acquire its chief triumphs by those who seem the least to have paid deference to its forms.

It is some comfort, amidst the declamations of Starch, to think

1. It is not often very easy to trace the manner in which an author is indebted to the spirit of a foreign literature, and which he may not even know in the original. Wordsworth, Coleridge and Scott, knew German, and their knowledge is manifest in their own writings. Byron was unacquainted with German; yet he was deeply imbued with the German intellectual spirit. A vast number of German fictions had been translated at the beginning of the century. They ran the round of the circulating libraries, and coloured and prepared the minds of the ordinary reading public, unknowingly to themselves, for the favourable reception of the first English writer in a similar school. I have heard from a relation of Byron's, that he had read these fictions largely in his youth, and that which swayed his mind in its cast of sentiment, laid the train in the general mind for the effect that he produced.

that the system of intellectual commerce with foreign languages is somewhat like the more vulgar trade, and if it corrupts, must be allowed at least to enrich.

You know, my dear sir, that in France, that lively country, where they always get up a dispute for the amusement of the spectators, where the nobles encouraged a democracy, for the pleasurable excitement of the controversy; and religion itself has been played like a game at shuttlecock, which is lost the moment the antagonists cease their blows;—in France, the good people still divert themselves with disputing the several merits of the Classical School, and the Romantic. They have the two schools—*that* is certain—let us be permitted to question the excellence of the scholars in either.

The English have not disputed on the matter, and the consequence is, that their writers have contrived to amalgamate the chief qualities of *both* schools. Thus, the style of Byron is at once classical and romantic; and, the Edinburgh reviewers have well observed, may please either a Gifford or a Shelley. And even a Shelley, whom some would style emphatically of the Romantic School, has formed himself on the model of the Classic. His genius is eminently Greek: he has become romantic, by being peculiarly classical.[2]

Thus while the two schools abroad have been declaring an union incompatible, we have united them quietly, without saying a word on the matter. Heaven only knows to what extremes of absurdity we should have gone in the spirit of emulation, if we had thought fit to set up a couple of parties, to prove which was best![3]

2. This observation will extend even to Keates himself, the last of the new school. 'Endymion' and 'Saturn' are both modelled from the casts of antiquity.

3. The question of the difference between the Romantic School and the Classic, has been merely that of forms. What, in the name of common sense, signify disputes about the Unities and such stuff,—the ceremonies of the Muses? The Medea would have been equally Greek if all the unities had been disregarded. The Faust equally romantic, if all the unities had been preserved. It is among the poems of Homer and Pindar, or Æschylus and Hesiod, that you must look for the spirit of antiquity; but these gentlemen look to the rules of Aristotle: it is as if a sculptor, instead of studying the statue of the Apollo, should study the yard measure that takes its proportions.

V

The Drama

"One may always leave the amusements to the care of the public; they are sure to pay for *those* well": thus said a mathematician to me, the other day, with the air of a man who wished benevolently to insinuate, that one made too much by one's novels, and that the king ought to give such a good mathematician as he was, five thousand a year at the least.

"The deuce you may, sir!—What then do you say to the drama? —Actors, authors, managers, singers, painters, jugglers, lions and elephants from Siam, all are working night and day to amuse you. And I fancy that the theatres are nevertheless but a poor speculation."

"Yes, but in this country—monopoly; no protection to the authors;—theatres too big;—free trade," mumbled the mathematician.

"Certainly, you are quite right—but look to France. No legislature can be more polite to the drama, than is the legislature of France. Authors protected, a Dramatic Board, plenty of theatres, no censor; and yet the poor Drama is in a very bad way even there. The Government are forced to allow the theatres several thousands a year; without that assistance they would be shut up. Messieurs the Public pay something to the piper, but not all the requisite salary; so that you see it is not quite true, that the public will always pay well for their own amusements."

If this be the case in France, I fear it must be still more the case in England. For in France, amusement is a necessary, while here it is scarcely even a luxury. "L'amusement est un des besoins de l'homme," said Voltaire. *Oui, Monsieur de Voltaire,—de l'homme François!* In England, thanks to our taxes, we have not yet come to reckon amusements among our *absolute* wants.

But everywhere throughout Europe the glory of the theatre is beginning to grow dim, as if there were certain arts in the world which blaze, and have their day, and then die off in silence and darkness, like an exhausted volcano. In France it is not only that the theatre is not prosperous, but that, with every advantage and stimulus, the talent for the theatre is degenerate. The French authors have started a new era in Art, by putting an end to Nature. They now try only to write something eccentric. They want to excite terror, by showing you bugbears that cannot exist. When Garrick wished to awe you, he had merely to change the expression of his countenance; a child wishing to terrify you, puts on a mask. The French authors put on a mask.

The French dramatists have now pretty nearly run through the whole catalogue of out-of-the-way crimes, and when that is completed, there will be an end of their materials. After the *Tour de Nesle,* what more can they think of in the way of atrocity? In this play, the heroine poisons her father, stabs and drowns all the lovers she can get (number unknown); intrigues with one son, and assassinates the other! After such a selection from the fair sex, it is difficult to guess, from what female conception of the Beautiful the French Poets will form their next fashionable heroine!

The French Theatre is wretched; it has been made the field for the two schools to fight in, and the combatants have left all their dead bodies on the stage.

If the French Theatre lives upon murders, the English exists upon robberies; it steals every thing it can lay its hands upon; to-day it filches a French farce, to-morrow it becomes sacrilegious, and commits a burglary on the Bible. The most honest of our writers turn up their noses at the rogues who steal from foreigners, and with a spirit of lofty patriotism confine their robberies to the literature of their own country. These are they, who think that to steal old goods is no theft: they are the brokers of books, and their avowed trade is second-hand. They hunt among the Heywoods and Deckers, pillage a plot from Fletcher or

Shirley; and as for their language, they steal *that* every where; these are they who fill every page with "go to" and "peradventure." If a lady asks her visiters to be seated, it is

> Pray ye, sit down, good gentles;

if a lover admires the fashion of his mistress's gown;—she answereth:—

> Ay, by my faith, 'tis quaint!

if a gentleman complains of a wound,

> It shall be look'd to, sir, right heedfully.

A dramatic author of this nature is the very Autolycus of plagiarists; "an admirable conceited fellow, and hath ribbons of all the colours of the rainbow"; he sayeth, indeed, that he derives *assistance only* from the elder dramatists—he robbeth not; no! *he catcheth the spirit!* verily this he doth all in the true genius of Autolycus, when he assists himself with the Clown, as thus:—

CLOWN.

How now! Can'st stand?

AUTOLYCUS.

Softly, dear Sir, (*picks his pocket:*) good Sir, softly. You ha' done me a charitable office.

Jack Old-Crib is a dramatic author of this class; you never heard of a man so bitter against the frivolity of those who filch from the French vaudevilles. Their want of magnanimity displeases him sadly. He is mightily bitter on the success of Tom Fribble, who lives by translating one-act farces from Scribe; he calls *that* plagiarism: meanwhile, Jack Old-Crib steals from all the loftiness of a five-act poet, and, worse than Fribble—does not even acknowledge the offence. No; he steals plot, character, diction and all, from Dodsley's Collection, but calls *that,* with a majestic smile, "reviving the Antient Drama."

Certainly there have been many reasons for the present deterioration of dramatic literature to be ascribed solely to the state of the laws. In the first place, what men that can write popularly anything else, would write for the stage, so long as, while they were damned if they might fail, they could get nothing if they succeeded? Does any fruit, even a crab-apple, flourish in that land where there is no security for property? The drama has been that land. In the second place, the two large theatres, having once gorged the public with show, have rendered themselves unfit for dignified comedy and sober entertainments, because they have created a public unfit to relish them. The minor theatres being against the law, few persons of capital have been disposed to embark property in illegal speculations. The sites of many of these theatres, too, are ill-chosen, and the audience not sufficiently guided in their tastes by persons of literary refinement. Some of these evils we may hope to reform. You know, sir, that I have introduced into Parliament two bills, one of which will give protection to authors, and the other encourage competition in theatres. The first has received the royal assent, and become law. I trust for the same good fortune for the second. Doubtless these improvements in legislation may be extremely beneficial in their ultimate consequences.

But there are causes of deterioration which the law cannot control; and, looking to the state of the drama abroad, while our experiment ought to be adventured, we must confess its success to be doubtful. Still more doubtful is it when we recollect that, if the state of the law were the only cause of the deterioration of the drama, by removing the cause you cannot always remove the effect which the cause has engendered. The public being once spoiled by show, it is not easy to bring them back to a patient love of chaste composition. The public, also, being once rendered indifferent to the drama, it is not easy to restore the taste. "Tardiora sunt remedia quàm mala, et, ut corpora lente augescunt cito exstinguuntur, sic ingenia studiaque oppresseris, facilius quàm revocaris." A very profound remark, which means simply that when the Drama has once gone to the dogs, it will be a matter of time to heal the marks of their teeth. It is easier to create a taste than to revive one. Most of us, how simple men soever, can beget life without any extraordinary exertion; but it requires a very able physician to restore the dying. At present let us remove the obstacles to the operations of nature, and trust that *she* will be the physician at last. And, at least, we must admit that the present age has shown no lack of dramatic talent. Of dramatic talent suited to *the taste of the day,* it assuredly has; but not of dramatic talent examined by the criteria of high art. I have already spoken of the magnificent tragedies of Byron: I may add to those the stern and terrible conception of the Cençi. Nor ought we to forget the Mirandola of Barry Cornwall, or the Evadne of Sheil—both works that, if written at an earlier period, would have retained a permanent and high station on the stage. The plays of Mr. Knowles, though at one time overlauded by the critics, and somewhat perhaps disfigured by imitations of the elder dramatists, testify considerable mastery of effect, and, with the exception of Victor Hugo's *chef-d'œuvres,* are undeniably superior to the contemporaneous dramas of France.

The greater proportion of prose fictions amongst us, too, have been written by the dramatic rules, rather than the epic, and evince an amplitude of talent for the stage, had their authors been encouraged so to apply it. In fine, then, the theatre wants good dramas; but the age shows no want of dramatic ability. Let us hope for the best, but not expect too speedy a realization of the hope. The political agitation of the times is peculiarly unfavourable to the arts: when people are busy, they are not eager to be amused. The great reason why the Athenians, always in a sea of politics, were nevertheless always willing to crowd the theatre, was this—*the theatre with them was political;* tragedy embodied the sentiment, and comedy represented the characters, of the times. Thus theatrical performance was to the Athenian a newspaper as well as a play. We banish the Political from the stage of the most vivid of its actual sources of interest. At present the English, instead of finding politics on the stage, find their stage in politics. In the testimony of the witnesses examined before the Dramatic Committee, it is universally allowed that a censor is not required to keep immorality from the stage, but to prevent political allusions. I grant that in too great a breadth of political allusions there is a certain mischief: politics addressed to the people should not come before the tribunal of their imagination, but that of their reason; in the one you only excite by convincing—in the other you begin at the wrong end, and convince by exciting. At the same time, I doubt if the drama will become thoroughly popular until it is permitted to embody the most popular emotions. In these times the public mind is absorbed in politics, and yet the stage, which should represent the times, especially banishes appeals to the most general feelings. To see our modern plays, you would imagine there were no politicians among us: the national theatre, to use a hacknied but appropriate jest, is like the play of Hamlet "with the part of Hamlet left out by the particular desire"—of the nobility!

But as the censor will be retained, and politics will still be banished from the stage, let us endeavour to content ourselves with the great benefits that, ere another year, I trust we shall have affected for the advancement of the Stage. By the one law already enacted, authors will have nothing material to complain of; a successful and standard play, bestowing on them some emolument every time it is performed, will be a source of permanent income. Some of the best writers of the age (for the best are often the poorest) will therefore be encouraged to write plays, and to write not for the hour only, but for permanent fame. By the second law, which I trust will soon be passed, every theatre will be permitted to act the legitimate drama: there will therefore be no want of competition in the number of theatres, no just ground of complaint as to their disproportionate size. There will be theatres enough, and theatres of all dimensions. I imagine the two large theatres will, however, continue to be the most important and influential. Monopoly misguided their efforts,— emulation will rectify the direction. These are great reforms. Let us make the most of them, and see, if despite the languor of the drama abroad, we cannot revive its national vigour at home.

And to effect this restauration, let us examine what are the true sources of dramatic interest which belong to this age. Let us borrow the divining rod, and see to what new fountains it will lead us.

Heaven and yourself, dear sir, know how many years ago it is since the members of the poetical world cried out, "Let us go back to the old poets." Back to the old poets accordingly they went—the inspiration revived them. Poetry bathed in the youth of the language, and became once more young. But the most sacred inspiration never lasts above a generation or two, and the power of achieving wonders wears itself out after the death of the first disciples. Just when the rest of the literary world began to think the new poets had made quite enough out of the old, just when they had grown weary of transfusing the spirit of chivalry and ballads into the genius of modern times, just when they had begun to allow that what was a good thing once, was beginning to grow too much of a good thing now, up starts our friend the Drama, with the wise look of a man who has suddenly perceived the meaning of a *bon mot,* that all the rest of the company have already admired and done with, and says, "Go back to the old poets. What an excellent idea!" The Drama, which ought to be the first intellectual representative to reflect every important change in the literary spirit of the world, has with us been the last, and is now going back to Elizabeth's day for an inspiration which a more alert species of poetry has already exhausted of the charm of freshness. It seizes on what is most hacknied, and announces its treasure as most new. When we are palled with the *bon mot,* it begins to din it into our ears as a capital new story. This will never do. To revive the Stage we must now go forward, the golden bridge behind us is broken down by the multitude of passengers who have crossed it. The darkness closes once more over the lovely Spirit of the departed Poetry, and like the fairy of her own wells and waterfalls, the oftener she has revisited the earth, the fainter has become her beauty, and the less powerful her charm.

> Like to a child o'erwearied with sweet toil,
> On its own folded wings and wavy hair
> The spirit of the earth is laid asleep!

There are two sources from which we should now seek the tragic influence, viz. the Simple and the Magnificent. Tales of a household nature, that find their echo in the hearts of the people —the materials of the village tragedy, awakening an interest common to us all; intense yet homely, actual—earnest—the pathos and passion of every-day life; such as the stories of Jeannie Deans or of Carwell, in prose fiction;—behold one great source of those emotions to which the dramatic author of this generation ought to apply his genius! Originally the personages of tragedy were rightly taken from the great. With a just propriety, Kings stalked the scenic boards; the heroine was a queen, the lover a warrior:—*for in those days there was no people!* Emotions were supposed to be more tragic in proportion as the station of their victims was elevated. This notion was believed in

common life, and to represent it was therefore natural and decorous to the Stage. But we have now learnt another faith in the
actual world, and to that faith, if we desire to interest the spectator, we must appeal upon the stage. We have learnt to consider that emotions are *not* the most passionately experienced in
a court; that the feelings of Kings are not more intense than
those of persons who are more roused by the stern excitements
of life, nor the passions of a Queen less freed from frivolity,
than the maiden of humbler fortunes, who loves from the depths
of a heart which hath no occupation but love. We know the
great now as persons assuredly whom it is wise and fitting to
respect; incarnations of the august ceremonies in which a nation
parades its own grandeur, and pleases its own pride. For my part
I do not profess a vulgar intolerance of belief that Kings must
be worse than other men;[1] but we know at least, amidst a round
of forms, and an etiquette of frivolities, that their souls cannot
be so large, nor their passions so powerful, nor their emotions
so intensely tragic as those of men in whom the active enterprises
of life constantly stimulate the desires and nerve the powers.
The passions are the elements of tragedy. Whatever renders the
passions weak and regulated is serviceable to morals, and unfitted for the Stage. A good man who never sins against reason
is an excellent character, but a tame hero. But morals alone do
not check the passions; frivolities check them also. And the nature of a King is controlled and circumscribed to limits too narrow for the Tragic, (which demands excess,) not perhaps by
the virtues that subdue, but the ceremonies which restrain, him.
Kings of old were the appropriate heroes of the stage; for all the
vastest of human ideas circled and enshrined them. The heroic
and the early Christian age alike agreed in attributing to the
Crowned Head a mysterious and solemn sanctity. Delegates of
supernatural agents, they were the gods or dæmons of the earth;
the hearts of mankind were compelled to a dread and irresistible
interest in their actions. They were the earthly repositories of
human fate; when their representatives appeared upon the stage,
habited and attended as *they* were, it was impossible that the

---

1. Nay, if they were so, they would be—terrible scourges, it is true, to the
world—but *quelquechose de bon* for the Stage. It really is because Kings are
now so rarely guilty of gigantic crime, that they cease to awe and terrify us on
the Stage.

interest of the spectator, so highly wrought at the reality, should not be prepared to transfer itself to the likeness. Then indeed that interest itself assumed a grand and tragic dignity. What vivid and awful emotions must those have experienced who surveyed the fate of beings who were the arch dispensers of the fates themselves![2]

The belief which attached to a Sovereign something of the power and the sanctity of a god, necessarily beheld a superhuman dignity in his love, and a terrible sublimity in his woe. The misfortunes that happened to the monarch were as punishments upon the people; the spectators felt themselves involved in the consequences of his triumph or his fall. Thus kings were the most appropriate heroes of the tragic muse, because their very appearance on the stage appealed to the Sublime—the superstition of the beholder stamped a gigantic grandeur on the august sufferer—and united with the pathos of human interest the awe of religion itself. The habits of monarchy in the elder age strengthened this delusion. For both in the remote classic and the later feudal time, the people did not represent themselves so much as they were represented in their chief. And when Shakspeare introduces Henry V. upon the stage, the spectators beheld not a king only, but the type of their own triumphs—the breathing incarnation of the trophies of Agincourt, and the abasement of France. To add yet more to the interest that encircled the tragic hero—the people, as I have just said, were *not*—Wisdom, Education, and Glory were alike the monopoly of the great. Then knowledge had not taught to the mass of mankind the mighty sources of interest which lay, untouched by the poet, in their own condition. The popular heart was only known in its great convulsions—it was the high-born and the knightly who were alone represented as faithful in love—generous in triumph —and magnanimous in adversity. The people were painted as a mob—fickle, insolent, and cruel; perhaps in that state of civilization they were nothing more. It may be that the great, being the best educated, were really the noblest part of the community.

In former times then, there were reasons which do not exist at present—that rendered the Great the fitting heroes of the tragic stage. Kings do not awaken the same awful and mysterious

2. "Princes are like to heavenly bodies, which cause good or evil times." —Bacon.

emotions that they once inspired—if not without the theatre, neither will they within its walls. You may go back to the old time, you may present to us an Œdipus or an Agamemnon, a Richard or a Henry; but you will not revive in us the same feelings with which their representatives were once beheld. Our reason tacitly allows that these names were clothed with associations from those which surround modern Sovereigns. But our feelings do not obey our reason—we cannot place ourselves in the condition of those who would have felt their blood thrill as the crowned shadows moved across the stage. We cannot fill our bosoms with the emotions that sleep in the dust of our departed fathers. We gaze upon the purple of past kings with the irreverent apathy of modern times. Kings are no longer Destinies. And the interest they excited has departed with their power. Whither? —to the People! Among the people, then, must the tragic author invoke the genius of Modern Tragedy, and learn its springs.

If this principle be true, down falls at once all the old fabric of criticism upon the tragic art! Down falls the pile of reasonings built to tell us why Kings, Princesses, Generals, and "the nobility in general" must be the characters of true tragedy! Down go the barriers which so rigidly shut out from the representation of elevated nature—the classes in which her elements are the most impassioned and their operations the most various! A new order of things has arisen in the actual world, and the old rules[3] instituted for the purpose of illustrating the actual world by the ideal, crumble to the dust!

In Shelley's noble thought, the Spirit of Power and Poesy passes into the Universal Heart:

It interpenetrates the granite mass;—

beings are called forth "less mighty but more mild," and

Familiar acts grow beautiful through Love!

---

3. I grant that the stage must not only represent but ennoble Nature—its likenesses must be spiritualized; but this it can effect equally from whatever grade its characters are drawn. Clarissa Harlowe is taken from the middle ranks—could the character of any queen have been more spiritualized? Goldsmith's Country Clergyman is nature—but nature ennobled. Faust is a German scholar; but partakes more largely of the grand idea than any Prince (save Hamlet) idealized by the magic of Shakspeare himself.

The SIMPLE, then, is one legitimate (and I hold the *principal*) source of the modern tragedy—its materials being woven from the woes—the passions—the various and multiform characters —that are to be found in the different grades of an educated and highly civilized people;—materials a thousand times more rich, subtle, and complex, than those sought only in the region of royal existence, the paucity of which we may perceive by the monotonous sameness of the characters into which, in the regal tragedy, they are moulded. The eternal prince, and his eternal confidant; the ambitious traitor, and the jealous tyrant; the fair captive, and her female friend!—We should not have had these *dramatis personæ* so often, if authors had not conceived themselves limited to the intrigues, the events, and the creations of a court.

Another and totally distinct source of modern tragedy may be sought in the MAGNIFICENT. True art never rejects the materials which are within its reach. The Stage has gained a vast acquisition in pomp and show—utterly unknown to any period of its former history. The most elaborate devices of machinery, the most exquisite delusions of scene, may indeed be said to snatch us

> From Thebes to Athens when and where you will.

The public have grown wedded to this magnificence. Be it so. Let the dramatist effect, then, what Voltaire did under a similar passion of the public, and[4] marry the scenic pomp "to immortal verse." Instead of abusing and carping at the public for liking the more gorgeous attractions, be it the task of our dramatists to elevate the attractions themselves. Let them borrow all they can from the sister arts, (in this they have the advantage of other poets, who must depend on the one art alone,) but let them make their magnificent allies subservient to the one great art they profess. In short, let them employ an equal gorgeousness of effect; but instead of wasting it on a spectacle, or a melodrama, make it instrumental to the achievements of tragedy herself. The astonishing richness and copiousness of modern stage illusion

4. Helvetius complains, however, that in his day, their full effect could not be given to magnificence and display, on account of the fashion of the spectators to crowd the stage.

opens to the poet a mighty field, which his predecessors could not enter. For him are indeed "the treasures of earth, and air, and sea." The gorgeous Ind with her mighty forests, and glittering spires; "Fanatic Egypt and her priests"; the stern superstitions of the North—its wizard pine glens—its hills of snow and lucid air

Clad in the beauty of a thousand stars:—

whatever Nature hath created, whatever history hath bequeathed, whatever fancy can devise—all now are within the power of the artist to summon upon the Stage. The poet of the drama hath no restrictions on his imagination from the deficiency of skill to embody corporeally his creations, and that which the epic poet can only describe by words, the tragic poet can fix into palpable and visible life. The MAGNIFICENT, then, is the second source of modern dramatic inspiration, combining all the attractions of scenery, embracing the vastest superstitions and most glowing dreams of an unbounded imagination. We may see that these two are the real sources of modern dramatic art, by the evidence, that even performances below the mediocre which have resorted to either source, have been the most successful with the public, —have struck the most powerfully on the sentiment of the age. The play of "The Gamblers," or "The Soldier's Wife," or of "Clari," or "The Maid and the Magpie"—all, however differing each from each, partake of the one attribute of the popular or domestic tragedy; and though of a very inferior order of poetical talent, invariably excite a vivid emotion in the audience. So, on the other hand, the splendour of an Easter spectacle, or the decorations of an almost pantomimic melodrame, produce an admiration which wins forgiveness to the baldness of the dialogue and the absurdity of the plot. How then would performances of either class attract, supposing their effect were aided by proportionate skill in the formation of character, the melody of language, and the conception of design;—by the witchery of a true poet, and the execution of a consummate artist! Not then by pondering over inapplicable rules,—not by recurring to past models,—not by recasting hacknied images, but by a bold and masterly adaptation of modern materials to modern taste, will an author revive the glories of the drama.

In this, he will in reality profit by the study of Shakspeare, who addressed *his* age, and so won the future. He will do as all the master-minds of his own day have done in other regions of poetry. Byron and Scott, Göthe and Schiller, all took the germ of a popular impulse, and breathed into it a finished and glorious life, by the spirit of their own genius. Instead of decrying the public opinion which first manifested itself in a love for the lower and more frivolous portion of a certain taste, those great masters cultivated that taste to the highest, and so at once conciliated and exalted the public mind. What the ballads of Monk Lewis were to Scott, the melodrames, whether simple or gorgeous, should be to the future Scott of the drama.

A true genius, however elevated, is refreshed by the streams that intersect the popular heart, just as, by the mysterious attraction of Nature, high peaks and mountains draw up, through a thousand invisible tubes, the waters that play amidst the plains below!

VI

Moral Philosophy

Every great Movement in a civilized age has its reflection—that reflection is the Philosophy of the period. The Movement which in England commenced by the Church Reformation, and slowly progressed during the reign of Elizabeth and James, till it acquired energy for the gigantic impulse and mighty rush of the Republican Revolution, had (as the consequence of the *one* part of its progress, and the prophet of the *other*)—its great philosophical representative—in the profound, inquisitive, and innovating soul of Bacon. The Movement which restored Charles II. to the throne, which filled the Court—whose threshold had been so lately darkened by the sombre majesty of Cromwell—with men without honour and women without shame—demanded a likeness of itself; it exacted its own philosophy; a moral mirror of the growing reaction from the turbulence of a fanatical freedom to the lethargy and base contentment of a profligate despotism;—a system that should invent slavery as the standard of legislation, and selfishness as the criterion of morals:—that philosophy, that reflection, and that system, had their representative in Hobbes. The Leviathan which charmed the Court, and was even studied by the King, was the moral of Restoration—it embodied the feelings that first produced and afterwards coloured that event. A sterner era advanced. A bolder thought demanded a new likeness—the Movement advanced from the Restoration to the Revolution—the Movement once more required its philosophy, and received that philosophy in Locke. In his mind lay the type of the sentiments that produced the Revolution—in his philosophy, referring all things to Reason only, its voice was heard. As diverted from the theory of governments—the Spirit of Research was stimulated by a multiplied and encreasing commerce, as the middle class increased into power; and the activity of Trade, disdaining the theories of the closet, demanded a philosophy for the mart; a more extensive if less visible Movement in civilization, required also its reflection, and the representative of the new movement was the author of the Wealth of Nations.

Each philosophy, vast and profound enough to represent its epoch, endures for a certain time, and entails upon us a succession of spirits more or less brilliant, that either by attacking or defending, by imitating, or illustrating that peculiar philosophy, continue its influential prevalence amongst us for a longer or shorter period—when at last it darkens away from the actual and outer world, banished like the scenes of a by-gone play from the glare of the lamps and the gaze of the audience, falling into the silence of neglected lumber, and replaced by some new system, which a new necessity of the age has called into existence. We as yet live under the influence of the philosophy of Adam Smith. The minds that formerly would have devoted themselves to metaphysical and moral research, are given up to inquiries into a more material study. Political economy replaces ethics; and we have treatises on the theory of rents, instead of essays on the theory of motives. It is the age of political economists; and while we see with regret the lamp of a purer naphtha almost entirely extinct in England, we must confess that foreigners have been unjust to us when they contend that for the last half century we have been producing little or nothing to the service of the human mind.—We have produced Ricardo!—When they accuse us of the want of speculative industry, let us confront them with the pamphlets upon pamphlets that issue monthly from the press, upon speculative points alone. As in the three celebrated springs in Iceland, the stream rushes at once into one only, leaving the others dry; so the copiousness of investigation upon Political Science, leaves exhausted and unfreshed the fountains of Metaphysics and of Ethics. The spirit of the age demands political economy now, as it demanded moral theories before. Whoever will desire to know hereafter the character of our times, must find it in the philosophy of the Economists.

But the influence of a prevailing monopoly of speculative inquiry, while it deadens the general tendency towards the other branches of intellectual commerce, cannot wholly silence the few devoted and earnest minds which refuse to follow in the common current, and pursue apart and alone their independent meditations. It cannot silence—but I apprehend it will *affect* them;—the fashion of materialism in one branch of inquiry will materialize the thought that may be exercised in another. Thus all our *few* recent English moralists are of the Material School. Not touching now upon the *Scotch* schools, from which the spirit of Adam Smith has (comparatively speaking) passed, and grown naturalized with us; nor commenting on the beautiful philosophizing rather than philosophy of Dugald Stewart—the most exquisite critic upon the systems of others that our language has produced—fulfilling to philosophy the office that Schlegel fulfilled to literature,—I shall just point out, in my way to the most celebrated moralist of the time, the few that have dignified similar pursuits. Mr. Bailey of Sheffield, has produced some graceful speculations upon Truth, and the Formation of Opinions, written in a liberal spirit and a style of peculiar purity. Mr. Mill has, in a work of remarkable acuteness, but written in so compressed and Spartan a form that to abridge it would be almost to anatomize a skeleton—followed out certain theories of Hartley into a new analysis of the Human Mind. His work requires a minute and painful study—it partakes of the severe logic of his more famous treatises on Government and Education; it is the *only* purely metaphysical book attracting any notice, which to my knowledge has been published in England for the last fifteen years.[1]

Mr. Hazlitt has also left behind him an early work, entitled, "An Essay on the Principles of Human Action"; little known, and rarely to be met with, but full of original remarks, and worthy a diligent perusal.[2]

In the science of Jurisprudence, Mr. Austen has thrown con-

1. See some additional remarks upon this eminent writer in Appendix C.

2. I do not here comment on the writings of Mr. Godwin; they belong, in their character and their influence, rather to the last century than the present. Mr. Hope (the author of Anastasius) left behind him a philosophical work,

siderable light upon many intricate questions, and has illustrated a sterile subject with passages of a lofty eloquence—another proof, be it observed, of the value of Professorships;—the work is the republication of lectures, and might never have been composed in these days, but for the *necessity* of composing it.

But in legislative and moral philosophy, Bentham must assuredly be considered the most celebrated and influential teacher of the age—a master, indeed, whom few have acknowledged, but from whom thousands have, mediately and unconsciously, imbibed their opinions.

The same causes which gave so great a fertility to the school of the Economists, had their effect upon the philosophy of Bentham; they drew his genius mainly towards examinations of men rather than of man—of the defects of Law, and of the hypocrisies and fallacies of our Social System; they contributed to the material form and genus of his code, and to those notions of Utility which he considered his own invention, but which had been incorporated with half the systems that had risen in Europe since the sensualism of Condillac had been grafted upon the reflection of Locke. But causes far more latent, and perhaps more powerful, contributed also to form the mind and philosophy of Bentham. He had preceded the great French Revolution—the materials of his thoughts had been compounded from the same foundations of opinion as those on which the more enlightened advocates of the Revolution would have built up that edifice which was to defy a second deluge, and which is but a record of the confusion of the workmen. With the philosophy of the eighteenth century, which first adopted what the French reasoners term the Principle of Humanity—(that is, the principle of philanthropy—a paramount regard for multitudes rather than for sectarian interests,)—with this philosophy, I say, the whole mind of Bentham was imbued and saturate. He had no mercy, no toleration for the knots and companies of men whom he considered interrupters or monopolists of the power of the many—to his mind they were invariably actuated by base and designing motives, and such motives, according to his philosophy, they

---

which has since been suppressed—it may be difficult to say whether the style or the sense of it be the less worthy the fine genius of the author. Lady Mary Shepherd has shown no ordinary acuteness in her Essay upon "The Relation of Cause and Effect."

were even *compelled* to entertain. His intellect was as the aque-
duct which bore aloft, and over the wastes and wrecks below, the
stream of the philosophy of one century to the generations of
the other. His code of morals, original in its results, is in many
parts (unconsciously to himself) an eclecticism of nearly all the
best parts of the various theories of a century. "The system of
Condillac required its *'moral'* code, and Helvetius supplied it."
The moral code of Helvetius required its legislative, and in
Bentham it obtained it. I consider, then, that two series of causes
conspired to produce Bentham—the one national, the other belonging to all Europe; the same causes on the one hand which
produced with us the Economists—the same causes on the other
hand which produced in France, Helvetius and Diderot, Volney,
Condorcet, and Voltaire. He combined what had not been yet
done, the spirit of the Philanthropic with that of the Practical.
He did not declaim about abuses; he went at once to their root:
he did not idly penetrate the sophistries of Corruption; he smote
Corruption herself. He was the very Theseus of legislative reform,—he not only pierced the labyrinth—he destroyed the
monster.

As he drew his vigour from the stream of Change, all his writings tended to their original source. He collected from the Past
the scattered remnants of a defeated innovation, and led them on
against the Future. Every age may be called an age of transition
—the passing on, as it were, from one state to another never
ceases; but in our age the transition is *visible,* and Bentham's
philosophy is the philosophy of a visible transition. Much has
already happened, much is already happening every instant, in
his country—throughout Europe—throughout the world, which
might not have occurred if Bentham had not been; yet of all his
works, none have been read by great numbers; and most of them,
from their difficulties of style and subject, have little chance of
ever being generally popular. He acted upon the destinies of
his race by influencing the thoughts of a minute fraction of the
few who think—from them the broad principles travelled onward—became known—(their source unknown)—became familiar and successful. I have said that we live in an age of visible
transition—an age of disquietude and doubt—of the removal of
time-worn landmarks, and the breaking up of the hereditary
elements of society—old opinions, feelings—ancestral customs

and institutions are crumbling away, and both the spiritual and temporal worlds are darkened by the shadow of change. The commencement of one of these epochs—periodical in the history of mankind—is hailed by the sanguine as the coming of a new Millennium—a great iconoclastic reformation, by which all false gods shall be overthrown. To me such epochs appear but as the dark passages in the appointed progress of mankind—the times of greatest unhappiness to our species—passages into which we have no reason to rejoice at our entrance, save from the hope of being sooner landed on the opposite side. Uncertainty is the greatest of all our evils. And I know of no happiness where there is not a firm unwavering belief in its duration.

The age then is one of *destruction!* disguise it as we will, it must be so characterized; miserable would be our lot were it not also an age of preparation for reconstructing. What has been the influence of Bentham upon his age?—it has been twofold—he has helped to destroy and also to rebuild. No one has done so much to forward, at least in his country, the work of destruction, as Mr. Bentham. The spirit of examination and questioning has become through him, more than through any one person besides, the prevailing spirit of the age. For he questioned all things. The tendencies of a mind at once sceptical and systematic, (and both in the utmost possible degree,) made him endeavour to trace all speculative phenomena back to their primitive elements, and to reconsider not only the received conclusions, but the received premises. He treated all subjects as if they were virgin subjects, never before embraced or approached by man. He never set up an established doctrine as a thesis to be disputed about, but put it aside altogether, commenced from first principles, and deliberately tasked himself systematically to discover the truth, or to re-discover it if it were already known. By this process, if he ever annihilated a received opinion, he was sure of having something either good or bad to offer as a substitute for it; and in this he was most favourably distinguished from those French philosophers who preceded and even surpassed him, as destroyers of established institutions on the continent of Europe. And we shall owe largely to one who reconstructed while he destroyed, if our country is destined to pass more smoothly through this crisis of transition than the nations of the continent, and to lose less of the good it already enjoys in working itself free from the evil;—his be the merit, if while the wreck of the old vessel is still navigable, the masts of the new one, which brings relief, are dimly showing themselves above the horizon! For it is certain, and will be seen every day more clearly, that the initiation of all the changes which are now making in opinions and in institutions, may be claimed chiefly by men who have been indebted to his writings, and to the spirit of his philosophy, for the most important part of their intellectual cultivation.

I had originally proposed in this part of my work to give a slight sketch of the principal tenets of Bentham, with an exposition of what I conceive to be his errors; pointing out at once the benefits he has conferred, and also the mischief he has effected. But slight as would be that sketch, it must necessarily be somewhat abstract; and I have therefore, for the sake of the general reader, added it to the volume in the form of an appendix.[3] I have there, regarding him as a legislator and a moralist, ventured to estimate him much more highly in the former capacity than the latter; endeavouring to combat the infallibility of his application of the principle of Utility, and to show the dangerous and debasing theories, which may be, and are, deduced from it. Even, however, in legislation, his greatest happiness principle is not so clear and undeniable as it is usually conceded to be. "The greatest happiness of the greatest number" is to be our invariable guide! Is it so?—the greatest happiness of the greatest number of men living, I suppose, not of men to come; for if of all posterity, what legislator can be our guide? who can prejudge the future? Of men living, then?—well—how often would *their* greatest happiness consist in concession to their greatest errors.

In the dark ages, (said once to me very happily the wittiest writer of the day, and one who has perhaps done more to familiarize Bentham's general doctrines to the public than any other individual,) in the dark ages, it would have been for the greatest happiness of the greatest number to burn the witches; it must have made the greatest number, (all credulous of wizardry,) very uncomfortable to refuse their request for so reasonable a conflagration; they would have been given up to fear and disquietude—they would have imagined their safety disregarded

3. See Appendix B.

and their cattle despised—if witches were to live with impunity, riding on broomsticks, and sailing in oyster-shells;—*their happiness* demanded a bonfire of old women. To grant such a bonfire would have been really to consult the greatest happiness of the greatest number, yet ought it to have been the principle of wise, nay, of perfect, (for so the dogma states,) of unimpugnable legislation? In fact, the greatest happiness principle, is an excellent general rule, but it is not an undeniable axiom.

We may observe, that whatever have been the workings of English philosophy in this age, they have assumed as their characteristic a *material* shape. No new, idealizing school has sprung up amongst us, to confute and combat with the successors of Locke; to counterbalance the attraction towards schools, dealing only with the unelevating practices of the world—the science of money-making, and the passionate warfare with social abuses. And this is the more remarkable, because, both in Scotland and in Germany, the light of the Material Schools has already waxed dim and faint, and Philosophy directs her gaze to more lofty stars, out of the reach of this earth's attraction.

But what is it that in Germany sustains the undying study of pure ethical philosophy? and what is it that in Scotland has kept alive the metaphysical researches so torpid here? It is the system of professorships and endowments. And, indeed, such a system is far more necessary in the loud and busy action of a free commercial people, than it is in the deep quiet of a German state. With us it is the sole means by which we shall be able to advance a science that *cannot* by any possible chance remunerate or maintain its poorer disciples in all its speculative dignity, preserved from sinking into the more physical or more material studies which to greater fame attach greater rewards. Professorships compel a constant demand for ethical research, while they afford a serene leisure for its supply; insensibly they *create* the taste upon which they are *forced,* and maintain the moral glories of the nation abroad, while they contribute to rectify and to elevate its character at home.[4]

4. Since writing the above, I have had great pleasure in reading a Petition from Glasgow, praying for endowed Lectureships in Mechanics' Institutes. I consider such a Petition more indicative of a profound and considerate spirit of liberalism than almost any other, which, for the last three years, has been presented to the Legislative Assembly.

VII

Patronage

Before touching upon the state of science, and the state of art in England, it may be as well to settle one point, important to just views of either. It is this—What is the real influence of patronage? Now, Sir, I hold that this question has not been properly considered. Some attribute every efficacy to patronage, others refuse it all; to my judgment, two distinct sorts of patronage are commonly confounded: there is the patronage of individuals, and there is the patronage of the State. I consider the patronage of individuals hurtful *whenever it is neither supported nor corrected by diffused knowledge among the public at large*—but that of the state is usually beneficial. In England, we have no want of patronage, in art at least, however common the complaint; we have abundant patronage, but it is all of one kind; it is individual patronage; the State patronizes nothing.

Now, Sir, I think that where the Public is supine, the patronage of individuals is injurious; first, because wherever, in such a case, there is individual patronage, must come the operation of individual taste. George the Fourth (for with us a king is an individual, not as the state) admired the low Dutch school of painting, and Boors and candlesticks became universally the rage. In the second place, and this has never been enough insisted upon; the domestic habits of a nation exercise great influence upon its arts. If people do not live in large houses, they cannot ordinarily purchase large pictures. The English aristocracy, wealthy as they are, like to live in angular drawing-rooms thirty feet by twenty-eight, they have no vast halls and long-drawn galleries; if they buy large pictures, they have no place wherein to hang them. It is absurd to expect them to patronize the grand historical school, until we insist upon their living in grand historical houses. Commodiousness of size is therefore the first requisite in a marketable picture. Hence, one very plain reason why the Historical School of painting does not flourish amongst us. Individuals are the patrons of painting, individuals buy pictures for private houses, as the State would buy them for public buildings. An artist painted an historical picture for a nobleman, who owned one of the few large houses in London; two years afterwards the nobleman asked him to exchange it for a little cabinet picture, half its value. "Your Lordship must have discovered some great faults in my great picture," said the piqued artist. "Not in the least," replied the nobleman very innocently, "but the fact is, *I have changed my house*."

There was no longer any room for the historical picture, and the ornament in one house had become lumber in the other.

Individual patronage in England is not therefore at this time advantageous to high art: we hear artists crying out for patronage to support art; they have had patronage enough, and it has crippled and attenuated art as much as it possibly could do; add to this that individual patronage leads to jobbing; the fashionable patron does every thing for the fashionable artist. And the job of the Royal Academy at this day, claims the National Gallery as a jobbing appendix to itself!—Sir Martin Shee asks for patronage, and owns in the same breath, that it would be the creature of "interest or intrigue." But if it promote jobbing among fashionable artists, individual patronage is likely to pervert the genius of great ones—it commands, it bows, it moulds its protégé to whims and caprices; it set Michael Angelo to make roads, and employed Holbein in designs for forks and salt-cellars.

No! individual patronage is not advantageous to art, but there is a patronage which *is*—the patronage of the State, and this only to a certain extent. Supposing there were in the mass of this country a deep love and veneration for art or for science, the State could do nothing more than attempt to perpetuate those feelings; but if that love and veneration do not exist, the State can probably assist to create or impel them. The great body of the people must be filled with the sentiments that produce science or art, in order to make art and science become thoroughly naturalized among us. The spirit of a state can form those sentiments among its citizens. This is the sole beneficial patronage it can bestow. How is the favour of the people to be obtained? by suiting the public taste. If therefore you demand the public encouragement of the higher art and loftier science, you must accordingly train up the public taste. Can kings effect this—can individual patrons? They can at times, when the public taste has been long forming, and requires only development or an impetus; not otherwise. It has been well observed, that Francis I., a true patron of art, preceded his time; he established patronage at the court, but could not diffuse a taste among the people; therefore his influence withered away, producing no national result; fostering foreigners, but not stimulating the native genius. But a succession of Francis the Firsts, that is, the perpetuating effect and disposition of a *State,* would probably have produced the result at last of directing the public mind towards an admiration of art; and that admiration would have created a discriminating taste which would have made the people *willing* to cultivate whatever of science or art should appear amongst them.

Art is the result of inquiry into the Beautiful, Science into that of the True. You must diffuse throughout a people the cultivation of Truth and the love of Beauty, before science and art will be generally understood.

This would be the natural tendency of a better and loftier education—and education will thus improve the influence of patronage, and probably act upon the disposition of the State. But if what I have said of endowments be true, viz. that men must be courted to knowledge—that knowledge must be obtruded on them: it is true also that Science should have its stimulants and rewards. I do not agree with Mr. Babbage, that places in the Ministry would be the exact rewards appropriate to men of science. I should be sorry to see our Newtons made Secretaries for Ireland, and our Herschels turned into whippers-in of the Treasury. I would rather that honours should grow out of the natural situation in which such men are placed, than transplant them from that situation to one demanding far less exertion of genius in general, and far less adapted in itself to the peculiar genius they have displayed. What I assert is this,—that the State should not seem insensible to the services and distinction of any class of men—that it should have a lively sympathy with the honour it receives from the triumphant achievements either of art or science,—and that if it grant reward to any other species of merit, it should (not for the sake of distinguishing immortality, but for the sake of elevating public opinion,) grant honours to those who have enforced the love of the beautiful, or the knowledge of the true. I agree with certain economists—that patronage alone cannot produce a great artist or a great philosopher; I agree with them that it is only through a superficial knowledge of history, that seeing at the same time an age of patrons and an age of art and science, vain enthusiasts have asserted that patronage produced the art; I agree with them that Phidias was celebrated through Greece *before* he was honoured by Pericles; I agree with them that to make Sir Isaac Newton Master of the Mint was by no means an advancement to Astronomy; I agree with them that no vulgar hope of patronage can produce a great discovery or a great picture: that so poor and mercenary an inspiration is not even present to the conceiving thought of those majestic minds that are alone endowed with the power of creation. But it is not to produce a few great men, but to diffuse throughout a whole country a respect and veneration for the purer distinctions of the human mind, that I desire to see a State bestowing honours upon promoters of her science and art; it is not for the sake of stimulating the lofty, but refining the vulgar, mind, that we should accustom ourselves to behold rank become the natural consequence of triumphant intellect. If it were the custom of this country to promote and honour art and science, I believe we should probably not create either a Newton or a Michael Angelo; but we should by degrees imbue the public mind with a respect for the unwordly greatness which yet acquires worldly distinction (for it is the wont of the commercial spirit to regard most those qualities which enable the possessor to get on the most in the world); and we should diffuse throughout the community a respect for intellect, just as, if we honoured virtue, we should diffuse throughout a community a respect for virtue. That Humboldt should be a Minister of State has not produced new Humboldts, but it has created throughout the circles around him (which in their turn act upon general society,) an attention to and culture of the science which Humboldt adorns. The King of Bavaria is attached to art: he may not make great artists, but he circulates through his court a general knowledge of art itself. I repeat, the true object of a State is less to produce a few elevated men than to diffuse a respect for all principles that serve to elevate. If it were possible, which in the present state of feeling must be merely a philosophical theory and suggestion, to confer peerages merely for life upon men of eminent intellectual distinction, it would gradually exalt the character of the peerage; it would popularize it with the people, who would see in it a reward for all classes of intellect, and not for military, legal, and political adventurers only; it would diminish, in some respect, the vulgar and exclusive veneration for mere birth and mere wealth, and though it would not stimulate the few self-dependent minds to follow art or science for itself, it would create among the mass, (which is a far more important principle of the two,) that general cultivation of art and science which we find is ever the consequence of affixing to any branch of human acquirement high worldly rewards.[1] The best part of the celebrated book of Helvetius is that which proves that the honours of a state direct the esteem of the people, and that according to the esteem of the people is the *general* direction of mental energy and genius: "the same desire of glory," says the philosopher, "which in the early ages of the Republic produced such men as Curtius and Decius, must have formed a Marius and Octavius, when glory, as in the latter days of the republic, was only connected with tyranny and power; the love of esteem is a diminutive of the love of glory"; the last actuates the few, the first the multitude. But whatever stimulates in a nation the love

---

1. "Oh," but say some, "these peerages would become the result of mere Court favour." I doubt it. Wherever talent forces itself into our aristocracy, not having wealth to support it, the talent, however prostituted, is usually the most eminent of its class. Whatever soldiers, whatever sailors, whatever lawyers, or whatever orators, climbing, not buying their way upward, ascend to the Upper House, are usually the best soldiers, sailors, lawyers, and orators of the day. This would probably be yet more the case with men whose intellect dabbles less in the stirring interests of the world, and of whose merits Europe is the arbiter.

of glory, acts also on the love of esteem, and the honours granted to the greater passion direct the motives of the lesser one.

A Minister was asked why he did not promote merit: "Because," replied the statesman drily, "merit did not promote *me!*" It is ridiculous to expect honours for men of genius in states where honours are showered upon the men of accident;—men of accident indeed amongst us especially,—for it is not to be high-born alone that secures the dignified emoluments of state,—but to be born in *a certain set*. A gentleman without a shilling proposed the other day to an heiress. Her father delicately asked his pretensions.

"I have little at present," said he, "but my expectations are very great."

"Ah, indeed—expectations!"

"Yes; you may easily conceive their extent, when I tell you that I have one cousin a Grenville and another a Grey."

To conclude, it seems, then, that the patronage of wealthy individuals, (when the public is so far unenlightened that it receives a fashion without examining its merits) a patronage, which cannot confer honours, but only confers money, is not advantageous to art or science,—that the patronage of the State is advantageous, not in creating great ornaments in either, but in producing a general taste and a public respect for their cultivation: For the minds of great men in a civilized age are superior to the influence of laws and customs; they are not to be made by ribands and titles—their world is in themselves, and the only openings in that world look out upon immortality. But it is in the power of law and custom to bring those minds into more extensive operation—to give a wider and more ready sphere to their influence; not to create the orators, but to enlarge and still the assembly, and to conduct, as it were, through an invisible ether of popular esteem, the sound of the diviner voices amidst a listening and reverent audience.

VIII

The State of Science

I shall follow out through this chapter a principle advanced in the last.

Whatever is addressed to man's wants, man's wants will pay for; hence the true wisdom of that doctrine in political economy which leaves the useful to be remunerated by the public.

Because, 1st. Those who consume the article are better judges of its merits than a Government.

2nd. The profit derived from the sale of the commodity is proportioned to the number of persons who derive advantage from it. It is thus naturally remunerated according to its utility.

3rd. The inventor will have a much greater inducement to improve his invention, and adapt it to the taste or want of his customers than he would have were he rewarded by a Government which pays for the invention, but not for each subsequent improvement. Whatever, therefore, addresses the necessities of the people, the Government may safely trust to the public requital.

But it so happens that that part of science which addresses itself to immediate utility is not the highest. Science depends on some few great principles of a wide and general nature; from these arise secondary principles, the partial application of whose laws to the arts of life improves the factory and creates the machine. The secondary principles are therefore the parents of the Useful.

For the comprehension, the discovery, or the full establishment of the primary and general principles, are required habits of mind and modes of inquiry only obtained by long years of profound thought and abstract meditation. What the alchymist imagined of the great secret applies to all the arcana of nature. "The glorified spirit," "the mastery of masterships," are to be won but by that absorbed and devout attention of which the greater souls are alone capable; and the mooned loveliness and divinity of Nature reveals itself only to the rapt dreamer upon lofty and remote places.

But minds of this class are rare—the principles to which they are applied are few. No national encouragement could perhaps greatly increase the number of such minds or of such principles.

There is a second class of intellect which applies itself to the discovery of less general principles.

There is a third class of intellect, which applies successfully principles already discovered to purposes of practical utility. For this last a moderate acquaintance with science, aided by a combining mind, and a knowledge of the details of the workshop, joined perhaps to a manual dexterity in mechanic or chemical arts, are, if essential, commonly sufficient.

The third class of intellect is rarely joined to the second, still more rarely to the first; but *though the lowest, it is the only one that the public remunerate, and the only one therefore safely to be left to public encouragement.*

Supposing, too, a man discover some striking and most useful theory, the want of capital, or the imperfect state of the mechanical arts may render it impossible for him to apply his invention to practical purposes. This is proved by the whole history of scientific discovery. I adduce a few examples.

The doctrine of latent heat, on which the great improvement of the steam-engine rested, was the discovery of a chemist, Dr. Black. Its successful application to the steam-engine required vast mechanical resources, and was reserved for the industry of Watt and the large capital of Mr. Boulton.

The principle of the hydrostatic paradox was known for two centuries before it was applied to the practical purposes of manufactures.

The press of Bramah, by which almost all the given pressures required in our arts are given, was suggested by that principle, but the imperfect state of the art of making machinery prevented its application until very recently.

The gas called chlorine was discovered by a Swedish chemist about the year 1770. In a few years another philosopher found out that it possessed the property of destroying infection, and it has since formed the basis of most of the substances employed for disinfecting. In later times another philosopher found out its property of whitening the fibre of linen and woollen goods, and it shortly became in the hands of practical men a new basis of the art of bleaching.

The fact that fluids will boil at a lower temperature in a vacuum than when exposed to the pressure of the air, has long been known, but the application of that principle to boiling sugar produced a fortune to its inventor.

It is needless to multiply similar instances; they are of frequent occurrence.

The application of science to useful purposes may then be left to the public for reward; not so the *discovery* of the theories on which the application is founded. Here, then, there should be something in the constitution of society or the state, which, by honouring science in its higher grades, shall produce a constant supply to its practical results in the lower. What encouragement of this nature is afforded to Englishmen? Let us consider.

In every wealthy community, a considerable number of persons will be found possessed of means sufficient to command the usual luxuries of their station in society, without the necessity of employing their time in the acquisition of wealth. Pleasures of various kinds will form the occupations of the greater part of this class, and it is obviously desirable to direct, as far as possible, that which constitutes the pleasures of one class to the advantage of all. Amongst the occupations of persons so situated, literature and science will occasionally find a place, and the stimulus of vanity or ambition will urge them to excel in the line they have chosen. The cultivators of the lighter elements of literature will soon find that a profit arises from the sale of their works, and the new stimulus will convert that which was taken up as an amusement into a more serious occupation. Those who pursue science will find in the demand for elementary books a similar source of profit, although to a far less extent. But it is evident that the highest walks both in literature and science can derive no stimulus from this source. In the mean time, the profits thus made will induce a few persons of another class to enter the field. These will consist of men possessing more moderate means, whose taxes are decidedly and strongly directed either to literature or to science, and who thus hope to make some small addition to their income. If any Institutions exist in the country, such as lectureships or professorships, or if there are any official situations, which are only bestowed on persons possessing literary or scientific reputation, then there will naturally arise a class of such duties, and the number of this class will depend in some measure on the number of those official situations, and on the fairness with which they are filled up. If such appointments are numerous, and if they lead to wealth or rank in society, then literature or science, as the case may be, will be considered as a profession. In England, the higher departments of science are pursued by a few who possess independent fortune, by a few more who hope to make a moderate addition to an income itself but moderate, arising from a small private fortune, and by a few who occupy the very small number of official situations, dedicated to the abstract sciences; such are the chairs at our universities: but in England the cultivation of science is not a profession. In France, the institutions of the country open a considerable field of ambition to the cultivators of science; in Prussia the range of employments is still wider, and the policy of the state, as well as the personal disposition of the sovereign, gives additional effect to those institutions. In both those countries science is considered a profession; and in both its most successful cultivators rarely fail to be rewarded with wealth and honours.

The contrast between England and the Continent is in one respect most singular. In our own country, we occasionally meet with persons in the station of private gentlemen, ardently pursuing science for its own sake, and sometimes even acquiring a European reputation, whilst scarcely a similar instance can be produced throughout the Continent.

As the annual income received by men of science in France

has been questioned, I shall select the names of some of the most eminent, and give, from official documents, the places they hold, and the salaries attached to them. Alterations may have taken place, but about two years ago this list was correct.

M. Le Baron Cuvier, (Pair de France.)

	Francs	£
Conseiller d'état	10,000	400
Membre du Conseil Royal	12,000	480
Professeur de College de France	5,000	200
Professeur Jardin des Plantes, with a house.	5,000	200
Secrétaire Perpétuel de l'Académie des Sciences	6,000	240
Directeur des Cultes Protestants	unknown	
	38,000	1520

M. Le Baron Thenard, (Pair de France.)

	Francs	£
Membre du Conseil Royal	12,000	480
Professeur à l'Ecole Polytechnique	5,000	200
Doyen de la Faculté des Sciences	6,000	240
Professeur au College de France	5,000	200
Membre du Comité des Arts et Manufactures.	2,400	96
Membre de l'Institût	1,500	60
	31,900	1276

M. Gay Lussac,	Francs	£
Professeur à l'Ecole Polytechnique	5,000	200
———— à la Faculté	4,500	180
———— au Tabacs	3,000	120
Membre du Comité des Arts et Manufactures.	2,400	96
———— du Conseil des Poudres et Salpetres, with a house at the Arsenal	4,000	160
Essayeur à la Monnoie	20,000	800
Membre de l'Institût	1,500	60
	40,400	1616

M. Le Baron Poisson,	Francs	£
Membre du Conseil Royal	12,000	480
Examinateur à l'Ecole Polytechnique	6,000	240
Membre du Bureau des Longitudes	6,000	240
Professeur de Mécanique à la Faculté		
Membre de l'Institût	1,500	60
	25,500	1020

These are the fixed sources of income of some of the most eminent men of science in France; they receive some additions from being named as members of various temporary commissions, and it appears that these four persons were two years back paid annually 5432*l.* and that two of them had houses attached to their offices.

Without meaning to compare their merits with those of our countrymen, let us take four names well known in England for their discoveries in science, Professor Airy, Mr. Babbage, Sir David Brewster, and Sir John Herschel: without entering into detail, the amount of the salaries of all the official situations, which any of them hold, is 700*l.*—and a residence is attached to one of the offices!

Having thus contrasted the pecuniary encouragement given to science in the two countries, let us glance at the social position it enjoys in each.[1] The whole tone of public opinion in either country, is different upon the subject of science. In France, two of the persons alluded to were peers, and in the late law relative to the peerage, amongst the classes out of whom it must be recruited, members of the Institute, who are distinguished by their discoveries, are included. The legion of honour is also open to distinguished merit, in the sciences as well as in civil life; and the views of Napoleon in the institutions of that order are remarkable as coming from the military head of a nation, whose attachment to military glory is proverbial.

1. The sordid and commercial spirit of our aristocracy may be remarked in the disposition of its honours. It is likely enough that there will soon be a numerous creation of Peers:—in France, such a creation would be rendered popular and respectable, by selecting the most distinguished men of the necessary politics;—*here*, neither the minister nor the public would ever dream of such a thing—we shall choose the *richest men!*

The following extracts from the speech of the First Consul in 1802, to the Council of State, deserve attention:—

> La découverte de la poudre à canon eut aussi une influence prodigieuse sur le changement du système militaire et sur toutes les conséquences qu'il entraîna. Depuis cette révolution, qui est-ce qui a fait la force d'un général? Ses qualités civiles, le coup-d'œil, le calcul, l'esprit, les connaissances administratives, l'éloquence, non pas celle du jurisconsulte, mais celle qui convient à la tête des armées, et enfin la connaissance des hommes: tout cela est civil. Ce n'est pas maintenant un homme de cinq pieds dix pouces qui fera de grandes choses. S'il suffisait pour être général d'avoir de la force et de la bravoure, chaque soldat pourrait prétendre au commandement. Le général qui fait de grandes choses est celui qui réunit les qualités civiles. C'est parce qu'il pas été Bey. Quand il me vit, il ne concevait pas comment je respecte. Il faut l'entendre raisonner au bivouac; il estime plus le général qui sait calculer que celui qui a le plus de bravoure. Ce n'est pas que le soldat n'estime la bravoure, car il mépriserait le général qui n'en aurait pas. Mourad-Bey était l'homme le plus forte et le plus adroit parmi les Mamelucks; sans cela il n'aurait pas été Bey. Quand il me vit, il ne concevait pas comment je pouvais commander à mes troupes; il ne le comprit que lorsqu'il connut notre système de guerre. . . . Dans tous les pays, la force cède aux qualités civiles. Les baïonnettes se baissent devant le prêtre qui parle au nom du Ciel, et devant l'homme qui en impose par sa science. . . . Ce n'est pas comme général que je gouverne, mais parce que la nation croit que j'ai les qualités civiles propres au gouvernement; si elle n'avait pas cette opinion, le gouvernement ne se soutiendrait pas. Je savais bien ce que je faisais, lorsque, général d'armée, je prenais la qualité de *membre de l'Institut*; j'étais sûr d'être compris, même par le dernier tambour.
>
> Le propre des militaires est de tout vouloir despotiquement; celui de l'homme civil est de tout soumettre à la discussion, à la vérité, à la raison. Elles ont leurs prismes divers, ils sont souvent trompeurs: cependant la discussion produit la lumière. Si l'on distinguait les hommes en militaires et en civils, on établirait deux ordres, tandis qu'il n'y a qu'une nation. Si l'on ne décernait des honneurs qu'aux militaires, cette préférence serait encore pire, car dès-lors la nation ne serait plus rien.

It is needless to remark, that these opinions are quite at variance with those which prevail in England, and that military or

political merit is almost the only kind which our institutions recognize.

Neither then by station nor by wealth does the practice and
custom of the State reward the English student of the higher
sciences; the comparison between England and the Continent in
this point is startling and decisive. Two consequences follow;—
the one is, that science is the most cultivated by the first order
of mind, which no discouragement can check; and by the third
order of intellect which, applied merely to useful purposes, or
the more elementary and popular knowledge, is rewarded sufficiently by the necessities of the Public; by that intermediate class
of intellect which pursues the discovery of the lesser speculative
principles, science is the most disregarded. On men of this class
the influences of society have a natural operation; they do not
follow a pursuit which gives them neither a respected station,
nor the prospect of even a decent maintenance. The second consequence is, that theoretical science amongst us had great luminaries, but their light is not generally diffused; science is not
higher on the Continent than with us, but being more honoured,
it is more generally cultivated. Thus when we hear some complaining of the decline of science in England, others asserting
its prosperity, we have only to keep these consequences in view,
in order to reconcile the apparent contradiction. We have great
names in science: a Babbage, an Herschel, a Brewster, an Airy,
prove that the highest walks of science are not uncultured; the
continuous improvement in machinery adapted to the social arts,
proves also that practical and popular science is not disproportioned to the wants of a great commercial people. But it is nevertheless perfectly true, that the circle of *speculative* science is narrow and contracted; and that useful applications of science would
be far *more* numerous, if theoretical speculators were more common. This deficiency we can repair, only (in my mind) by increasing the number and value of endowed professorships, and
by that vigilant respect from the honours of the State, which
improves and elevates the tone of public opinion, makes science
a profession, and allures to its rewards a more general ambition
by attaching to them a more external dignity.

We may observe too, that the aristocratic influence in England
has greatly adulterated the destined Reservoir of science, and the

natural Fountain of its honorary distinctions—I speak of the Royal Society. In order to make the Society "respectable"—it has been considered in the first place, necessary to pay no trifling subscription for admission. "It should be observed," says Mr. Babbage, "that all members contribute equally, and that the sum now required is fifty pounds; it used until lately to be ten pounds on entrance, and four pounds annually." Now men of science have not yet found the philosopher's stone, and many whom the society ought most to seek for its members, would the most shrink from its expense. In the second place, to make it "respectable" the aristocratic spirit ordains that we should crowd the society as full as possible with men of rank and property. Imagine seven hundred and fourteen fellows of the Royal Society! How can it possibly be an honour to a man of science to be one of seven hundred and fourteen men;[2] five-sixths of whom, too, have never contributed papers to the Transactions!—the number takes away emulation, the admittance of rank and station indiscriminately, and for themselves alone, lowers and vulgarises the standard whereby merit is judged. Mr. Davies Gilbert is a man at most of respectable endowments, but he is of large fortune—the Council declare him "*by far* the most fit person for president." An agreeable compliment to the great men in that society, to whom Mr. Gilbert in science was as a child! But, perhaps you may imagine it an honour to the country, that so many men of rank are desirous of belonging to a scientific society? Perhaps you may deem it a proof that they cultivate science?—as well might you say they cultivate fish-selling, because by a similar courtesy they belong to the Fishmongers' Company; they know as much of science as of fishmongery: judge for yourself. In 1827, out of one hundred and nine members *who had contributed to* the Transactions, there were—how many peers, think you?—there was—ONE!

A sun-beam that had gone astray!

I have said that the more popular and more useful sciences are

2. But the most remarkable thing, according to Mr. Babbage, is, that a candidate of moderate scientific distinction is pretty sure of being blackballed, whilst a gentleman of good fortune perfectly unknown, is sure to be accepted. Thus is a society of science the mimic of a fashionable club!

encouraged amongst us, while speculations in the higher and more abstruse are confined only to the few whom, in all ages, no difficulties can discourage. A proof of this is in the number and flourishing state of societies which are supported chiefly by the middle classes, and which mere vanity could not suffice therefore to create. In the metropolis, even in provincial towns, numerous societies for cultivating Botany, Geology, Horticulture, &c. assemble together those of similar tastes; and elementary tracts of all sizes upon all sciences, are a part of fashionable literature. But what I have said of letters generally, is applicable yet more to science,—viz. that encouragement to new, to lofty, and to abstruse learning is more than ever necessary, when the old learning becomes popularized and diffused.

Ambition is of a more various nature than the shallow suppose. All biography tells us that men of great powers will turn early from one pursuit not encouraged, to other pursuits that are. It is impossible to calculate how much Science may lose if to all its own obstacles are added all social determents. Thus we find that the same daring inventor who has ennobled our age with the construction of the celebrated calculating machine,[3] after loudly

3. One word upon this,—the most remarkable discovery of the time.
The object of the calculating machine is not to answer individual questions, but to produce multitudes of results following given laws. It differs remarkably from all former attempts of the kind in two points.

    1. It proposes to construct mathematical tables by the *Method of Differences*.
    2. It proposes to print on plates of copper the tables so computed.

It is not within my present plan to attempt even briefly any explanation of its mechanical principles, but the views which mechanism has thus opened respecting the future progress of mathematical science, are too striking to be passed over.

In this first attempt at substituting the untiring efforts of machinery, for some of the more simple, but laborious exertions of the human mind, the author proposed to make an engine which should tabulate any function whose sixth difference is constant. Regarding it merely in this light, it would have been a vast acquisition by giving to mathematical tables a degree of accuracy which might vainly have been sought by any other means; but in that small portion which has yet been put together, other powers are combined—tables can be computed by it, having no difference constant; and other tables have been produced by it, so complicated in their nature, that mathematical analysis must itself be improved before it can grasp their laws. The existence of the engine in its present state, gives just reason to expect that in its finished form, instead of tabulating the *single* equation of differences, which its author proposed, it will tabulate large classes of that species comprised in the general form of *linear equations with constant co-efficients*.

avowing his dissatisfaction at the honours awarded to science, has proclaimed practically his discontent at these honours, by courting the votes of a metropolitan district. Absolute monarchs have been wise in gratifying the ambition that is devoted to *peaceful* pursuits; it diverts the ambition of many working and brooding minds from more stirring courses, and steeps in the contented leisure of philosophy the faculties that might otherwise have devoted the same process of intrepid questioning and daring thought to the more dangerous career of action.

The future steps of machinery of this nature are not so improbable, now that we see realised before us the anticipations of the past. One extensive portion of mathematical analysis has already fallen within the controls of wheels. Can it be esteemed visionary to suppose that the encreasing demands of civilized man, and the constantly improving nature of the tools he constructs, shall ultimately bring within his power the whole of that most refined instrument of human thought—the pure analysis?

IX

The State of the Arts

Every one knows that the Art of Painting cannot be said to have taken root among us before the last century;—till then we believed ourselves to be deficient in the necessary imagination.— *We* who had produced a Milton and a Shakspeare! But the art commencing with Thornhill, took a vigorous stride to perfection, and to popular cultivation, from the time of Hogarth; and, corrupted on the Continent during the eighteenth century, it found in that era its regeneration in England.

From 1734, the number of English artists increased with so great a rapidity, that in 1760 we far surpassed our contemporaries in Italy and France, both in the higher excellence of painting and the general cultivation of the art. The application of the fine arts to manufactures, popularized and domesticated them amongst us. And the delft ware manufactured by the celebrated Wedgewood, carried notions of grace and beauty to every village throughout the kingdom. Many of Flaxman's first designs were composed for Wedgewood; and, adapting his conceptions to the pure and exquisite shapes of Grecian art, he at once formed his own taste, and created that of the public. Never did Art present fairer promise in any land than when Reynolds presided over Portraiture, Barry ennobled the Historical School, and Flaxman breathed its old and lofty majesty into Sculpture. Just at that time the Royal Academy (subsequent to the Chartered Society of Artists) was established. I shall reiterate none of the just attacks which of late have been made against that institution. It is sufficient to state, that the Royal Academy was intended for the encouragement of historical paintings—that it is filled with landscapes and portraits; that it was intended to incorporate and to cheer on all distinguished students—that it has excluded and persecuted many of the greatest we possess, and that at this moment, sixty-five years after its establishment, our greatest living artists, with scarcely any exceptions, have *not* been educated at an academy, intended of course *to* educate genius, even more than to support it afterwards![1] With the assumption of a public body, it has combined the exclusiveness of a private clique. I do not however agree with its assailants, that it has been very effectively injurious to art; on the contrary, I think that in some respects art has been unconsciously assisted by it. In the first place, though it has not fostered genius, it has diffused through a large circle a respectable mediocrity, that is, it has made the standard of the Mediocre several degrees higher than it was before. And secondly, its jealousy and exclusiveness, though in some instances repressing the higher art they refused to acknowledge, have nerved it in others to new flights by the creative stimulus of indignation. For nobly has Haydon said, though, alas! the aphorism is not universally just, "Look down upon Genius and he will rise to a giant—attempt to crush him and he will soar to a god!"

The pictorial art is at this moment as high perhaps in this country as in any other, despite the rivalry of Munich and of Paris. I call to witness the names of Martin, Haydon, Wilkie, Landseer, Turner, Stanfield. It is also more generally cultivated and encouraged. Witness the number of artists and the general prices of pictures. It is rather a singular fact, that in no country abroad do you see many pictures in the houses of the gentry or lesser nobles. But with us they are a necessary part of furniture. A house-agent taking a friend of mine over a London house the other day, and praising it to the skies, concluded with, "And when, sir, the dining-room is completely furnished—handsome

---

1. Martin was a pupil of Musso. Flaxman studied with his father, and at the Duke of Richmond's gallery. He studied, indeed a short time at the Academy, where he was refused the gold medal. Chantrey learned carving at Sheffield; Gibson was a ship-carver at Liverpool. When Sir Thomas Lawrence became a probationer for admission to the schools of the Academy, his claims were not allowed. The Academy taught not Bonnington—no—nor Danby, nor Stanfield. Dr. Monro directed the taste of Turner.—See an article in the *New Monthly Magazine,* on the Royal Academy, May 1833.

red curtains, sir—and twleve good 'furniture pictures'—it will be a perfect nonpareil." The pictures were as necessary as the red curtains.

But as in the connexion between literature, art, and science, whatever affects the one affects also the other, so the prevalent characteristic of the English school of painting at this moment is the MATERIAL. You see bold execution and glaring colours, but there is an absence of sentiment—nothing raises, elevates, touches, or addresses the soul, in the vast majority of our artists. I attribute this, indeed, mainly to the little sway that Religion in these days exercises over the imagination. It is perfectly clear that Religion must, in painting and in sculpture, inspire the most ideal conceptions; for the artist seeking to represent the images of Heaven, must necessarily raise himself beyond the earth. He is not painting a mere mortal—he cannot look only to physical forms—he must darken the chamber of his mind, and in meditation and fancy image forth something beyond the Visible and Diurnal. It is this which imparts the unutterable majesty to the Capitolian Jove, the voluptuous modesty to the Venus de' Medici, and breathes over the angry beauty of the Apollo, the mystery and the glory of the God. Equally in the Italian schools, the sentiment of Religion inspired and exalted the soul of the artist, and gave the solemn terror to Michael Angelo, and the dreamlike harmony to Raffaelle. In fact, it is not Religion alone that inspires the sentiment, but it is the habit of rousing the thought, of nurturing the imagination, which he who has to paint some being not "of earth earthy," is forced to create and to sustain. And this sentiment, thus formed by the severe tasking of the intellect, is peculiarly intellectual; and once acquired, accompanies the artist even to more common subjects. His imagination having caught a glory from the sphere which it has reached, retains and reflects it everywhere, even on its return to earth.[2] Thus, even in our time, the most striking and powerful painter we possess owes his inspiration to a deep and fervid sentiment of the Religious. And the dark and solemn shadow of the Hebrew God rests over the towers of Babylon, the valleys of Eden, and the awful desolation of the Universal Deluge.

If our houses are too small for the Historical School, they are

2. "Omnia profecto cum se à celestibus rebus referet ad humanas, excelsius magnificentiusque et dicet et sentiet."—CICERO.

yet still more unfitted for SCULPTURE: these two branches of art are necessarily the least generally encouraged. It is said, indeed, that sculpture is too cold for us,—it is just the reverse; *we* are too cold for sculpture! Among the sculptors of the present day, Chantrey and Gibson are pre-eminent: the first for portraits, the other for fancy subjects. The busts of Chantrey possess all those qualities that captivate the originals, and content their friends. He embellishes at once nature and art. If, however, the costume of his whole-length figures is in most cases appropriate and picturesque, (witness the statue of James Watt,) the statue of Pitt, in Hanover-square, is a remarkable exception, in which commonplace drapery sits heavy on a disagreeable figure. It is much to be regretted that, since this eminent artist has been loaded with orders for portraits, the monuments that issue from his factory possess none of that simple beauty which distinguishes his early productions,—such as the Sleeping Children at Lichfield Cathedral, and the Lady L. Russell. The intention and execution of those performances raised him at once to a pitch of fame that *mere* portraits, however beautiful, cannot maintain. The highest meed of praise is, therefore, fast settling on Gibson, who now and then sends to our Exhibition, from Rome, the most classical specimens of sculpture that modern times have produced: they possess the grace—they sometimes approach—the grandeur of the Past. Next to the above, Gott and Campbell, at Rome, and Westmacott, Baily, Behnes, Carew, Nicholl, Lough, Pitts, and Rossi, in London, possess considerable talent.

In hurrying over the catalogue of names that have enriched the HISTORICAL department of PAINTING, I can only indicate, not criticise. The vehement action, the strength of colour, and the individualising character of Haydon, are well known. Hilton, more successful in pictures of half-size life than the colossal, exhibits in the former an unusual correctness of outline. A certain delicacy, and a romance of mind, are the characteristics of Westall. But too great a facility in composition, and a vagueness of execution, make us regret that very luck of the artist which, by too great a prosperity in youth, forced and forestalled the fruits his natural genius, by slow and more painful culture, would have produced. Etty, practised in the colours of the Venetian painters, if not strictly of the Historical School, can be classed in no other.

His beauties are in a vigorous and fluent drawing, and bursts of brilliancy and light, amidst an imitative affection of the errors as well as excellence of the Venetian School.

The Foggos (T. and G.) are men of considerable talent—nor have they sacrificed their own judgment to the fashions of the day.

But I hasten to Martin,—the greatest, the most lofty, the most permanent, the most original genius of his age. I see in him, as I have before said, the presence of a spirit which is not of the world—the divine intoxication of a great soul lapped in majestic and unearthly dreams. He has taken a range, if not wholly new, at least rarely traversed, in the vast air of religious contemplation; he has gone back into the drear Antique; he has made the *Old* Testament, with its stern traditionary grandeur—its solemn shadows and ancestral terrors—his own element and appanage. He has looked upon "the ebon throne of Eld," and imbued a mind destined to reproduce what is surveyed, with

> A mighty darkness
> Filling the Seat of Power—as rays of gloom
> Dart round.

Vastness is his sphere—yet he has not lost or circumfused his genius in its space; he has chained, and wielded and measured it, at his will; he has transfused its character into narrow limits; he has compassed the Infinite itself with mathematical precision. He is not, it is true, a Raffaelle, delineating and varying human passion, or arresting the sympathy of passion itself in a profound and sacred calm; he is not a Michael Angelo, the creator of gigantic and preternatural powers,—the Titans of the ideal heaven. But he is more original, more self-dependant than either: they perfected the style of others; of Massaccio, of Signiorelli;—*they* perfected others; Martin has borrowed from none. Alone and guideless, he has penetrated the remotest caverns of the past, and gazed on the primæval shapes of the gone world.

Look at his DELUGE—it is the most simple of his works,—it is, perhaps, also the most awful. Poussin had represented before him the dreary waste of inundation; but not the inundation of a world. With an imagination that pierces from effects to the ghastly and sublime agency, Martin gives, in the same picture, a possible solution to the phenomenon he records, and in the gloomy and perturbed heaven you see the conjunction of the sun, the moon, and a comet! I consider this the most magnificent alliance of philosophy and art of which the history of painting can boast. Look, again, at the Fall of Nineveh; observe how the pencil seems dipped in the various fountains of light itself: here the moon, there the electric flash; here torch upon torch, and there "the smoldering dreariment" of the advancing conflagration;—the crashing wall—the rushing foe—the dismay of some, the resignation of others;—in front, the pomp, the life, the brilliant assemblage, the doomed and devoted beauty gathered round the monarch, in the proud exultation of his immortalising death! I stop not to touch upon the possible faults, upon the disproportionate height of these figures, or upon the theatrical effect of those; upon the want of some point of contrasting repose to augment the general animation, yet to blend with it a softer sympathy; or upon occasional errors in the drawing, so fiercely denounced by rival jealousies;—I speak of the effect which the picture produces on all,—an effect derived from the sublimest causes,—the most august and authentic inspiration. They tell us of the genius that the Royal Institution may form—it thrust this man from its bosom: they tell us of the advantage to be found in the patronizing smiles of aristocratic favour—let them ask the early history of Martin! If you would know the victorious power of enthusiasm, regard the great artist of his age immersed in difficulty, on the verge of starvation, prying in the nooks and corners of an old trunk for one remaining crust to satisfy his hunger, returning with unsubdued energy to his easel, and finding in his own rapt meditations of heaven and heaven's imagery, every thing that could reconcile him to earth! Ask you why *he* is supported, and why the lesser genii droop and whine for the patronage of Lords?—it is because *they* have NO rapt meditations!

I have heard that one of Martin's pictures was undertaken when his pecuniary resources could not bear him through the expenses of the task. One after one his coins diminished; at length he came to a single bright shilling, which *from* its brightness he had, in that sort of playfulness which belongs to genius, kept to the last. The shilling was unfaithful as it was bright—it was taken with a sigh to the baker's, declared to be a counterfeit, and the loaf just grasped, plucked back from the hand of the immortal artist.

In PORTRAIT-PAINTING—Lawrence, Owen and Jackson are gone; the ablest of their successors (in oil) are Pickersgill and Philips: but it may show the rottenness of individual patronage to note, that while this department is far the most encouraged, it has produced amongst us far fewer painters of worth and eminence. The habit, perhaps, of painting so many vulgar faces in white cravats, or velvet gowns, has toned down the minds of the artists to a correspondent vulgarity.

In FANCY-PAINTING we have the light grace and romantic fancy of Parris; the high-wrought elegance and chaste humour of Leslie (that Washington Irving of the easel); the pleasant wit of Webster; the quick facility and easy charm of Newton. In Boxall, there is a tender and melancholy sentiment, which excels in the aspect of his women. Howard reminds us of Flaxman's compositions in a similar school—more the pity for Howard; and Clint, though employed in scenic representation, is dramatic—not theatrical. The most rising painter of this class, is Mr. Maclise: his last picture, "Mokanna raising the veil," is full of talent; but the face wants the sublimity of ugliness; it is grotesque, not terrible; it is the hidiousness of an ape, not a demon.

But when touching on this department of the art, who does not feel the name of Wilkie rush to his most familiar thoughts? Who does not feel that the pathos and the humour of that most remarkable painter have left on him recollections as strong and enduring as the *chef-d'œuvres* of literature itself; and that every new picture of Wilkie—in Wilkie's own vein—constitutes an era in enjoyment? More various, more extensive in his grasp than even Hogarth, his genius sweeps from the dignity of history to the verge of caricature itself. Humour is the prevalent trait of all minds capable of variety in character; from Shakspeare and Cervantes, to Goldsmith and Smollett. But of what shades and differences is not Humour capable? Now it loses itself in terror—now it broadens into laughter. What a distance from the Mephistophiles of Göthe to the Sir Roger de Coverley of Addison, or from Sir Roger de Coverley to Humphrey Clinker! What an illimitable space from the dark power of Hogarth to the graceful tenderness of Wilkie! And which can we say with certainty is the higher of the two? Can we place even the "Harlot's Progress" beyond the "Distraining for Rent," or the exquisite beauty of "Duncan Grey"? And if, indeed, upon mature and critical consideration, we must give at length the palm to the more profound, analytic, and epic grandeur of Hogarth's fearful humour, we have again to recollect that Wilkie reigns also in the graver domain to which Hogarth aspired only to record the limit of his genius. The Sigismunda of Hogarth, if not indeed so poor a performance as Lord Orford esteems it, is at least immeasurably beneath the fame of its wonderful artist. But who shall say that "Knox," if also below the breadth and truth of character which Wilkie carries into a more familiar school, is not, for boldness of conception, and skill in composition, an effort of which any master might be proud? Wilkie is the Goldsmith of painters, in the amiable and pathetic humour, in the combination of smiles and tears, of the familiar and the beautiful; but he has a stronger hold, both over the more secret sympathies and the springs of a broader laughter, than Goldsmith himself. If the Drama could obtain a Wilkie, we should hear no more of its decline. He is the exact illustration of the doctrine I have advanced—of the power and dignity of the popular school, in the hands of a master; dignified, for truth never loses a certain majesty, even in her most familiar shapes.

In LANDSCAPE-PAINTING, England stands pre-eminent in the present age: for here no academic dictation, no dogma of that criticism which is born of plagiarism, the theft of a theft, has warped the tendency of genius, or interfered with the simple advice of Nature, *whose face teaches*. Turner, Danby, and Martin, Stanfield, Copley Fielding, Dewint, Collins, Lee, Callcott, John Wilson, Harding, and Stanley, are true pastoralists of the art. Turner was once without a rival; all that his fancy whispered, his skill executed. Of late, he has forsaken the beautiful and married the fantastic. His genius meant him for the Wordsworth of description, he has spoilt himself to the Cowley! he no longer sympathizes with Nature, he coquets with her. In Danby, a soft transparency of light and shade floating over his pictures accords well with a fancy almost Spenserian in its cast of poetical creation. In Stanfield, who does not acknowledge the precision of sight, the power of execution, the amazing scope and variety of design?

In MISCELLANEOUS PAINTINGS—I pass over the names of Roberts, Prout, Mackensie, Challond, eminent for architectural drawings; of Lance and Derby, who almost rival the Dutch painters in the line of dead game, fruits, &c.; of Cooper, Hancock, Davis, distinguished in the line of Edwin Landseer, in order to come to Landseer himself. The extreme facility of this singular artist, renders his inferior works too sketchy, and of a texture not sufficiently characteristic; but in his best, we have little if any thing to desire. He reminds us of those metaphysicians, who have given animals a soul. He breathes into the brute world a spiritual eloquence of expression beyond all literary power to describe. He is worth to the "Voice of Humanity," all the societies in England. You cannot gaze on his pictures and ill-use an animal for months afterwards. He elevates your sympathies for them to the level of human interest. He throws a poetry over the most unpoetical; nay, he has given a pathos even to "a widowed duck"; he is a sort of link to the genius of Wilkie, carrying down the sentiment of humane humour from man to man's great dependant family, and binding all creation together in one common sentiment of that affection whose wisdom comprehends all things. Wilkie and Landseer are the great benevolists of painting: as in the quaint sublimity of the Lexicon of Suidas, Aristotle is termed "the Secretary of Nature, who dipped his pen in intellect," so each of these artists may be called, in his several line, the Secretary also of Nature, who dips his pencil in sympathy: for both have more, in their genius, of the heart's philosophy than the mind's.

PAINTING IN WATER-COLOURS—forms a most distinguishing part of English art. About the end of the last century, a new style of water-colour drawing or painting was adopted: till then, whatever talent was observable in the works of Sandby, Hearne, &c. there was no particular difference in their method and the works of foreign artists. At the period above mentioned, Dr. Monro, of the Adelphi, an eminent amateur in that peculiar line, invited several young men to study from the drawings in his valuable collection, and under his guidance: Turner, Girtin, Varley, and others acquired a power of depicting nature in transparent water-colours, that far outstrips every thing of the like manner previously produced. Depth of tone, without blackness; aërial distances, the "glow of sunshine and the cool of shade," have been accomplished in a surprising degree, not only by the three artists above mentioned, but also by Glover, Fielding, Barret, Heaphy, Richter, Stanfield, Cox, Holland, Harding and the German and wild and mystic pencil of Cattermole. But in many respects, the large heads of expression, &c. by Sir Charles Bell are the most extraordinary works in this department; and it is not a little remarkable, that, in this style, a medical gentleman should have pointed the goal to excellence, and an anatomist have obtained it.

The art of ENGRAVING was in its infancy among us a century ago; in the course of a few years, Strange, Woollett, Earlom, and Sharp carried it to its utmost vigour; but in our time, the application of machinery, and the system of division of labour, give to the practice perfection of line at the expense of sentiment and variety; the same means being applied on all occasions. This is observable in the Annuals and other works by the majority of our engravers. The sacrifice of the nobler qualities to mechanism reduces engraving to a trade; for the higher denomination of art can only be allowed where the unconstrained mind pervades the whole, keeping each part subordinate to and in character with the subject. John Landseer, Doo, the elder Engleheart, &c. still, however, support engraving as an art. The like may be said of Reynolds the mezzotinto engraver. But this century may boast of having, in Bewick of Newcastle, brought wood-engraving to perfection; his pupil Harvey continues the profession with reputation.

One word on the ARTS applied to MANUFACTURES. There have for some time past been various complaints of a deficiency of artists capable of designing for our manufactures of porcelain, silk, and other articles of luxury in general use: we are told, that public schools are required to supply the want. It may be so, yet Wedgewood, Rundell, and Hellicot the watch-maker, found no such difficulty, and now that a Royal Academy has existed sixty-five years, the complaint has become universal. One would imagine that the main capacity of such institutions was to create that decent and general mediocrity of talent, which appeals to trade and fashion for encouragement. In truth, the complaint is not just. How did Wedgewood manage without a public school for designers? In 1760, our porcelain wares could not stand competition with those of France. Necessity prompts, or, what is quite as good, allows the exertions of genius. Wedgewood applied chemistry to the improvement of the material of his pottery, sought the most beautiful and convenient specimens of antiquity, and caused them to be imitated with scrupulous nicety; he *then had recourse to the greatest genius of the day, for designs and advice.* He was of course successful. But now the manufacturers of a far more costly material, without availing themselves of the example of Wedgewood, complain of want of talent in those whom they never sought, and whom they might as easily command, if they were as willing to reward. But the worst of fashion in its operation on art is its sudden caprices. China-painting was at its height about 1806. Mr. Charles Muss, afterwards celebrated for his enamelling, was at that time a painter on porcelain: this application of colours was then a fashion, and ladies willingly gave him a guinea or more per lesson for his instructions. Within three years the taste subsided; ladies not only purchased less, but to a fashion for painting on china, had succeeded the fashion for painting on velvet. Thence the fair students progressed to japanning, and at length settled with incredible ardour on the more feminine mysteries of shoe-making.

> With varying vanities from every part,
> They shift the moving toy-shop of the heart.

Trembling at his approaching fate, Muss by a vigorous effort turned from china to glass, (the art of painting on which was then little cultivated or understood,) but ere he could taste the fruits of his ingenuity, his family was in want of bread. On a stormy night, drenched with rain, he anxiously pursued his way from Adam-street to Kensington, in hope of borrowing a shilling. His friend was in a nearly similar state of destitution; fortunately the latter, however, had still the blessed and English refuge of credit; and by this last remaining possession, he procured a loaf, with which the victim of these sudden reverses in feminine taste returned to his half-starved children. But, alas!

the destinies of nations have their influence upon porcelain! Peace triumphed on the Continent, and

The tottering china shook without a wind!

Compared with the foreign ground of China, that on which we paint is too coarse to allow equal beauty, whatever artist we employ: the fault is not with the painter, but in those who have not energy to ascertain and remedy the imperfection. They, it is true, have however the excuse, that in fashion every thing is novelty; to-day all must be ponderous and massive ornament; to-morrow all must be fillagreed and minute.

A man whose service of plate is refashioned every ten years, will scarcely allow the silversmith to expend the same price for designing and modelling, that was obtained when Rundell and Bridge, by employing the ablest designers in this country, supplanted competition. "Something handsome must be got up," and a meretricious and overloaded display is cheaper than exquisite execution; in some cases drawings have been sent abroad, to be there got up in metal at a cheaper rate.

With regard to silk-working: a few years ago a committee of gentlemen of rank and distinction, who took an active interest in the productions of British manufactures, obtained from France a sample of figured silk representing the departure of a young soldier; they felt confident that our own manufacturers could equal, or even surpass its excellence; but where could they procure a pattern with similar beauty and national interest? They applied to a foreign gentleman in London, who immediately called on an English artist whom he considered adequate to the performance. The subject undertaken was a young sailor returned from a successful cruise: he hears that an old and valued friend is in prison for debt; he hastens to the gaol; he finds his friend tended by one, only visiter, (his young daughter,) in sickness and despair. The composition gave great and general satisfaction; but will it be believed that the idea of a British tar in a prison (even though visiting it for so noble a purpose) appeared to our sages in silk to be shockingly ominous? they therefore wished the background to be changed into *a cottage!* The artist insisted very properly on the prison, and heard no more of the patronage of the committee. It is also an anecdote that for many years an aristocratic feeling prevented Wilkie's "Distraining for Rent" being engraved—*lest it should excite an unpleasant feeling towards the country gentlemen!*

In nothing, Sir, to my mind, is the material and unelevated character which belongs generally to the intellectual spirit of our times more developed than in our national ARCHITECTURE. A stranger in our streets is struck with the wealth, the gaud, the comfort, the bustle, the animation. But how rarely is he impressed with the vast and august simplicity, that is the result in architecture, as in letters, of a lofty taste, and the witness of a people penetrated with a passion for the *great!* The first thing that strikes us in England is the lowness of all the public buildings —they appear uncompleted; you would imagine a scythe had been drawn across them in the middle: they seem dedicated to St. Denis, after he had lost his head. The next thing that strikes you in them is the want of originality—they are odd, but unoriginal. Now, wherever an architecture is not original, it is sure to be inappropriate: we transplant what belongs to one climate to another wholly distinct from it—what is associated with one history or religion, to a site in which the history and religion are ludicrously opposed to it.

The celebrated Stuart, who sought to introduce amongst us the knowledge of the Grecian principles of architectural elegance, has in reality corrupted rather than corrected taste. Even he himself, laying down "The Appropriate," as a necessary foundation in the theory of architecture, neglects it in his practice. Look at yonder chapel: it is perfectly unconnected and inharmonious with the character of the building attached to it; assuredly it is the most elegant chapel we can boast of—but you would imagine it must be designed for the devotions of some fastidious literary institution, or the "daintie oratoire" of a Queen. No! it is designed for our jolly tars, and the most refined temple is dedicated to the rudest worshippers. The followers of Stuart have made this want of suiting the design to the purpose still more ridiculous. On a church dedicated to St. Philip we behold the ox heads typical of Jupiter; and on the frieze of a building consecrated to a quiet literary society, with whom prancing

horses and panting riders have certainly no connexion, we see
the bustling and fiery procession of a Grecian cavalcade. The
Greek architecture, even in its purity, is not adapted to a gloomy
and chilling climate; all our associations connect it with bright
skies and "a garden life"; but when its grand proportions are
omitted, and its minute details of alien and *unnaturalizable* mythology are carefully preserved, we cannot but think that we
have adopted one at least of the ancient deities, and dedicated all
our plagiarised blunders in stucco to—the Goddess of Laughter!

Few, indeed, amidst the wilderness of houses in which common sense wanders distracted, are the exceptions of a better
taste in imitation. But the portico of St. Pancras and the London
University are beautiful copies from antient temples, if nothing
more, and it is impossible not to point out to the favour of
foreigners the small Ionic chapel in North Audley Street, and
the entrance to Exeter Hall, in which last there is even a lofty as
well as an accurate taste.

But as a proof of the sudden progress which art makes, when
divorced from imitation, I instance to you our bridges: Waterloo
and Southwark bridges are both admirable in their way—they
are English; we may reasonably be proud of them, for they are
our own.

For my part I candidly confess, however I may draw down on
myself the languid contempt of the would-be amateurs of the
portfolio—that I think, in architecture as in poetry, we should
seek the germ of beauty in the associations that belong to the
peculiar people it is addressed to. Every thing great in art must
be national. Wherever we are at a loss for invention, let us not
go back to the past of other countries, but the past of our own—
not to imitate, not to renew, but to adapt, to improve; to take the
old spirit, but to direct it to new uses. If a great architectural genius were to rise among us, a genius that should combine the
Beautiful with the Appropriate, satisfy the wants, suit the character, adapt itself to the life, and command, by an irresistible
sympathy, the admiration of the people, I am convinced that his
inspiration would be derived from a profound study of *our own*
national monuments of architecture from the Saxon to the Eliza-
bethan. He should copy neither, but produce a school from both,
—allied at once to our history, our poetry, our religion, and our

climate. Nothing is so essentially patriotic as the arts; they only permanently flourish amongst a people, when they spring from an indigenous soil.

From this slight and rapid survey of the state of the arts in England, we may observe, first, that there is no cause to complain of their decline;—secondly, that as those efforts of art most adapted to private favour have succeeded far more amongst us than those adapted to the public purposes of a state; so the absence of state encouragement, and the preponderance of individual patronage, have operated prejudicially on the grander schools. Even (with a few distinguished exceptions) our finest historical paintings, such as those of Martin, are on a small scale of size, adapted more for the private house than the public hall. And it is mostly on achievements which appeal not to great passions, or to pure intellect—but to the household and domestic interests—that our higher artists have lavished their genius. We see Turner in landscape, and Landseer in animals, Stanfield in scenes, and Wilkie, whose sentiment is purer, loftier, and deeper than all, (save Martin's,) addressing himself, in the more popular of his paintings, to the most fire-side and familiar associations. The rarer and more latent, the more intellectual and immaterial sources of interest, are not those to which English genius applies itself. We may note also a curious coincidence between the Royal Academy for Art, and the Royal Academy for Science; both ridiculous for their pretensions, but eminent for their inutility—the creatures of the worst social foibles of jealousy and exclusiveness—severe to genius, and uxorious to dotage upon the Mediocrity which has produced them so numerous a family.

But as I consider that the architecture of a nation is one of the most visible types of its prevalent character, so in that department all with us is comfortable and nothing vast. A sense of poetry is usually the best corrector and inspiration of prose—so a correspondent poetry in the national mind not only elevates the more graceful, but preserves also a noble and appropriate harmony in the more useful, arts. It is the POETRY OF MIND which every commercial people should be careful to preserve and to refresh.

X

Supplementary Characters

Lord Plume is one of those writers of the old school of whom so few are at present existing—writers who have a great notion of care in composition—who polish, who elaborate, who are hours over a sentence, which, after all, is, nine times out of ten, either a fallacy or a truism. He writes a stiff, upright hand, and values himself upon being a witty correspondent. He has established an unfortunate target in every court in Europe, at which he shoots a monthly despatch. He is deep read in memoirs, and has Grammont at his fingers'-ends: he swears by Horace Walpole, who would have made a capital butt of him. He reads the Latin poets, and styles himself F.R.S. He asks you how you would translate *'simplex munditiis'* and *'copia narium'*—takes out his handkerchief while you consider the novel question, sighs, and owns the phrases are indeed untranslatable. He is full of anecdotes and the by-gone scandal of our grandmothers: he will give you the history of every crim. con. which took place between a wig and a farthingale. He passes for a man of most elegant mind—sets up for a Mæcenas, and has a new portrait of himself painted every year, out of a tender mindfulness, I suppose, for the convenience of some future Grammont. Lord Plume has dabbled greatly in reviews—not a friend of his ever wrote a book that he did not write *to* him a letter of compliment, and *against* him an article of satire: he thinks he has the Voltaire turn, and can say a sharp thing or two. He looks out for every new book written by a friend with the alacrity of a wit looking out for a repartee. Of late years, indeed, he has not, however, written much in the Quarterlies, for he was found out in a squib on his uncle, and lost a legacy in consequence: besides, he is editing memoirs of his own ancestors. Lord Plume thinks it elegant to write, but low to confess it; the anonymous, therefore, has great charms for him: he throws off his jealousy and his wit at the same time, and bathes in the Castalian stream with as much secrecy as if he were one of its nymphs. He believes, indeed, that it would be too great a condescension in his genius to appear in the glare of day—it would create too great a sensation—he thinks men would stop each other in the street to exclaim, "Good God! have you heard the news?—Plume has turned author!" Delightedly, then, in his younger day, crept he, nameless and secret, into the literary world. He is suspected of having written politics as well as criticism, and retailed all the tattle of the court by way of enlightening the people. Plume is a great man.

From this gentle supporter of the anonymous press, turn for one moment to gaze on the most dirty of its disgraces. Sneak "keeps a Sunday newspaper" as a reservoir for the filth of the week; he lets out a *cabinet d'aisance* for any man who wishes to be delivered of a lie. No trader of the kind can be more obliging or more ill-savoured: his soul stinks of his profession, and you spit when you hear his name. Sneak has run through all the circle of scoundrelism: whatever is most base, dastardly, and contemptible, Sneak has committed. Is a lie to be told of any man? Sneak tells it. Is a Countess to be slandered? Sneak slanders her. Is theft to be committed? Sneak writes to you—"Sir, I have received some anecdotes about you, which I would not publish for the world if you will give me ten pounds for them." Sneak would declare his own mother a drab, and his father a hangman, for sixpence-halfpenny. Sneak sets up for a sort of Beau Sneak— crawls behind the scenes, and chats with the candle-snuffer: when he gets drunk, Sneak forgets himself, and speaks to a gentleman; the gentleman knocks him down. No man has been so often kicked as Sneak—no man so often horsewhipped; his whole carcase is branded with the contumely of castigation:—methinks there is, nevertheless, another chastisement in reserve for him at the first convenient opportunity. It is a pity to beat one so often beaten—to break bones that have been so often broken; but why deny oneself a luxury at so trifling an expense?—it will be some honour to beat him worse than he has been beaten yet! Sneak is at heart the most miserable of men; he is poisoned by the stench of his own disgrace: he knows that every man loathes him; he strives to buoy himself from "the graveolent abyss" of his infamy by grasping at some scamp of a lord. One lord, with one shred of character left to his back, promised to dine with him, and has been stark naked of character ever since. Sneak has stuck up a wooden box in a nursery garden between Richmond and London, exactly of that description of architecture you would suppose him to favour: it is for all the world like the temple which a Cit erects to the Roman Goddess of Sewers; here "his soul still sits at squat." The little house stares you in the face, and reminds you at once of the nightman its owner. In vain would ingenuity dissociate the name of Sneak from the thought of the scavenger. This beautiful effect of the anonymous system I have thus honoured with mention, in order that posterity may learn to what degree of rottenness rascality can be corrupted.

Mendlehon is a man of remarkable talent, and of that biting wit which tempts the possessor into satire. Mendlehon set up a journal, the vein of which ran into personal abuse; Mendlehon then went nowhere, and himself and his authorship were alike unknown: he became courted—he went into society, his journalism was discovered and avowed. Since then the gossips say that the journal has grown dull, for it runs no longer into scurrility. When the anonymous was dropped, the writer came under the eye of public opinion, and his respectability forbids him to be abusive.

Of all melancholy and disappointed persons, a young poet in this day is perhaps the most. Observe that pale and discontented countenance, that air at once shy and proud. St. Malo is a poet of considerable genius; he gives himself altogether up to the Muse—he is consumed with the desire of fame; the loud celebrity of Byron yet rings in his ears: he asketh himself, why he should not be equally famous: he has no pleasure in the social world: he feels himself not sufficiently made of: he thinketh "by and by they will run after my genius": he is awkward and gloomy; for he lives not in the present: he plunges into an imaginary future never to be realized. He goes into the world thinking the world must admire him, and ask "Who is that interesting young man?" He has no sympathy with other men's amusements, unless they either write poetry themselves or read *his* own: he expects all men to have sympathy with *him;* his ear and taste were formed early in the school of Byron; he has now advanced to the schools of Wordsworth and Shelley. He imitates the two last unconsciously, and then wonders why his books do not sell: if the original did not sell, why should the copy? He never read philosophy, yet he affects to write metaphysics, and gives with considerable enthusiasm into the Unintelligible. Verse-writing is the serious occupation of his life; he publishes his poems, and expects them in his heart to have an enormous sale. He cannot believe that the world has gone round; that every time has its genius; that the genius of *this* time is wholly antipoetic. He throws away thought and energy, and indomitable perseverance, and the enviable faculty of concentrating ambition upon a barren and unprofitable pursuit. His talents whisper him "success,"— their direction ensures him "disappointment." How many St. Malos have I known!—but half of them, poor fellows, have married their first cousins, gone into the church, and are now cultivating a flower-garden!

But who is this dry and austere young man, with sneer on lip and spectacles on nose? He is the opposite to the poet—he is Snap, the academical *philosopherling.* Sent up to Cambridge to learn theology, he has studied Locke, and become materialist. I blame him not for that; doubtless he has a right to his opinion, but he thinks nobody else has a right to any *other* opinion than *his:* he says with a sneering smile, "Oh, of course, Locke was too clever a man not to know what his principles must lead to; but he did not dare to speak out for fear of the bigots." You demur —he curls his lip at you—he has no toleration for a believer; he comprehends not the vast philosophy of faith; he cannot get beyond Hume upon Miracles; he looks down if you utter the word "soul," and laughs in his sleeve; he is the most intolerant of men; he cannot think how you can possibly believe what seems to him such evident nonsense. He carries his materialism into all his studies; he is very fond of political economy, and applies its principles to all things; he does not think that government should interfere with education, because it should not interfere about money. He is incapable of seeing that men must be induced to be good, but that they require no inducement to get rich; that a poor man will strive for wealth, that an immoral man will *not* strive for morality; that an ignorant man will *not* run after knowledge; that governments should tempt to virtue, but human passions will tend to wealth. If our philosopherling enters the House of Commons, he sets up for a *man of business;* he begs to be put upon the dullest committees; he would not lose an hour of twaddle for the world; he affects to despise eloquence, but he never speaks without having learnt every sentence by heart. And oh! such sentences, and such delivery! for the Snaps have no enthusiasm! It is the nature of the material philosophy to forbid that beautiful prodigality of heart; he unites in his agreeable style, the pomp of apathy with the solemnity of dulness. Nine times out of ten our philosopherling is the son of a merchant, his very pulse seems to enter its account in the ledger-book. Ah Plato! Ah Milton! did you mean the lute of philosophy for hands like these!

"And how, Sir, do you like this engraving of Martin's?" Go, my dear reader, put that question to yon gentleman with the powdered head—that gentleman is a Royal Academician. I never met with an Academician who did not seem to think you insulted him by an eulogy on Martin. Mr. Gloss Crimson is one of those who measure all art by the Somerset-house Exhibition. He ekes out his talk from Sir Joshua Reynold's discourse—he is very fond of insisting on the necessity of study and labour, and of copying the antique. "Sir," quoth he, one day, "painting is the synonym of perseverance." He likes not the company of young artists; he is angry if invited to meet them; he calls them indiscriminately "shallow coxcombs." He is a great worshipper of Dr. Johnson, and tells you that Dr. Johnson extolled the project of the Academy. Alas, he little knows that the good doctor somewhere wonders what people can be thinking of to talk of such trifles as an Academy for Painting! He is intensely jealous, and more exclusive than a second-rate Countess; he laments the decay of patronage in this country; he believes every thing in art depends upon lords; he bows to the ground when he sees an earl; and thinks of Pericles and Leo X. His colours are bright and gaudy as a Dutchman's flower-garden, for they are put on with an eye to the Exhibition, in which every thing goes by glare. He has a great notion of the dignity of portrait-painting. He would like to say to you, "Sir, I have painted four Earls this year, and a Marchioness, and if that's not a high school of painting, tell me what is!" He has a great contempt for Haydon, and is sure "the nobility won't employ him." He thinks the National Gallery a necessary perquisite of the Royal Academicians. "Lord, Sir," saith he, "if *we* did not manage the matter, there would be no discrimination, and you might see Mr. Howard's pictures in no better a situation than"—

"Mr. Martin's—that *would* be a shame!"

And so much, dear Sir, for characters that may serve to illustrate a few of the intellectual influences of the time.

Book the Fifth

A View of Our Political State

INSCRIBED TO

THE ENGLISH PEOPLE

Since the affairs of men rest still uncertain,
Let's reason with the worst that may befall.
SHAKESPEARE

Si quid novisti rectius istis
Candidus imperti—si non, his utere mecum.
HORAT.

I

If, my dear countrymen, you can spare a few minutes from the very great bustle in which you all seem to be at present; if you can cease for awhile from the agreeable duties of abusing the Ministry, reckoning up your bad debts, deploring the state of the markets, and wondering what is to become of you; if you can spare a few minutes to listen to your neighbour, who has your interest always at heart; he flatters himself that you will possibly find you have not entirely thrown away your time.

I inscribe to you this, my fifth, book, which comprehends a survey of our political state, because, between you and me, I shrewdly suspect that the condition of the country is more your concern than that of any one else. Certain politicians, it is true, are of opinion that patriotism is an oligarchical virtue, and that the people are only anxious to go to the Devil as fast as they possibly can. To hear them, one must suppose that you are the greatest fools in existence, and that every piece of advice you are in the habit of giving to your rulers tends only to implore them to ruin you with all convenient dispatch. For my part, I do not believe these gentlemen; without thinking you either saints or sages, you have always seemed to me sensible good sort of persons, who have a very quick eye to your own interests, and seldom insist much upon any thing that, if granted, would operate greatly to your disadvantage. I inscribe this book to you, and we will now proceed to its contents.

I am obliged to suppose that you have read the preceding sections of the work—it is a bold hypothesis, I know, but we reasoners cannot get on without taking something for granted. Now, in all states, there is some one predominant influence, either monarchical or sacerdotal, or popular, or aristocratic. What is the influence which, throughout the previous sections of this work, I have traced and proved to be the dominating influence of England; colouring the national character, pervading every grade of our social system, ruling our education, governing our religion, operating on our literature, our philosophy, our sciences, our arts? You answer at once, that it is the ARISTOCRATIC. It is so. Now then observe, many of your (perhaps) inconsiderate friends insinuate the disadvantages of a Monarchy and the vices of an Established Church—*those* are the influences which they assert to be hostile to your welfare. You perceive by the examination into which we have entered, that this is not the fact; whatever be the faults in any part of our moral, social, or intellectual system, we have not traced the causes of those faults to the monarchical influences. I grant that, in some respects, (but those chiefly the effects of a clumsy machinery,) we have something to complain of in certain workings of the Established Church. Tithes are unpleasant messengers between our pastors and ourselves, but, as we are about to substitute for these a more agreeable agency, we will not talk any longer of the old grievance: in the true English spirit, when the offence is over, we will forget and forgive. The custom of Squirearchical patronage in the Church, of making the cure of souls a provision for younger sons, gives us, as I have attempted to prove, many inactive and ineffective pastors. But this, you will observe, is not the necessary consequence of an establishment itself, but of the aristocratic influence which is brought to bear on the establishment: just as those vast expenses, which we have managed to incur, have not been the fault of the representative system, but of the aristocracy by which the system has been corrupted: the two instances are parallel. In penetrating every corner of the island, in colonizing every village with the agents of civilization, in founding schools, in enlightening squires, in operating unconsciously on the moral character and spiritual teaching of dissenters; in curbing to a certain limit the gloomy excesses of fanaticism—in all this you behold the redeeming effects of an ecclesiastical establishment,—

effects which are sufficient, let us acknowledge, to atone tenfold for all its abuses, and which even the aristocratic deteriorations have not been baneful enough to destroy.

It is not therefore, my friends, against a Monarchy or against an ecclesiastical establishment, that it becomes us, as thinking and dispassionate men, to direct the liberalism of the age. No, it is against a very peculiar and all-penetrative organization of the aristocratic spirit! This is very important for us thoroughly to understand and fully to acknowledge. This is a first principle, to be firmly established if we do not desire to fight in the dark against imaginary thieves while the real marauders are robbing us with impunity.

Between ourselves, I see a large portion of the aristocracy ready at any opportunity to throw the blame of their own misdeeds upon the king or the unfortunate bishops. Be on your guard against them!

II

In examining the national character and our various social system, we do not find the monarchical influence pernicious; I might venture to say more,—we shall generally find the monarch the most efficient check to the anti-popular interests. Look to our later history! Do you not remark that, in all popular measures, the King has taken part with yourselves?—has taken part with the people? The concurrence of two branches of the legislature —the executive and the representative—has compelled the reluctant assent of the hereditary chamber. What interest has a monarch in the perpetuation of abuses? He, unlike the aristocracy, has nothing to lose by concession to the popular advantage. What interest has he in the preservation of game laws and corn laws— of corporations and monopolies, or of the vast and complicated ramifications from which aristocratic nepotism raises a forest of corruption out of a single banyan?—An easy people makes a powerful King, but a weak Noblesse. No, my friends, no—a king has nothing to gain by impoverishing his people; but every lord has a mortgage to pay off, or a younger son to provide for, and it is for the aristocracy, not the king, that corruption is a lucrative system. Compare, at this moment, that which a prime minister "does for his family" with that which his royal master can do for his own. Heavens! what a storm was raised when the King's son obtained the appointment of the Tower! Was he not compelled to resign that petty command—so great was the popular clamour—so silent the ministerial eloquence? But, my

Lord Grey! what son—what brother—what nephew—what cousin—what remote and unconjectured relative in the Genesis of the Greys has not fastened his limpet to the rock of the national expenditure? Attack the propriety of these appointments, and what haughty rebukes from the Minister will you not receive! The tongue so mute for the King's son, rolls in thunder about the revered heads of the innumerable and unimpugnable Greyides. A king stands aloof and apart from the feuds and the jealousies—the sordid avarice—the place-hunting ambition— which belong to those only a little above the people. The aristocracy have been no less his enemies than ours—they have crippled his power while they have encroached on our resources. For the nature of that freedom which results from a privileged order partakes rather of the pride of arrogance than the passion for liberty. Observe how natural a generous loyalty is to you, and how selfishness distorts the loyalty of an aristocracy. When the Reform Bill was at length to receive the royal assent, were you not all breathless with a hope that the King would assent to it *in person?*—were you not all anxious for an event, which should, after an interval of doubt and jealousy, restore William the Reformer to your affections? You saw in so natural an opportunity for the King to proclaim his heartiness in your cause, a fitting and a solemn occasion for both King and people to renew an uninterrupted confidence; your loyalty expected—demanded this gratification; it was the loyalty of a generous people. But his Majesty did *not* confirm the Bill in person. Now, ask yourselves this question, Ought not my Lord Grey, if unaffectedly and sincerely loyal—ought he not to have prevailed upon his Majesty to win to himself such golden opinions at so easy a price?—can we believe that he had not the power to prevail? When the King had assented to the creation of peers, if necessary, can we suppose that his Majesty would have refused a concession so much more reasonable, had it been urged with an equal force? No. Lord Grey had the power, and he cared not to exert it. He ought to have resolved that his sovereign, who had borne the odium of one party, should receive the gratitude of the other: generously sinking his own pomp of popularity, he should have resolved that the King should appear first and prominent in the great act of grace; he must have known that the appearance of a lukewarm consent was a sign of weakness in the crown—the appearance of zealous assent was a token of its magnanimity and its power. But Lord Grey loved to stand forth the prime agent of good; he was willing that the curtain should be drawn across the throne, and leave himself in the front-ground, unrelieved and alone, in all the stiffness of condescending ostentation; he was willing to monopolize the honours of reform, and to appear to have gained a victory over the King himself. My friends, see the loyalty of an aristocrat!

An aristocracy like ours is, I say, equally hostile to the King's just power and popularity as it is hostile to the welfare of the people. "Ah, but," cry some, "if you weaken the aristocracy, you weaken the crown." Is that necessarily the case? Is a powerful aristocracy necessary to the safety of the throne? Look round the world, and see. Are not those monarchies the most powerful and the most settled in which the influence of the aristocracy is least strong, in which the people and the king form one state, and the aristocracy are the ornaments of the fabric, not the foundations? Look at Prussia, the best governed country in the world, and one in which the happiness of the people reconciles us to despotism itself. Believe me, my friends, where a people are highly educated, absolute monarchy is more safe and less corrupting than a grasping nobility.

Look again to the history of the states around you; so far from a king deriving strength from an aristocracy, it is the vices of an aristocracy, and not of a monarch, that usually destroy a kingdom: it is the nobles that take popularity from a court— their scandal and their gossip—their backstairs-creeping and gliding, their ridicule of their master behind his back, their adulation to his face—these are the causes that dim the lustre of royalty in man's eyes, and vulgarize the divinity that should hedge a king. Impatient of the abuses of authority, the people do not examine nicely from *what quarter of authority* the abuses proceed, and they concentrate on the most prominent object the odium which belongs of right to objects more subordinate and less seen. I say that an aristocracy, when corrupted, destroys, and does not preserve a monarchy, and I point to France for an example: had the French aristocracy been less strong and less odious, Louis XVI. would not have fallen a victim to that fearful glamoury which conjured a scaffold from a throne. That unfortunate king may justly be called a martyr;—he was a martyr to the vices of his *noblesse!*

I deny, then, the assertion of those who term it dangerous to weaken the aristocracy on the ground that by so doing we should weaken the monarchy. Henry VII. and Louis XI. may teach us wiser notions of the foundations of monarchical sway. I deny still more strongly that we require the undiminished power of the aristocracy as a check to the prerogative of the king. My good friends, you all know the old dogma, that a strong nobility prevents monarchical encroachment. Now, tell me candidly, do you think we can take care of ourselves? Do we want these disinterested proxies to attend to our interests? For my part, I fear that we can but imperfectly afford such very expensive stewards. When we were minors in education, they might have been necessary evils; but now we are grown up, and can take care of our own concerns. Can you fancy, my dear friends, that if the aristocracy were not, "if it had bowed the head and broke the stalk, and fallen into the portion of weeds and wornout faces,"[1] can you fancy that you would not be equally vigilant against any very dangerous assumptions on the part of the monarch? Trust me, while the looms of Manchester are at work—while the forges of Sheffield ring upon our ears—while morning and night the PRESS unfolds her broad banner, visible from John o' Groats to the Land's-end, there is but little fear that the stout heart of England should fall into so lethargic a slumber that a king could gather armies without her consent, construct dungeons without her knowledge, raise taxes without her connivance, and wake her at last to behold a sudden tyranny, and mourn for the departed vigilance of incorruptible courtiers!

In truth, my friends, all those ancient arguments on the necessity of a strong aristocracy, to check the king on the one side, and the commons on the other, are utterly inapplicable now. The checking power is not content to be a check alone; it is like the sea, and gains in every place where it does not recede: as we have seen, it has entered, penetrated, suffused every part of the very influences which ought to have opposed it; and I tell you once

---

1. Jeremy Taylor.

for all, my friends, that most of the ancient maxims of polity dragged forth from garbled extracts of half-read classics— maxims of polity which were applicable to the world before the invention of printing, are for that very reason inapplicable now. Perfectly right, perhaps, were the statesmen of old in their scoffs and declamations against the people: the people were then uneducated, a mere brute physical force; but the magic of Gutten-burg and Füst hath conjured a wide chasm between the past and the future history of mankind: the people of one side the gulf are not the people of the other; the physical force is no longer sepa-rated from the moral; mind has by slow degrees crept into the mighty mass—the popular Cymon has received a soul! In the primal and restless consciousness of the new spirit, Luther ap-pealed to the people—the first, since Christ, who so adventured. From that moment all the codes of classic dogmatists were worth-less—the expired leases to an estate just let to new tenants, and upon new conditions.

There is an era in civilization, when an aristocracy may be safely allowed a disproportionate strength, because an aristocracy is then composed of the best educated men; and because their very haughtiness which fears liberty resists servitude.

In that era, men set apart from the baser drudgeries of life, and devoted to the pursuit of arms, which in all times links itself with certain principles of honour, can scarcely fail of inspiring somewhat of refinement and of gallantry into the stubborn masses of an unenlightened society; their very ostentation promotes in-dustry;—and industry, in diffusing wealth, expedites civilization. But, as it is profoundly laid down by Montesquieu, "there is a very great difference between a system which *makes* a State great, and a system which *preserves* its greatness." The era in which it is wise to promote a dominant aristocracy ceases when monarchs are not military chiefs, and the people of themselves can check whatever excess of power in the sovereign they may deem dangerous; it ceases when nobles become weak, but the spirit of aristocracy becomes strong; (two consequences, the re-sult of a *numerous* peerage which leaves half of the order men-dicants upon corruption, but confirms the spirit which the order has engendered, by insensibly extending its influence through-out the subordinate grades with which it seeks intermarriage, and from which it receives its supplies; at that time chivalry has abandoned the nobles, and corruption has supplied its place;) —it ceases when an aristocracy is no longer in advance of the people, and a king and his subjects require no obstacle to their confidence in each other.

Thus then, neither for the safety of the king nor for that of the people, is it incumbent upon us to preserve undiminished, or rather uncorrected, the Aristocratic power. But while both people and king can even do without an aristocracy, could you, my friends, do equally well without a king? Come, let us suppose that the wish of certain politicians were gratified; let us suppose that a republic were established to-morrow? I will tell you what would be the result—your republic would be the very worst of aristocracies!

Do not fancy, as some contend, that the aristocracy would fall if the king fell. Not a whit of it. You may sweep away the House of Lords if you like; you may destroy titles; you may make a bonfire of orb and ermine, and after all your pains, the aristocracy would be exactly as strong as ever. For its power is not in a tapestried chamber, or in a crimson woolsack, or in ribbons and stars, in coronets and titles; its power, my friends, is in yourselves; its power is in the aristocratic spirit and sympathy which pervade you all. In your own hearts while you shout for popular measures, you have a reverential notion of the excellence of aristocratic agents; you think rich people alone "respectable"; you have a great idea of station; you consider a man is the better for being above his fellows, not in virtue and intellect, but in the good things of life. The most eminent of your representatives is accustomed to boast "that he owes his station to his father's industry in cotton-spinning"; you admire him when he does so—it is but a few weeks since that you rent the air when the boast was uttered; you fancied the boast was democratic and truth-loving. It was just the reverse—very aristocratic (though in a vulgar mode of aristocracy) and very false. Owes his station to cotton-spinning! Observe that the boast implies a pride of wealth, an aristocracy of feeling much more offensive than the pride of birth. Owes his station to cotton-spinning! If a man did so owe it, to my mind there is nothing to boast of, nothing very ennobling in the process of cotton-spinning. But what your Representative means to say, is this,—that

371

the industry of his father in amassing an immense fortune is praiseworthy, and he is therefore proud of it; and, you, my dear friends, being most of you employed in money-getting, are very apt to be charmed with the compliment. But successful industry in amassing money, is a very poor quality in the eyes of men who cherish high notions of morality; it is compatible with the meanest vices, with the paltriest exertions of intellect, with servility, with cunning, with avarice, with over-reaching! Compatible! Nay, it is by those very qualities, that, nine times out of ten, a large fortune is made! They were doubtless not the failings of your Representative's father. I know nothing about that gentleman now no more; he enjoyed a high character; he may have had every virtue under the sun; I will willingly suppose that he had; but, let us stick to the point; it was only of one virtue that Sir Robert Peel boasted—namely, the virtue of making money. If this was an aristocratic boast, if it showed a poor comprehension of morality, so, on the other hand, it was not true in itself. And your Representative must have known it was not true while he uttered it. It is not true, that that disinguished man owes his station in the world to his father's industry; it is not true, that cotton-spinning has anything at all to do with it; he owes his station to his own talents, to his own eloquence, to his own perseverance—these are qualities to be proud of; and a great man might refer to them with a noble modesty; but *to please you,* my dear friends, the crafty orator only talks of the *to kalon* of cotton-spinning, and the *to prepon* of money-making.

Believe me then, that if you were to institute a republic tomorrow, it would be an aristocratic republic; and though it would be just as bad if it were an aristocracy of shopkeepers, as if it were an aristocracy of nobles, yet I believe on the whole it would be an aristocracy very much resembling the present one (*only without the control* which the king's prerogative at present affords him). And for one evident reason—namely, the *immense property* of our nobles and landed gentry! Recollect, that in this respect they differ from most other aristocracies, which are merely the shadows of a court and without substance in themselves. From most other aristocracies, sweep away the office and the title, and they themselves are *not;* but banish from court a Northumberland, a Lonsdale, a Cleveland, a Bedford, or a Yarborough; take away their dukedoms and their earldoms, their ribbons or their robes, and they are exactly as powerful, with those broad lands and those mighty rent-rolls, as they were before. In any republic you can devise, men with this property will be *uppermost;* they will be still your rulers, as long as you yourselves think that property is the legal heir to respect.

I always suppose, my friends, in the above remarks, that you would not *take away* the property, as is recommended by some of the unstamped newspapers, to which our Government will permit no reply, and which therefore enjoy a monopoly over the minds of the poor; I always imagine, that, republican or monarchical, you will still be English; I always imagine that, come what may, you will still be honest, and without honesty it is useless to talk of republics. Let possessions be insecure, and your republic would merge rapidly into a despotism. All history tells us, that the moment liberty invades property, the reign of arbitrary power is at hand;—the flock fly to a shepherd to protect them from wolves. Better one despot, than a reign of robbers.

If we owe so much to our faults and imperfections to the aristocratic influence, need I ask you if you would like an unrelieved aristocracy? If not, my friends, let us rally round the Throne.

III

But the Throne is expensive. Ah! hark to the popular cry:—

> That's the wavering Commons; for their love
> Lies in their purses, and whoso empties them
> By so much fills their hearts with deadly hate,
> Wherein the King stands generally condemned.[1]

The belief that the Throne costs something quite enormous is generally received in the manufacturing towns—thanks again to the unstamped publications, to which Lord Althorp, (desiring a republic, I suppose,) compels the poor—never will I be weary of urging the Government on that point!—And men, afraid to avow that republicanism is a good thing, delicately insinuate that it is an exceedingly cheap one. Let us see how far this is true; let us subject our constitution to the multiplication table; let us count up, my friends, what a King costs us.

The whole of our yearly expenditure, including our National Debt, is somewhat more than fifty millions; out of this vast sum you may reckon that a King costs as follows:—

Civil list	411,800
Three regiments of Horse Guards	80,000
Pensions to Royal Family	220,000
For servants to different branches of the Royal Family	24,000
	£735,800

1. Richard II.

These are the main expenses of royalty; I can not find, by any ingenuity, that we can attach to it a much larger sum;—but let us be liberal and reckon the whole at a million. What then? Why the King would only cost us just one fiftieth part of our yearly outgoings, or one twenty-eighth part of our National Debt!

I think, indeed, the royal expenditure might be somewhat lessoned without diminishing the royal dignity. I see not why we should have three regiments of Horse Guards; but let this pass. Suppose we do not cut down a shilling of the King's expenses, is it not idle to talk of the oppressive cost of a King when it amounts only to a fiftieth part of our yearly incumbrances?

Ah, say some, but supposing the King were not, we should be better able to cut down the other expenses. I fancy they are very much mistaken! those expenses are the expenses that have no connexion with the Monarchy—expenses that are solely for the convenience of the aristocracy.

Do you find that the King himself resists retrenchment? on the contrary, was not retrenchment the very principle established between himself and his ministers? Republics, I allow, are generally cheap; but then Republics have not generally run into debt as you have. I suppose, by being Republicans, we should not get whitewashed, and that we should be equally obliged to discharge our pecuniary obligations. But how was that debt incurred? My dear friends, that is quite another question; I am not arguing whether you might not be richer had you established a Republic a century ago, (thought I doubt it exceedingly, for I could prove your aristocracy, more than your monarch, to blame for your debt,) but whether you would be much richer *now* by establishing a Republic? It is cheaper to build a plain house than a fine one; but having once built your fine house, it is a false economy to take it down for the purpose of building a plain one.

Some one pulls me by the arm and asks me, why I defend a Monarchy which the Whigs assure us that nobody attacks. Hark you, my good friends, the reason is this—I see much farther than the Whigs do, and I speak more conscientiously,—I hate the policy that looks not beyond the nose of the occasion. I love to look far and to speak boldly. I have no place to gain, no opinion to disguise—nothing stands between me and the Truth. I put it to you all, whether, viewing the temper of the age, the discontent of the multitude, the example of foreign states, the restlessness of France, the magnificent affluence of North America, the progress of an unthinking liberalism, the hatred against ostensible power—I put it to you all whether, unless some great and dexterous statesman arise, or unless some false notions are removed, some true principles are explained, you do not perceive slowly sweeping over the troubled mirror of the Time the giant shadow of the coming Republic?

IV

But since it seems that our jealousy must be directed mainly against the aristocratic power, how shall we proceed in order to resist and diminish it? That is a question not easily answered. Do not, my friends, do not let us confound a House of Lords, which is but a part of the aristocracy, with the aristocracy itself: there is just as much aristocracy in the House of Commons as there is in the House of Lords, only at this moment you are very justly displeased with the Lords. If you were to destroy that assembly, it would not be long before you would be quite as much displeased with the House of Commons!

Could I persuade you take my advice, you would look with considerable suspicion on the leading articles of newspapers; especially when their writers seem very earnestly to take your view of the question. You know it is a common trick among thieves, when they see a green-horn engaged in a broil, to affect to be all on his side; so in Roderick Random, an honest fellow offers very good-naturedly to hold Strap's coat for him while Strap enjoys a comfortable round or two at reciprocal fisticuffs. When the battle is done, Strap's coat has disappeared! My dear friends, there are certain journalists who seem passionately in your favour—all willing to pat you on the back, and give you a knee, while you show your manhood on the House of Lords! but recollect poor Strap, and keep your coats on your shoulders. This is the homely advice of your friend and neighbour.

Yes! I see certain journalists strongly recommending a numerous creation of peers. Somehow or other, those journalists are very fond of the ministers: it is true they scold them now and then in a conjugal way; but they make it up on a pinch, because like man and wife, the journalist and minister often have an interest in common. There was a time when I advocated a numerous creation of peers—a creation that should bring the two Houses of Parliament into tolerable concord; but that time is past. New objections have arisen to such a policy, and I confess that on my mind those objections have considerable weight. Are you willing, my compatriots, to give the Whig ministers such a majority in both houses, that you will never be able without revolution to have any other administration? If so, then go on, clap your hands, and cry out with the Morning Chronicle for new peers! Do not fancy that measures would be more liberal if this creation were made! it is a delusion! What would be this creation? it would be a *Whig creation!* Ah! I see that, sooner than such a creation, you would consent to have chaos a little longer! You are right. Measures would not be more liberal; on the contrary, it is from the despair of pleasing the Lords that the only really liberal measure of the Whigs (the Reform Bill) was insisted upon! Do you not observe, the moment the two Houses may be brought pretty nearly to the same temper, that the Whigs are willing to pare down and smooth away any popular proposition, so that it may glide quietly from one House through the other? If there were but little difference between the two chambers, depend upon it, in that little difference the people would invariably go to the wall. Do you not mark, that as the ministers now cannot govern by the House of Lords, so they *must* govern somewhat by the people? But suppose they had secured the House of Lords, the people would not be half so necessary to them. It is the very opposition of the Tory aristocracy that has compelled the Whigs to be liberal. Let them break that opposition entirely, and you will see the Whigs themselves rapidly hardening and encrusting into Tories. There was a time, I say, when I thought a creation of peers desirable; but at that time I imagined we might safely trust the Whigs with so enormous a power. I think otherwise now. Give them the command of both the chambers, and you reduce the King to a cipher. You make a Whig aristocracy perpetual. "Oh!" cry some of the mob-orators, or our friends the journalists, "the people have now the power to get good government, and they will use it, let there be what ministry there may!" No such thing, my dear friends, no such thing; we have *not* that power. You have chosen your House of Commons, it is true, and a pretty set of gentlemen you have chosen! "You talk," said one of the most enlightened of the ministers to a friend of mine, "you talk of our fear of a collision with the Lords, if we should be very popular in our measures. Faith, in that case we should be equally afraid of a collision with the Commons. Look at the scatterlings of the Mountain Bench; run your eye over Mr. Hume's divisions; count the number of Radicals in Parliament, and confess that we have *not* a House of Commons prepared to receive with joy any *very* popular propositions." Was not the minister right? Where, O English people! where are your friends—where your supporters—where those securers of good government that the coat-holders talk of! Yon few violent theorists, all quarrelling with each other, full of crotchets and paper-money chimeras,—are *those* your friends? Yon ministerial benches, of whom, were it not for yells and groans which savour but little of humanity, one might apply the line once applied to the stoics—

Rarus sermo in illis, et magna libido tacendi,—

are *they* your friends? "No," you say; "but if we had a dissolution!" Ah, *but in the mean while?*—the next five years? Are we to throw *those* years away by granting Whig measures a certain monopoly of the whole legislature? I think the experiment would be unwise in us! But between ourselves, I fear greatly that if Parliament were dissolved next week, though you would return many more Tories, and a few more independent members, you would still, under the present Reform Bill, return a sufficient majority of Whigs. The basis of the Reform Bill is property; your own minds incline to the representation of property; the Whigs possess the great proportion of that sort of property which is brought to bear in elections; their property will return them. So that were you to swamp the Lords, and then to proceed to a new election, you would still perpetuate the Whig dynasty. It is true that you might pledge your representatives; but I think you have seen enough of pledges. Do you know an excellent pair of caricatures called "Before and After?" In the first caricature the lover is all ardour, in the second he is all frigidity. For a lover read a member—members' pledges are like lovers' oaths —possession destroys their value!

I beseech you then to pause well and long before you swell the cry for new peers, or before you are cajoled into believing that to strengthen a Whig ministry is the best mode of weakening an aristocratic domination.

A second mode of dealing with the House of Lords has occurred to some bolder specualtors—they propose not to swamp it, but to wash it away altogether. Mighty well! What would be the consequence? Why you would have all the Lords taking their seats in the House of Commons. You would have no popular assembly at all; you would transfer the Wellingtons, and the Winchelseas, and the Northumberlands, and the Exeters, and the Newcastles, to the Lower House, as the representatives of yourselves. Their immense property would easily secure their return, to the exclusion of poorer but more popular men, for the divided counties in which it is situated; and all you would effect by destroying the existence of one chamber, would be a creation of a Tory majority in the other.

It was this which the sagacious mind of the Duke of Wellington foresaw, when he declared—as he is reported to have done in private—that he would rather the House of Lords were destroyed than swamped; and that in the former case he would be more powerful as Mr. Wellesley, than in the latter as the Duke of Wellington.

Trust me then, neither of these modes of treating the Lords will be found to our advantage: a third mode might be devised —but I think we are not yet prepared for it, viz.—the creation of an elective, not an hereditary senate, which might be an aristocracy in the true sense of the world—that is, an essembly of the best men—the selected of the country—selected from the honest as the rich, the intelligent as the ignorant—in which property would cease to be the necessary title, and virtue and knowledge might advance claims equally allowed. But I say no more on this point. For nothing could give rise or dignity to such an assembly, but the enlightened opinion among ourselves which legislation alone cannot effect!

V

It appears then, upon the whole, that the only safe, practical, and uncharlatanic resistance you can offer to the influences which are so pernicious, is in a thorough understanding of the extent and nature of those influences—in a perpetual and consistent jealousy of their increase—in wise, unceasing, but gradual measures for their diminution. You have observed that the worst part of these influences is in a *moral* influence. This you can counteract by a *new* moral standard of opinion—once accustom yourselves to think that

> Rank is but the guinea stamp,
> The mon 's the gowd for a' that;

once learn to detach respectability from acres and rent-rolls—once learn indifference for fashion and fine people; for the 'whereabouts' of lords and ladies; for the orations of men boasting of the virtue of making money; once learn to prize at their full worth—a high integrity, and a lofty intellect—once find yourselves running to gaze, not on foreign Princes and Lord Mayors' coaches, but on those who elevate, benefit, and instruct you, and you will behold a new influence pushing its leaves and blossoms from amidst the dead corruption of the old. To counteract a bad moral influence, never let us omit to repeat that you must create a good moral influence. Reformed opinion precedes reformed legislation. Now is the day for writers and advisers; *they* prepare the path for true lawgivers; they are the pioneers of good; no reform is final, save the reform of mind. Hence it is that I have written this book, instead of devoting the same time, like our philosopherling Mr. Snap, to the compilation of a score or two of speeches. The speeches would perish in a week; but the subject of this book must make it live, till its end be fulfilled. Others, with greater effect, because with higher genius, will follow in my track—"Je serais le mouche du coche qui se passera bien de mon bourdonnement. Il va, mes chers amis—et ne cesse d'aller. Si sa marche nous parait lente, c'est que nous vivons un instant. Mais que de chemin il a fait depuis cinq ou six siecles! A cette heure, en pleine roulant, rien ne le peu plus arrêter."[1]

1. Pamphlet des Pamphlets.

VI

The State of Parties

Having defined, through the mists of political delusion, the outline of the hostile and the friendly encampments—having ascertained what powers we shall attack and what defend, let us approach somewhat closer to the actual field, and examine the state of those contending parties, who, not sharing our views, nor actuated by our motives, fight without knowing wherefore or for what end, save, perhaps, that to the vulgar mass of the soldiery there is some guiding and consolatory recollection that plunder is the perquisite of conquest.

THE STATE OF PARTIES: it is an interesting survey, and you, my dear friends, ought to think it peculiarly interesting; for, as formerly men burnt each other out of pure affection for God, so now they all attack each other like furies for no other motive in the world but a disinterested attachment to the People. Heaven grant that you may be better served by *your* fanatics than our good Maker has been by his!

Don't believe the coat-holders, my friends, when they tell you with so assured an air that the Tories, as a party, are extinct. They are *not* extinct; the spirit of Toryism never dies. "You may kill men," said a French friend of your's once, and the saying is full of the pith of that wit which is another word for truth, "you may kill men, but you cannot kill things." The Tories in a year or two hence will perhaps be as formidable as ever. It is true that Wetherell may wander seatless; it is true that Croker's sarcastic lip may no longer lavish compliments on the treasury benches; it is true that Gatton is a ghost, and Old Sarum a tradition; but, my dear friends, till the future itself is no more, the past will have its bigoted defenders, and the world will be in no want of a Wetherell. And what though Gatton be defunct? Trust me, the corruption of a Norwich will engender the same fungi that sprouted forth from the rottenness of Gatton. But the Tories, even as a body of men so known and termed, are not extinct; they have a majority in the Lords, and in the Commons they are at least three times as numerous as the ultra Radicals. Take the Tories at the lowest, there are a hundred and fifty of them in your own assembly: take the ultra Radicals at the highest, and you cannot number above fifty. Better, therefore, might you say, that the Radicals were extinct, than that the Tories were extinct. The last, I grant you, seem lethargic enough at present; but, like the hare, they sleep with their eyes open, and, like the snake, they are hoarding venom.

But the main feature of all parties at this moment is, that in every party there are divisions. The Tories are weakened by bitter though unacknowledged schisms among themselves: in the Commons they fall into two main bands, the one following Sir Robert Peel, the other regarding him with suspicion, and half disposed to revolt from his side. "The following" of Sir Robert Peel are composed of men of a certain semi-enlightenment, of moderate passions, and a regard for peace above all things: they would rather retain the ministers than discard them; they have no desire for perilous experiments of Tory rule; they have a horror of revolution, and possess more of the timorous prudence of merchants than the haughty courage of aristocrats. Whatever is Tory among "the more respectable" of the metropolitan population—the bankers, the traders, the men who deem it a virtue in their fathers to make money by cotton-spinning— all these are with Sir Robert Peel: they extol his discretion and confide in his judgment: And, in truth, Sir Robert Peel is a remarkable man—confessedly a *puissance* in himself, confessedly the leading member of the representative, yes, even of your reformed, assembly: he is worth our stopping in our progress for a moment in order to criticize his merits.

It is a current mistake in the provinces to suppose that Sir Robert Peel is rather sensible than eloquent. If to persuade, to bias, to soothe, to command the feelings, the taste, the opinions of an audience, often diametrically opposed to his views—if *this* be eloquence, which I, a plain man, take it to be, then Sir Robert Peel is among the most eloquent of men. I am not one of those who think highly of the art of oratory; I laugh at the judgment of such as rank its successful cultivation among the great efforts of mind: it depends mainly upon physical advantages and a combination of theatrical tricks; a man may therefore have but ordinary intellectual powers, and yet be exceedingly eloquent to a popular assembly; nay, we need only analyse calmly the speeches which have delighted an audience, to be aware of their ordinary lack of all eminently intellectual qualifications. That sentence which reads to you so tame, was made emphatic by the most dexterous pronunciation—that sarcasm which seems to you so poor, took all its venom from the most significant smile—that fallacy which strikes you as so palpable, seemed candour itself by the open air of sincerity with which it was delivered. Pronunciation, smile, air! They are excellent qualities in an orator, but may they not be achieved without any wondrous depth of the reason, or any prodigous sublimity of the imagination? I am speaking, therefore, in admiration of Sir Robert Peel's eloquence, and not of his mind; though even in the latter he excels the capacity of orators in general.

Physical advantages are one component of successful oratory; there Sir Robert Peel possesses—a most musical voice—a tall and stately person—a natural happiness of delivery, which though not wholly void of some displeasing peculiarities, is more than ordinarily commanding and impressive. A combination of theatrical tricks is another component of successful oratory, and this also Sir Robert Peel has most dexterously acquired; by a wave of the hand, by a bow across the table, by an expression of lip, by a frankness of mien, he can give force, energy, wit, or nobility— to nothings! Oratory is an art—he is an elaborate artist. In the higher qualities of mind, he must be considered a man of remarkable accomplishments. With a wide range of ornamental, he combines a vast hoard of practical, knowledge; he is equally successful in a speech on the broadest principle, or on the narrowest detail. He has equally the information of a man of letters, and of a man of business. He is not philosophical, but he skims the surface of philosophy; he is as philosophical as the House will bear any *effective* orator to be. He is not poetical, but he can command the embellishments of poetry, and suits an assembly which applauds elegance but recoils from imagination. In his deficiencies, therefore—if we note the limit of the mind—we acknowledge the skill of the artist—he employs every tool necessary to his work, and no man with a more happy effect. To his skill as an orator, he adds certain rare qualities as a leader; he has little daring, it is true, but he has astonishing tact—he never jeopardiezs a party by any rash untowardness of phrase—he is free from the indiscretion habitual to an orator. Another eminent characteristic of his mind is accuracy. I do not remember ever to have heard him misstate a fact, and I have heard almost every other public speaker misstate a hundred facts. It is probably this constitution of mind which gifts him with his faculty for business. Assuredly no man who, in times of wide and daring speculation, pertinaciously resolved to narrow his circle, and be

Content to live in decencies for ever,

has been able to invest the existence with more dignity, and to hide with a better effect the limited circumference of his range. There seems to me little doubt but that this accomplished statesman is enthralled and hampered by the early ties which it is now and henceforth impossible for him, without worldly dishonour, to break. His mind evidently goes beyond the tether of his companions—his arguments are not theirs—to illiberal conclusions he mostly applies liberal reasonings. He describes his narrow circle with compasses disproportionately large, and seems always to act upon that saying of Mirabeau's,—"La politique doit raisonner même sur des suppositions aux quelles elle ne croit pas." It is one of the phenomena of our aristocratic customs, that a man especially marked out by birth and circumstance to be the leader of the popular, should be the defender of the oligarchical party. Sprung from the people, he identifies himself with the patricians. His pure and cold moral character, untinctured by the vices, unseduced by the pursuits of an aristocracy, seems to ally him naturally to the decorous respectabilities of the great middle class to which his connexions attach him; and even ambition might suggest that his wealth would have made him the first of the one class, though it elevates him to no distinction in the other. Had he placed himself in his natural position among the ranks of the people, he would have been undeniably what

he now just fails of being—a GREAT MAN. He would not have
been a Secretary for Ireland at so early an age, but he would now
have been prime minister, or what is a higher position, the leader
and centre of the moral power of England. As it is, he has knit
himself to a cause which requires passion in its defenders, and
is regarded with suspicion by his allies, because he supports it
with discretion.

You observe then, my friends, that his good qualities themselves displease and disgust a large body of the Tories, and they
would adhere to him more zealously if he were less scrupulous
in his politics. For you will readily perceive that, by the more
haughty, vehement, and aristocratic of the Tories, *the Whigs
can never be forgiven!* Those who possessed boroughs, consider
themselves robbed of their property; those who *zealously* loved
the late form of government, deem themselves defrauded of a
Constitution. Thus insulted self-interest in some, and even a
wounded patriotism in others, carry the animosities of party into
the obstinacy of revenge. This division of the Tories care little
for your threats of rebellion or fears of revolution; they are willing to hazard any experiment, so discontented are they with the
Present. As the more prudent Tories are chiefly connected with
the trading interest, so the more daring Tories are mainly connected with the agricultural; they rely on their numerous tenantry
—on their strongholds of clanship and rustic connexions, with a
confidence which makes them shrink little from even an armed
collision with the people. Claiming amongst them many of that
old indomitable band of high-born gentry—the true chivalric
noblesse of the country, (for to mere titles there are no ancestral
recollections, but blood can bequeath warlike and exciting traditions,) they are stimulated by the very apprehensions which dis-
arm the traders. They are instinct with the Blackwood spirit of
resistance; and in that perverted attachment to freedom, which
belongs to an aristocracy, they deem it equally servile to obey a
people they despise, as to succumb to a ministry they abhor. And
of these, many are convinced, surrounded as they are in their
visits to their estates by admiring subordinates, that their cause
is less unpopular and more powerful in mere numerical force
than it is represented. How can a Chandos, the idol of his county,
full of courage and of pride, and equally respected and beloved
by the great agricultural body he represents,—how can *he* be-

lieve you when you tell him that the Tories are hated?—how can
he listen with patience to the lukewarm concessions of Sir Robert
Peel?—to the threats of the Journalists?—and to the self-lau-
datory assertion of the Whigs, that order and society itself rest
solely on their continuance in office? It is this party, of which,
though he appears but rarely, I consider Lord Chandos the legitimate and natural head, that Sir Robert Peel must perpetually disgust. Willing to hazard all things to turn out the ministry, they
must naturally divide themselves from a leader who is willing to
concede many things to keep the ministry in power.

Such is the aspect of the once united and solid Tory party,—
such the character of its two great divisions, between which the
demarcation becomes daily more visible and wide.

Turn your eyes now to the ultra Radicals, what a motley, confused, jarring, miscellany of irreconcilable theorists! Do two of
them think alike? What connexion is there between the unvary-
ing Warburton and the contradictory Cobbett? What harmony
betwixt the French philosophy of this man, and the English
prejudices of that? here all is paper money and passion, there all
frigidity and fund-holding. Each man, ensconced in his own
crotchets, is jealous of the crotchets of the other. Each man is
mad for popularity, and restless for position. Vainly would you
hope to consolidate a great national party that shall embrace all
these discordant materials; the best we can do is to incorporate
the more reasonable, and leave the rest as isolated skirmishers,
who are rather useful to harass your enemy, than to unite with
your friends. For do not believe that all who call themselves
your friends are so in reality; never cease to recollect poor Strap
and the runaway coat-holder!

Turn next to the great ministerial party, with its body of gold
and its feet of clay; what a magical chemistry is there not in a
treasury bench! What scattered particles can it not conglomerate!
What antipathetic opposites does it not combine! A Palmerston
and a Brougham, a Grant and an Althorp, the wavering indolence
of a Melbourne, and the dogged energy of an Ellice! I have read
in a quack's advertisement, that gold may be made the most
powerful of cements—I look to the ministry and I believe it!
The supporters are worthy of the cabinet; they are equally various
and equally consolidated; they shift with the ministers in every
turn; bow, bend, and twist with every government involution—

to-day they repeal a tax, to-morrow restore it; now they insist on a clause in the Irish Tithe Bill, as containing its best principle—and now they erase it as incontestably the most obnoxious; they reflect on the placid stream of their serene subserviency every shadow in the April heaven of ministerial supremacy. But we shall find on a more investigating observation, that by the very loyalty of their followers, the Whig ministers are injuring themselves, *"they are dragging their friends through the mire,"* they are directing against them the wrath of their constituents, they are attracting to every sinuosity of creeping complaisance, the indignation and contempt of the country;—in one homely sentence, *they are endangering the return of their present majority to the next Parliament!* That a Whig majority of one sort or another will be for some years returned by the operations of the Reform Bill, I have before said that I cannot doubt; but the next majority will be less vast and less confiding than the present! The great failing of the ministers is want of unity,—the Reform Bill united them, and during its progress they were strong; the Reform Bill passed, they had no longer a rallying point; they seem divided in opinion upon every thing else, nay, they allow the misfortune. What mysterious hints do you not hear from every minister, that he is not of the same mind as his brethren. Did not Mr. Stanley declare the other night, that on the principle of rendering church property at the disposal of Parliament, he would be disposed to divide on one side, and some of his companions on the other? On what an important question are these declared divisions!

This want of unity betrays itself in all manner of oscillations, the most ludicrous and undignified! Now the ministerial pendulum touches the Mountain Bench; now it vibrates to the crimson seat of his Grace of Wellington. Planning and counter-planning, bowing and explaining, saying and unsaying, bullying to-day and cringing to-morrow, behold the melancholy policy of men who clumsily attempt what Machiavel has termed the finest masterpiece in political science, viz. "to content the people and to manage the nobles."

Pressed by a crowd of jealous and hostile suitors, the only resource of our political Penelopes is in the web that they weave to conciliate each, and unravel in order to baffle all! My friends, as long as a Government lacks unity, believe me it will be ever weak in good, and adherent to mischief. A man must move both legs in order to advance; if one leg stands still, he may flourish with the other to all eternity without stirring a step. We must therefore see if we cannot contrive to impart unity to the Government, should we desire really to progress. How shall we effect this object? It seems to me that we might reasonably hope to effect it in the formation of a new, strong, enlightened, and rational party, on which the Government, in order to retain office, must lean for support. If we could make the ministers as afraid of the House of Commons as they are of the House of Peers, you have no notion how mightily we should brighten their wits and spirit up their measures!

But the most singular infatuation in the present Parliament is, that while ministers are thus daily vacillating from every point in the compass, we are eternally told that we must place unlimited confidence in them. My good friends, is it not only in something firm, steady, and consistent, that any man ever places confidence?—you cannot confide in a vessel that has no rudder, and which one wind drives out of sight, and another wind as suddenly beats back into port. I dare say the ministers are very honest men, I will make no doubt of it. God forbid that I should. I am trustful in human integrity, and I think honesty natural to mankind; but political confidence is given to men not only in proportion to their own honesty, but also in proportion to the circumstances in which they are placed. An individual may repose trust where there is the inclination to fulfill engagement; but the destinies of a people are too grave for such generous credulity. A nation ought only to place its trust where there is no *power* to violate the compact. The difference between confidence in a despotism, and confidence in a representative government is this: in the former we hope every thing from the virtues of our rulers, in the latter, we would leave nothing we can avoid leaving, to the chance of their errors.

This large demand upon our confidence in men who are never two days the same, is not reasonable or just. *You* have lost that confidence; why should your representatives sacrifice every thing to a shadow, which, like Peter Schemil's, is divorced from its bodily substance—yourselves?

VII

A Picture of the Present House of Commons

It seems, then, that an independent party ought to be formed, strong enough in numbers and in public opinion, to compel the ministers to a firm, a consistent, a liberal, and an independent policy. If so compelled, the Government would acquire unity of course, for those of their present comrades who shrank from that policy which, seemingly the most bold, is in troubled times really the most prudent, would naturally fall off as the policy was pursued. But does the present House of Commons contain materials for the formation of such a party? I think we have reason to hope that it may; there are little less than a hundred members of liberal opinions, yet neither tamely Whig nor fiercely Radical, a proportion of whom are already agreed as to the expediency of such a party, and upon the immediate principles it should attempt to promote. At the early commencement of the session (the first session of the reformed Parliament) such a party ought to have formed itself at once. But to the very name of Party, many had a superstitious objection. Others expected more from the Government than the Government has granted. Some asked who was to be leader, and some thought it a plan that might be *disagreeable to the feelings of Lord Althorp.*

Rusticus expectat dum defluat amnis.

The stream of time has flowed on, and Rusticus, perhaps, thinks it advisable to wait no longer. As a theory, I dislike the formation of parties. I will show you, my good friends why, if you wish that independent men shall be useful men, a party at this moment is necessary in practice.

Just walk with me into the House of Commons—there! mount those benches; you are under the Speaker's gallery. The debate is of importance—it is six o'clock—the debate has begun—it goes on very smoothly for an hour or two, during which time most of the members are at dinner, and half the remaining members are asleep. Aware of the advantage of seizing this happy season of tranquillity, some experienced prosers have got the ball of debate in their own hands; they mumble and paw, and toss it about, till near ten o'clock. The House has become full, you resettle yourselves in your seats, you fancy *now* the debate will begin in earnest; those gentlemen who have just entered will give new life to the discussion, they are not tired with the prosing *you* have heard, they come fresh to the field, prepared to listen and applaud. Alas, you are much mistaken! these gentlemen do not come to improve the debate, but to put an end to it as soon as they possibly can. They cluster round the bar in a gloomy galaxy;—like the stars; "they have neither speech nor language, but their voices are heard among them." Hark! a low murmur of question, it creeps, it gathers, and now—a cough!—fatal sound! —a general attack of phthisis seizes upon the House. All the pulmonary diseases of pathology seem suddenly let loose on the unfortunate senators. Wheezing and sneezing, and puffing and grunting, till at last the ripening symphony swells into one mighty diapason of simultaneous *groans!* You would think the whole assembly smitten with the plague. Sounds so mournful, so agonizing, so inhuman, and so ghastly, were never heard before! Now and then a solemn voice proclaims "order," a momentary silence succeeds, and then, with a tumultuous reaction, rush once more from nook to nook the unutterable varieties of discord;

Venti velut agmine facto,
Quà data porta, ruunt, et terras turbine perflant.

But who is the intrepid and patient member, whom at short and dreary intervals you hear threading with wearied voice, the atmospherical labyrinth of noise. My good friends, it is an independent member, *he has no party to back him!* Exhausted and vanquished, the orator drops at length. Up starts a Tory, dull, slow, and pompous; the clamour recommences, it is stopped short by indignant cries of "hear, hear!" the sound of "order" grows stern and commanding.

> Rex Æolus antro
> Luctantes ventos, tempestatesque sonoras
> Imperio premit.

Minister and Tory look round, and by menacing looks enjoin attention from their followers "for an *old* member of *such* respectability!" The noisier of the Æolian group escape in sullen silence through the side doors.

> Una Eurusque Notusque ruunt, creberque procellis Africus.

And for the next half hour the Tory orator, with uninterrupted authority, "vexes the dull ears of the drowsy men." To him succeeds a Whig, perhaps a Minister; the same silence, and the same security of prosing. Mark, by friends, both these gentlemen had a party at their backs!

I assure you that I am a very impartial witness on these facts, and write not at all sorely; for, being very well contented to be silent, save when I have any thing to say, I speak but seldom, as becomes a young member, and at the early part of the evening among the prosers, as becomes a modest one. It has never therefore been my lot to fall a victim to that ferocity of dissonance which I have attempted to describe. But members more anxious to display their eloquence than I am, have been made so sensible of the impossibility of addressing the House often, without any party to appeal to from the uproarious decisions of the bar, that I believe this cause, more than any other, has driven speech-loving gentlemen into the idea of forming an independent national party. A second reason that has, no doubt, had its weight with them is this; if a member, unsupported by others, bring forward any motion that he considers of importance, he is accused of preventing the business of the night,[1] and up rises my Lord

1. In order to expedite business, it is a party custom to *count out* the House on an independent member's motion, and so lose a night to the nation. The other day, six gentlemen put off their motions one after another, in order "not to take up the time of the House at so late a period of the session." When all these had thus resigned their right in favour of ministers, what did the House do?—proceed with the ministerial business? No, it adjourned till the next day!

Althorp, and benevolently puts it to him, whether he will per-
severe in his motion "against the general sense of the House?"
Whereupon the Whigs open their mouths, and emit a considerable cheer. Perhaps the member, if he be a very bold fellow,
perseveringly proceeds, the House being excessively thin and
excessively sulky. He sits down, the minister rises, and shuffles
the whole question out of discussion, by observing that the
honourable gentleman has brought it forward at a time so
obviously unfavourable, that, without giving a negative to the
principle, he shall think it *(totidem verbis)* his duty to throw
as much cold water upon it as he possibly can. The minister
having thus discharged his bucket, every Whig member adds a
thimbleful; the cry of question commences by *cock-crow,* and
the motion is washed out of the House as fast and as fearfully as
if it were poison!

No wonder, my dear friends, that you have been complaining
of silence and want of energy in your independent members;
they must have been stubborn spirits indeed, the very Molochs
of manhood, to resist such discouraging chills, and such powerful
combinations. Depend upon it, that so far as energy and talk are
concerned, the independent members will not displease you, if
they once resolve to unite. For my part, I have great hopes, should
this party be ever properly formed, that the stream will work
itself tolerably clear from the muddiness of its source, and that
your reformed Parliament, which disappoints you now, will in a
year or two sufficiently content you.

VIII

And what manner of men will they be who shall compose this national party?—My friends, they cannot be the aristocrats. The aristocracy on either side are pledged to old and acknowledged factions, one part to the Tories, another to the Whigs: the party to which I refer must necessarily consist chiefly of new members, and of men wedded to no hereditary affections. So far so well; and what objects will they embrace?—That is more than I can pretend to affirm; but I know what objects they *ought* to embrace.

In the first place, you may remember that in a previous section I observed, that of late years the intellectual spirit of the time has merged in the political spirit; so, still more lately, the political has merged in the economical—you only think at present of what you can save. Well, then, a party that shall obtain your opinion and represent your wishes, must consider economy before all things; not looking to niggard and miserly retrenchments alone, not converting themselves into save-alls of candle-ends and graters of cheese-parings; but advocating a vigorous and large retrenchment, extending from the highest department of state to the lowest. Never mind what the ministers tell us, when they say they have done their possible and can retrench no more. So said the Canning administration; and yet the Duke of Wellington retrenched some millions. So said the Duke of Wellington after his retrenchment; and yet the Whigs have retrenched a few millions more. So say the Whigs now; I fancy, if we look sharp, and press them hard, that we shall again find some snug *terra incognita* in the map of economy—the whole of that chart is far from being thoroughly explored. Retrenchment should be the first object of this party,—a retrenchment that shall permit the repeal of the most oppressive of the taxes, the assessed taxes, the malt-tax, the stamp duty on political knowledge. I say boldly RE-TRENCHMENT; for, between you and me, my friends, I have little faith in the virtue of any commutation of taxes. I have studied the intricacies of our finance, I have examined the financial systems of other countries, and I cannot discover any very large *fiscal* benefit as the probable result of new combinations of taxation. I own to you that I think you are inclined to over-rate the merits of a property-tax; depend upon it that, before such a tax existed three years, you would be as loud for its repeal as you are now for the repeal of the house and window-taxes; *they* are property-taxes,—of a less just nature, I grant, on the one hand, but of a less onerous and inquisitorial nature on the other:—an immense national debt renders direct taxation a dangerous experiment. No; I should vote for a property-tax, in lieu of other taxes, merely as a temporary expedient—as an expedient that would allow us time to breathe, to look round, to note well what retrenchments we can effect. In a year or two the retrenchments already made will come more into sensible operation; in a year or two, if your minds were made easy on your affairs, quiet and hope would increase our trade, and therefore our revenue; in a year or two new savings could be effected, and the property-tax, if imposed, be swept away; this is the sole benefit I anticipate from its imposition. I am for bold and rigid economy, not for its own sake alone, but because I believe, my friends, that, until you get this cursed money-saving out of your heads, until you are sensible that you are fairly treated, and can look at something else than your pockets, you will not be disposed to examine into higher and better principles of government than its mere cheapness. In vain pleads the head till the stomach is satisfied; in vain shall we entreat you to regard your intellectual and moral advancement, till we set at rest your anxiety not to be ruined.

Economy, then, should be the first principle of such a party; but not at that point should its duties be limited. It is from a profound knowledge of the character of the people to whom legislation is to be applied, that statesmen should legislate. I have said, in my first book, that the main feature of your character is industry; industry, therefore, should be supported and encouraged. I have said next, that the *present* disposition of the aristocratic influence weakens and degrades you; that disposition should be corrected and refined. I have said, thirdly, that a monarchy is your best preservative from entire deliverance to the domination of brute wealth and oligarchical ascendancy; the monarchy should be strengthened and confirmed. I have said, again, that an established Church preserves you from fanaticism and the worst effects of your constitutional gloom: an established Church should be jealously preserved; mark me, its preservation does not forbid —no, it necessitates its reform. I have said that a material and sordid standard of opinion has formed itself in the heart of your commercial tendencies; and this standard, by organized education, by encouragement to that national spirit which itself gives encouragement to literature, to science, and to art,—by a noble and liberal genius of legislation, we ought to purify and to exalt. This last object neither Whig nor Tory has ever dreamt of effecting. Lord Brougham, indeed, when the Whigs disowned him, comprehended its expediency, and pledged himself to its cause; but, since he has been the member of a Whig cabinet, he seems to have slipped from his principles, and forgotten his pledge. These are the main objects which your national party should have in view. A more vast and a more general object, to which, I fear, no party is yet prepared to apply itself, seems to me to be this,—to merge the names of People and of Government, to unite them both in the word STATE. Wherever you see a good and a salutary constitution, *there* you see the great masses of the population wedded to and mingled with the state; there must be energy to ensure prompt and efficient legislation: energy exists not where unity is wanting. In Denmark and Prussia is the form of absolute monarchy; but nowhere are the people happier or more contented, because in those countries they are utterly amalgamated with the state, the state protects, and educates, and cherishes them all. In America you behold republicanism; but the state is equally firm as it is in Denmark or Prussia, the people equally attached to it, and equally bound up in its existence. In these opposite constitutions you behold equal energy, because equal unity. Antient nations teach us the same truth: in Rome, in

Athens, in Tyre, in Carthage, the people were strong and prosperous only while the people and the state were one. But away with antient examples! let us come back to common sense. Can the mind surrender itself to its highest exertions when distracted by disquietude and discontent?—The mind of one individual reflects the mind of a people, and happiness in either results from the consciousness of security;—but you are never secure while you are at variance with your government. In a well-ordered constitution, a constitution in harmony with its subjects, each citizen confounds himself with the state; he is proud that he belongs to it; the genius of the whole people enters into his soul; he is not one man only, he is inspired by the mighty force of the community; he feels the dignity of the nation in himself— he beholds himself in the dignity of the nation. To unite, then, the people and the Government, to prevent that jealousy and antagonism of power which we behold at present, each resisting each to their common weakness, to merge, in one word, both names in the name of state, we must first advance the popular principle to satisfy the people, and then prevent a conceding government by creating a directive one. At present, my friends, you only perceive the Government when it knocks at your door for taxes; you couple with its name the idea not of protection, but of extortion; but I would wish that you should see the Government educating your children, and encouraging your science, and ameliorating the condition of your poor; I wish you to warm while you utter its very name, with a grateful and reverent sense of enlightenment and protection; I wish you to behold all your great Public Blessings repose beneath its shadow; I wish you to feel advancing towards that unceasing and incalculable amelioration which I firmly believe to be the common destiny of mankind, with a steady march and beneath a beloved banner; I wish that every act of a beneficent Reform—should seem to you neither conceded nor extorted,—but as a pledge of a sacred and mutual love;—the legitimate offspring of one faithful and indissoluble union between the Power of a People and the Majesty of a State!

This is what I mean by a *directive* government; and a government so formed is always strong—strong not for evil, but for good. I know that some imagine that a good government *should* be a weak government, and that the people should thus sway and mould it at their will; you cannot have a weaker government than at present, and I do not see how you are the better for it! But you, the people, do *not* sway a feeble government—I should be delighted if you did; for the people are calm and reasoning, and have a profound sense of the universal interest. But you have a false likeness, my dear friends; a vile, hypocritical, noisy, swaggering fellow, that is usually taken for you, and whom the journalists invariably swear by,—a creature that is called "THE PUBLIC": I know not a more pragmatical, conceited animal than this said PUBLIC. YOU are immortal, but the PUBLIC is the grub of a day; he floats on the mere surface of time; he swallows down the falsest opinions; he spouts forth the noisiest fallacies; what he says one hour he unsays the next; he is a thing of whims and caprices, of follies and of frenzies. And it is this wrangling and shallow pretender, it is the Public, and not the People, that dictates to a feeble government!

You have been misled if you suppose a strong government is necessarily hostile to you; *coercive* governments are not *strong* ones; governments are never strong save when they suit the people, but a government truly strong would be efficient in good; it would curb arrogance as well as licentiousness. Government was strong when it carried your Reform Bill through the House of Lords; Government was weak when it sacrificed to the Lords the marrow of the Irish Tithe Bill. An united State, and a strong Government, such should be the ulterior objects of a national party really wise and firmly honest. But the members of such a party should dismiss all petty ambition, all desire of office for themselves; they are not strong enough, for years they cannot be strong enough, without base and unnatural alliances, to nourish the hope of coming into power with the necessary effect. They should limit their endeavours to retain the best of the present Ministers in office, and to compel them to a consistent and generous policy. They should rather imitate the watch-dog, than aspire to the snug cottage of the shepherd.

This, my friends, is the outline of what, in my poor opinion, a national party *ought* to be; but I own to you that when I look to the various component parts of such an association; when I reflect how difficult it must be to unite the scruples of some, and to curb the desires of others, I limit my present hopes to a very small portion of the benefit it could attain. It is for you to widen the sphere of that benefit by a vigilance towards its efforts, and an approbation of its courage. Should it remain unformed after all—should its elements jar prematurely—should it dissolve of itself—should it accomplish none of its objects; and, for want of some such ground of support to good Government, and of fear to bad, should our present Ministers continue their oscillatory politics, weakening the crown, irritating the people, declining to enlighten, and incapable to relieve; shifting from rashness to cowardice, and cowardice to rashness, I behold the most serious cause of apprehension and alarm. I look beyond the day; I see an immense expenditure, an impoverished middle class, an ignorant population, a huge debt, the very magnitude of which tempts to dishonesty; I behold a succession of hasty experiments and legislative quackeries—feuds between the agriculturist[1] and the fund-holder—"scrambles" at the national purse; tamperings with the currency, and hazardous commutations of taxes; till having run through all the nostrums which Ignorance can administer to the impatience of Disease, we shall come to that last dread operation, of which no man can anticipate the result!

1. I firmly believe that if the National Debtor be ever in danger, the fatal attack will come less from the radicals than the country gentlemen, who are jealous of the fund-holder, or crippled with mortgages. The day after the repeal of half of the Malt Tax (leaving a large deficit in the Revenue) was carried, I asked one of its principal supporters, (a popular and independent country gentleman,) how he proposed to repair the deficit?—"By a tax of 2 per cent." quoth he, "upon Master Fund-holder!"—"And if that does not suffice?" asked I.—"Why, then, must tax him 4 *per cent.*" was the honest rejoinder!

Chapter the Last
The Author's Apology

And now, my dear friends, but little remains for me to say. Your welfare has ever been to me that object, which above all others has excited my ambition, and linked itself with my desires. From my boyhood to this hour, it is to the condition of great masses of men that my interest and my studies have been directed; it is for their amelioration and enlightenment that I have been a labourer and an enthusiast. Yes, I say, enthusiast!—for when a man is sincere, enthusiasm warms him; when useful, enthusiasm directs. Nothing can sustain our hopes for mankind, amidst their own suspicion of our motives and misconstructions of our aims, —amidst the mighty obstacles that oppose every one who struggles with old opinion,—and the innumerable mortifications, that are as the hostile winds of the soul, driving it back upon the haven of torpor and self-seeking;—save that unconquerable and generous zeal which results from a hearty faith in our own honesty, and a steady conviction of that tendency and power TO PROGRESS, which the whole history, as well of Philosophy as of Civilization, assures us to be the prerogative of our race! If I have, in certain broad and determined opinions, separated myself from many of your false and many of your real friends; if I have not followed the more popular leaders of the day against our ecclesiastical establishment, or against a monarchical constitution of government, it is not because I believe that any minor interests should be consulted before your own; it is not because I see a sanctity in hereditary delusions, or in the solemn austerities of power; it is not because I deny that in some conditions of society a republic may be the wisest government,[1] or because I maintain that where certain standards of moral opinion be created, an endowed establishment is necessary to the public virtue; but it is, because I consider both Institutions subordinate to your welfare; it is because I put aside the false mists and authorities of the past, and regard diligently the aspect of the present; it is because on the one hand I feel persuaded, viewing the tendencies which belong to our time, and the moral bias of the general feeling, which while often seeming to oppose an aristocracy, inclines equally (in its opposition) to aristocratic fallacies whether of wealth or of station, that your republic would *not* be a true and sound democracy, but the perpetuater of the worst influences which have operated on your character and your laws;—and because on the other hand, I dread, that the effects of abolishing an endowed Church would be less visible in the reform of superstitions, than in the gloomy advances of fanaticism. If I err in these opinions, it is for your sake that I err; if I am right, let us look with some what of prudent jealousy at the declamations and sarcasms which spring from a partial and limited survey of the large principles of practical polity; a survey which confounds every unpopular action of a king with the question of a monarchy; every failing of a priest, with the consideration of an establishment; which to-day insinuates a republic, because the King dines with a Tory, and to-morrow denounces an establishment, because a bishop votes against the Whigs.[2] These are the

---

1. Were I, in this work, giving myself up to the speculative and conjectural philosophy of Politics, I should be quite willing to allow my conviction that, as yet, we have scarce passed the threshold of Legislative Science; and that vast and organic changes will hereafter take place in the elements of Government and the social condition of the World. But I suspect that those changes will be favourable to the concentration, not of power, but the executive *direction* of power, into the *fewest* possible hands; as being at once energetic and responsible in proportion to such a concentration. I think *then* that the Representative System itself will not be found that admirable invention which it is now asserted to be. But these are distant theories, not adapted to this age, and must be reserved for the visions of the closet. He *now* is the most useful Politician, who grapples the closest with the time.

2. Whether or not the Bishops should have the privilege to vote in Parliament, is a question I shall not here attempt to decide. For the sake of removing the establishment itself from the perpetual danger of jarring, in its ostensible heads, against the opinions and passions of the people, the privation of that

cries of party, and have no right to response from the more deep and thoughtful sympathies of a nation. Believe me, once more, and once for all, if there be a pretender of whom the People should beware, it is that stage mummer—the Public!

Come what may in the jar and conflict of momentary interests, it is with the permanent and progressive interest of the people, that the humble writer who addresses you stands or falls, desiring indeed to proportion your power to your knowledge, but only because believing that all acquisitions of authority, whether by prince or people, which exceed the capacity to preserve and the wisdom to direct, are brief and perilous gains; lost as soon as made; tempting to crude speculations, and ending possibly in ruin. Every imprudence of the popular power is a step to despotism, as every excess of the oligarchical power is the advance of the democratic.

Farewell, my dear friends. We part upon the crisis of unconjecturable events.

> From this shoal and sand of Time
> We leap the life to come.

Gladly indeed would I pass from dealings with the policy of the present, to the more tempting speculations upon the future; but the sky is uncertain and overcast; and as, my friends, you may observe on a clouded night, that the earth gathers no dew, even so it is not in these dim and unlighted hours that the prophetic thirst of Philosophy may attain to those heavenlier influences which result from a serener sky, and enable her to promise health and freshness to the aspect of the morrow.

---

privilege might be desirable, and tend even to the preservation and popularity of the Church; but I beseech the reader to mark that nothing can be more unjust than the present cry against "the time-serving" and "servility" of the episcopal bench! What! when for the first time the prelates have refused all dictation from the Government, have separated themselves wholly from ministerial temptation, have, with obstinate fidelity, clung fast to a falling party, which cannot for years longer than those which usually remain to men who have won to episcopal honours, be restored to power!—what, *now* do you accuse them of time-serving and servility! Alas! it is exactly because they refuse to serve the time; exactly because they abjure servility to the dominant powers, that the public assail and the ministers desert them.

Appendix B
Remarks on Bentham's Philosophy

It is no light task to give an abridged view of the philosophical opinions of one, who attempted to place the vast subjects of morals and legislation upon a scientific basis: a mere outline is all that can be attempted.

The first principles of Mr. Bentham's philosophy are these;—that happiness, meaning by that term pleasure and exemption from pain, is the only thing desirable in itself; that all other things are desirable solely as means to that end: that the production, therefore, of the greatest possible happiness, is the only fit purpose of all human thought and action, and consequently of all morality and government; and moreover, that pleasure and pain are the sole agencies by which the conduct of mankind is in fact governed, whatever circumstances the individual may be placed in, and whether he is aware of it or not.

Mr. Bentham does not appear to have entered very deeply into the metaphysical grounds of these doctrines; he seems to have taken those grounds very much upon the showing of the metaphysicians who preceded him. The principle of utility, or as he afterwards called it "the greatest-happiness principle," stands not otherwise demonstrated in his writings, than by an enumeration of the phrases of a different description which have been commonly employed to denote the rule of life, and the rejection of them all, as having no intelligible meaning, further than as

This appendix was written for Bulwer by John Stuart Mill—ed.

they may involve a tacit reference to considerations of utility. Such are the phrases "law of nature," "right reason," "natural rights," "moral sense." All these Mr. Bentham regarded as mere covers for dogmatism; excuses for setting up one's own *ipse dixit* as a rule to bind other people. "They consist, all of them," says he, "in so many contrivances for avoiding the obligation of appealing to any external standard, and for prevailing upon the reader to accept the author's sentiment or opinion as a reason for itself."

This, however, is not fair treatment of the believers in other moral principles than that of utility. All modes of speech are employed in an ignorant manner, by ignorant people; but no one who had thought deeply and systematically enough to be entitled to the name of a philosopher, ever supposed that his *own* private sentiments of approbation and disapprobation must necessarily be well-founded, and needed not to be compared with any external standard. The answer of such persons to Mr. Bentham would be, that by an inductive and analytical examination of the human mind, they had satisfied themselves, that what we call our moral sentiments, (that is, the feelings of complacency and aversion we experience when we compare actions of our own or of other people with our standard of right and wrong,) are as much part of the original constitution of man's nature as the desire of happiness and the fear of suffering: That those sentiments do not indeed attach themselves to the same actions under all circumstances, but neither do they, in attaching themselves to actions, follow the law of utility, but certain other general laws, which are the same in all mankind naturally; though education or external circumstances may counteract them, by creating artificial associations stronger than they. No proof indeed can be given that we ought to abide by these laws; but neither can any proof be given, that we ought to regulate our conduct by utility. All that can be said is, that the pursuit of happiness is natural to us; and so, it is contended, is the reverence for, and the inclination to square our actions by, certain general laws of morality.

Any one who is acquainted with the ethical doctrines either of the Reid and Stewart school, or of the German metaphysicians (not to go further back), knows that such would be the answer of those philosophers to Mr. Bentham; and it is an answer of which Mr. Bentham's writings furnish no sufficient refutation. For it is evident, that these views of the origin of moral distinctions are *not,* what he says all such views are, destitute of any precise and tangible meaning; nor chargeable with setting up as a standard the feelings of the particular person. They set up as a standard what are assumed (on grounds which are considered sufficient) to be the instincts of the species, or principles of our common nature as universal and inexplicable as instincts.

To pass judgment on these doctrines, belongs to a profounder and subtler metaphysics than Mr. Bentham possessed. I apprehend it will be the judgment of posterity, that in his views of what, in the felicitous expression of Hobbes, may be called the *philosophia prima,* it has for the most part, even when he was most completely in the right, been reserved for others to *prove* him so. The greatest of Mr. Bentham's defects, his insufficient knowledge and appreciation of the thoughts of other men, shows itself constantly in his grappling with some delusive shadow of an adversary's opinion, and leaving the actual substance unharmed.

After laying down the principle of Utility, Mr. Bentham is occupied through the most voluminous and the most permanently valuable parts of his works, in constructing the outlines of practical ethics and legislation, and filling up some portions of the latter science (or rather art) in great detail: by the uniform and unflinching application of his own greatest-happiness principle, from which the eminently consistent and systematic character of his intellect prevented him from ever swerving. In the writings of no philosopher, probably, are to be detected so few contradictions—so few instances of even momentary deviation from the principles he himself has laid down.

It is perhaps fortunate that Mr. Bentham devoted a much larger share of his time and labour to the subject of legislation, than to that of morals; for the mode in which he understood and applied the principle of Utility, appears to me far more conducive to the attainment of true and valuable results in the former, than in the latter of these two branches of inquiry. The recognition of happiness as the only thing desirable in itself, and of the production of the state of things most favourable to happiness as the only rational end both of morals and policy, by no means necessarily leads to the doctrine of expediency as professed by Paley; the ethical canon which judges of the morality of an act or a class of actions, solely by the probable *consequences* of that particular kind of act, supposing it to be generally practised. This is a very small part indeed of what a more enlarged understanding of the "greatest-happiness principle" would require us to take into the account. A certain kind of action, as for example, theft, or lying, would, if commonly practised, occasion certain evil consequences to society: but those evil consequences are far from constituting the entire moral bearings of the vices of theft or lying. We shall have a very imperfect view of the relation of those practices to the general happiness, if we suppose them to exist singly, and insulated. All acts suppose certain dispositions, and habits of mind and heart, which may be in themselves states of enjoyment or of wretchedness, and which must be fruitful in *other* consequences, besides those particular acts. No person can be a thief or a liar without being much else: and if our moral judgments and feeling with respect to a person convicted of either vice, were grounded solely upon the pernicious tendency of thieving and of lying, they would be partial and incomplete; many considerations would be omitted, which are at least equally "germane to the matter"; many which, by leaving them out of our general views, we may indeed teach ourselves a habit of overlooking, but which it is impossible for any of us not to be influenced by, in particular cases, in proportion as they are forced upon our attention.

Now, the great fault I have to find with Mr. Bentham as a moral philosopher, and the source of the chief part of the temporary mischief which in that character, along with a vastly greater amount of permanent good, he must be allowed to have produced, is this: that he has practically, to a very great extent, confounded the principle of Utility with the principle of specific consequences, and has habitually made up his estimate of the approbation or blame due to a particular kind of action, from a calculation solely of the consequences to which that very action, if practised generally, would itself lead. He has largely exemplified, and contributed very widely to diffuse, a tone of thinking, according to which any kind of action or any habit, which in its own specific consequences cannot be proved to be necessarily or probably productive of unhappiness to the agent himself or to others, is supposed to be fully justified; and any disapprobation or aversion entertained towards the individual by reason of it, is set down from that time forward as prejudice and superstition. It is not considered (at least, not habitually considered,) whether the act or habit in question, though not in itself necessarily pernicious, may not form part of a *character* essentially pernicious, or at least essentially deficient in some quality eminently conducive to the "greatest happiness." To apply such a standard as this, would indeed often require a much deeper insight into the formation of character, and knowledge of the internal workings of human nature, than Mr. Bentham possessed. But, in a greater or less degree, he, and every one else, judges by this standard: even those who are warped, by some partial view, into the omission of all such elements from their general speculations.

When the moralist thus overlooks the relation of an act to a certain state of mind as its cause, and its connexion through that common cause with large classes and groups of actions apparently very little resembling itself, his estimation even of the consequences of the very act itself, is rendered imperfect. For it may be affirmed with few exceptions, that any act whatever has a tendency to fix and perpetuate the state or character of mind in which itself has originated. And if that important element in the moral relations of the action be not taken into account by the moralist as a cause, neither probably will be taken into account as a consequence.

Mr. Bentham is far from having altogether overlooked this side of the subject. Indeed, those most original and instructive, though, as I conceive, in their spirit, partially erroneous chapters, on *motives* and on *dispositions,* in his first great work, the Introduction to the Principles of Morals and Legislation, open up a direct and broad path to the most important topics. It is not the less true that Mr. Bentham, and many others, following his example, when they came to discuss particular questions of ethics, have commonly, in the superior stress which they laid upon the specific consequences of a class of acts, rejected all contemplation of the action in its general bearings upon the entire moral being of the agent; or have, to say the least, thrown those considerations so far into the background, as to be almost out of sight. And by so doing they have not only marred the value of many of their speculations, considered as mere philosophical enquiries, but have always run the risk of incurring, and in many case have in my opinion actually incurred, serious practical errors.

This incompleteness, however, in Mr. Bentham's general views, was not of a nature materially to diminish the value of his speculations through the greater part of the field of legislation. Those of the bearings of an action, upon which Mr. Bentham bestowed almost exclusive attention, were also those with which almost alone legislation is conversant. The legislator enjoins or prohibits an action, with very little regard to the general moral excellence or turpitude which it implies; he looks to the consequences to society of the particular kind of action; his object is not to render people incapable of *desiring* a crime, but to deter them from actually *committing* it. Taking human beings as he finds them, he endeavours to supply such inducements as will constrain even persons of the dispositions the most at variance with the general happiness, to practise as great a degree of regard to it in their actual conduct, as can be obtained from them by such means without preponderant inconvenience. A theory, therefore, which considers little in an action besides that action's *own* consequences, will generally be sufficient to serve the purposes of a philosophy of legislation. Such a philosophy will be most apt to fail in the consideration of the greater social questions—the theory of organic institutions and general forms of polity; for those (unlike the details of legislation) to be duly estimated, must be viewed as the great instruments of forming the national character; of carrying forward the members of the community towards perfection, or preserving them from degeneracy. This, as might in some measure be expected, is a point of view in which except for some partial or limited purpose, Mr. Bentham seldom contemplates these questions. And this signal omission is one of the greatest of the deficiencies by which his speculations on the theory of government, though full of valuable ideas, are rendered, in my judgment, altogether inconclusive in their general results.

To these we shall advert more fully hereafter. As yet I have not acquitted myself of the more agreeable task of setting forth some part of the services which the philosophy of legislation owes to Mr. Bentham.

The greatest service of all, that for which posterity will award most honour to his name, is one that is his exclusively, and can be shared by no one present or to come; it is the service which can be performed only once for any science, that of pointing out by what method of investigation it may be *made* a science. What Bacon did for physical knowledge, Mr. Bentham has done for philosophical legislation. Before Bacon's time, many physical facts had been ascertained; and previously to Mr. Bentham, mankind were in possession of many just and valuable detached observations on the making of laws. But he was the first who attempted regularly to deduce all the secondary and intermediate principles of law, by direct and systematic inference from the one great axiom or principle of general utility. In all existing systems of law, those secondary principles or dicta in which the essence of the systems resided, had grown up in detail, and even when founded in views of utility, were not the result of any scientific and comprehensive course of enquiry; but more frequently were purely technical; that is, they had grown out of circumstances purely *historical,* and, not having been altered when those circumstances changed, had nothing left to rest upon but fictions, and unmeaning forms. Take for instance the law of real property; the whole of which continues to this very day to be founded on the doctrine of feudal tenures, when those tenures have long ceased to exist except in the phraseology of Westminster Hall. Nor was the *theory* of law in a better state than the practical systems; speculative jurists having dared little more than to refine somewhat upon the technical maxims of the particular body of jurisprudence which they happened to have studied. Mr. Bentham was the first who had the genius and courage to conceive the idea of bringing back the sciences to first principles. This could not be done, could scarcely even be attempted, without, as a necessary consequence, making obvious the utter worthlessness of many, and the crudity and want of precision of almost all, the maxims which had previously passed everywhere for principles of law.

Mr. Bentham, moreover, has warred against the errors of existing systems of jurisprudence, in a more direct manner than by merely presenting the contrary truths. The force of argument with which he rent asunder the fantastic and illogical maxims on which the various technical systems are founded, and exposed the flagrant evils which they practically produce, is only equalled by the pungent sarcasm and exquisite humour with which he has derided their absurdities, and the eloquent declamation which he continually pours forth against them, sometimes in the form of lamentation, and sometimes of invective.

This then was the first, and perhaps the grandest achievement of Mr. Bentham; the entire discrediting of all technical systems; and the example which he set of treating law as no peculiar mystery, but a simple piece of practical business, wherein means were to be adapted to ends, as in any of the other arts of life. To have accomplished this, supposing him to have done nothing else, is to have equalled the glory of the greatest scientific benefactors of the human race.

But Mr. Bentham, unlike Bacon, did not merely prophesy a science; he made large strides towards the creation of one. He was the first who conceived with anything approaching to precision, the idea of a Code, or complete body of law; and the distinctive characters of its essential parts,—the Civil Law, the Penal Law, and the Law of Procedure. On the first two of these three departments he rendered valuable service; the third he actually created. Conformably to the habits of his mind, he set about investigating *ab initio,* a philosophy or science for each of the three branches. He did with the received principles of each, what a good code would do with the laws themselves;—extirpated the bad, substituting others; re-enacted the good, but in so much clearer and more methodical a form, that those who were most familiar with them before, scarcely recognized them as the same. Even upon old truths, when they pass through his hands, he leaves so many of his marks, that often he almost seems to claim the discovery of what he has only systematized.

In creating the philosophy of Civil Law, he proceeded not much beyond establishing on the proper basis some of its most general principles, and cursorily discussing some of the most interesting of its details. Nearly the whole of what he has published on this branch of law, is contained in the *Traités de Législation,* edited by M. Dumont. To the most difficult part, and that which most needed a master-hand to clear away its difficulties, the nomenclature and arrangement of the Civil Code, he contributed little, except observations, and criticisms upon the errors of his predecessors. The "Vue Générale d'un Corps Complet de Législation," included in the work just cited, contains almost all which he has given to us on this subject.

In the department of Penal Law, he is the author of the best attempt yet made towards a philosophical classification of offences. The theory of punishments (for which however more had been done by his predecessors, than for any other part of the science of law) he left nearly complete.

The theory of Procedure (including that of the constitution of the courts of justice) he found in a more utterly barbarous state than even either of the other branches; and he left it incomparably the most perfect. There is scarcely a question of practical importance in this most important department, which he has not settled. He has left next to nothing for his successors.

He has shown with the force of demonstration, and has enforced and illustrated the truth in a hundred ways, that by sweeping away the greater part of the artificial rules and forms which obtain in all the countries called civilized, and adopting the simple and direct modes of investigation, which all men employ in endeavouring to ascertain facts for their own private knowledge, it is possible to get rid of at least nine-tenths of the expense, and ninety-nine hundredths of the delay, of law proceedings; not only with no increase, but with an almost incredible diminution, of the chances of erroneous decision. He has also established irrefragably the principles of a good judicial establishment: a division of the country into districts, with *one* judge in each, appointed only for a limited period, and deciding all sorts of case; with a deputy under him, appointed and removable by himself: an appeal lying in all cases whatever, but by the transmission of papers only, to a supreme court or courts, consisting each of only *one* judge, and stationed in the metropolis.

It is impossible within the compass of this sketch, to attempt any further statement of Mr. Bentham's principles and views on the great science which first became a science in his hands.

As an analyst of human nature (the faculty in which above all it is necessary that an ethical philosopher should excel) I cannot

rank Mr. Bentham very high. He has done little in this department, beyond introducing what appears to me a very deceptive
phraseology, and furnishing a catalogue of the "springs of action," from which some of the most important are left out.

That the actions of sentient beings are wholly determined by
pleasure and pain, is the fundamental principle from which he
starts: and thereupon Mr. Bentham creates a *motive,* and an
interest, corresponding to each pleasure or pain, and affirms that
our actions are determined by our *interests,* by the *preponderant*
interest, by the *balance* of motives. Now if this only means what
was before asserted, that our actions are determined by pleasure
and pain, that simple and unambiguous mode of stating the
proposition is preferable. But under cover of the obscurer phrase
a meaning creeps in, both to the author's mind and the reader's,
which goes much farther, and is entirely false: that all our acts
are determined by pains and pleasures *in prospect,* pains and
pleasures to which we look forward as the *consequences* of our
acts. This, as a universal truth, can in no way be maintained.
The pain or pleasure which determines our conduct is as frequently one which *precedes* the moment of action as one which
follows it. A man *may,* it is true, be deterred, in circumstances
of temptation, from perpetrating a crime, by his dread of the
punishment, or of the remorse, which he fears he may have to
endure *after* the guilty act; and in that case we may say with
some kind of propriety, that his conduct is swayed by the balance
of motives; or, if you will, of interests. But the case *may* be, and
is to the full as likely to be, that he recoils from the very thought
of committing the act; the idea of placing himself in such a situation is so painful, that he cannot dwell upon it long enough to
have even the physical power of perpetrating the crime. His
conduct is determined by pain; but by a pain which precedes the
act, not by one which is expected to follow it. Not only *may* this
be so, but unless it be so, the man is not really virtuous. The fear
of pain *consequent* upon the act, cannot arise, unless there be
deliberation; and the man as well as "the woman who deliber-
ates," is in imminent danger of being lost. With what propriety
shrinking from an action without deliberation, can be called
yielding to an *interest,* I cannot see. *Interest* surely conveys, and
is intended to convey, the idea of an *end,* to which the conduct

(whether it be act or forbearance) is designed as the *means*. Nothing of this sort takes place in the above example. It would be more correct to say that conduct is *sometimes* determined by an *interest*, that is, by a deliberate and conscious aim; and sometime by an *impulse*, that is, by a feeling (call it an association if you think fit) which has no ulterior end, the act or forbearance becoming an end in itself.

The attempt, again, to *enumerate* motives, that is, human desires and aversions, seems to me to be in its very conception an error. Motives are innumerable: there is nothing whatever which may not become an object of desire or of dislike by association. It may be desirable to distinguish by peculiar notice the motives which are strongest and of most frequent operation; but Mr. Bentham has not even done this. In his list of motives, though he includes sympathy, he omits conscience, or the feeling of duty: one would never imagine from reading him that any human being ever did an act merely because it is right, or abstained from it merely because it is wrong. In this Mr. Bentham differs widely from Hartley, who, although he considers the moral sentiments to be wholly the result of association, does not therefore deny them a place in his system, but includes the feelings of "the moral sense" as one of the six classes into which he divides pleasures and pains. In Mr. Bentham's own mind, deeply imbued as it was with the "greatest-happiness principle," this motive was probably so blended with that of sympathy as to be undistinguishable from it; but he should have recollected that those who acknowledge another standard of right and wrong than happiness, or who have never reflected on the subject at all, have often very strong feelings of moral obligation; and whether a person's standard be happiness or anything else, his attachment to his standard is not necessarily in proportion to his benevolence. Persons of weak sympathies have often a strong feeling of justice; and others, again, with the feeling of benevolence in considerable strength, have scarcely any consciousness of moral obligations at all.

It is scarcely necessary to point out that the habitual omission of so important a spring of action in an enumeration professing to be complete, must tend to create a habit of overlooking the same phenomenon, and consequently making no allowance for it, in other moral speculations. It is difficult to imagine any more fruitful source of gross error; though one would be apt to suppose the oversight an impossible one, without this evidence of its having been committed by one of the greatest thinkers our species has produced. How can we suppose him to be alive to the existence and force of the motive in particular cases, who omits it in a deliberate and comprehensive enumeration of all the influences by which human conduct is governed?

In laying down as a philosophical axiom, that men's actions are always obedient to their interests, Mr. Bentham did no more than dress up the very trivial proposition that all persons do what they feel themselves most disposed to do, in terms which appeared to him more precise, and better suited to the purposes of philosophy, than those more familiar expressions. He by no means intended by this assertion to impute universal selfishness to mankind, for he reckoned the motive of sympathy as an *interest,* and would have included conscience under the same appellation, if that motive had found any place in his philosophy, as a distinct principle from benevolence. He distinguished two kinds of interests, the self-regarding and the social: in vulgar discourse, the name is restricted to the former kind alone.

But there cannot be a greater mistake than to suppose that, because we may ourselves be perfectly *conscious* of an ambiguity in our language, that ambiguity therefore has no effect in perverting our modes of thought. I am persuaded, from experience, that this habit of speaking of all the feelings which govern mankind under the name of *interests,* is almost always in point of fact connected with a tendency to consider *interest* in the vulgar sense, that is, purely self-regarding interest, as exercising, by the very constitution of human nature, a far more exclusive and paramount control over human actions than it really does exercise. Such, certainly, was the tendency of Mr. Bentham's own opinions. Habitually, and throughout his works, the moment he has shown that a man's *selfish* interest would prompt him to a particular course of action, he lays it down without further parley that the man's interest lies that way; and, by sliding insensibly from the vulgar sense of the word into the philosophical, and from the philosophical back into the vulgar, the conclusion which is always brought out is, that the man will act as the selfish interest prompts.

The extent to which Mr. Bentham was a believer in the predominance of the selfish principle in human nature, may be seen from the sweeping terms in which, in his Book of Fallacies, he expressly lays down that predominance as a philosophical axiom.

"In *every* human breast (rare and shortlived ebullitions, the result of some extraordinarily strong stimulus or excitement, excepted) self-regarding interest is predominant over social interest; each person's own individual interest over the interests of all other persons taken together."

In another passage of the same work (p. 363) he says, "Taking the whole of life together, there exists not, *nor ever can exist,* that human being in whose instance any public interest he can have had will not, in so far as depends upon himself, have been sacrificed to his own personal interest. Towards the advancement of the public interest, all that the most public-spirited (which is as much as to say the most virtuous) of men can do, is to do what depends upon himself towards bringing the public interest, that is, his own personal share in the public interest, to a state as nearly approaching to coincidence, and on as few occasions amounting to a state of repugnance, as possible, with his private interests."

By the promulgation of such views of human nature, and by a general tone of thought and expression perfectly in harmony with them, I conceive Mr. Bentham's writings to have done and to be doing very serious evil. It is by such things that the more enthusiastic and generous minds are prejudiced against all his other speculations, and against the very attempt to make ethics and politics a subject of precise and philosophical thinking; which attempt, indeed, if it were necessarily connected with such views, would be still more pernicious than the vague and flashy declamation for which it is proposed as a substitute. The effect is still worse on the minds of those who are not shocked and repelled by this tone of thinking, for on them it must be perverting to their whole moral nature. It is difficult to form the conception of a tendency more inconsistent with all rational hope of good for the human species, than that which must be impressed by such doctrines, upon any mind in which they find acceptance.

There are, there have been, many human beings, in whom the motives of patriotism or of benevolence have been permanent

steady principles of action, superior to any ordinary, and in not a
few instances, to any possible, temptations of personal interest.
There are, and have been, multitudes, in whom the motive of
conscience or moral obligation has been thus paramount. There
is nothing in the constitution of human nature to forbid its being
so in all mankind. Until it is so, the race will never enjoy one-
tenth part of the happiness which our nature is susceptible of.
I regard any considerable increase of human happiness, through
mere changes in outward circumstances, unaccompanied by
changes in the state of the desires, as hopeless; not to mention
that while the desires are circumscribed in self, there can be no
adequate motive for exertions tending to modify to good ends
even those external circumstances. No man's individual share
of any public good which he can hope to realize by his efforts,
is an equivalent for the sacrifice of his ease, and of the personal
objects which he might attain by another course of conduct. The
balance can be turned in favour of virtuous exertion, only by the
interest of *feeling* or by that of *conscience*—those "social interests," the necessary subordination of which to "self-regarding" is
so lightly assumed.

But the power of any one to realize in himself the state of
mind, without which his own enjoyment of life can be but poor
and scanty, and on which all our hopes of happiness or moral
perfection to the species must rest, depends entirely upon his having faith in the actual existence of such feelings and dispositions
in others, and in their possibility for himself. It is for those in
whom the feelings of virtue are weak, that ethical writing is
chiefly needful, and its proper office is to strengthen those feelings. But to be qualified for this task, it is necessary, first to
have, and next to show, in every sentence and in every line, a
firm unwavering confidence in man's capability of virtue. It is by a
sort of sympathetic contagion, or inspiration, that a noble mind
assimilates other minds to itself; and no one was ever inspired
by one whose own inspiration was not sufficient to give him faith
in the possibility of making others feel what *he* feels.

Upon those who *need* to be strengthened and upheld by a
really inspired moralist—such a moralist as Socrates, or Plato, or
(speaking humanly and not theologically) as Christ; the effect
of such writings as Mr. Bentham's, if they be read and believed

and their spirit imbibed, must either be hopeless despondency and gloom, or a reckless giving themselves up to a life of that miserable self-seeking, which they are there taught to regard as inherent in their original and unalterable nature.

Mr. Bentham's speculations on politics in the narrow sense, that is, on the theory of government, are distinguished by his usual characteristic, that of beginning at the beginning. He places before himself man in society without a government, and, considering what sort of government it would be advisable to construct, finds that the most expedient would be a representative democracy. Whatever may be the value of this conclusion, the mode in which it is arrived at appears to me to be fallacious; for it assumes that mankind are alike in all times and all places, that they have the same wants and are exposed to the same evils, and that if the same institutions do not suit them, it is only because in the more backward stages of improvement they have not wisdom to see what institutions are most for their good. How to invest certain servants of the people with the power necessary for the protection of person and property, with the greatest possible facility to the people of changing the depositaries of that power, when they think it is abused; such is the only problem in social organization which Mr. Bentham has proposed to himself. Yet this is but a part of the real problem. It never seems to have occurred to him to regard political institutions in a higher light, as the principal means of the social education of a people. Had he done so, he would have seen that the same institutions will no more suit two nations in different stages of civilization, than the same lessons will suit children of different ages. As the degree of civilization already attained varies, so does the kind of social influence necessary for carrying the community forward to the next stage of its progress. For a tribe of North American Indians, improvement means, taming down their proud and solitary self-dependence; for a body of emancipated negroes, it means accustoming them to be self-dependent, instead of being merely obedient to orders: for our semi-barbarous ancestors it would have meant, softening them; for a race of enervated Asiatics it would mean hardening them. How can the same social organization be fitted for producing so many contrary effects?

The prevailing error of Mr. Bentham's views of human nature

appears to me to be this—he supposes mankind to be swayed by only a part of the inducements which really actuate them; but of that part he imagines them to be much cooler and more thoughtful calculators than they really are. He has, I think, been, to a certain extent, misled in the theory of politics, by supposing that the submission of the mass of mankind to an established government is mainly owing to a reasoning perception of the necessity of legal protection, and of the common interest of all in a prompt and zealous obedience to the law. He was not, I am persuaded, aware, how very much of the really wonderful acquiescence of mankind in any government which they find established, is the effect of mere habit and imagination, and, therefore, depends upon the preservation of something like continuity of existence in the institutions, and identity in their outward forms; cannot transfer itself easily to new institutions, even though in themselves preferable; and is greatly shaken when there occurs anything like a break in the line of historical duration—anything which can be termed the end of the old constitution and the beginning of a new one.

The constitutional writers of our own country, anterior to Mr. Bentham, had carried feelings of this kind to the height of a superstition; they never considered what was best adapted to their own times, but only what had existed in former times, even in times that had long gone by. It is not very many years since such were the principal grounds on which parliamentary reform itself was defended. Mr. Bentham has done much service in discrediting, as he has done completely, this school of politicians, and exposing the absurd sacrifice of present ends to antiquated means; but he has, I think, himself fallen into a contrary error. The very fact that a certain set of political institutions already exist, have long existed, and have become associated with all the historical recollections of a people, is in itself, as far as it goes, a property which adapts them to that people, and gives them a great advantage over any new institutions in obtaining that ready and willing resignation to what has once been decided by lawful authority, which alone renders possible those innumerable compromises between adverse interests and expectations, without which no government could be carried on for a year, and with difficulty even for a week. Of the perception of this important truth, scarcely a trace is visible in Mr. Bentham's writings.[1]

It is impossible, however, to contest to Mr. Bentham, on this subject or on any other which he has touched, the merit, and it is very great, of having brought forward into notice one of the faces of the truth, and a highly important one. Whether on government, on morals, or on any of the other topics on which his speculations are comparatively imperfect, they are still highly instructive and valuable to any one who is capable of supplying the remainder of the truth; they are calculated to mislead only by the pretension which they invariably set up of being the whole truth, a complete theory and philosophy of the subject. Mr. Bentham was more a thinker than a reader; he seldom compared his ideas with those of other philosophers, and was by no means aware how many thoughts had existed in other minds, which his doctrines did not afford the means either to refute or to appreciate.

1. It is necessary, however, to distinguish between Mr. Bentham's practical conclusions, as an English politician of the present day, and his systematic views as a political philosopher. It is to the latter only that the foregoing observations are intended to apply: on the former I am now called upon to pronounce any opinion. For the just estimation of his merits, the question is not what were his conclusions, but what was his mode of arriving at them. Theoretical views most widely different, may lead to the same practical corollaries: and that part of any system of philosophy which bodies itself forth in directions for immediate practice, must be so small a portion of the whole as to furnish a very insufficient criterion of the degree in which it approximates to scientific and universal truth. Let Mr. Bentham's opinions on the political questions of the day be as sound or as mistaken as any one may deem them, the fact which is of importance in judging of Mr. Bentham himself is that those opinions rest upon a basis of half-truth. Each enquirer is left to add the other half for himself, and confirm or correct the practical conclusion as the other lights of which he happens to be in possession, allow him.

Appendix C

A Few Observations on Mr. [James] Mill

Mr. Mill has been frequently represented as the disciple of Bentham. With truth has he been so represented in this respect —he was one of the earliest in adopting—he has been one of the most efficient in diffusing—many of the most characteristic of Bentham's opinions. He admits without qualification—he carries into detail with rigid inflexibility, the doctrine that the sole ground of moral obligation is *general utility*. But the same results may be reached by minds the most dissimilar; else why do we hope for agreement amongst impartial inquirers?—else why do we hope to convert one another? why not burn our lucubrations, or wait to establish a principle until we have found an exact resemblance of ourselves?

In some respects Mr. Mill's mind assimilates to Bentham's, in others it differs from it widely. It is true that Mr. Mill's speculations have been influenced by impressions received from Bentham; but they have been equally influenced by those received from the Aristotelian Logicians, from Hartley, and from Hobbes. He almost alone in the present age revived the study of those writers—he has preserved, perhaps, the most valuable of their doctrines—he is largely indebted to them for the doctrines which compose, for the spirit which pervades his philosophy. The character of his intellect seems to partake as much of that of either of those three types of speculative inquiry, as it does of the likeness of Bentham.

As a searcher into original truths, the principal contribution which Mr. Mill has rendered to philosophy, is to be found in his most recent work, "The Analysis of the Phenomena of the Human Mind." Nothing more clearly proves what I have before asserted, viz.—our indifference to the higher kind of philosophical investigation, than the fact, that no full account—no *criticism* of this work has appeared in either of our principal Reviews.

The doctrine announced by Hartley, that the ideas furnished by Sense, together with the law of association, are the simple elements of the mind, and sufficient to explain even the most mysterious of its phenomena, is also the doctrine of Mr. Mill. Hartley, upon this principle, had furnished an explanation of *some* of the phenomena. Mr. Mill has carried on the investigation into all those more complex phychological facts which had been the puzzle and despair of previous metaphysicians. Such, for instance, as Time and Space—Belief—the Will—the Affections—the Moral Sentiments. He has attempted to resolve all these into case of association. I do not pause here to contend with him— to show, or rather endeavour to show, where he has succeeded— where failed. It would be a task far beyond the limits of this Book—it is properly the task of future metaphysicians.

The moment in which this remarkable work appeared is unfortunate for its temporary success. Had it been published sixty years ago—or perhaps sixty years hence, it would perhaps have placed the reputation of its author beyond any of his previous writings.

There is nothing similar to these inquiries in the writings of Mr. Bentham. This indicates one principal difference between the two men. Mr. Mill is eminently a metaphysician; Bentham as little of a metaphysician as any one can be who ever attained to equal success in the science of philosophy. Every moral or political system must be indeed a corollary from some general view of human nature. But Bentham, though punctilious and precise in the premises he advances, confines himself, in that very preciseness, to a few simple and general principles. *He seldom analyses*—he studies the human mind rather after the method of natural history than of philosophy. He enumerates—he classifies the facts—but he does not *account* for them. You read in his works an enumeration of pains and pleasures—an enumeration of motives—an enumeration of the properties which constitute the value of a pleasure or a pain. But Bentham does not even attempt to *explain* any of the feelings or impulses enumerated —he does not attempt to show that they are subject to the laws of any more elementary phenomena of human nature. Of human nature indeed in its rarer or more hidden parts, Bentham knew but little—wherever he attained to valuable results, which his predecessors had missed, it was by estimating more justly than they the action of some outward circumstance upon the more obvious and vulgar elements of our nature—not by understanding better than they, the workings of those elements which are not obvious and not vulgar. Where but a moderate knowledge of these last was necessary to the correctness of his conclusions, he was apt to stray farther from the truth than even the votaries of common place. He often threw aside a trite and unsatisfactory truism, in order to replace it with a paradoxical error.

If, then, the power of analysing a complex combination into its simple elements be in the mental sciences, as in the physical, a leading characteristic of the philosopher, Mr. Mill is thus far considerably nearer to the philosophic ideal than Mr. Bentham. This, however, has not made so great a difference as might have been expected in the practical conclusions at which they have arrived. Those powers of analysis which, by Mr. Bentham, are not brought to bear upon the phenomena of our nature at all, are applied by Mr. Mill almost solely to our *common universal* nature, to the general structure which is the same in all human beings; not to the differences between one human being and another, though the former is little worthy of being studied except as a means to the better understanding of the latter. We seldom learn from Mr. Mill to understand any of the varieties of human nature; and, in truth, they enter very little into his own calculations, except where he takes cognizance of them as aberrations from the standard to which, in his opinion, all should conform. Perhaps there never existed any writer, (except, indeed, the ascetic theologians,) who conceived the excellence of the human being so exclusively under one single type, to a conformity with which he would reduce all mankind. No one ever made fewer allowances for original differences of nature, although the existence of such is not only compatible with, but a necessary consequence of, his view of the human mind, when combined with the extraordinary differences which are known to exist between one individual and another in the kind and in the degree of their nervous sensibility. I cannot but think that the very laws of association, laid down by Mr. Mill, will hereafter, and in other hands, be found (while they explain the diversities of human nature) to show, in the most striking manner, how much of those diversities is inherent and inevitable; neither the effect of, nor capable of being reached by, education or outward circumstances.[1] I believe the natural and necessary differences among mankind to be so great, that any practical view of human life, which does not take them into the account, must, unless it stop short in generalities, contain at least as much error as truth; and that any system of mental culture, recommended by such imperfect theory in proportion as it is fitted to natures of one class, will be entirely unfitted for all others.

Mr. Mill has given to the world, as yet, on the subject of morals, and on that of education, little besides generalities: not "barren generalities," but of the most fruitful kind; yet of which the fruit is still to come. When he shall carry his speculations into the details of these subjects, it is impossible that an intellect like his should not throw a great increase of light upon them: the danger is that the illumination will be partial and narrow; that he will conclude too readily that, whatever is suitable food for one sort of character, or suitable medicine for bringing it back, when it falls from its proper excellence, may be prescribed for *all,* and that what is *not* needful or useful to one of the types of human nature, is worthless altogether. There is yet another danger, that he will fail, not only in conceiving sufficient variety of excellence, but sufficiently *high* excellence; that the type to which he would reduce all natures, is by no means the most perfect type; that he conceives the ideal perfection of a human being, under *some* only of its aspects, not under all; or at least that he would frame his practical rules as if he so conceived it.

The faculty of drawing correct conclusions from evidence, together with the qualities of moral rectitude and earnestness, seem to constitute almost the whole of his idea of the perfection

1. I venture to recommend to the notice of the Reader an able paper on the character of Dr. Priestley, published in several recent numbers of Mr. Fox's excellent *Monthly Repository.*

of human nature; or rather, he seems to think, that with all other valuable qualities mankind are already sufficiently provided, or will be so by attending merely to these. We see no provision in his system, so far as it is disclosed to us, for the cultivation of any other qualities; and therefore, (as I hold to be a necessary consequence,) no *sufficient* provision for the cultivation even of these.

Now there are few persons whose notion of the perfection to which a human being may be brought, does not comprehend much more than the qualities enumerated above. Most will be prepared to find the practical views founded upon so narrow a basis of theory, rather fit to be used as part of the materials for a practical system, than fit in themselves to constitute one. From what cause, or combination of causes, the scope of Mr. Mill's philosophy embraces so partial a view only of the ends of human culture and of human life, it belongs rather to Mr. Mill's biographer than to his mere reader, to investigate. Doubtless the views of almost all inquirers into human nature are necessarily confined within certain bounds by the fact, that they can enjoy complete power of studying their subject only as it exists in themselves. No person can thoroughly appreciate that of which he has not had personal consciousness: but powers of metaphysical analysis, such as Mr. Mill possesses, are sufficient for the understanding and appreciation of all characters and all states of mind, as far as is necessary for practical purposes, and amply sufficient to divest our philosophic theories of everything like narrowness. For this, however, it is necessary that those powers of analysis should be applied to the details, not solely to the outlines, of human nature; and one of the most strongly marked of the mental peculiarities of Mr. Mill, is, as it seems to us, impatience of details.

This is another of the most striking differences between him and Mr. Bentham. Mr. Bentham delighted in details, and had a quite extraordinary genius for them: it is remarkable how much of his intellectual superiority was of this kind. He followed out his inquiries into the minutest ramifications; was skilful in the estimation of small circumstances, and most sagacious and inventive in devising small contrivances. He went even to great excess in the time and labour which he was willing to bestow on minutiæ, when more important things remained undone. Mr. Mill, on the contrary, shuns all nice attention to details; he attaches himself exclusively to great and leading points; his views, even when they cannot be said to be enlarged, are always on a large scale. He will often be thought by those who differ from him, to overlook or undervalue great things,—never to exaggerate small ones; and the former, partly from not being attentive *enough* to details, when these, though small, would have suggested principles which are great.

The same undervaluing of details has, I think, caused most of the imperfections, where imperfections there are, in Mr. Mill's speculations generally. His just contempt of those who are incapable of grasping a general truth, and with whom the grand and determining considerations are always outweighed by some petty circumstance, carries him occasionally into an opposite extreme: he so heartily despises those most obtuse persons who call themselves Practical Men, and disavow theory, as not always to recollect that, though the men be purblind, they may yet "look out upon the world with their dim horn eyes" and see something in it, which, lying out of his way, he may not have observed, but which it may be worth while for him, who *can* see clearly, to note and *explain*. Not only a dunce may give instruction to a wise man, but no man is so wise that he can, in all cases, do without a dunce's assistance. But a certain degree of intellectual impatience is almost necessarily connected with fervour of character and strength of conviction. Men much inferior to Mr. Mill are quite capable of setting limitations to his propositions, where any are requisite; few in our own times, we might say in any times, could have accomplished what he has done.

Mr. Mill's principal works besides the "Analysis" already mentioned, are, 1, "The History of British India," not only the first work which has thrown the light of philosophy upon the people and upon the government of that vast portion of the globe, but the first, and even now the only work which conveys to the general reader even that knowledge of facts, which, with respect to so important a department of his country's affairs, every Englishman should wish to possess. The work is full of instructive comments on the institutions of our own country, and abounds with illustrations of many of the most important principles of government and legislation.

2. "Elements of Political Economy." Mr. Mill's powers of concatenation and systematic arrangement peculiarly qualified him to place in their proper logical connexion the elementary principles of this science as established by its great masters, and to furnish a compact and clear exposition of them.

3. Essays on Government, Jurisprudence, Education, &c. originally written for the Supplement to the Encyclopædia Britannica; the most important of them have been several times reprinted by private subscription.

These little works, most of which are mere outlines to be filled up, though they have been both praised and animadverted upon as if they claimed the character of complete scientific theories, have been, I believe, more read than any other of Mr. Mill's writings, and have contributed more than any publications of our time to generate a taste for systematic thinking on the subject of politics, and to discredit vague and sentimental declamation. The Essay on Government, in particular, has been almost a text-book to many of those who may be termed the Philosophic Radicals. This is not the place to criticise either the treatise itself or the criticisms of others upon it. Any critical estimate of it thoroughly deserving the name, it has not yet been my fortune to meet with; for Mr. Macaulay—assuming, I suppose, the divine prerogative of genius—only entered the contest, in order to carry away the argument he protected in a cloud of words.

Mr. Mill's more popular writings are remarkable for a lofty earnestness, more stern than genial, and which rather flagellates or shames men out of wrong, than allures them to the right. Perhaps this is the style most natural to a man of deep moral convictions, writing in an age and in a state of society like that in which we live. But it seems, also, to be congenial to the character of his own mind; for he appears, on most occasions, much more strongly alive to the evil of what is evil in our destiny, than to the good of what is good. He rather warns us against the errors that tend to make us miserable, than affords us the belief that by any means we can attain to much positive happiness. He does not hope enough from human nature—something despondent and unelevating clings round his estimate of its powers. He saddens the Present by a reference to the Past—he does not console it by any alluring anticipations of the Future;—he rather discontents us with vice than kindles our enthusiasm for virtue. He possesses but little of

> The vision and the faculty divine;—

nor is it through his writings, admirable as they are, that we are taught

> To feel that we are greater than we know.

Index

431

Fonblanque, Albany, 236
Fox, Charles James, 108
Francis I, 90, 324
Fraser's Magazine, xv

Garrick, David, 302
George IV, 322
Gibbon, Edward, vii, 91 n.i., 184
Gibson, John, 340, 342
Gifford, William, 300
Gilbert, Davies, 336
Girtin, Thomas, 347
Glover, John, 348
Godwin, William, 50, 316 n.2
Goethe, Johann Wolfgang von, 282, 286, 313, 345
Goldsmith, Oliver, 262, 298, 345, 346
Gore, Catherine Grace, 85–86
Gott, Joseph, 342
Grant, Charles, 388
Grey, second Earl (Charles Grey), xx, 28, 367–68

Harding, James, 346, 348
Harrow, 157
Harrowby, first Earl of, and Viscount Sandon (Dudley Ryder), 28
Hartley, David, 316, 415, 422, 423
Harvey, William, 348
Haydon, Benjamin Robert, 342, 359
Hazlitt, William, x, 243, 259, 316
Heaphy, Thomas, 348
Hearne, Thomas, 347
Helvetius, Claude Adrien, 213, 311 n.4, 318, 326
Henry VII, 369
Hershel, Sir John, 324, 333, 335
Hesiod, 300 n.3
Hilton, William, 342
Hobbes, Thomas, 314, 407, 422
Hogarth, William, 339, 345, 346
Holbein, Hans, 323

Holland, James, 348
Homer, 122, 300 n.3
Hook, Theodore, xiv
Hooker, Richard, 194 n.4
Howard, Frank, 345
Hugo, Victor, 305
Humboldt, Wilhelm von, 325
Hume, David, vii, 195, 298, 357, 379
Hunt, Henry, 26
Hunt, Leigh, 259
Hutcheson, Francis, 208

Ingersoll, Robert G., 176 n.7
Irish Coercion bill, 88
Irish Tithe Bill, 389, 399

Jackson, John, 345
Jeffrey, Lord (Francis Jeffrey), xvi, 261, 263
John Bull, 191
Johnson, Samuel, 246 n.5, 262, 298, 358
Junius, 240

Kant, Immanuel, 164, 213
Kay (Shuttleworth), James, 222
Kean, Edmund, 51, 212
Keats, John, 300 n.2
King's College, Cambridge, 174
King's College, London, 168–71

LaFontaine, Jean de, 258, 299
Lamb, William, 259
Lancastrian system of education, 160–61 n.6, 176
Lance, George, 347
Landseer, Sir Edwin H., 340, 347, 353
Landseer, John, 348
Latimer, Hugh, 175, 194 n.4
Lawrence, Sir Thomas, 340 n.1, 345
Lee, William, 346
LeSage, Alain René, 287
Leslie, Charles Robert, 345